The Process
of Stratification

TRENDS AND ANALYSES

STUDIES IN POPULATION

Under the Editorship of: H. H. WINSBOROUGH

Department of Sociology
University of Wisconsin
Madison, Wisconsin

The Process of Stratification

TRENDS AND ANALYSES

ROBERT M. HAUSER
Department of Sociology
University of Wisconsin
Madison, Wisconsin

DAVID L. FEATHERMAN
Department of Rural Sociology
University of Wisconsin
Madison, Wisconsin

ACADEMIC PRESS   New York   San Francisco   London
A Subsidiary of Harcourt Brace Jovanovich, Publishers

To Tess and Jo-Anna

ACADEMIC PRESS, INC.
111 Fifth Avenue, New York, New York 10003

United Kingdom Edition published by
ACADEMIC PRESS, INC. (LONDON) LTD.
24/28 Oval Road, London NW1

Library of Congress Cataloging in Publication Data

Hauser, Robert Mason.
    The process of stratification.

    (Studies in population)
    Bibliography: p.
    1.   Social mobility—United States.   2.   Occupa-
tional mobility—United States.   I.   Featherman,
David L., joint author.   II.   Title.   III.   Series.
HN90.S65H38   301.44'044'0973   76-19487
ISBN 0−12−333050−5

Contents

Contents

List of Figures

List of Tables

Preface

The publication in 1967 of *The American Occupational Structure,* by Peter M. Blau and Otis Dudley Duncan, began a new phase in research on social mobility and socioeconomic inequality in the United States. While acknowledging the significance of other indicants of social class, status, and power, Blau and Duncan followed other sociologists in making occupational positions and movements among them the central foci of their research. From the end of childhood and schooling until retirement, disability, or death, job-holding is the major activity of almost all men and an increasing fraction of women in industrial societies. There is nothing hierarchical in the concept of an occupation, which merely invokes the differentiation of work from other activities and a certain division of labor among those who work. Yet there is an almost universal and moderately consistent hierarchy of occupations, which is expressed in variables like the educational requirements for occupational entry, the typical level of remuneration, and the esteem with which occupational incumbents are held by the public. Indeed, these hierarchical characteristics of occupations are so pervasive that the distinction between occupational roles and attendant statuses is often lost.

Blau and Duncan regarded occupational incumbency as a key variable in their investigations of social mobility. Moreover, they thought of stratification as inherently dynamic—a concept referring to a social process—rather than static, as in earlier descriptive studies of status layers and class influence in single communities. The process of stratification was the mechanism by which the socioeconomic statuses of one generation were linked to those of the next. Without offering a theory of the sociogenesis of class and status inequalities in modern society, they drew attention to the regime under which inequalities in social standing (strata or classes) persist or change.

Blau and Duncan postulated that familial origins represent a set of social constraints and resources that affect the status mobility or inheritance of successive cohorts in the population. The relevant initial conditions include social categories defined by race, nativity, regional and farm origin, and family size; they also include social resources of money and capital; tastes and life style preferences; knowledge and abilities; and social connections and prestige. As children mature, their social origins are reflected in their schooling, and together social background and schooling affect jobs, occupational careers, earnings, and other socioeconomic statuses. The movement from the social conditions of childhood to achievement in adulthood is typically punctuated by such contingencies as geographic mobility, marriage, child-rearing, and military service. The ultimate distribution of a cohort over the array of social statuses is conditioned in large part on opportunities whose genesis is exogenous to the mobility process. Yet the linkage among status positions in a model of the socioeconomic life cycle may accurately be described as a process of stratification. With this model of the socioeconomic mobility of individuals from generation to generation, Blau and Duncan measured and interpreted the degree of stratification in American society. Further, they characterized inequality of opportunity as variation in stratification by race, ethnicity, and other social categories.

In calling this monograph *The Process of Stratification*, we acknowledge the profound influence on our work of the conceptual scheme developed by Blau and Duncan. Our objective has been to elaborate their description and analysis of socioeconomic inequality, stratification, and inequality of opportunity in American society in the early 1960s, as evidenced in the "Occupational Changes in a Generation" (OCG) data from March 1962. Further, we offer provisional calculations of trend and change in mobility patterns and opportunities between 1962 and 1972. In this latter aspect of our work, we have taken advantage of a distinguishing feature of the Blau and Duncan research. Unlike the early community studies and the various subnational mobility studies of the 1950s, the OCG study provided national benchmark measurements of social stratification and mobility in the United States. The study's conceptual approach to this question and its analytic methods have motivated others in the United States and elsewhere to undertake replicate or parallel researches in order to establish benchmarks, where there were none, or to assess change (cf. Featherman, Hauser, and Sewell, 1974).

This report is a product of the initial phase of our research on temporal changes in stratification and inequality in the United States. The central component of that program is a replicate of the 1962 OCG survey (Featherman and Hauser, 1975), which we commissioned the U.S. Bureau of the Census to field as a supplement to the March 1973 Current Population Survey (CPS). Together with the data from the 1962 benchmark, the OCG replicate will provide definitive estimates of change in social stratification. In preparation for this comparative analysis, we acquired the microrecords from the March 1962 CPS and from its OCG supplement. At the time of the Blau and Duncan project, the U.S. Bureau of the Census was prohibited from releasing the microrecords to the investigators, who, perforce, had to prespecify the analytic tabulations of the OCG and CPS data which were to be executed by the census bureau. Fortunately, bureau policies changed regarding the release of demographic surveys. Without extensive new tabulations, there would have been little new information to be gleaned about stratification from the 1962 data, and this book could never have been written. Moreover, the microrecords are essential to the extensive diachronic analysis we plan in conjunction with the 1973 replicate survey.

Details of the design and properties of the March 1962 CPS sample and the OCG supplement are discussed by Blau and Duncan (1967:13). The target population was civilian males aged 20 to 64 in the noninstitutional population, including as "civilians" about 900,000 men in the armed forces living in families on military posts or off-post in civilian quarters. Within the approximately 35,000 households in the CPS sample, about 25,000 men in the target population were located. Of these, 20,700 men completed and returned the two-page OCG questionnaire (cf. Blau and Duncan, 1967: Appendix B) which was left behind by the CPS interviewer; with extensive follow-up, the completion rate was 83%.

Throughout our analyses of the 1962 data, we have weighted the sample cases to reflect population frequencies, taking into account nonresponse in both the CPS and OCG surveys. The average sample weight was 2173.14 (see Appendix F). Where our tabulations show sample frequencies, these have been calculated by inflating each case by its unique weight and dividing by the average weight. In addition, the sampling design of the CPS was less efficient than a simple random sample. We calculated a design factor of .62 to correct estimated sampling variances of proportions for departure from simple random sampling (see Appendix F). Our estimates of standard errors in the following chapters reflect this adjustment for the sample design, which is conservative in the sense that we have typically overestimated the probability of falsely rejecting a null hypothesis. We believe this conservatism is justified by the massive size of the OCG sample, but the reader should be careful to take the reported standard errors and probability levels as no more than a rough guide to the interpretation of results.

We have arranged *The Process of Stratification* into three parts, corresponding to primary emphases on methods and assumptions (Chapters 1 and 2), mobility trends (Chapters 3–7), and cross-sectional analyses (Chapters 8–11). Part I addresses several assumptions, concepts, and methods that were implicit in *The American Occupational Structure* and which some of its critics found problematic. Inasmuch as our replicate study was planned to incorporate these assumptions, we undertook their explicit examination. Part II is both an exposition of a method and a description of trends in stratification and socioeconomic achievement. We regard these analyses as provisional, inasmuch as trend and change are inferred deductively from assumptions and methods elaborated in Chapter 3. Fortunately, the results alert us to relationships and issues which we can and shall explore directly in the comparison of the 1962 and 1973 OCG surveys. Part III summarizes analyses of socioeconomic status allocation which broaden our understanding of the process of stratification in the benchmark period. While each chapter is self-contained, the book has several themes in method and substance to which we would alert the reader at the outset.

The importance of high-quality information about occupations and the facility to order occupations in metrics of social standing are highlighted in Part I. Throughout our stratification research, we give a central place to occupation, on the rationale provided earlier, even though in this volume (Chapter 11) and elsewhere, we have examined the intergenerational persistence of income and earning levels. A principal assumption in the OCG studies of occupational stratification has been that socioeconomic status (here indexed by the Duncan (1961) SEI scale) is a central feature of occupational incumbency and of occupational mobility. In Chapter 1, we lend credibility to this assumption in a comparative study of Australia and the United States. At least in these two societies, the mobility of men among occupations, between or within generations, is generally explicable in terms of the socioeconomic differences and similarities among jobs. That is, a hierarchy of occupations that reflects educational prerequisites and monetary remuneration (i.e., occupational socioeconomic status) captures the major axis of occupational preference, aspiration, and inter-

and intragenerational mobility. The methodological implication is that
a socioeconomic index for occupations is substantively, and statistically, preferable to prestige indexes in stratification research.

Another important methodological conclusion is that valid and reliable information about a person's location in the industrial and occupational structures can be elicited from large-scale social surveys
(Chapter 2). We provide guidelines and conventions that would en-
gender a high order of comparability among studies of occupational
stratification and that assure that detailed examinations of interoccupa-
tion and interindustry moves are warranted by the quality of the data.
In addition, we develop a set of prestige and socioeconomic status
scores for 1970 census detailed occupation titles (Appendix B).

In Part II, we show several ways in which a single baseline survey
of intergenerational and career mobility can be employed to infer
temporal change in the process of stratification. This is feasible when
the same cohorts (not necessarily the same persons) are represented in
a survey from which the distribution of persons by occupation or other
socioeconomic characteristics can be estimated (Chapters 3, 4, 5, and
7). While this idea is not new (Duncan, 1965), we are surprised that it
has not been used more in projective and retrojective analyses of
change, especially where a regular series of mobility studies would be
prohibitively expensive. Chapter 7 suggests that mobility analysts
might capitalize on a single baseline study to forecast the impacts on
social mobility of demographic shifts in labor force participation and in
the sectorial (industrial) and occupational divisions of labor. This is
supported by our finding in Chapter 6 that little, if any, change has
taken place in intergenerational mobility in the U.S. in the last 30 to 40
years that cannot be attributed to shifts in the occupation distributions
of successive cohorts. That is, the fundamental associations between
occupations of origin and destination (for example, father's and son's
occupations) are constant across time, so earlier or later mobility tables
can be estimated from a single mobility table by a statistical adjustment for proportional changes in the origin and destination distributions. However, this empirical invariance and the resulting analytic
and projective possibilities do not obviate the need for replicate
studies of social mobility. The apparent constancy in the endogenous
association of social origins and destinations (in the instance of occupational mobility) could dissolve, were the nexus of institutional ar-
rangements involving the family, the school, and the labor market
altered from their historical configurations. How revolutionary these
rearrangements would need to be in order to affect the endogenous
mobility regime is unknown.

A substantive finding that affects the interpretations in several other chapters of Part II emerges from Chapter 6. Despite considerable evidence that elements of the process of stratification have changed since 1962 (Chapter 5) and that the volume of (upward) social mobility via occupation has not diminished since the early 1950s (Chapter 3), the maintenance of these shifts and patterns into the future is not guaranteed. The regime of mobility at any point in history and, obversely, changes in the amount and pattern of mobility, bear the impact of growth and decline of industrial and occupational groups. Indeed, most of the change we observe in *gross* mobility trends is structurally induced by compositional shifts in industry and occupation. Therefore, future research into the relationship between structural and circulation (endogenous) mobility is warranted. This work awaits the comparative analysis of the OCG replicate survey and of the new round of studies of stratification in capitalist and socialist nations (Featherman, Hauser, and Sewell, 1974).

Within our provisional analysis of trends in American stratification in Part II, there are some consistencies worthy of summary here. First, growth and decline across occupations have been uneven in the decade 1962 to 1972. White-collar jobs in the professions and in technical pursuits and skilled or supervisory blue-collar jobs have grown disproportionally. Second, declines in farming and in self-employment in business and the professions (versus growth in salaried positions in these broad groups) were quite marked. Together, these shifts in the occupational structure comprised a net upward shift in the mean level of socioeconomic status; and within both the white- and blue-collar sectors the average socioeconomic status rose as a function of the redistribution of workers. From the 1962 OCG mobility statistics, we believe a primary component of this redistribution is a change in career mobility from first jobs to the current occupations of men in the labor force. Third, commensurate with the status upgrading of the occupational structure was an educational upgrading, as greater proportions of young, large birth cohorts undertook higher education and began working. As a result, the relationship between schooling and occupational achievement was changed. In the more recent period, white males with given "qualifications" of social background and education held lower-status jobs than did men of the same age in 1962.

A fourth trend is the persistence of racial discrimination in the labor market. While advances in socioeconomic status among blacks have surpassed those among whites, differences in mean levels of occupational status and earnings remain. Moreover, occupational status and income are still lower for blacks than for whites of equivalent background and schooling. In short, inequality of opportunity by race persists, and such discrimination is no less important in explaining mean differences in occupational status and earnings in the recent years than it was in the early 1960s. At the same time, the process of stratification for young workers (ages 25–34) appears to be less dissimilar than for older cohorts; this may imply some amelioration of unequal socioeconomic opportunity (Featherman and Hauser, 1976a; Hauser and Featherman, 1976).

While racial discrimination in the labor market is in some respects similar to sexual discrimination, we argue in Chapters 4 and 8 that there are also fundamental dissimilarities between racial and sexual inequalities. Elsewhere, we have demonstrated, using OCG data, that married women in the labor force fail to convert their resources (e.g., social origins, educational attainment, and work experience) into earnings at the same rate as men in the same occupations (Featherman and Hauser, 1976c). However, we found no evidence of inequality of opportunity by sex for educational and occupational status among married persons in the experienced labor force. Not only are the processes that allocate married male and female workers from their social origins to educational levels and occupational statuses alike, but men's and women's mean levels of schooling and occupational status are virtually the same.

Another of the themes in our work, therefore, is that racial discrimination in the process of stratification is primarily socioeconomic, whereas sexual discrimination is not socioeconomic in the same sense, except in the case of earnings. Among both male and female workers, blacks attain lower levels of education and occupational standing than do whites, and the returns to "qualifications" are less for blacks. The occupational segregation of the sexes is actually greater than that between the races, but it does not result in socioeconomic differences among married persons who work. Historically, female workers have been allocated to jobs that apparently are less attractive to men, and shifts in the occupational distributions of the sexes suggest that men are preferred over women for employment in growing sectors of the economy.

Another major feature of the process of status allocation that distinguishes men from women and racial from sexual stratification also distinguishes persons in the labor force from those outside it. That is, the traditional sex-role patterns which allocate women to roles outside the regular labor force are the primary basis of difference between the regimes that distribute women from their socioeconomic origins to their own occupations (including housewifery) and the intergenerational mobility of men.

In Chapters 9 and 10, we develop the notion that socioeconomic achievement occurs in contexts that may organize the process of stratification in distinctive ways. Industry, or situs, and size of place of residence are two such contexts. Intergenerational movements among industries are much like those among occupations, showing an appreciable degree of "inheritance." In addition, a man's industrial history is another resource on which he can trade in pursuing his occupational career. However, there were few differences in processes of occupational and economic achievement by size of urban place within the nation in the early 1960s.

In Chapter 11, we broaden our treatment of the intergenerational transmission of social statuses to include the persistence of incomes from generation to generation. Using a structural equation model to deduce how a measure of parental income might have behaved, if one had been included in the 1962 OCG survey, we conclude that the persistence of economic status across generations is probably similar in character and magnitude to that of occupational status. The correlation between incomes of fathers and sons is positive, but undoubtedly less than those among schooling, occupational status, and income within the generations of fathers and sons. Of course, these conclusions are speculative, even if based on manipulations of quantitative data. As in the case of our preliminary trend analyses, Chapter 11 should be read partly as an illustration of a method and partly as an invitation to more direct and conclusive inquiry.

The several lines of research reported here are commonly motivated and guided by a concept of social stratification as a life cycle process. We think that concept has proved to be a powerful stimulus to research on social mobility and inequality, while, at the same time, it encourages a desirable eclecticism in methodological approaches to a broad range of substantive questions. We strongly caution the reader not to view this monograph as a systematic or comprehensive effort to exploit the utility of that concept. Rather, we have been deliberately selective and opportunistic in exploring assumptions, methods, and theoretic issues. Our efforts have been bounded on one side by earlier comprehensive analyses of the 1962 OCG data, and they have been limited in another way by our anticipation of the 1973 OCG survey.

Acknowledgments

This book is a product of our program of research on trends in social stratification and mobility in the United States. The heart of our program is a replicate survey of social mobility conducted in 1973 (Featherman and Hauser, 1975), which was designed to measure changes in social mobility in the decade following the 1962 benchmark study, "Occupational Changes in a Generation" (Blau and Duncan, 1967). The present volume does not report findings from the 1973 replicate, but its chapters were drafted while the U.S. Bureau of the Census was collecting and coding the 1973 survey data. This work was primarily supported by the same grant from the National Science Foundation (GI-31604X) under which we commissioned the Bureau of the Census to execute the replicate survey. At the same time the Bureau prepared unit record tapes from the 1962 survey which had not previously been available. Several units of the University of Wisconsin-Madison provided material and financial support for our work. These include the Center for Demography and Ecology, which has core support from the National Institute for Child Health and Human Development (HD-05876); the Institute for Research on Poverty, under a grant from the Office of Economic Opportunity pursuant to the Economic Opportunity Act of 1964; and the College of Agricultural and Life Sciences (Experiment Station).

Several of our faculty and student colleagues have contributed to the thinking of the coauthors. Others have carried out important statistical analyses or have drafted chapters or major portions of chapters. Among the most central of our collaborators are F. Lancaster Jones (Chapter 1); Michael Sobel and David Dickens (Chapter 2); Peter J. Dickinson, Harry P. Travis, and John N. Koffel (Chapters

6 and 7); Dennis P. Hogan (Chapters 8 and 9); Charles W. Mueller (Chapter 10); and Donald J. Treiman (Chapter 11). Other associates and assistants include Neil Fligstein, David Dickens, Michael Sobel, James Kluegel, Hernando Gomez-Buendia, Armona Livneh, Nancy Scott, Andrew Karman, Thomas Di Prete, and Jenny Camper. We are singularly grateful to Edward Knowles and Alphonso Episcopo of the Demographic Surveys Division of the U.S. Bureau of the Census who provided essential technical assistance in the acquisition and preparation of the data tapes for the March 1962 CPS and OCG surveys. John M. Bregger of the Bureau of Labor Statistics, U.S. Department of Labor, supplied unpublished tabulations which were helpful in preparing Chapter 3. In addition to his contribution as a sociologist, Peter J. Dickinson designed the local computer files and oversaw an efficient and effective analysis of the 1962 data on the computer at the Center for Demography and Ecology.

Without the editorial and clerical skills of Mary Balistreri, Kathy Reynolds, and Christine Waldo, this book would still be an idea rather than a reality.

In its organization, the book reflects new writings (Chapters 4, 8, 9, 10, and 11) and expansions or reprints of earlier publications. In the latter category, permissions to reprint were kindly provided by Academic Press (Chapter 1), Sage Publications, Inc. (Chapters 1 and 2), and The American Sociological Association (Chapters 3, 6, and 7).

Throughout our work on this volume we have benefited immensely from the encouragement and criticism of William H. Sewell and Halliman H. Winsborough. Otis Dudley Duncan, Paul Duncan-Jones, Carl Frederickson, Arthur S. Goldberger, Leo A. Goodman, Keith Hope, Christopher S. Jencks, Margaret Martin, Natalie Rogoff-Ramsøy, Kenneth Spenner, Ross M. Stolzenberg, R. Blair Wheaton, and Harrison White have read one or more of our draft chapters, and we thank them for friendly advice and criticism. Any opinions, findings, conclusions or recommendations are those of the authors and do not necessarily reflect the views of the National Science Foundation or other agencies supporting our work.

I

ASSUMPTIONS AND METHODS

1

Commonalities in Social Stratification and Assumptions about Status Mobility in the United States

Recent commentaries on mobility research within the United States (Haller and Portes, 1973; Featherman, Hauser, and Sewell, 1974) have noted the prominent influence of Blau and Duncan (1967) on both the conceptualization and the conduct of American stratification inquiries. The impact of these approaches has transcended academe to influence the structuring of public policy questions on social and economic inequalities in the United States. Jencks *et al.* (1972) in *Inequality,* for example, draw generously from *The American Occupational Structure* (Blau and Duncan, 1967), from later extensions of that work (Duncan, Featherman, and Duncan, 1972), and from the pioneering work of Sewell, Haller, and Ohlendorf (1970) and Sewell and Hauser (1975), on the "process of status attainment." Since the influence of the Duncan and Sewell approaches is widely appreciated, we shall not dwell

This chapter was prepared by David L. Featherman and Robert M. Hauser. It synthesizes materials that appeared in Featherman, Jones, and Hauser (1975), and in Featherman and Hauser, "Prestige or socioeconomic scales in the study of occupational achievement," *Sociological Methods and Research,* Vol. 4, No. 4 (May 1976), pp. 403–422, reprinted by permission of the publisher, Sage Publications, Inc. An earlier version was delivered at the International Conference on Theory and Research on Social Structure and Mobility, Institute of Philosophy and Sociology, Polish Academy of Sciences, Warsaw, Poland, in March 1974. Professor F. Lancaster Jones of Australian National University was a collaborator in this research.

3

upon it here. However, inasmuch as these perspectives pervade a broad sweep of American studies of inequality and mobility,[1] and in view of the increasing adoption of similar sociological approaches in comparative mobility researches at the national level (cf. Featherman, Hauser, and Sewell, 1974), it is useful to review assumptions of the status attainment "school." In this chapter, we address assumptions about occupational status and mobility which critics, friendly and otherwise, find problematic or limiting.

Some American sociologists lament the preponderance of occupation and, particularly, of occupational status in studies of inequality and social mobility. Pease, Form, and Rytina (1970) ask why, after nearly 80 years of attention to these fundamental issues of American society, analysts foresake power and economic inequalities, devoting nearly exclusive attention to the measurement of occupational status. However, few sociologists would deny the central place of occupational roles within the structure of industrialized societies or the linkage of individuals to the society through such roles. These relationships involving occupations are especially clear in capitalist economies (Parkin, 1971), with high proportions of the population employed and where more than three-quarters in total income derives from salaries, wages, and self-employment. Moreover, if one conceives of "power" as "control over resources" (cf. Titmuss, 1962; Parkin, 1971; Weber, 1958), then studies of social inequality and mobility in the U.S., framed as they often are in terms of occupational mobility, tap the major stratifying process, yielding information simultaneously (albeit, indirectly) on status power, economic power, and political (authority) power.

If the structure of capitalist industrial societies justifies the focus on occupations, then what justifies the use of prestige and socioeconomic metrics to scale occupations and to measure social mobility qua occupational stratification and inequality? There is mounting evidence in the U.S. and elsewhere that the hierarchical structure underlying occupational roles is largely socioeconomic. Students of social inequality acknowledge the cross-validated evidence for a hierarchy of occupational prestige. This occupational structure essentially is invariant

---

[1] Clearly not all current American researches treat mobility as a process of achievement, after Duncan and Sewell. Notable exceptions include the continuing analysis of mobility tables (i.e., Goodman, 1969a; McFarland, 1969, 1970; Fararo, 1973), scrutiny of job vacancy chains (White, 1970), and dynamic assessments of occupational life histories (Sørensen, 1974). For a partial overview of major U.S. inquiries incorporating status attainment approaches, see Duncan, Featherman, and Duncan, 1972:Epilogue.

across spans of several decades, among societies and regions, among the sociocultural characteristics of rankers, and over dimensions of ranking (Hodge, Treiman, and Rossi, 1966; Hodge, Siegel, and Rossi, 1964; Siegel, 1971). Undeniably, American (and probably other) studies represent a congeries of interpretations of prestige, both on the part of the study designers and on that of the rankers of occupational titles (cf. Reiss, 1961). We would not dispute an interpretation of the emergent prestige ranking as a hierarchy of *desirability* rather than of *prestige*, in its strictly interpreted classical sense (Goldthorpe and Hope, 1972), for the social organization of modern capitalist societies (and perhaps others as well) may preclude normatively prescribed prestige groups (viz., symbolically legitimated groups, with patterned relationships of deference, acceptance, and derogation) except at the most microsocial levels. However, to agree with this interpretation is *not* to concur with those who assert that such a state of affairs is theoretically uninteresting (cf. Goldthorpe and Hope, 1974). We examine this argument and the evidence.

WHAT DO PRESTIGE SCALES SCALE?

We first address the question of how populations of raters structure occupations in hierarchical space. To put it another way, what do so-called prestige scales, as conventionally derived, actually scale? Evidence accumulated most recently in Britain (Goldthorpe and Hope, 1974) joins that available for the United States (Reiss, 1961; Siegel, 1971) to indicate that the dimensions underlying occupational inequality in the minds of popular raters are manifold, only some of which correspond to the classical, sociological conceptions of prestige (see Goldthorpe and Hope, 1972:27–33, for a review of this evidence). Despite the evidence that occupational "prestige" rests upon a congeries of dimensions, the common core and dominant dimension of occupational status is socioeconomic in nature. Naturally, this assertion is a postulate and not an axiom, as it rests on an admittedly thin body of evidence in societies whose institutional forms are not strikingly dissimilar (although rough calculations of the socioeconomic correlates of occupational prestige for places such as West Malaysia and Singapore (Featherman, 1974) do not provide disconfirming data for this assertion).

One can conceive of small social systems and some nations (perhaps such as Israel, Cuba, and China) in which this postulate may not hold. These would be systems in which the social organization of jobs, arranged into occupations based on unit relationships of economic function (e.g., working with things, people, or ideas; control over production, employment, or time), and the allocation of socioeconomic resources would be misaligned, relative to current circumstances in many capitalist and industrial societies. For example, explicit efforts to minimize earnings inequalities through taxation in Israel could alter the equivalence of "desirable" with high-paying occupations (subject to the constraint that the "desirable" occupations are not able to convert their (otherwise nonsocioeconomically) desirable qualities into "income" in the form of subsidized housing, vacations; into varieties of "in-kind" payments (e.g., medical care, loans); or into amenities in the physical conditions of work, to cite just a few examples). In the face of such evidence (now largely conjectural), we may need to alter the postulate to say that the core and dominant dimension of occupational status is power—Titmuss' (1962) "command over resources over time," as a function of occupation. For most capitalist and industrial nations, this occupational power would manifest itself in the conjunction of income, authority relationships within and between occupation groups, and education, to fashion the observed socioeconomic nature of occupational status ("desirability" or "prestige"). In other systems, occupational power may fashion other configurations such that occupational status is truly nonsocioeconomic, but instances of these conditions are too under-researched to bring us to disclaim our initial (albeit provisional) assertion. Nevertheless, studies of occupational "prestige" are theoretically interesting, if only to show the societal variation (or lack thereof) in the dimensionality of occupational desirability.

Evidence for the dominance of socioeconomic factors in occupational desirability in the U.S. is well known. When an individual is queried as to why he or she wants to change jobs, the most typical reasons offered are socioeconomic (e.g., financial, educational reasons) rather than ones indicative of the social prestige of the occupations (Reiss, 1961:29–30). Or, when asked to account for the fact that some occupations are ranked high and others low in social standing, raters again give socioeconomic reasons as the major factors (Reiss, 1961:30–31). It is not surprising, therefore, that Duncan finds some 83% of the variance in the "prestige" of 90 U.S. occupational titles to represent socioeconomic predictors (Duncan, 1961:124). Furthermore, with the rather stable rank-ordering of occupational education and income in the U.S. (cf. Siegel, 1971), one expects and does find near invariance in the ratings of occupational "prestige" over several decades. We have little doubt that similar invariance may be uncovered in other industrialized countries. For example, Routh (1965:147–148) reports high rigidity in relative earnings across a wide array of British occupations between 1906 and 1960.

The most extensive U.S. studies of occupational prestige are reported by Siegel (1971), who, like Duncan, finds an overwhelming socioeconomic basis to occupational prestige. From Siegel (1971:265), one can calculate the following regression equation, relating prestige scores for several hundred U.S. occupations to selected characteristics, each measured in standard form:

$$\hat{P} = -.026M - .061L + .543E - .097C \\ + .018S + .014F - .068N + .422I; \ R^2 = .812, \quad (1)$$

where M is the percentage of employed males in manufacturing; L is percentage of employed males self-employed; E is mean education, male experienced civilian labor force (ECLF); C is percentage of employed males urban; S is percentage of male ECLF in South; F is percentage of ECLF female; N is percentage of male ECLF Negro; and I is mean income, male ECLF. The *Beta* coefficients indicate the clear dominance of occupational education and income. Siegel argues that the deviations of prestige ratings for occupations from a strictly socioeconomic regression line bespeak explicable "true" prestige deviations—that is, those titles enjoying higher or lower social standing than their occupational education and income levels would imply. Still, he finds few measures that explain this "true" prestige variance; note, for example, that the *Beta* coefficients in the regression above for the percentages female or Negro (which we might interpret as indicating the effects of social honor) are quite small.

For Britain, Goldthorpe and Hope (1974) offer cross-validating evidence for the socioeconomic basis of occupational prestige. On the basis of earlier research, one can expect that the newest popular estimates of the social standing of occupations in Britain will correlate highly with those in the U.S., and for the British sample the emergent "prestige" hierarchy is a linear combination (to the extent of 97% of its variance) of four rating dimensions: standard of living, power and influence, qualifications, and value to society. (Goldthorpe and Hope do not report the covariances necessary to compute a regression of the prestige scale on the four dimensions, although the correlations among the dimensions indicate that "qualifications" and "power and influence" are the most central components. These data are consistent with the proposition of Svalastoga (1972) that occupational prestige reflects two dimensions: occupational education and authority.)

While Goldthorpe and Hope (1974:13) are dismayed by the sociological potential of this congruity between two or more societies in the structure of occupational inequality, we find this fact to be of some substantial theoretical import. We shall elaborate more on this interpretation in later discussion. Suffice to say here that people perceive rather accurately that professional and administrative occupations, by their very definition or organization, call for the exercise of greater authority and control and apparently require for their exercise native and trained capacities and personality traits which craft or operative occupations, by their organization, do not (in degree or kind). That the organization of occupations across societies (at least of an industrialized type) is so similar and that persons in them, regardless of their social circumstances, perceive this organization as "socially desirable" (i.e., normative in an existential sense, rather than a legitimatory one) is not without sociological interest.

Additionally, it may be the case that the congruity of ranking and of the basis for that ranking of occupations across societies devolve from sources complementary to the similarity of the organization of occupations in industrial, and especially capitalist, economies. To examine this possibility, we inquire about the structure of social qua occupational mobility in the U.S. We ask if the basis on which such mobility occurs is unique or common among capitalist, industrial societies. Our provisional answer is that it is common in large measure, and that the basis of this mobility is socioeconomic. Again we find this observation to be interesting sociologically, but also it sustains the validity of studying social mobility qua movement among categories of occupational socioeconomic status, a basic assumption in American mobility research. We turn now to the evidence.

BASES AND AMOUNT OF OCCUPATIONAL
MOBILITY: TWO CASE STUDIES

In a rarely cited publication, Klatzky and Hodge (1971) have demonstrated that the pattern of occupational mobility for the United States is ordered according to the socioeconomic distances among occupational categories. Applying canonical correlation techniques to a 17-category classification of extended major occupation groups in the Occupational Changes in a Generation (OCG) data, Klatzky and Hodge conclude that the socioeconomic scaling used in the OCG study by Blau and Duncan (1967) captured the essential relationship in both inter- and intragenerational mobility.[2] The canonical correlations were quite close in magnitude to the product–moment correlations reported by Blau and Duncan, and the canonical weights for the occupational variates correlated highly with aggregate occupational education and income. Furthermore, they reaffirmed that the relative statuses of occupational categories have remained constant, at least over the period of time encompassed by the OCG data. For the U.S., it would seem that (1) the structure of occupational hierarchies is fundamentally socioeconomic, (2) that this structure in its relationships of relative super- and subordination in a socioeconomic sense has remained constant (at least) within this century, and (3) the major dimension of social distance on which mobility is conducted in the U.S. is socioeconomic.

While these observations are themselves interesting to the sociologist, they would become even more so were we able to demonstrate consistencies across societies and/or systematic societal variations in these elements of stratification systems. In fact, research underway by Treiman (e.g., Treiman and Terrell, 1975b) and by Featherman and Hauser in the U.S. joins that in other nations which works toward this end. In this chapter, we report similarities uncovered in our reanalysis of data for Australia, kindly provided for this purpose by L. Broom and F. L. Jones of the Australian National University (ANU). The ANU data are from a 1965 mobility survey conducted among adult male workers. Our purpose in reanalysis is to effect more comparable analyses than were possible earlier, especially prior to Jones' (1971) comparison of U.S.–Australian path models.[3] The

---

[2] Klatzky and Hodge report a second canonical variate for the U.S., which they do not interpret. Moreover, Duncan-Jones (1972), independently analyzing the OCG and other national mobility data, finds discrepancies between the canonical and least-squares (ordinary correlations) structures, especially for the father-to-son's first occupation matrices. These observations demonstrate that social mobility is not purely a matter of socioeconomic processes, although they do not detract from the socioeconomic interpretation of the major common feature of mobility which we advance subsequently.

[3] Jones did not have at his disposal the unit-record tape from the OCG survey as he attempted the earlier comparison of the two stratification systems. This precluded computations of metric regressions based on comparably coded educational and occupational classifications. Moreover, the occupational scale used by Jones was a constructed prestige scale consisting of 16 hierarchically ordered groups (Broom, Jones, and Zubrzycki, 1965; Broom and Jones, 1969a). Although not based explicitly on popular ratings of the social standing of occupations, the scale was constructed to simulate such a scale; it was not a socioeconmic index constructed like the Duncan SEI (Duncan, 1961) or the Blishen (1967) index for Canada. Indeed, the fact that income data are not col-

following comparison rests upon a reconciliation of the occupational detail in the ANU and OCG data sets into a single classification at the level of 10 major occupation groups and into (nominally) the same educational categories.[4] We would note that, while now the two surveys are substantially more comparable with respect to the classifica-

---

lected in the Australian census precluded the construction of an explicit socioeconomic scale.

A major difference between socioeconomic and prestige scales is that farm occupations obtain lower relative scores in the former than in the latter. For example, Broom and Jones (1969a) place graziers (large-scale farmers) second highest on their list, and other farmers and farm managers sixth highest. Similarly, in the NORC scale (Siegel, 1971), farmers and farm managers have a major group score of 41, ranking between managers, officials and proprietors, and clerical workers, whereas in the Duncan SEI scale, they score only 14 SEI points, a position higher only than laborers (nonfarm or farm). So it seems that the public, when rating the social standing of farmers, gives them a much higher position than is the case when one measures their socioeconomic position.

There are several possible reasons for this discrepancy between the two methods of scaling. First, the public may ignore the fact that many farmers eke out a marginal existence, little above subsistence level, and focus rather on the large-scale, prosperous farmer. Second, there may be still something of a cultural lag in social perception, such that rural images are rated higher than urban images (the devaluation of urban life syndrome). Third, there may be a tendency for socioeconomic indices to understate the position of farmers because they do not measure income in kind. We cannot arbitrate among these possible explanations or resolve which combination of factors accounts for the discrepancy. The main point, however, is that the earlier comparison by Jones (1971) was clouded by the fact that the Australian study used a prestige scale, whereas the United States study used the SEI. By reducing both studies to a common metric, we can examine the effect that different types of metric have on our comparison, and also evaluate whether an SEI index fits the data better than a prestige index.

To effect such a comparison, we have no alternative but to use prestige and socioeconomic scales derived from U.S. data. We justify this procedure on the grounds that a detailed comparison of Australian occupation scales with scales for Canada gives high interscale correlation, both with the prestige scale constructed by Pineo and Porter and with the Blishen index (Jones and Jones, 1972). Inasmuch as the Pineo–Porter scale correlates .98 with the NORC scale and .87 with the Australian ANU scale, while the Australian scale correlates .83 with the Blishen scores (Jones and Jones, 1972:79), we are satisfied that our procedure does not introduce any systematic errors of importance into the comparison.

[4] The 10 major occupation groups are (1) professional, technical, and kindred workers, (2) managers, officials, and proprietors, (3) clerical workers, (4) sales workers, (5) craftsmen and foremen, (6) operatives, (7) service workers, (8) nonfarm laborers, (9) farmers and farm managers, and (10) farm laborers and foremen. In reconciling the roughly 100 categories of Australian occupations into their U.S. detailed census counterparts, prior to regrouping at the major group level, we were not uniformly successful. For example, owing to the treatment of apprentices as craftsmen in Australia and as operatives in the 1960 U.S. Census classification, some (but not all) of the Australian apprentices were misclassified (i.e., those not listed as craftsmen's assistants in groups that we classified as containing basically operatives).

tion of educational and occupational information, there remain conceptual differences between the two studies. The most marked is the definition of "father's occupation," which in the OCG data is given by the occupation of father at the son's age 16, and which in the ANU data is father's current occupation (circa 1965) or longest job (if deceased or not then at work).

Table 1.1 summarizes the 10-category inter- and intragenerational mobility tables (not reported here). Briefly, in all three mobility matrices, we observe greater net mobility (structural mobility, as given in

TABLE 1.1

Occupational Mobility Statistics for U.S. Men Aged 20-64 in 1962 and Australian Men Aged 20 and Over in 1965

Type of Mobility and Society	Percent Changing Major Occ Group			Mobility Index[d]
	Minimum[a]	Observed[b]	Expected[c]	
Father's Occ to				
Current Occ				
U.S.	21.8	77.1	88.0	83.5
Australia	14.9	71.0	86.6	78.2
Father's Occ to				
First Occ				
U.S.	43.7	78.9	90.2	75.7
Australia	32.2	73.3	88.5	73.0
First Occ to				
Current Occ				
U.S.	31.2	72.3	89.3	70.7
Australia	23.2	59.7	87.8	56.5

[a]Net mobility; coefficient of dissimilarity comparing row and column marginals.

[b]Percentage off main diagonal.

[c]Percentages off the main diagonal under model of independence of rows and columns.

$$^d \text{Mobility Index} = \left(\frac{\text{Observed} - \text{Minimum}}{\text{Expected} - \text{Minimum}}\right).$$

the marginal distributions) in the U.S. than in Australia, coupled with somewhat greater observed (gross) mobility, especially in career mobility. Were we to subtract minimum from observed mobility to calculate "circulation" mobility in the fashion of Broom and Jones (1969a), we would find *greater* circulation mobility in Australia than in the U.S., except in the case of career mobility (cf. Broom and Jones, 1969a). If we take the model of complete independence of origins and destinations as a norm for comparison, the mobility indices of Table 1.1 argue for no major societal difference in the relationship of observed to expected mobility (which is really a ratio of "circulation" mobility observed to "circulation" mobility expected on the model of complete independence), save in the case of career mobility. In the latter instance, there is some more predictability, or rigidity, in the Australian intragenerational transition matrix.

Are the ANU and OCG matrices the same or different? Table 1.2 offers some insight into the question of whether the bivariate mobility patterns bespeak two societies with one mobility regime or with two different ones. We have applied log-linear models explicated recently by Leo Goodman (1972a) to a three-dimensional data matrix for each of the three mobility matrices. Dimension one is occupation of origin (father's or first occupation), dimension two is occupation of destination (first or current occupation), and dimension three is place (Australia or U.S.); overall each matrix is $10 \times 10 \times 2$. The data are completely nominal, and the purpose is to apply models of interest to the end of predicting or estimating the observed frequencies in each matrix. Goodness of fit of a model is given by testing against a likelihood-ratio Chi-square. Table 1.2 reports on two models: Model A estimates the frequencies on the assumption that differences in mobility between the two places are solely a function of different structure, as given in the origin and destination marginals; Model B estimates the frequencies on the assumption of different marginals, but it also assumes that relative mobility chances (i.e., mobility relationships between origins and destinations) are the same in both places. It is important to note that a significant Chi-square value for the fit of this model indicates that Model B does not fit the data well, implying that mobility patterns in the two places are not the same.

Table 1.2 is clear about the fit of Model A: There is far more to the pattern of mobility in the two societies than is given in the fact of their differing (marginal) structures. Actually, we have no great interest in Model A except as it serves as a baseline for assessing the fit of Model B, which hypothesizes (as null) that there is no difference in mobility

TABLE 1.2

Applications of *Log-Linear Models to Mobility Matrices for U.S. Men Aged 20-64 in 1962 and Australian Men Aged 20 and Over in 1965*

Matrix and Models	TOTAL MEN				NONFARM ORIGINS			
	Index of dis-similarity	X^2_{LR}	df	p	Index of dis-similarity	X^2_{LR}	df	p
Father's Occ by Son's Current Occ								
A. Model of variable marginals	19.00	5630.6	162	.00	16.05	2260.6	126	.00
B. Model of variable marginals and place-constant interactions	1.79	128.3	81	.00	1.91	89.6	63	.02
Father's Occ by Son's First Occ								
A. Model of variable marginals	24.86	8344.8	162	.00	15.02	2248.0	126	.00
B. Model of variable marginals and place-constant interactions	1.44	126.9	81	.00	1.56	87.9	63	.02
Son's First Occ by Current Occ								
A. Model of variable marginals	26.37	10542.8	162	.00	24.81	6610.1	162	.00
B. Model of variable marginals and place-constant interactions	2.26	210.7	81	.00	2.55	192.2	81	.00

regimes. We must reject null (no difference), since the deviations of observed from expected frequencies are statistically significant. This means that, in each of the three mobility matrices, there are interactions that are attributable to place, holding constant the differences in (marginal) structure and the additive mobility effects of place. However, it is important to note that the departures of the observed from expected frequencies under Model B are but a small percentage of both the total Chi-square for each matrix and the values under Model A. In fact, Chi-square values for net inter-place differences in mobility (128.3, 126.9, and 210.7 from Table 1.2) are but some 2% of the Chi-square under Model A; therefore, about 98% of the "variance" in each matrix, net of the inter-place differences stemming from their marginals, is attributable to additive effects, that is, place-constant mobility patterns. So, despite a significant inter-place difference, the significant effect of inter-place similarity is dominant.

We now block the origin categories for farmers and farm laborers and rerun our log-linear models on the $8 \times 10 \times 2$ intragenerational matrices and $10 \times 10 \times 2$ career matrices for men of nonfarm origin. This strategy reveals a major source of the imperfect fit of Model B. About 60 to 73% of the original Chi-square in the two intergenerational inter-place matrices is a function of the differential effects of farm origins in the two societies' mobility regimes, although the remaining Chi-square indicates a continuing, sometimes significant, but substantively small (4% of Chi-square under Model A), inter-place effect within the nonfarm population.

We conclude from this analysis of contingency tables that the bivariate process of mobility in Australia and the U.S. in the mid-1960s was largely the same, with minor but significant idiosyncratic patterns, originating in the main from the unique mobility patterns for men from farm origins. Having established a case for the similarity of stratification as a process in the two societies, we inquire into the foundation of that process. Given our knowledge of the socioeconomic basis of occupational stratification in the U.S., it would be surprising were it to be otherwise for Australia. Before proceeding to examine the specifics of the process of status attainment in the two societies, we pause to relate our findings on father-to-son mobility to earlier generalizations about rates of intergenerational mobility in industrial society. In a recent overview, Boudon (1974) has asserted that the conclusion of Lipset and Bendix (1960), that overall rates of father-to-son mobility seem to be much the same in industrial societies, "does not seem to have been seriously challenged by studies conducted since the publication of the theory." This claim, however, neglects the fact that, as early as 1960, S. M. Miller (1960) seriously qualified the generality of the Lipset–Bendix conclusion. Moreover, Jones (1969) has shown that the quality of the data on which Lipset and Bendix relied was so seriously deficient as not to justify any sound conclusion. If Lipset and Bendix were right, they were right in spite of the poor quality of their evidence.

We believe that industrial societies can be shown not to have the same rates of *observed* mobility (cf. Broom and Jones, 1969a, 1969b). However, there is reason to suppose that they may have similar patterns of *circulation* mobility. For two societies where adequate longitudinal data are available, it seems that, once structural mobility has been taken into account, circulation mobility has been nearly constant over time. For the United States, we have reanalyzed seven bodies of data covering national surveys from 1947 to 1972 as well as Rogoff's (1953a) Indianapolis study for 1910 and 1940 (see Chapter 6). Our conclusion is that "empirically, we have observed that in several bodies of data for U.S. men the multiplicative associations between father's and son's occupation are largely invariant with respect to time." That is to say, the intrinsic pattern of generational mobility has been the same over the period considered. What has varied is the occupational structure, or environment, within which that pattern has been expressed.

To this finding for the U.S. we can now add an identical finding for England and Wales. Despite substantial difficulties in reconciling occupational classification, Hope (1974) has compared the "splice" between the 1959 and 1972 studies of occupational mobility in England and Wales (the splice consists of men born between 1910 and 1929, a cross-section of whom was interviewed by Glass as young men in 1949 and by the Nuffield mobility group as older men in 1972). From the results of this and other comparisons, "it may be concluded that, so far as men are concerned, the occupational structure of England and Wales is no more open today than it was fifty or sixty years ago" (Hope, 1974:35). Taken together, these findings suggest that there exists a relatively stable process of status transmission in a class of industrial societies, a process presumably rooted in the family system, and that this process changes its expression according to the rate at which the occupational system is transformed over time.

To this constancy *within* countries, we can now add a constancy *between* at least two different countries, Australia and the United States. Our comparison of father-to-son mobility indicates that, once differences in the respective occupational opportunity structures have been taken into account, the pattern of circulation mobility is basically the same. We therefore venture a new, provisional hypothesis to replace the falsified Lipset–Bendix hypothesis about total rates of mobility. This new hypothesis differs in that it is specified in terms of *circulation* mobility, and states the genotypical pattern of mobility (circulation mobility) in industrial societies with a market economy and a nuclear family system is basically the same. The phenotypical pattern of mobility (observed mobility) differs according to the rate of change in the occupational structure, exogenously determined (so far as any individual family is concerned) by (for example) technological change, the supply and demand for specific kinds of labor (e.g., educated labor, women), and changing social values affecting (among other things) the demand for higher education, the rate of economic change, family size, and the spacing of children. How widely this generalization can be applied beyond the two countries included in this analysis (which is, we remind the reader, far more detailed in terms of its occupational classification than Lipset and Bendix's original study) will be clearer when the results of the present round of national mobility studies conducted between 1972 and 1975 in upward of a dozen nations become available (Featherman, Hauser, and Sewell, 1974). We should also add that if the above hypothesis is suppported by these data, one implication is that mobility analysts will need to give much more attention to unraveling the factors involved in structural change than has been the case in the past. To be able to make this assertion likewise implies an analytical ability to distinguish circulation from structural mobility.

THE PROCESS OF STATUS ALLOCATION
IN TWO SOCIETIES

Tables 1.3 through 1.8 report on an extensive examination of the process of stratification as revealed in the ANU and OCG data. We have classified and scaled both data sets equivalently, running correlations and regressions for both the total and nonfarm populations (viz., men whose fathers were not farmers, farm laborers, farm managers or farm foremen) and altering the analysis by rescaling occupation variables (at the level of major groups) into Duncan's socioeconomic index (1961), Siegel's (1971) new prestige scores, and Treiman's (1975) standard international prestige index.[5] Since we have expected somewhat greater similarity between societies among the men of nonfarm origin than in the total male population, we have run separate analyses for these groups.

Table 1.3 contains interscale correlations for two of the three occupational variables from the basic Blau and Duncan model which we have estimated (in its fully recursive form) for both societies. By and large, the two prestige scales correlate more highly with each other than does either with the socioeconomic scale. In both societies, the Duncan and Siegel scales are more highly collinear than are the Duncan and Treiman scales, perhaps indicating somewhat less validity in Treiman's version of prestige in both places. Inasmuch as the largest difference between socioeconomic and prestige scales involves the treatment of farm occupations (because of the higher ranks of farming on the prestige scales), it is not surprising that the two SES-prestige correlations are higher when calculated over the nonfarm rather than the total population; however, there is no change in the Treiman–Siegel correlations. Finally, there are no apparent systematic differences attributable to place in Table 1.3.

Tables 1.4 and 1.5 render product–moment correlations for the five variables of a Blau–Duncan stratification model, along with means and standard deviations. We shall not dwell on these summary statistics, except to note that, apart from the Treiman scores, the correlations for Australia, based on the reconciled major occupation group classification, are much closer to their U.S. counterparts than are the correlations reported by Jones (1971), which rested upon a different educa-

[5] The major group scale scores are as follows:

| Occupation group | Scales | | |
	Duncan	Siegel	Treiman
Professional, technical, and kindred	75	60	57
Managers, officials, proprietors	57	50	64
Clerical and kindred	45	39	44
Sales and kindred	49	34	40
Craft and kindred	31	39	41
Operatives	18	29	33
Service	17	25	31
Nonfarm labor	7	18	19
Farmers and farm managers	14	41	47
Farm laborers	9	19	27

N.B.: Treiman scores were calculated from an early appendix kindly supplied by the author.

TABLE 1.3

*Interscale Correlations[a] over Major Occupation Groups, Duncan (1961),
Siegel (1971), and Treiman (Forthcoming) Scores, Australian Men Aged
20 and Over in 1965 and U.S. Men Aged 20-64 in 1962*

Scale Comparisons	Populations and Occupations			
	TOTAL MEN			
	Father's Occupation		Current Occupation	
	Australia	U.S.	Australia	U.S.
Duncan-Siegel	.7904	.7224	.8585	.9013
Duncan-Treiman	.7629	.6794	.8036	.8441
Siegel-Treiman	.9486	.9404	.9277	.9272
	NONFARM MEN			
	Father's Occupation		Current Occupation	
	Australia	U.S.	Australia	U.S.
Duncan-Siegel	.9599	.9454	.9192	.9467
Duncan-Treiman	.9296	.9111	.8654	.8940
Siegel-Treiman	.9478	.9373	.9239	.9255

[a]Correlations reflect population frequencies as weights.

tional and occupational classification. More importantly, for both
societies and in each population of both places, the correlations calculated over Duncan's socioeconomic index are uniformly higher than
those computed over either of the prestige scales. We shall take advantage of this last observation later.

For total men in Australia (Table 1.6) and in the U.S. (Table 1.7), the
process of stratification, as depicted by occupational variables encoded
in any of the three metrics of status, is much the same. Comparing
Panels A, B, and C of standardized regression coefficients within each
of Tables 1.6 and 1.7 reveals no striking departures from the now
familiar relationships in this three-equation stratification model, irrespective of the metric in which occupation is scaled. However, in each
of the three equations for both Australia and the U.S., the R^2 value is
higher if we have scaled occupations in units of socioeconomic status
rather than in units of prestige (Siegel or Treiman). This finding is
consistent with an argument that rests the process of stratification on an
underlying socioeconomic base, irrespective of place.

TABLE 1.4

Coefficients of Correlation for OCG Males Aged 20-64 (Above Diagonal) and Australian Males Aged 20 and Older (Below Diagonal), Based on Reconciled Classification of Occupations into U.S. Major Occupation Groups, with Categories Scored in Selected Metrics of Status

Variables	FAED	FAOCC	EDUC	FJOB	OCC	Mean	Std. Dev.
(a) Socioeconomic Status (Duncan, 1961) Metric							
Father's education	--	.501	.445	.325	.298	2.27	1.55
Father's occupation	.462	--	.426	.402	.380	28.06	18.77
R's education	.472	.340	--	.512	.564	3.42	1.56
R's first job	.284	.315	.498	--	.523	26.68	20.23
R's current occupation	.324	.339	.518	.545	--	35.66	21.48
Mean	2.45	28.22	3.13	29.66	34.05		
Standard Deviation	1.30	18.95	1.26	18.49	20.35		
(b) NORC Prestige (Siegel, 1971) Metric							
Father's education	--	.360	.445	.298	.261	2.27	1.55
Father's occupation	.370	--	.234	.219	.236	37.46	10.06
R's education	.472	.223	--	.472	.503	3.42	1.56
R's first job	.245	.176	.451	--	.444	31.58	11.82
R's current occupation	.266	.223	.451	.438	--	38.28	12.08
Mean	2.45	36.64	3.13	34.52	38.44		
Standard Deviation	1.30	10.56	1.26	10.50	10.89		
(c) International Prestige (Treiman, forthcoming) Metric							
Father's education	--	.305	.445	.283	.237	2.27	1.55
Father's occupation	.264	--	.219	.216	.240	42.58	11.58
R's education	.472	.189	--	.435	.442	3.42	1.56
R's first job	.210	.163	.403	--	.371	35.52	10.98
R's current occupation	.226	.204	.345	.339	--	42.77	12.98
Mean	2.45	41.70	3.13	38.47	43.21		
Standard Deviation	1.30	12.87	1.26	9.82	12.47		

In his earlier comparison based on unreconciled occupational classifications, Jones (1971) noted two apparent differences in the process of status attainment in the two countries: the relative weakness of father's occupation as a determinant of son's status in Australia, and a looser articulation between educational and occupational statuses. The first difference is now shown to be entirely an artifact of differences in the methods of classifying and scaling occupations: When SEI scores are used, the correlations between father's occupation and son's first and present occupation are raised, and although father's occupation is still the weakest correlating variable in the Australian case, it is now much closer in importance to father's education. It is interesting

TABLE 1.5

Coefficients of Correlation for OCG Males Aged 20-64 of Nonfarm Background
(Above Diagonal) and Australian Males Aged 20 and Over of Nonfarm Background
(Below Diagonal), Based on Reconciled Classification of Occupations into U.S.
Major Occupation Groups, with Categories Scored in Selected Metrics of Status

Variables	FAED	FAOCC	EDUC	FJOB	OCC	Mean	Std. Dev.
(a) Socioeconomic Status (Duncan, 1961) Metric							
Father's education	--	.494	.419	.300	.274	2.49	1.61
Father's occupation	.458	--	.384	.336	.337	34.10	19.32
R's education	.454	.306	--	.487	.562	3.69	1.50
R's first job	.250	.238	.493	--	.504	30.18	20.79
R's current occupation	.299	.292	.520	.517	--	38.80	21.64
Mean	2.60	32.57	3.27	32.51	36.65		
Standard Deviation	1.31	19.52	1.26	18.32	20.34		
(b) NORC Prestige (Siegel, 1971) Metric							
Father's education	--	.449	.419	.282	.247	2.49	1.61
Father's occupation	.434	--	.342	.289	.291	36.87	11.17
R's education	.454	.274	--	.459	.514	3.69	1.50
R's first job	.240	.194	.464	--	.464	33.31	11.81
R's current occupation	.261	.246	.486	.472	--	39.33	12.33
Mean	2.60	36.10	3.27	35.30	38.71		
Standard Deviation	1.31	11.35	1.26	10.28	11.26		
(c) International Prestige (Treiman, forthcoming) Metric							
Father's education	--	.392	.419	.276	.228	2.49	1.61
Father's occupation	.316	--	.340	.284	.303	41.54	13.10
R's education	.454	.242	--	.437	.454	3.69	1.50
R's first job	.219	.176	.427	--	.389	36.74	11.19
R's current occupation	.228	.224	.381	.373	--	43.70	13.14
Mean	2.60	40.79	3.27	38.82	43.24		
Standard Deviation	1.31	14.10	1.26	9.69	12.70		

to note that, whereas using the SEI scores for major groups reduces the
U.S. correlations fractionally by only .02 points (illustrating Blau and
Duncan's (1967) observation that the use of detailed occupations
rather than major groups "offers a useful refinement but not radically
different pattern of grading"), it raises the Australian correlations by an
average of .11 points, thus reducing the intersocietal differences previously noted by Jones. So far as the second difference is concerned
(the looser articulation between the educational and occupational systems), the original relative difference does persist: Son's education
still has a weaker direct effect on current occupation than does first job

TABLE 1.6

Standardized and Metric Regression Coefficients for Three-Equation Stratification Model, Australian Men Aged 20 and Over, 1965, by Selected Scales of Socioeconomic Status and Prestige

| Dependent Variables | Independent Variables | | | | α | R^2 |
	FAED	FAOCC	EDUC	FJOB		
	Standardized Coefficients					
A. Duncan SES Scores						
1. Education	.401 [a] (.022)	.156 (.022)				.242
2. First Occupation	-.001 (.024)	.165 (.022)	.442 (.023)			.272
3. Current Occupation	.036 (.022)	.113 (.021)	.285 (.023)	.357 (.021)		.392
B. Siegel Prestige Scores						
1. Education	.452 (.021)	.056 (.021)				.226
2. First Occupation	.016 (.024)	.075 (.022)	.427 (.023)			.210
3. Current Occupation	.023 (.023)	.099 (.021)	.290 (.024)	.283 (.022)		.283
C. Treiman Prestige Scores						
1. Education	.454 (.021)	.069 (.021)				.228
2. First Occupation	.006 (.025)	.089 (.022)	.383 (.024)			.170
3. Current Occupation	.048 (.024)	.114 (.021)	.212 (.025)	.225 (.022)		.184
	Metric Regression Coefficients					
A. Duncan SES Scores						
4. Education	.388	.001			1.84	
5. First Occupation	.015	.161	6.53		4.76	
6. Current Occupation	.562	.122	4.63	.393	3.07	
B. Siegel Prestige Scores						
4. Education	.438	.006			1.81	
5. First Occupation	.128	.075	3.59		20.3	
6. Current Occupation	.193	.103	2.53	.294	16.2	
C. Treiman Prestige Scores						
4. Education	.440	.007			1.76	
5. First Occupation	.044	.068	3.01		26.1	
6. Current Occupation	.463	.111	2.11	.286	19.9	

[a] Standard errors in parentheses.

TABLE 1.7

Standardized and Metric Regression Coefficients for Three-Equation Stratification Model, U.S. Men Aged 20-64, March 1962, by Selected Scales of Socioeconomic Status and Prestige

Dependent Variables	Independent Variables				α	R^2
	FAED	FAOCC	EDUC	FJOB		

Standardized Coefficients

	FAED	FAOCC	EDUC	FJOB	α	R^2
A. Duncan SES Scores						
1. Education	.309 (.007)[a]	.272 (.007)				.253
2. First Occupation	.040 (.007)	.210 (.007)	.405 (.007)			.305
3. Current Occupation	-.020 (.007)	.113 (.007)	.376 (.007)	.292 (.007)	(.006)	.401
B. Siegel Prestige Scores						
1. Education	.414 (.007)	.085 (.007)				.204
2. First Occupation	.080 (.007)	.093 (.007)	.415 (.007)			.240
3. Current Occupation	-.014 (.007)	.100 (.006)	.367 (.007)	.253 (.007)		.317
C. Treiman Prestige Scores						
1. Education	.417 (.006)	.092 (.006)				.206
2. First Occupation	.083 (.007)	.109 (.007)	.374 (.007)			.210
3. Current Occupation	-.005 (.007)	.126 (.006)	.328 (.007)	.203 (.007)		.250

Metric Regression Coefficients

	FAED	FAOCC	EDUC	FJOB	α	R^2
A. Duncan SES Scores						
4. Education	.311	.023			2.08	
5. First Occupation	.521	.226	5.25		1.20	
6. Current Occupation	-.284	.129	5.17	.310	6.72	
B. Siegel Prestige Scores						
4. Education	.417	.013			1.98	
5. First Occupation	.608	.110	3.14		15.3	
6. Current Occupation	-.106	.120	2.84	.258	16.2	
C. Treiman Prestige Scores						
4. Education	.419	.012			1.94	
5. First Occupation	.592	.103	2.64		20.8	
6. Current Occupation	-.045	.141	2.73	.240	19.0	

[a] Standard errors in parentheses.

22

in Australia than in the U.S. However, we hasten to observe that the
metric estimates for these same equations show that, in terms of raw
units of socioeconomic status or prestige (as the case may be), the
current occupational returns to education and first job in the two
places are quite similar. Moreover, in an analysis of age cohorts not
replicated in this analysis, Jones (1971) noted some convergence in the
pattern of these coefficients. In sum, while there may be some (minor)
difference in the effective role of educational attainment in determining current job in the two countries, the overall pattern is seen to be
very similar when more nearly comparable methods of classification
are used. Moreover, the fact that apprentices are coded as operatives
in the 1960 U.S. Census classification but as craftsmen in the Australian may account for the small differences that remain.

The men of nonfarm origin in the U.S. and Australia are perhaps
most comparable, and they appear in Table 1.8; we pause to note from
the metric coefficients some minor differences in the process of
achievement as given therein. From the equation intercepts, it is clear
that the Americans attain somewhat higher average years of schooling
than do the Australians, controlling for background factors. While the
Australians typically are better able to enter higher-status first jobs,
U.S. men hold more prestigious current occupations. Among the regression estimates, we find in Equations 4 of Panels A and B that
Australian father's education is nearly half again as efficacious for son's
education as is the case in the U.S., although in terms of real consequences of this difference, the net advantage to the Australians is trivial. In Equations 5 of Panels A and B, the Australians appear to benefit
some .8 Duncan score points more than the Americans from equal
(net) schooling. While the societal differences in the effects of paternal
education in Equations 5 and 6 are large enough to be significant, the
coefficients themselves are either statistically nonsignificant or negligible in their substantive bearing.

We return to our earlier observation that in both places the correlations for the basic model are higher when run over socioeconomic status
than over prestige; additionally, R^2 values in regression equations for
each society are larger when calculated for socioeconomic scores.
These data, which replicate earlier observations within the U.S. (Duncan, Featherman, and Duncan, 1972), are consistent with the interpretation that prestige scales are fallible indexes of socioeconomic status.
If what underlies the apparent fundamental similarity of social mobility among some societies is a socioeconomic process, then to study that
process via prestige scales is to misspecify its essence and to err
(though not by a large arithmetic factor, given the usually high correla-

TABLE 1.8

Standardized and Metric Regression Coefficients for Three-Equation Stratification Model, Australian Men Aged 20 and Over in 1965 with Nonfarm Background and U.S. Men Aged 20-64 in March 1962 with Nonfarm Background

Dependent Variables	Independent Variables					
	FAED	FAOCC SES	EDUC	FJOB SES	α	R^2
Standardized Coefficients						
A. Australia						
1. Education	.397 [a] (.026)	.124 (.025)				.218
2. First Occ SES [b]	.004 (.028)	.102 (.026)	.440 (.026)			.233
3. Current Occ SES	.023 (.026)	.104 (.024)	.319 (.027)	.336 (.024)		.377
B. United States						
1. Education	.303 (.008)	.234 (.008)				.217
2. First Occ SES	.054 (.008)	.154 (.008)	.405 (.008)			.265
3. Current Occ SES	-.028 (.008)	.104 (.008)	.395 (.008)	.286 (.007)		.393
Metric Regression Coefficients						
A. Australia						
4. Education	.382	.008			2.02	
5. First Occ SES	.050	.095	6.40		8.34	
6. Current Occ SES	.349	.109	5.15	.373	3.25	
B. United States						
4. Education	.282	.018			2.37	
5. First Occ SES	.696	.165	5.62		2.08	
6. Current Occ SES	-.380	.116	5.69	.297	5.80	

[a] Standard errors in parentheses.

[b] Duncan SES scores assigned to all occupations, classified in major groups.

tion between scales of prestige and socioeconomic status) in statistical estimation of cause and effect.[6]

In taking this interpretation seriously, we have specified the causal

[6] Surely there are analyses in which a purified prestige scoring of occupations makes more sense conceptually than does a socioeconomic scoring. However, in models of status attainment wherein individual-level achievements of economic (earnings), educational, and occupational status are problematic, we argue here that a socioeconomic scoring is preferable. Clearly, in adopting a major occupation group classification, we

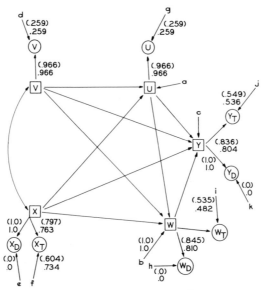

Figure 1.1 Confirmatory factor model of the process of socioeconomic achievement, United States and Australian men. Coefficients in parentheses ( ) are for United States. □ denotes unmeasured variable; ○ denotes measured variable; V = father's education; U = R's education; X = father's status; X_D = father's occupation (Duncan); X_T = father's occupation (Treiman); W = first job status; W_D = first job (Duncan); W_T = first job (Treiman); Y = current occupational status; Y_D = current occupation (Duncan); Y_T = current occupation (Treiman). For estimates of unmarked paths, see Table 1.9.

model in Figure 1.1, obtaining the estimates that appear in Table 1.9 for both societies, using a technique developed by K. Jöreskog (Jöreskog, Gruvaeus, and van Thillo, 1970). Essentially Figure 1.1 represents a factor model in which each of the boxed variables is unmeasured in either the OCG or ANU data but is reflected in variables

---

have assumed the theoretical import of skill levels and "head-work/hand-work" distinctions; this is consistent with standing notions about the characteristics of industrialized societies. By scoring major occupation groups in the metric of socioeconomic status (i.e., assigning aggregate, group-specific socioeconomic scores), we uncover two interesting relationships in models of status attainment, estimated over individuals. First, we estimate the relationship of individuals' educational achievements (years of schooling) to their occupational levels, based on knowledge of the expected educational (i.e., skills) and earnings (i.e., performance, productivity) characteristics of average role incumbents. Second, we estimate the relationship of individuals' earnings to their occupational levels, based on expectations in the aggregate of the educational and earnings of "typical" role incumbents. Were we to score occupations in the metric of prestige, we would be faced with the theoretical dilemma that prestige is ordinarily thought to be an *outgrowth* (among other determinants) of education- and wealth-based criteria.

TABLE 1.9

Standardized Regression Coefficients for Stratification Model Based on Figure 1.1, U.S. and Australian Men in 1962 and 1965, Respectively

Dependent Variables	Independent Variables					
	FAED[a]	FAOCC STATUS	EDUC	FJOB STATUS	R^2	$\sqrt{1-R^2}$
AUSTRALIA, 1965						
R's Education	.438 [b] (.022)	.143 (.022)			.272	.853
First Job Status	-.019 (.025)	.159 (.022)	.470 (.023)		.287	.845
Current Occ Status	.026 (.023)	.110 (.021)	.306 (.024)	.345 (.021)	.398	.776
UNITED STATES, 1962						
R's Education	.340 (.007)	.265 (.007)			.279	.849
First Job Status	.036 (.007)	.180 (.007)	.433 (.007)		.312	.829
Current Occ Status	-.029 (.007)	.095 (.006)	.414 (.007)	.268 (.007)	.406	.771

[a]See text for definition of variables.

[b]Standard errors in parentheses.

for which we have measurements (indicators). For simplicity we have taken the Duncan and Treiman scores as reflections of each unmeasured occupational variable, and we have estimated the validity of each from the data matrix. In the case of the two education variables, we have assumed a constant validity coefficient of .966, based on earlier analysis (Siegel and Hodge, 1968). The estimation procedure conforms to a confirmatory factor model, and Figure 1.1 assumes all residuals are uncorrelated. If we are correct in asserting that the process of achievement in both the U.S. and Australia is a socioeconomic one and that prestige scales are fallible indicators of socioeconomic status, we should estimate higher validity coefficients for the Duncan scale reflections than for the Treiman scale variables.

In fact, Figure 1.1 confirms our expectations, with validities of unity (these validity coefficients were free parameters) for all Duncan variables in both societies and substantially lower ones for the Treiman variables. The standardized regression estimates in Table 1.9 do not deviate in their descriptive character from those in Tables 1.6 and 1.7, save for the larger R^2 values; hence we shall not discuss them.

ARTIFACTUAL OR REAL DIFFERENCES BETWEEN PRESTIGE AND SOCIOECONOMIC SCORES?

In advancing the hypothesis that prestige scores are less valid indicators of the dimension of status which underlies occupational mobility than are SEI scores, we do not neglect the possibility that our correlational results reflect artifacts of metric. (We are indebted to O. D. Duncan for reminding us of this possibility.) One may recall Duncan's efforts to transform the 1947 NORC prestige scale into his SEI scores (Reiss, 1961:119) and the "S-shaped" functional relationship between rankings of equivalent titles. Moreover, the SEI scale tends to accentuate the distinction between white-collar and blue-collar occupations, and it has a longer upper tail than does the prestige metric. To illustrate these points, we list the Duncan SEI and Siegel NORC prestige scores for U.S. Census major occupation groups:

	SEI	1965 NORC
Professional, technical, and kindred	75	60
Managers, officials, proprietors, excluding farm	57	50
Sales workers	49	34
Clerical and kindred workers	45	39
Craftsmen and foremen	31	39
Operatives and kindred workers	18	29
Service workers		
Other	17	25
Private household	8	20
Farmers and farm managers	14	41
Farm laborers and foremen	9	19
Nonfarm laborers	7	18

The relevance of these relationships for our conclusion that prestige is an "error-prone" proxy for socioeconomic status is obvious upon its statement. The socioeconomic metric accentuates correlations relative to the metric of prestige, which has an attenuated variance and more regular intervals among ranked occupation titles. Therefore, the patterns of correlations and regressions calculated over SEI and prestige reported for both Australia and the U.S. may be an artifact of expansions or contractions of a single (ordinal) metric rather than of real differences in the relative ranking of occupation titles by prestige versus socioeconomic status.

In order to reduce these sources of artifactuality in our scale comparisons, we normalize all three scales—Duncan's, Siegel's, and Treiman's—against a percentile distribution of occupation titles in the 1970 U.S. Census classification (some 400 specific titles); for this exercise, we use only the 1962 OCG data for men aged 25–64. We use or develop Duncan, Siegel, and Treiman raw scores to rank titles; then, we calculate the percentage of all titles having Duncan, Siegel, and Treiman scores below the title of interest. After transformation, titles are ranked by percentile scores having means of 50 on all three scales; there are equal variances among titles in each new scale, but not in the scaled occupation distributions. What differentiates the position of a particular occupation on, say, Duncan's versus Siegel's scale is now solely the ranking properties of the socioeconomic as opposed to the prestige scale. For example, the title "farmer" is assigned a raw value of 14 on Duncan's SEI and of 41 on the 1965 NORC scale. After transformation, these values are 12.2 and 52.8, respectively.

When normalized to a common percentile metric, the sample variances of the three scales are more similar than when they are in their untransformed (raw) metrics. This holds for each of the three occupation variables, and it holds among men of nonfarm background (Table 1.11) as well as among all men aged 25–64 (Table 1.10). Comparing corresponding triangles of correlations among scales for each occupation in Tables 1.10 and 1.11, we find a small improvement in the correlations of the two prestige scales under transformation, with the exception of the first-job correlations r_{78}. For all men (Table 1.10), transformation generally increases the correlations between the distributions of respondents over ranks on the Duncan and Siegel scales, with the correlations over occupations of father being an exception; however, the Duncan–Treiman correlations are smaller in all three occupations. In view of the rather high correspondence in ranking between the prestige scales (especially under transformation), we compute the average correlation between Duncan SEI and Siegel–Treiman prestige scales for each occupation and in both halves of Table 1.10. This comparison between SEI and "averaged" prestige shows a somewhat *larger* difference between the two types of scales in the transformed data than in the raw scales for all three occupations.

Ideally we would want to decompose the variation in raw interscale correlations into components attributable to metric and ranking properties. Without undertaking this detailed analysis, we can derive some inference about the relative magnitudes of these components from a comparison of Tables 1.10 and 1.11. We focus on the differential ranking of farm occupations on prestige and socioeconomic scales and the

TABLE 1.10

Coefficients of Correlation among Five Stratification Variables with Occupations in Three Metrics (Below Diagonal) and in a Single Percentile Metric (Above Diagonal): U.S. Men Aged 25-64 in March 1962

Variables	1	2	3	4	5	6	7	8	9	10	11	M̄	S.D.
1. Father's Education	1.0	.431	.419	.294	.200	.294	.259	.213	.295	.255	.221	7.79	3.88
2. R's Education	.431	1.0	.412	.239	.142	.522	.474	.385	.577	.522	.456	10.78	3.58
3. Father's Occ - Duncan	.477	.429	.943	.695	.488	.378	.312	.235	.369	.301	.258	28.55	26.38
4. Father's Occ - Siegel	.378	.261	.698	.943	.907	.208	.214	.205	.201	.225	.221	41.46	24.82
5. Father's Occ - Treiman	.293	.173	.525	.882	.941	.112	.139	.171	.108	.157	.176	45.70	27.57
6. First Job - Duncan	.316	.555	.420	.269	.183	.960	.831	.674	.487	.408	.353	28.85	26.06
7. First Job - Siegel	.269	.492	.340	.254	.182	.826	.968	.869	.409	.394	.350	28.65	24.96
8. First Job - Treiman	.239	.426	.278	.247	.212	.752	.889	.964	.320	.337	.326	31.53	25.49
9. Current Occ - Duncan	.316	.610	.402	.236	.149	.537	.445	.384	.947	.839	.710	42.73	28.42
10. Current Occ - Siegel	.277	.559	.331	.248	.183	.473	.455	.414	.831	.934	.911	46.54	25.93
11. Current Occ - Treiman	.246	.499	.295	.241	.198	.423	.405	.392	.748	.889	.946	47.53	27.26
Mean	7.79	10.78	27.06	37.86	40.55	26.30	30.67	33.52	37.66	39.35	40.83		
Standard Deviation	3.88	3.58	20.98	11.56	11.88	20.98	13.19	12.13	24.50	13.82	13.84		

29

TABLE 1.11

Coefficients of Correlation among Five Stratification Variables with Occupations in Three Metrics (Below Diagonal) and in a Single Percentile Metric (Above Diagonal): U.S. Men of Nonfarm Background Aged 25-64 in March 1962

Variables	1	2	3	4	5	6	7	8	9	10	11	$\overline{M}$	S.D.
1. Father's Education	1.0	.398	.422	.392	.356	.273	.254	.224	.270	.245	.225	8.30	3.97
2. R's Education	.398	1.0	.401	.368	.339	.510	.480	.421	.574	.535	.490	11.42	3.43
3. Father's Occ – Duncan	.496	.414	.930	.895	.816	.337	.301	.254	.344	.311	.288	35.59	28.52
4. Father's Occ – Siegel	.465	.357	.834	.939	.917	.310	.295	.250	.312	.294	.271	38.30	27.76
5. Father's Occ – Treiman	.432	.339	.770	.892	.934	.281	.269	.246	.282	.262	.250	38.59	28.26
6. First Job – Duncan	.304	.555	.385	.334	.312	.958	.844	.707	.468	.413	.378	33.40	26.80
7. First Job – Siegel	.265	.499	.322	.311	.289	.844	.963	.882	.414	.412	.380	31.62	25.36
8. First Job – Treiman	.251	.465	.293	.284	.279	.781	.906	.962	.357	.362	.352	32.87	25.93
9. Current Occ – Duncan	.293	.610	.367	.307	.286	.525	.445	.417	.944	.876	.776	47.50	28.03
10. Current Occ – Siegel	.268	.574	.327	.298	.273	.480	.477	.445	.856	.931	.914	48.84	26.33
11. Current Occ – Treiman	.246	.529	.311	.282	.270	.445	.435	.422	.793	.891	.945	48.87	27.53
Mean	8.30	11.42	33.37	37.36	38.35	29.74	32.32	34.25	41.49	40.72	41.75		
Standard Deviation	3.97	3.43	22.76	13.39	13.14	21.86	13.15	12.61	24.80	14.30	14.30		

data on father's occupation for illustration. The difference between r_{34} in the lower triangle of Table 1.10 represents differences between the Duncan and Siegel indexes over the distribution of father's occupation, which we attribute *both* to the differences in scale intervals and to differential ranking of fathers in farming; upon subtraction this difference is .136. Performing the same subtraction of r_{34} values in the upper triangles of Tables 1.10 and 1.11 yields a difference of .200, which represents changes in the interscale correlations under a common metric, but owing *solely* to differential ranking of farm occupations. Finally $1 - .895 = .105$ reflects the differential distribution of men over (and ranking of) all nonfarm paternal occupations on the Duncan and Siegel scales. Therefore, the overall *change* in the correlations between these scales from .698 to .895 under metric transformations and the removal of farm titles is most substantially influenced by the score of farm occupations in units of prestige relative to their score in (standardized) units of socioeconomic status; the differential metric properties of the two indexes play a lesser role in this change. In fact, normalizing the metrics tends to *amplify* the differential ranking properties and any corresponding substantive differences between socioeconomic status and that embodied in prestige scales.

We extend our treatment of correlations with the multivariate analyses of Tables 1.12 through 1.14, which give estimates of regression and beta coefficients for the five-variable basic Blau–Duncan model, taking in turn the scaling of detailed U.S. occupations in Duncan SEI, Siegel NORC prestige, and Treiman international prestige scores; occupation distributions are expressed over both raw and normalized metrics. We find no changes in the comparative scaling conclusions drawn from the earlier analyses within both the U.S. and Australia. That is, the higher R^2 values associated with model estimates based on socioeconomic rather than prestige scores cannot be assigned to metric differences among these indexes. Across Tables 1.12 through 1.14, in both raw and percentile data, more variance in occupational status attainment is explained when the process is measured by socioeconomic units than by prestige units. In addition, within each table (holding index constant) the R^2 values are generally *lower* for occupation regressions run over transformed rather than raw data. However, transformation into a common percentile metric does not in any appreciable manner alter the interpretation of the causal process of stratification adduced by the structural equations and coefficients, irrespective of the status index on which this interpretation rests.

We draw another observation from Tables 1.12 through 1.14 regarding frequent allegations that the Duncan SEI artifactually inflates

TABLE 1.12

Regression Analysis of Three Endogenous Variables in Blau-Duncan Basic Model with Occupations Scored on Duncan's Socioeconomic Index and under Transformed and Raw Metrics, U.S. Men Aged 25-64 in March 1962 and by Nonfarm Background Status

Dependent Variables	Independent Variables					
	Father's Education	Father's Occ Duncan SEI	Education (Years Completed)	First Job Duncan SEI	α	R^2
TOTAL MEN AGED 25-64						
Raw Occupation Metrics						
A. Standardized coefficients						
1. Education	.293	.289	--	--	--	.250
2. First Job - SEI	--	.223	.458	--	--	.348
3. Current Occ - SEI	--	.115	.417	.258	--	.439
B. Unstandardized coefficients						
1. Education	.270	.049	--	--	7.34	--
2. First Job - SEI	--	.223	2.68	--	-8.65	--
3. Current Occ - SEI	--	.134	2.85	.301	-4.52	--
Occupation Metrics in Percentiles						
C. Standardized coefficients						
1. Education	.314	.280	--	--	--	.251
2. First Job - SEI	--	.196	.441	--	--	.305
3. Current Occ - SEI	--	.113	.411	.230	--	.390
D. Unstandardized coefficients						
1. Education	.290	.038	--	--	7.42	--
2. First Job - SEI	--	.194	3.21	--	-11.2	--
3. Current Occ - SEI	--	.122	3.26	.250	-3.03	--

NONFARM MEN AGED 25-64

Raw Occupation Metrics

E. Standardized coefficients

1. Education	.255	.288	--	--	.221
2. First Job - SEI	--	.187	.477	--	.337
3. Current Occ - SEI	--	.091	.435	.249	.429

F. Unstandardized coefficients

1. Education	.215	.042	--	--	8.42
2. First Job - SEI	--	.180	3.11	--	-12.4
3. Current Occ - SEI	--	.099	3.21	.282	-7.00

Occupation Metrics in Percentiles

G. Standardized coefficients

1. Education	.278	.284	--	--	.224
2. First Job - SEI	--	.157	.446	--	.280
3. Current Occ - SEI	--	.102	.421	.219	.379

H. Unstandardized coefficients

1. Education	.240	.034	--	--	8.21
2. First Job - SEI	--	.148	3.48	--	-11.7
3. Current Occ - SEI	--	.100	3.44	.229	-2.97

TABLE 1.13

Regression Analysis of Three Endogenous Variables in Blau-Duncan Basic Model with Occupations Scored on Siegel's NORC Prestige Index and under Transformed and Raw Metrics, U.S. Men Aged 25-64 in March 1962 and by Nonfarm Background Status

Dependent Variables	Independent Variables					
	Father's Education	Father's Occ (Siegel NORC)	Education (Years Completed)	First Job (Siegel NORC)	α	R^2
TOTAL MEN AGED 25-64						
Raw Occupation Metrics						
A. Standardized coefficients						
1. Education	.388	.113	--	--	--	.197
2. First Job - Siegel	--	.134	.456	--	--	.258
3. Current Occ - Siegel	--	.080	.428	.225	--	.361
B. Unstandardized coefficients						
1. Education	.358	.035	--	--	6.66	--
2. First Job - Siegel	--	.153	1.68	--	6.79	--
3. Current Occ - Siegel	--	.095	1.65	.235	10.9	--
Occupation Metrics in Percentiles						
C. Standardized coefficients						
1. Education	.395	.123	--	--	--	.200
2. First Job - Siegel	--	.107	.448	--	--	.235
3. Current Occ - Siegel	--	.087	.416	.178	--	.307
D. Unstandardized coefficients						
1. Education	.365	.018	--	--	7.19	--
2. First Job - Siegel	--	.108	3.12	--	9.44	--
3. Current Occ - Siegel	--	.091	3.01	.185	5.04	--

NONFARM MEN AGED 25-64

Raw Occupation Metrics

E. Standardized coefficients

1. Education	.296	.219	--	--	.196
2. First Job - Siegel	--	.152	.445	--	.269
3. Current Occ - Siegel	--	.071	.428	.241	.382

F. Unstandardized coefficients

1. Education	.250	.055	--	--	7.49
2. First Job - Siegel	--	.154	1.80	--	5.69
3. Current Occ - Siegel	--	.075	1.82	.254	8.61

Occupation Metrics in Percentiles

G. Standardized coefficients

1. Education	.299	.251	--	--	.211
2. First Job - Siegel	--	.137	.430	--	.247
3. Current Occ - Siegel	--	.086	.413	.188	.324

H. Unstandardized coefficients

1. Education	.259	.031	--	--	8.08
2. First Job - Siegel	--	.125	3.17	--	-9.43
3. Current Occ - Siegel	--	.081	3.17	.196	3.36

TABLE 1.14

Regression Analysis of Three Endogenous Variables in Blau-Duncan Basic Model with Occupations Scored on Treiman's Standard International Prestige Index and under Transformed and Raw Metrics, U.S. Men Aged 25-64 in March 1962 and by Nonfarm Background Status

Dependent Variables	Independent Variables					
	Father's Education	Father's Occ (Treiman)	Education (Years Completed)	First Job (Treiman)	α	R^2

TOTAL MEN AGED 25-64

Raw Occupation Metrics

A. Standardized coefficients

	Father's Education	Father's Occ (Treiman)	Education (Years Completed)	First Job (Treiman)	α	R^2
1. Education	.416	.051	--	--	--	.188
2. First Job - Treiman	--	.143	.401	--	--	.201
3. Current Occ - Treiman	--	.086	.396	.204	--	.294

B. Unstandardized coefficients

	Father's Education	Father's Occ (Treiman)	Education (Years Completed)	First Job (Treiman)	α	R^2
1. Education	.384	.015	--	--	7.16	--
2. First Job - Treiman	--	.146	1.36	--	13.0	--
3. Current Occ - Treiman	--	.100	1.53	.233	12.5	--

Occupation Metrics in Percentiles

C. Standardized coefficients

	Father's Education	Father's Occ (Treiman)	Education (Years Completed)	First Job (Treiman)	α	R^2
1. Education	.420	.058	--	--	--	.189
2. First Job - Treiman	--	.119	.368	--	--	.162
3. Current Occ - Treiman	--	.094	.380	.163	--	.243

D. Unstandardized coefficients

	Father's Education	Father's Occ (Treiman)	Education (Years Completed)	First Job (Treiman)	α	R^2
1. Education	.388	.007	--	--	7.41	--
2. First Job - Treiman	--	.110	2.62	--	-.017	--
3. Current Occ - Treiman	--	.093	2.89	.175	6.67	--

NONFARM MEN AGED 25-64

Raw Occupation Metrics

E. Standardized coefficients

1. Education	.309	.205	--	--	.193
2. First Job - Treiman	--	.138	.419	--	.233
3. Current Occ - Treiman	--	.073	.406	.213	.324

F. Unstandardized coefficients

1. Education	.261	.052	--	--	7.44
2. First Job - Treiman	--	.132	1.58	--	10.9
3. Current Occ - Treiman	--	.080	1.73	.241	10.4

Occupation Metrics in Percentiles

G. Standardized coefficients

1. Education	.317	.226	--	--	.203
2. First Job - Treiman	--	.117	.382	--	.190
3. Current Occ - Treiman	--	.076	.393	.167	.270

H. Unstandardized coefficients

1. Education	.274	.028	--	--	8.08
2. First Job - Treiman	--	.107	2.88	--	-4.77
3. Current Occ - Treiman	--	.074	3.15	.178	4.29

education–occupation relationships, owing to the representation of aggregate educational characteristics of occupations within the SEI index. (Analyses elsewhere sought to allay this suspicion (Blau and Duncan, 1967:124–128; Duncan, Featherman, and Duncan, 1972:45–49).) Note that the standardized coefficients in Equations A.1 and E.1 for education across the scales in Tables 1.12 through 1.14 indicate a somewhat greater emphasis of the relative role of paternal occupation in units of SEI than in either of the prestige scales. However, when units are comparable (i.e., expressed in percentiles), as they appear in Equations D.1 and H.1, the unstandardized parameters are essentially identical across the indexes in the three tables. Moreover, we find no evidence for an accentuation of the education effect on either first job or current occupation, which is unique to the SEI scale.

We conclude that distortions of metric and ranking artifacts which may arise in the use of Duncan's SEI do not confound the analysis of occupational stratification to any noticeable, substantive extent. The chief differences in scales of prestige and socioeconomic status are substantive, leading to differential rank assignments for the same occupation title. We retain our provisional conclusion that the process of stratification in the U.S. and Australia (perhaps elsewhere, too) is essentially a socioeconomic one in which the fundamental (common, but not exclusive) dimension of occupation roles is socioeconomic status and not prestige (either in the classical sense or in the sense of occupation "desirability," apart from that which arises from socioeconomic status per se). In further support of this postulate, we estimate the structural equation model for U.S. men represented by Figure 1.2, which, like Figure 1.1, was estimated in a confirmatory factor analysis.

Figure 1.2 specifies that measurements of occupational stratification are imperfect to the extent that occupational status is less than perfectly reflected in indexes either of prestige or of socioeconomic status. It assumes that errors in the rankings of detailed occupations by status as provided by Siegel and Treiman prestige scales are correlated in three occupation variables, but that errors in socioeconomic rankings and prestige rankings are not correlated. Finally, errors in occupation rankings are random across variables, such that the sons' reports of paternal and filial occupations are unbiased, each with respect to the other (cf. Bielby, Hauser, and Featherman, 1976). We have estimated the structural coefficients of Figure 1.2 from correlations for total men aged 25–64 when occupation metrics for all three indexes are expressed in percentiles (Table 1.10, upper triangle).

Basing our estimates upon a normalized metric does not force us to reconsider our assessment of the process of occupational stratification

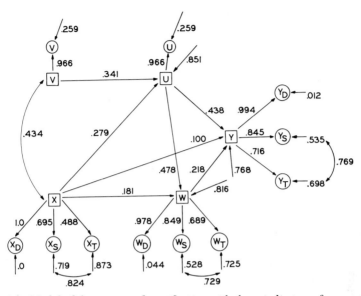

Figure 1.2 Model of the process of stratification with three indicators of occupational status, calculated for detailed titles and with scores in percentiles, United States men aged 25–64 in March 1962. □ denotes unmeasured variable; ○ denotes measured variable; V = father's education; U = R's education; X = father's status; X_D = father's occupation (Duncan); X_T = father's occupation (Treiman); X_S = father's occupation (Siegel); W = first job status; W_D = first job (Duncan); W_T = first job (Treiman); W_S = first job (Siegel); Y = current occupational status; Y_D = current occupation (Duncan); Y_T = current occupation (Treiman); Y_S = current occupation (Siegel).

in the U.S., which is best characterized as a distribution of persons both within and between generations over occupations hierarchically ordered by socioeconomic status rather than by prestige. Paternal oc- cupational status, but also first job and current occupational status, are well reflected in Duncan's SEI, and the pattern of structural coeffi- cients for the five-variable basic model are akin to those in Table 1.12. Siegel and Treiman (in that order) prestige scales offer less valid indi- cations of socioeconomic status, which we regard as the major dimen- sion underlying occupational mobility in the U.S. (and possibly Aus- tralia as well, especially among the nonfarm population). Hence, the (partial) correlations between the residuals to the Treiman and Siegel indexes are large and positive in Figure 1.2, especially for paternal occupational status. (Here the proportion of fathers in farm occupa- tions should heighten the different rankings of sons by prestige and socioeconomic status.)

While the model in Figure 1.2 reproduces with fair accuracy the

TABLE 1.15

Residual Coefficients Representing Difference between Observed Correlations and Correlations Estimated from Maximum Likelihood Solution of Figure 1.2 for U.S. Men Aged 25-64 in March 1962

Variables	1	2	3	4	5	6	7	8	9	10	11
1. Father's Education	.000										
2. R's Education	.000	.000									
3. Father's Occ – Duncan	.000	.000	.000								
4. Father's Occ – Siegel	.003	-.047	.000	.000							
5. Father's Occ – Treiman	-.004	-.059	.000	.051	.102						
6. First Job – Duncan	.000	-.003	.002	-.054	-.072	.000					
7. First Job – Siegel	.003	.018	-.015	-.013	-.021	.000	.000				
8. First Job – Treiman	.006	.015	-.030	.021	.042	.000	.005	.010			
9. Current Occ – Duncan	.000	-.001	.001	-.055	-.072	.002	-.013	-.022	.000		
10. Current Occ – Siegel	.004	.031	-.012	.007	.004	-.005	.036	.046	.000	.000	
11. Current Occ – Treiman	.008	.040	-.007	.037	.046	.003	.046	.080	-.001	.020	.040

correlations in Table 1.10 (cf. Table 1.15 of residual coefficients), the maximum likelihood Chi-square for the model is 3031.4 with 33 degrees of freedom ($p = .00$). However, this specification offers a better fit (taking as our criterion the matrix of residual coefficients) of the data than others we estimated, including (a) a three-indicator model with no correlated errors, (b) a three-indicator model with uncorrelated errors among the indexes of each variable but nonrandom co-variation in the scaling of all three occupations by each index in turn, and (c) a three-indicator model incorporating the error structure specification of Figure 1.2 with that in (b). We could entertain other hypotheses about errors in variables but have postponed this exercise until better estimates of the differential validities of own and proxy reports of occupational and educational characteristics are available from studies now in process under our direction (e.g., Bielby, Hauser, and Featherman, 1976).

THE COMMON BASIS OF MOBILITY IN AUSTRALIA AND THE UNITED STATES

To return to and conclude our analysis of the comparative structure of social mobility, in its common features across societies, and to offer additional credibility for our assertion as to its socioeconomic character, we conduct a series of canonical correlation analyses of the Australian and U.S. mobility tables at the level of 10 major occupation groups. In using this technique, we have retrenched from the superimposition of structure upon the process of mobility to the point of making such structure problematic. We know from our application of log-linear models that the two societies' occupational stratification systems are largely the same. The regression analysis has assumed that the basis of similarity was some common socioeconomic process. Can we establish independent support for this interpretation?

Table 1.16 gives the canonical weights for the first and second variates for each of the three mobility tables in each society; Table 1.17 reports weights for the first variates in both places from inter- and intragenerational mobility tables for the men of nonfarm origins. A summary and interpretation of these variates are contained in Tables 1.18 through 1.20; it is the latter tables that we shall discuss.

Table 1.18 establishes that mobility for total men in both societies involves at least two orthogonal variates which yield canonical correlations of some magnitude. When we compare the canonical correlations for the U.S. and those for Australia with their Duncan score counter-

TABLE 1.16

Canonical Weights on First and Second Variates of Occupations, Based on Intergenerational and Intragenerational Mobility Matrices, 1965 Australian and 1962 U.S. Men

	First Variate						Second Variate					
	FATHER'S		FIRST		CURRENT		FATHER'S		FIRST		CURRENT	
	A[a]	B	C	D	E	F	A	B	C	D	E	F
AUSTRALIA												
Professional, tech.	-.98	-.77	-.59	-2.89	-.87	-2.49	3.17	2.91	2.10	2.38	2.14	1.90
Mgrs., officials, prop.	-.46	-.54	-.34	-.55	-.26	-.26	1.06	.91	1.68	-.20	.79	-.36
Clerical	-.81	-.82	-.67	-.53	-.77	-.38	.89	1.21	1.15	-.38	.29	-.67
Sales	-.60	-.60	-.33	-.09	-.56	-.26	.96	1.24	.42	-.41	1.00	-.32
Craft	-.61	-.59	-.49	-.07	-.46	.04	-.76	-.41	-.43	-.80	-.93	-.87
Operatives	-.27	-.45	-.36	.11	.05	.27	-.87	-.87	-.94	-.45	-.79	-.29
Service	-.62	-.39	-.55	.01	-.44	.01	-.02	-.71	-.98	-.67	-.65	-.38
Nonfarm laborers	-.41	-.34	-.17	.16	-.05	.37	-.81	-.79	-1.00	-.33	-1.14	-.23
Farmers	1.95	1.94	2.82	2.00	2.63	1.86	.25	.33	1.05	2.16	.50	1.96
Farm laborers	.16	.83	1.36	1.03	1.24	1.09	-1.08	-2.30	-.84	.73	-.12	.75

UNITED STATES

Professional, tech.	1.63	.99	.88	2.74	1.38	2.26	1.48	2.43	2.23	1.59	.99	1.19
Mgrs., officials, prop.	1.28	.92	.79	.63	.76	.37	1.06	1.41	2.56	-.57	.85	-.53
Clerical	1.22	.88	.81	.63	.54	.36	.60	.77	.29	-.52	-.45	-.67
Sales	1.22	.88	.80	.50	1.10	.41	1.09	1.19	.98	-.74	.58	-.73
Craft	.42	.61	.44	-.07	-.11	-.38	-.74	-.62	-.33	-.60	-.72	-.49
Operatives	.11	.53	.29	-.25	-.43	-.51	-1.12	-1.12	-.90	-.61	-.85	-.41
Service	.29	.57	.43	-.15	-.26	-.42	-.94	-.85	-.86	-.62	-.88	-.38
Nonfarm laborers	-.27	.23	.02	-.37	-.79	-.69	-1.61	-1.26	-.80	-.46	-.93	-.11
Farmers	-1.31	-1.45	-2.16	-1.41	-2.51	-1.61	.82	.29	.84	2.64	2.43	2.92
Farm laborers	-1.43	-1.65	-2.01	-1.17	-2.30	-1.57	-.66	-.17	.39	1.44	.97	2.32

[a] Column:
A   from father to current matrix
B   from father to first matrix
C   from father to first matrix
D   from first to current matrix
E   from father to current matrix
F   from first to current matrix.

43

TABLE 1.17

Canonical Weights on First Variate of Occupations, Based on Intergenerational and Intragenerational Mobility Matrices, 1965 Australian and 1962 U.S. Men of Nonfarm Origins

| Occupation Groups | Australia, 1965 | | | | | | United States, 1962 | | | | | |
| | FATHER'S | | FIRST | | CURRENT | | FATHER'S | | FIRST | | CURRENT | |
	A[a]	B	C	D	E	F	A	B	C	D	E	F
Professional, tech.	2.88	2.80	2.02	3.38	1.96	2.79	1.57	2.01	2.03	2.66	1.26	2.12
Mgrs., officials, prop.	.96	.88	1.94	.42	.87	.04	1.35	1.26	2.18	.81	1.09	.32
Clerical	.79	1.21	1.18	.21	.31	.06	.91	.77	.39	.43	.02	.17
Sales	.92	1.10	.42	-.19	1.03	.03	1.21	1.13	1.13	.31	.11	.17
Craft	-.56	-.41	-.42	-.41	-.74	-.53	-.30	-.40	-.16	-.33	-.61	-.65
Operatives	-.85	-.84	-.91	-.38	-.93	-.44	-.79	-.79	-.68	-.54	-1.01	-.76
Service	.05	-.59	-.93	-.39	-.49	-.26	-.69	-.70	-.80	-.60	-.87	-.70
Nonfarm laborers	-.71	-.75	-.88	-.37	-1.08	-.53	-1.48	-1.21	-.87	-.66	-1.51	-.92
Farmers	--	--	-1.05	-1.22	-.08	-.99	--	--	.24	-.65	.34	-.86
Farm laborers	--	--	-.89	-.71	.18	-.72	--	--	-.86	-1.02	-1.48	-1.20

[a]Column: A   from father to current matrix
             B   from father to first matrix
             C   from father to first matrix
             D   from first to current matrix
             E   from father to current matrix
             F   from first to current matrix.

44

TABLE 1.18

Canonical Correlations among Occupation Variates, Australian and U.S. Mobility Matrices

Occupations	Australia		United States	
	First Variate	Second Variate	First Variate	Second Variate
	TOTAL MEN			
Father's and Current Occ	.525	.317	.423	.263
Father's and First Occ	.604	.253	.564	.297
First and Current Occ	.670	.587	.570	.428
	NONFARM ORIGIN			
Father's and Current Occ	.339		.359	
Father's and First Occ	.267		.351	
First and Current Occ	.635		.541	

SOURCE: Tables 1.16 and 1.17.

parts in Table 1.4, Panel A, it is apparent that the maximum correlations for the first variates exceed the Pearsonian correlations and that there is more variance in each of these tables than is captured under the assumption of socioeconomic (or prestige) dimensionality. The exception to this interpretation is the U.S., wherein the deviation of the two intergenerational canonical correlations from their socioeconomic, product–moment counterparts is slight. For men of nonfarm origin (compare Table 1.18 with Table 1.5, Panel A), the canonical correlations for the first variates compare rather favorably in both societies with the Pearsonian correlations.

That there is dissimilarity in the scaling of the first and second variates between societies is evidenced in Table 1.19, where the Pearsonian correlations of the weights of corresponding variates in the two places are reported. These correlation coefficients range from .67 to .98, with the highest correspondence arising in the intragenerational relationship (Rows D and F). Limiting our attention to men of nonfarm origins (lower panel of Table 1.19), we find cross-societal correlations in excess of .90, with the exception of the reflection of father on son's current occupation ($r = .81$) and the reflection of current occupation on father's occupation ($r = .86$).

Having achieved a scoring of major occupation group categories through induction from the mobility matrices, we now attempt to iden-

TABLE 1.19

Coefficients of Correlation of Occupational Variates between United States and Australia

		First Variate	Second Variate
		TOTAL MEN	
Father's Occ	A[a]	.77	.85
	B	.93	.85
First Occ	C	.95	.89
	D	.98	.94
Current Occ	E	.90	.67
	F	.97	.87
		NONFARM ORIGIN	
Father's Occ	A	.86	
	B	.96	
First Occ	C	.91	
	D	.95	
Current Occ	E	.81	
	F	.94	

SOURCE: Tables 1.16 and 1.17.

[a]Row: A from father to current matrix
        B from father to first matrix
        C from father to first matrix
        D from first to current matrix
        E from father to current matrix
        F from first to current matrix.

tify the emergent structure of mobility in the two societies. Table 1.20 arrays the correlations on the canonically scored variates with each of Duncan's and Siegel's status scores. If the canonical structure of mobility in either society is essentially a socioeconomic process or a phenomenon of prestige hierarchies, then the correlations should be rather high. If the common core of social mobility in both societies is movement through socioeconomic rather than prestige space, then in both societies the correlations between the canonical scores and the Duncan scores should be higher than those between the canonical weights and the Siegel scores.

In nearly every comparison, the column involving the Duncan socioeconomic scores contains higher correlations than the column with Siegel prestige scores, although in some instances the differences are minimal. (Generally the correlations of canonical weights with

TABLE 1.20

Correlations of Canonical Weights and Status Scores for Major
Occupation Groups, Australia and U.S. Men

Occupation Groups		Total Men		Nonfarm Origin	
		Duncan SEI	Siegel Prestige	Duncan SEI	Siegel Prestige
AUSTRALIA					
First Variate Father's Occ	A[a]	.51	.12	.92	.83
	B	.55	.20	.95	.84
First Occ	C	.48	.14	.95	.80
	D	.81	.61	.82	.70
Current Occ	E	.58	.22	.85	.72
	F	.83	.61	.81	.69
Second Variate Father's Occ	A	.90	.85		
	B	.89	.86		
First Occ	C	.83	.91		
	D	.23	.48		
Current Occ	E	.82	.78		
	F	.10	.36		
UNITED STATES					
First Variate Father's Occ	A	.87	.62	.97	.85
	B	.65	.40	.98	.88
First Occ	C	.64	.35	.92	.88
	D	.90	.71	.94	.85
Current Occ	E	.84	.55	.86	.95
	F	.92	.72	.94	.83
Second Variate Father's Occ	A	.80	.81		
	B	.89	.83		
First Occ	C	.78	.79		
	D	.06	.25		
Current Occ	E	.21	.44		
	F	.27	.03		

SOURCE: Tables 1.16 and 1.17.

[a]Row: A from father to current matrix
        B from father to first matrix
        C from father to first matrix
        D from first to current matrix
        E from father to current matrix
        F from first to current matrix.

Treiman's scale scores are lower than those with Siegel's.) The scores of the first variate in the U.S. more closely adhere to the occupational hierarchy of socioeconomic status than in Australia, although in both societies it is *intragenerational* mobility that most nearly approximates a unidimensional, socioeconomic process and that establishes commonality in the processes of stratification in the two societies. For the U.S., the structure of intergenerational mobility to first jobs apparently entails more than socioeconomic variance, as the reflection of father's occupation on son's first job, and vice versa, have the lowest correlations with occupational socioeconomic status. In Australia, it is only intragenerational mobility across categories defined by the first variate which clearly follows either a socioeconomic or prestige pattern, and it is the former which dominates this transition.

On the second variate, differences between the prestige and the socioeconomic correlations are smaller than on the first variate, in both Australia and the U.S. For Australia, both types of intergenerational mobility follow socioeconomic and prestige hierarchies, while intragenerational movements reflect neither one nor the other very sharply. Intragenerational mobility within the second U.S. variate repeats the Australian pattern, although intergenerational movements are somewhat less consistent with socioeconomic or prestige distances among occupational categories in the U.S. than in Australia.

When we look at the correlations run over the men of nonfarm origin in the two societies, differences across place in either inter- or intragenerational mobility are reduced, and the stronger set of correlations involving the socioeconomic scores of occupations (compared to the prestige scores) is the same in both places. In short, the canonical structure of social (qua occupational) mobility among Australian and U.S. men of nonfarm origin is given in the socioeconomic distances among major groups of occupations.

CONCLUSIONS

In closing, we propose that the fundamental core of occupational inequality in the United States and other capitalist, industrial societies is socioeconomic status, and not occupational prestige. Furthermore, across capitalist industrial (and possibly other) societies, the *common* structure of social mobility is occupational socioeconomic status. We assume that there are idiosyncratic features to each society's stratification system, for the U.S.–Australian comparison clearly has yielded evidence of such properties (namely in the mobility patterns associated with men of farm origins). Likewise, we readily acknowledge the variance in any society's process of stratification which stems from nonsocieconomic factors, strictly construed. In the American case, the interaction of race with the socioeconomic components of the basic model and the historically unique pattern of intergenerational mobility of blacks vis-à-vis whites are manifestations of cultural, social, and/or ideological elements of U.S. society which affect the operation of the process of stratification. Still, the basic model of socioeconomic stratification applies to blacks, although in some attenuated form.

We eschew the necessity of some legitimatory, normative system, either within an individual or within a total society, for the operation and maintenance of these largely similar socioeconomic processes of stratification. Whether or not the sociological facts of inequality and stratification in a given place are consensually validated and whether or not an individual's sense of distributive justice accords with these facts are interesting research questions with import for social change. However, in the final analysis, values may play a relatively minor role, relative to the impact of the economy, in shaping and sustaining the mobility processes in capitalist, industrial nations. Therefore, our research is not offered either as substantiation for or in refutation of a functionalist theoretic position, as it is usually understood.

We speculate quite tentatively (while similar analyses to those reported herein can be carried out in other places) that concurrence across societies on the hierarchical rating of occupations, and the apparent commonality of socioeconomic distance as the metric of measurement for this ordering, arise from quite similar economic forces of supply and demand which have noticeably parallel features in capitalist, industrial nations. Furthermore, these same economic relationships of supply and demand define the specific details of the process of stratification—that is, which variables are to be included in the basic model and the effect parameters among them. Popular evaluations of occupational prestige or desirability conducted in different places mirror the common features of their respective stratification processes, namely their socioeconomic elements.

Rather than fostering uninteresting theoretical questions, the emerging evidence for the cross-societal importance of socioeconomic status (among those places in which such research has been attempted) offers new lines of inquiry and speculation. These findings may lead us away from a preoccupation with personal and societal values to a focus on common and unique features of institutions—particularly economic and political ones—across societal boundaries and over time. In the spirit of this thought, we would hope that stratification research of the kind reported herein might be implemented in noncapitalist economies. If in such industrialized, noncapitalist societies the *major* basis of stratification is occupational socioeconomic status, as we provisionally conclude it is in capitalist economies, such a finding would have a profound impact on existing theories of social stratification. At least for the United States, we are not troubled by the standing assumption that occupational socioeconomic status is the primary basis of mobility.[7]

---

[7] We argue that common socioeconomic bases to occupational mobility, coupled with similarities in the (economic) functional organization of work and jobs, across capitalist industrial societies construct the "prestige" or desirability of occupation roles, as given in popular ratings. "Prestige" is a fallible index of occupational status and a fortiori socioeconomic status is a more valid status index, *only* with reference to occupational *mobility;* other occupational processes may be less responsive to the purely socioeconomic hierarchy of these roles than is mobility and may be more responsive to other desirable ("prestigious") but nonsocioeconomic occupational dimensions. Therefore, (occupational) "prestige" is indeed a multidimensional concept, and one needs to be quite specific about the (occupational) process one is discussing in identifying the most salient or valid dimension of status. Alternatively, one can construe the evidence as providing no universal, efficacious social meaning to prestige, since it implies at least both prestige in the classical sociological case of symbolically legitimated groups and "prestige" in the vulgar existential case of popular desirability. We think the matter is an empirical one and have phrased it as such. In any event, it is of high theoretic interest.

2

The Measurement of
Occupation in Social Surveys

Students of social inequality and social mobility sometimes come to the erroneous judgment that social survey data collected on current and retrospective occupations are subject to substantial reporting errors and errors of recall. They argue that reliability of occupation information is low and vitiates efforts to code data into the detailed occupation and industry titles or even into the 12 or 13 categories of major occupation and industry groups commonly associated with tabulations of the United States Bureau of the Census, or the Bureau of Labor Statistics. Finally, it is asserted that intertemporal analyses of occupational mobility which encode occupations in metrics of prestige or socioeconomic status founder on the inevitable shifts over time in the status position or social standing of particular occupational titles and in the status hierarchy in general.

Students of industrial societies commonly employ the concept of occupation to locate individuals in the social system, recognizing the high salience in such systems of complexly differentiated occupational roles for both the functioning of the society and for the allocation of scarce resources (status such as wealth, esteem, power) to per-

This chapter was prepared by David L. Featherman and Robert M. Hauser. Portions of this work appeared in Featherman and Hauser, "On the measurement of occupations in social surveys," *Sociological Methods and Research*, Vol. 2, No. 2 (November 1973), pp. 239–251, and are reprinted by permission of the publisher, Sage Publications, Inc. The manual for the coding of occupation and industry, developed by Featherman in collaboration with Michael Sobel and David Dickens, draws heavily from procedures and publications of the U.S. Bureau of the Census.

sons. We shall not pursue here any of the theories which attempt to explain the relationships between functional differentiation by occupational roles and inequality in the distribution of resources to roles and their occupants. Suffice it to say that sociologists attribute major importance to the characteristics of occupational roles as causal antecedents of economic and social inequalities among persons in industrial societies.

For more than a half century, sociologists have recognized the tendency of persons to accord differential status to various occupational roles. Systematic study of this social fact has been confined to the years since 1925 (Counts, 1925), and it has been just in the last decade that sociologists have learned something of the process whereby persons in the general population come to rather marked agreement in their ratings of the social standing of occupational roles (Duncan, 1961; Duncan and Hodge, 1963; Hodge, Siegel, and Rossi, 1964; Siegel, 1971; Goldthorpe and Hope, 1974). The concept of occupational prestige is applied to the phenomenon of differential popular evaluations of occupations according to their social standings.

What do sociologists know about occupational prestige? First, there is no variance in the rankings of occupational titles as the result of different instructions to samples of raters—rankings according to social standing, to honor, to requisite intelligence all correspond (Hodge, Siegel, and Rossi, 1964; Siegel, 1971; Duncan, Featherman, and Duncan, 1972). Second, any single study of occupational prestige in a cross-section sample of the population is devoid of significant variance in rankings owing to the sex, age, region, residence, education, and occupation of individual raters (Reiss, 1961). Third, since 1925 the structure of occupational prestige has remained constant. True, some individual titles apparently have shifted their relative positions in the hierarchy of prestige since 1925, but the overall transformation of the hierarchy in the last 50 years has been glacial in nature: Prestige scores in two surveys separated by about forty years correlate about .93 (Duncan, 1968d:704–709). Fourth, stability of the structure of prestige over time is matched by stability across space. Both in western and nonwestern countries and in developed and developing societies, there is apparent invariance in the prestige attributed to matching occupation titles (Hodge, Treiman, and Rossi, 1966; Treiman, 1975). Finally, about 83% of the variance in occupational prestige is accounted for by a linear combination of aggregate educational and income characteristics of detailed occupation titles (Duncan, 1961:124). This is to say that the status which inheres in an occupational role is largely a function of prerequisite certification (schooling) and the market value (income) of the persons who commonly exercise that role. Thus, the concept of occupational socioeconomic status, as developed by Duncan (1961) refers to an attribute of a specific occupation.

Duncan's index of socioeconomic status (SEI), when applied as an attribute of a person, denotes the status accorded to the individual as the incumbent of a particular occupation role. The status (SEI) is not correlated highly with either the individual's own years of schooling or the person's earnings; years of schooling and SEI correlate among men at about .6 and SEI and income correlate about .4 (Duncan, Featherman, and Duncan, 1972:38). A discussion of this point is found in Blau and Duncan (1967:117–128). See also Chapter 1 of this volume.

SOCIOECONOMIC AND PRESTIGE SCALES
OF OCCUPATIONAL STATUS

As a result of these developments in the measurement of occupation, sociologists have two metrics in which to array occupations hierarchically—prestige and socioeconomic status—and their relative utilities in the study of occupational stratification are discussed in Chapter 1. As one might anticipate, arrays of prestige and socioeconomic statuses are correlated in the range .86 to .91 (Duncan, Featherman, and Duncan 1972:45–49). Given the stable characteristics of the prestige structure in the U.S. and (apparently) throughout the world, scales based on these metrics can be used in time-series and comparative analyses as standardized, calibrated measures of the status which accrues to a person owing to his or her incumbency of a particular occupation.

While other scales of occupational status abound (cf. Robinson, Athanasiou, and Head, 1969: Chapter 14), none has been as widely standardized in the U.S. as that developed by Duncan (1961) and by Siegel (1971). Duncan's socioeconomic index and Siegel's prestige index have been developed for *all* occupations referenced by the *Alphabetical Index of Occupations and Industries* (U.S. Bureau of the Census, 1960). This manual contains some 20,000 jobs summarized by 296 detailed occupation titles and 18,000 industries summarized by 149 detailed industry titles. Were some analyst to have his or her data classified according to the conventions of the *Alphabetical Index, all* occupations could be assigned explicit SEI and prestige scale scores according to standardized conventions, eliminating nearly all subjec-

tive and ad hoc coding judgments and rendering far greater comparability to researches which include occupational status. Later we expli-
cate the conventions and the process of occupation coding as outlined
in the 1971 revision of the *Alphabetical Index* (U.S. Bureau of the
Census, 1971a). In addition, we have appended (Appendix B) sets of
Duncan SEI and Siegel prestige scores calculated for detailed titles in
the 1970 census classification of occupations (Appendix A).

REQUISITE OCCUPATION INFORMATION

In order to classify data according to the *Alphabetical Index* and to
obtain status scores for detailed occupational titles, what kinds of information about jobs would our hypothetical analyst have to collect
from his or her respondents? Three pieces of information are necessary: occupation, industry, and class of worker. Most survey organizations ordinarily collect some or all of this detail and often by questions
quite similar to items employed by the U.S. Bureau of the Census.
The census asks the following item for occupation: "What kind of
work were you doing?" The item for industry reads: "What kind of
business or industry was this?" Class of worker establishes whether
the person's pay in this employment was in the form of salaries and/or
wages, in terms of self-employment income, or whether the person
was working without pay; it also establishes whether the person was
employed in the private or government (public) sector:
Was this person—

An employee of PRIVATE company, business, or individual for
   wages, salary, or commission .... □
A FEDERAL government employee .... □
A STATE government employee .... □
A LOCAL government employee .... □
Self-employed in OWN business, profession, practice, or farm
   Is the business incorporated?   Yes .... □
                                         No (or farm) .... □
Working WITHOUT PAY in family business or farm .... □
NEVER WORKED .... □

In order to assign status scores to all occupations, the only distinction
the analyst would need to make about class of worker is between self-
employment versus salaried (wages). (A note of caution: As of 1967, the
U.S. Bureau of the Census has considered as salaried all nonfarm employment in which the respondent reported self-employment in his

own incorporated business. This technique of enumeration represents a change in procedure but not in the concept of self-employment.)

While most surveys collect similar detail about employment, few study directors specify procedures for the classification and storage of their data which parallel those of the Bureau of the Census. In perusing codebooks, it is not uncommon to find occupation and industry classified into a system somewhat akin to the census major occupation and industry groups, although frequently some of these 12 or 13 categories have been combined (e.g., clerical and sales) or class of worker has been treated as an attribute of the person's employment rather than of the person's employment in the particular occupation (e.g., person's general employment coded as self-employed, salaried, or both). Perhaps these unfortunate classification decisions are made in the absence of familiarity with the introductory pages of the *Alphabetical Index* which explain to naive coders how the census processes and classifies both industry and occupation information. (Our experience is that clerks can process such information with high reliability after a modest training period; an average coder can process about 10 occupations per hour, assigning three-digit codes for each of industry and occupation, a one-digit class of worker code, and the prestige and SEI status scores.) Again, the census manual makes explicit what otherwise is most often treated on an ad hoc basis. We argue that the benefit of comparability offsets the costs of effort.

ERRORS IN OCCUPATION REPORTS

"But why worry about comparability and about classifying occupation and industry in such great detail when reports of occupation and industry are subject to large errors?" We take strong exception to this frequent response to our suggestions as to procedures of treating occupation. Based on data which we shall cite subsequently, we find occupation reports of persons about their own occupations to be about as reliable as their reports of education and current income. Moreover, there appears to be marked ability of persons to report their occupations held five years in the past, with nearly the same reliability as they report current statuses. We reject the implication that occupation information is subject to unusual distortion and decay as a function of time. There is no basis, in issues of measurement, for the treatment of occupation in less than the detail which its importance in concept and theory recommends.

We draw our data on the reliability of reports of current social and economic statuses from Siegel and Hodge (1968) on causal approaches to measurement error. Siegel and Hodge matched respondents' reports of completed schooling, personal income, and occupational status (Duncan's SEI equivalents to census major occupation groups of titles) to the 1960 decennial census of population with subsequent reports by the same persons of these items to either the Post Enumeration Survey or the Current Population Survey. While the Siegel–Hodge estimates of test–retest reliability of socioeconomic items were calculated over slightly different populations (see the original source for details), we find no impairment of the comparison of relative reliabilities. Siegel and Hodge report a reliability correlation of .8726 for occupation, while the corresponding coefficients for education and income are .9332 and .8468, respectively (Siegel and Hodge, 1968:37). We agree that the reliability of occupation reports is about equivalent to that for personal income, and that both are less consistently reported than years of schooling completed. Students of social mobility, stratification, and inequality can conclude from these estimates that the phenomena of socioeconomic status which they study do not rest on grossly fragile indicators or ones with largely discrepant degrees of reliability, where these indexes are taken in the context of social surveys. Indeed, the Siegel–Hodge estimates give support to our notion that the proper collection, processing, and classification of socioeconomic (especially occupation) information will yield reliable data and sustain detailed analyses involving indicators of status. For analysts interested in correcting their socioeconomic data for attenuations in variance and other errors in variables, we recommend a close reading of Siegel and Hodge and of more recent and extensive elaborations of error structures (e.g., Mason *et al.*, 1976; Bielby, Hauser, and Featherman, 1976).

There are other issues in the measurement of status in social surveys. One major issue is whether retrospective reports of status (i.e., reports of occupations held in the past) are accurate and useful. A second issue is whether proxy reports (e.g., a person's reports of his or her father's occupation at the time the adult respondent would have been about 16 years of age) are subject to special measurement problems. We have more data on the former issue than on the latter, although several studies under way will repair this deficiency. On the issue of retrospective reports, we do know that the memory of occupations held 5 years in the past is nearly as good as the ability to report (accurately) current occupation, at the level of major occupation groups. In a working paper circulated within the Bureau of the Census, Walsh and Buckholdt (1970) reported results of a special survey in the summer of 1968 in which respondents who were a part of the Current Population Survey in July of 1963 were requested to report retrospectively about the occupation held five years in the past. Using the tables provided by this paper, we have computed Table 2.1, arraying the occupation reported in 1963 by the 5-year retrospective report in 1968; occupation is in major occupation groups, with Duncan SEI score equivalents. Calculating a product–moment correlation of .8020 for men aged 19 and over who reported in both surveys yields the conclusion that memory of occupation is not subject to much more decay in the long run (5 years) than it is in the short run (several months), as witnessed by the similarity of the reliability (.8726) and stability (.8020) correlation coefficients.

On the issue of quality of proxy reports, our data come from several sources, although at best they are suggestive. Treiman and Hauser (Chapter 11 of this volume) have calculated a validity correlation of .718 for adult son's report of father's occupation. Blau and Duncan (1967:462) reported a correlation of .74 between men's reports of paternal nonfarm occupations (the Rs were about age 16) and fathers' own reports to censuses; this estimate was obtained from a small case base within their study's pretest in Chicago. Jencks *et al.* (1972:334) calculate an estimated filial–paternal correlation for father's occupation of .769.

Kerckhoff, Mason, and Poss (1973) find little accuracy in the reports of young schoolchildren, but, by the time students leave Grade 12, they are as accurate in reporting paternal occupation as is the father himself. We take these data to mean that proxy reports may be rather accurate for current parental statuses, but retrospective reports by proxy decay with time somewhat more substantially than own retrospective reports. These conclusions are tentative and await the results of an exercise we are undertaking as part of a state of Wisconsin and a national study of social mobility (Featherman and Hauser, 1975). We are obtaining a sample of men aged 20–65 in 1973 who will report retrospectively the occupations and years of schooling of their fathers (or heads of families) in the census years closest to their (Rs) sixteenth birthdays. Having reports of these statuses in hand—in addition to fathers' (heads') names and addresses in those years—will permit us to match back to actual reports of the named fathers (heads) to the censuses in the precise years in question. We anticipate that the reliability of these reports will vary some by sons' ages. In any event, we look forward to assessing hypotheses regarding correlates of response accuracy, as we are collecting varied information on the respondent's career and his background.

TABLE 2.1

1968 Report of 1963 Occupation by 1963 CPS Report: Males 19 Years and Over Reporting in 1963 and 1968

Major Group 1963	Duncan SEI Score	Major Group in 1968 Report of 1963 Occupation											Total
		(1)	(2)	(3)	(4)	(5)	(6)	(7)	(8)	(9)	(10)	(11)	
(1) Professionals	75	143	-	6	4	-	7	4	-	-	-	2	166
(2) Farmers	14	4	80	4	-	-	-	4	-	3	8	2	102
(3) Managers	57	12	-	131	1	15	22	6	-	2	-	1	190
(4) Clerical	45	7	2	11	50	5	7	5	-	-	-	1	88
(5) Sales	49	5	-	11	3	53	2	6	-	1	-	1	82
(6) Craftsmen	31	5	2	18	3	3	219	25	-	5	0	12	292
(7) Operatives	18	8	3	5	9	2	38	172	-	5	2	10	254
(8) Private Household	7	-	-	-	-	-	-	1	2	-	-	-	3
(9) Other Services	17	2	-	3	4	1	9	5	-	66	-	1	91
(10) Farm Laborers	6	-	9	-	1	1	9	4	-	-	21	2	47
(11) Nonfarm Laborers	7	1	2	1	4	2	8	16	-	6	2	38	80
Total		184	98	190	79	82	321	248	2	88	33	70	1345

SOURCE: Walsh and Buckholdt, 1970.

58

SUMMARY

The structure of status associated with incumbency in occupational roles has remained stable over the last half century. There appear to be no methodological artifacts in popular evaluations of occupational prestige (or socioeconomic status) which would jeopardize the development of standardized instruments which yield status indexes comparable across time and societal boundaries. Moreover, the reports of occupation collected in social surveys are of comparable reliability to reports of income and education, and they appear durable when obtained retrospectively over periods of 5 years.

We argue from these data for the careful collection of information on occupation, industry, and class of worker and for the classification and storage of these details according to procedures outlined in the *Alphabetical Index* and elaborated below. With occupation and industry stored at the detailed level, any number of more summary classifications can be constructed to suit the analyst's special purposes. Both Siegel's prestige scale and Duncan's SEI index have been calibrated for the 1960 census classification of detailed titles; in Appendix B, we list both Duncan and Siegel scores reconciled to the 1970 census classification. Beyond these two scales, other indexes of occupation characteristics are available to the analyst if the data are stored according to U.S. Census conventions. For example, Trieman's (1975) international prestige scale has been standardized for categories of the occupation classification developed by the International Labor Organization (International Labor Office, 1969). It is possible to map all lines of the census detailed classification into the I.L.O. classification and to obtain Treiman prestige score equivalents.

A MANUAL FOR CODING SURVEY
INFORMATION ABOUT OCCUPATIONS

To illustrate the conventions that will insure more complete and accurate information about occupation within social surveys, we have constructed a prototype occupation coding manual.

This manual includes the coding and editing procedures that we have used in several household surveys and that ultimately classify job information into the detailed occupation and industry categories currently recognized by the Bureau of the Census (see Appendix A). These conventions are reproductions and minor modifications of the instructions for classification as found in the introductory pages of the *Alphabetical Index of Industries and Occupations* (U.S. Bureau of the Census, 1971a). Our format, however, is intended to be more didactic and to train unspecialized coders to process job information in standardized ways with a high order of intercoder reliability. In addition, we frequently have used this manual to train *interviewers* to elicit adequately codable occupational and industrial information by exposing them to the necessary requirements of the coding process; we have found this practice cuts down the fail-edits and our survey field costs.

Finally, in Appendix B, we include scores for socioeconomic status and prestige for detailed occupation categories of the 1970 census classification (i.e., Appendix A). *Caveat:* The Duncan Socioeconomic Status Index (SEI) for detailed 1970 categories is based on the occupational education and income characteristics circa *1950*, as estimated by O. D. Duncan and reported in Reiss (1961) for the 1950 census classification system; subsequently, Duncan reconciled these scores to the 1960 classification, *without* reestimating the socioeconomic characteristics of occupation titles.[1] In arriving at our SEI scores for detailed 1970 occupations, we have used Duncan's *original* (1950) scores for titles in the 1960 classification, reconciling the latter to the 1970 classification system, as provided by the transformation matrix found in Table 1 of Bureau of the Census Technical Paper 26, *1970 Occupation and Industry Classification Systems in Terms of Their 1960 Occupation and Industry Elements* (Priebe, Heinkel, and Greene, 1972).[2] Any occupation score therefore represents the weighted SEI average of the 1970 title's 1960 components, where the weights are the men and women in the experienced civilian labor force of 1960. (Technical Paper 26 is based on a double coding of a 1960 census sample.) Insofar as there has been rather general stability of occupational education and income (i.e., the rank ordering of occupations by these characteristics) *and* virtual invariance in the prestige hierarchy of occupation titles since 1925, we feel that the adaptation of the 1950 SEI scores for the 1970 classification system does not do great violence to the structure of occupational socioeconomic status of the present.

In parallel fashion, we have transformed the newest (1964–1965) NORC prestige scores reported in Siegel (1971) for the 1960 census

[1]For some occupation titles, the SEI scores depend upon industrial and/or class-of-worker distinctions.

[2]Initially, we collapsed all industrial and class of worker variations in SEI within detailed occupation titles of the 1960-basis system. For the NORC scores reported by Siegel (1971), we followed the same procedures.

detailed titles into the 1970 classification system, based on Technical Paper 26.[3]

Conventions of Occupation Coding

In survey research, the proper coding of occupations is of utmost importance; improper and arbitrary coding can destroy the validity of the final piece of research. This coding is also of utmost difficulty; it requires the ability to make fine distinctions, the perseverance to explore all possibilities, and the patience to defer the classification of an occupation until all the information is in.

Occupations are to be classified in a manner similar to that employed by the United States Bureau of the Census in 1970. All respondents are asked the following:

1A. What kind of work were you doing?

(For example: electrical engineer, stock clerk, farmer.)

1B. What were your most important activities or duties?

(For example: kept account books, filed, sold cars, operated printing press, finished concrete.)

1C. What kind of business or industry was this?

(For example: TV and radio mfg., retail shoe store, State Labor Dept., farm.)

1D. Were you: (Mark one.)
an employee of a PRIVATE company,
business or individual for wages,
salary, or commissions?.. □ PR

a GOVERNMENT employee (federal, state,
county, or local government)?.. □ GOV
self-employed in OWN business,
professional practice, or farm?

own business not incorporated (or farm) .... □ OWN
own business incorporated... □ INC

working WITHOUT PAY in a family
business or farm?... □ WP

[3] While we have made no use of the industry and class-of-worker information in producing status scores for the 1970-basis occupation classification, this reflects an interim state. In a few months, we hope to reestimate new scores for the Duncan index, based upon 1970 census information, which discriminate among occupations of the same title but in different industries (or among the various classes of worker). Our efforts along this line may be anticipated by work under way by Charles Nam at Flordia State University.

With these pieces of information, and the proper sources, it should be possible to classify almost all occupations. The main source for coding is the *Alphabetical Index of Industries and Occupations* (U.S. Bureau of the Census, 1971a). Sometimes, the information given there may not be detailed enough for proper classification. Then, the coder may wish to consult two other sources; these are (1) the *Classified Index of Industries and Occupations* (U.S. Bureau of the Census, 1971b), and (2) the *Dictionary of Occupational Titles* (U.S. Department of Labor, 1965).

Industry. The census has classified the 19,000 industries listed in the *Alphabetical Index* into over 200 detailed titles. Each detailed title represents a pool of industries which are similar to one another. Each category is represented either by a three-digit number ending in 7, 8, 9, or by one of the letters A–M. Each letter can be translated back into a three-digit number. For industrial categories, the letters represent the following numbers:

A = 017	G = 669
B = 069	H = 769
C = 319	J = 838
D = 407	K = 857
E = 609	L = 917
F = 628	M = 937

Notice that there is no entry "I." This is because the letter "I" might easily be confused with the number "1."

The census also classifies the detailed titles into 12 major industrial groups. Each major group represents a pool of industrial titles which are similar in function to one another.

The code ranges for the 12 major industrial groups are as follows:

Agriculture, forestry, fisheries	017–029; A
Mining	047–058
Construction	067–078; B
Manufacturing	107–399; C
Transportation, communication, and other public utilities	407–499; D
Wholesale and retail trade	507–699; E,F,G
Finance, insurance, and real estate	707–719
Business and repair services	727–767
Personal services	769–799; H
Entertainment and recreation services	807–817
Professional and related services	828–899; J,K
Public administration	907–947; L,M

Occupation. The census has classified the over 23,000 occupations listed in the *Alphabetical Index* into 429 detailed occupational titles. Each detailed title represents a pool of occupations that are similar to one another. Each title is represented either by a three-digit number ending in 0, 1, 2, 3, 4, 5, 6, or by one of the letters N–Z. Each letter can be translated back into a three-digit number. For occupational titles, the letters represent the following numbers:

N = 142	U = 715
P = 305	V = 751
Q = 372	W = 801
R = 415	X = 903
S = 473	Y = 915
T = 602	Z = 984

Notice that there is no entry "O." This is because the letter "O" might easily be confused with the number "0."

The census also classifies the 429 detailed occupational titles into 12 major occupation groups. Each group represents a pool of occupational titles that are related to one another.

The code ranges for the 12 major occupational groups are as follows:

Professional, technical, and kindred workers	001–196; N
Managers and administrators, except farm.	201–246
Sales workers	260–296
Clerical and kindred workers	301–396; P,Q
Craftsmen and kindred workers	401–586; R,S
Operatives, except transport	601–696; T
Transport equipment operatives	701–726; U
Laborers, except farm	740–796; V
Farmers and farm managers	801–806; W
Farm laborers and farm foremen	821–846
Service workers, except private household	901–976; X,Y
Private household workers	980–986; Z

Class of Worker. Sometimes the assignment of an industry or occupation depends on the class-of-worker distinction made by the census. The *Alphabetical Index* contains the following class-of-worker abbreviations:

Working for a private company, business or individual for wages, salary, or commission	Pr
Working for federal, state, or local government	Gov
In own business, professional practice, or farm (Unincorporated)	Own
In own business, professional practice, or farm (Incorporated)	Inc
Without pay in a family business or farm	WP

It is important to *remember always* that a person who incorporates his own business is technically an employee of that corporation. Therefore, he is *always* classified as an "Inc," not an "Own."

The Alphabetical Index

Coverage

The *Alphabetical Index* lists industry and occupation titles that have been reported in earlier censuses and surveys, and it covers the bulk of industry and occupation titles in the economy. Sometimes the title for which you are looking is not listed in the *Alphabetical Index*. There are two main reasons for this: New industries and occupations are constantly being developed, and new titles for existing industries and occupations are always arising.

Alphabetization

The titles listed in the *Alphabetical Index* are arranged according to the word system similar to telephone directories and encyclopedias. Under word alphabetizing, the position of a title may vary according to whether the title is shown as a single word or as two words. The following example will illustrate the word-system alphabetization:

> address list compilers
> address system, public
> addressing service
> addressograph plates
> addressographing service

Cross-Indexing

Many titles shown in the *Alphabetical Index* contain two or more words. In many cases, the multiword titles are listed in the *Alphabetical Index* in all possible orders. However, some multiword titles are listed only once in the *Alphabetical Index*.

For multiword industry and occupation titles, if the particular order of words cannot be found in the *Alphabetical Index*, it does not necessarily mean that the title has been omitted from the index. It is necessary to try all possible orders of words before deciding that the title is not in the *Alphabetical Index*.

Sometimes it is also important to try highly related possibilities. For example, an occupational entry might be "legal clerk." The *Alphabetical Index* does not list this as a possibility; however, the index does have a listing for "law clerk."

In order to save space, exceptions to this rule for occupations are made for nine "key words," selected because they occur frequently. Cross-indexing was eliminated for occupation titles containing any one of these nine selected words. Occupation titles containing these key words are listed only once in the *Alphabetical Index* under the key word. For example, one of the key words is "mechanic." For "auto mechanic," in looking under "mechanic, specific type" for "auto," you will not find "auto mechanic" listed under the A's. The list of *key words* is as follows:

Apprentice	Inspector
Assembler	Manager
Assistant	Mechanic
Engineer	Teacher
Helper	

Industry Coding

General. Industry entries are the first section of the *Alphabetical Index* and are arranged alphabetically. A typical industry entry looks like:

Dry cleaning 779

Therefore, for a schedule industry entry of "dry cleaning," the code "779" should be entered in the item 33 code box. The industry titles will have either a three-digit code or a single letter in the right-hand margin.

Abbreviations following Industry Titles. The following abbreviations are used in the *Alphabetical Index* with certain industry titles and are considered an essential part of the title so qualified:

(Const.)—for construction, building, excavating, etc.
(Mfg.) —for manufacturing, factory, mill, plant, etc.
(Ret.) —for retailing, retail store, retail shop, etc.
(Whsl.) —for wholesaling, wholesale company, wholesale store, etc.
(Ext.) —for mining, mine, well, quarry, etc.

For example:

Acetylene gas (Mfg.) 347
Acetylene gas (Whsl.) 508

Schedule entries such as "acetylene gas factory" and "acetylene gas plant" are to be coded "347." On the other hand, entries such as "wholesale acetylene gas company" and "acetylene gas wholesaling" are to be coded "508." Note that these abbreviations are also used with the industry titles shown in the center column of the occupation portion of the *Alphabetical Index.*

Any Not Listed above and Except (. . . .). In the industry section of the *Alphabetical Index,* there sometimes appears the listing "any not listed above (mfg.)." This line covers either specified or unspecified kinds of factories that are *not* shown in the preceding list. For example: "Yarn: Any not listed above (mfg.)" would apply to a schedule entry of either "yarn factory" or "nylon yarn factory," since the latter is not listed separately. In like manner, the *Alphabetical Index* will also contain an "except" line which covers all the cases except the preceding line. For example, the *Alphabetical Index* shows:

> Apparel, knit (mfg.)
> Apparel, exc. knit (mfg.)

which means that any apparel manufacturing that is not knit would use the second line.

Industry Returns of Self-Employed, Own Account, etc. Industry schedule entries of "self-employed," "own business," "self," "own practice," and the like are to be considered as equivalent to "own account." To cover these terms, a listing "own account" with occupation title has been included in the *Alphabetical Index*. To facilitate coding, the listing under "own account" presents occupations. On each line are two codes; the first code is the industry code which should be entered in the industry code box. The second code is the code for occupation which should be placed in the proper code box. Therefore, an industry–occupation combination of "own account" allows you to code both the industry and occupation at the same time without referring to the occupation portion of the *Alphabetical Index*. Many of these entries will require information from the occupation item for identifying the industries.

Occupation Coding

Occupation titles are listed in the *Alphabetical Index* in several ways. These are as follows.

Occupation Titles with No Restrictions. The following is an example of such.

> Ticket writer 394

This means that, if the schedule entry reads "ticket writer," the proper code to be entered in code box 34 would be "394."

Occupation Titles with Industry and/or Class-of-Worker Restrictions. There are a number of types of restrictions. In all cases, the occupation title is in the left column and the occupation code in the right column.

> (1) Title with one industry code in the center:
> Salesman.............287 705

This means that you can code your occupation "705" *only* when the industry has been assigned the code "287."

> (2)   Title in combination with range of industry codes:
> Compensation man 307–318   620

If the industry code had been assigned "308," you could code the "compensation man" as "620," because code 308 falls within the range 307–318. If the industry code does not fall within this range of codes in the middle column, you cannot use the code for occupation.

> (3)   Title in combination with several industry codes:
> Criminal investigator . . . . . .L, M, 907, 927   964

In identical fashion as the industry range, here the occupation code 964 can be used only if you have assigned as the industry one of the four codes in the center.

> (4)   Title in combination with a schedule entry:
> Field examiner . . . . .Veterans Administration L . . .   321

You can code the occupation entry "321," only if the industry entry on the schedule is "Veterans Administration."

> (5)   Residual middle entries:
> Motor man . . . . .Any not listed above   710

This entry completes a listing of similar occupation titles and is used when one of the preceding entries does not apply or where industry is blank. Other instructions similar to this are: "mfg., not listed above," "not specified," "except . . . '," and "mfg. except . . ."

> (6)   A middle entry of a class of worker description:
> Private duty nurse . . . . .Own, 848   075

"Own" means that you should note item 35 (class of worker). If this person was in industry 848 *and* checked either "own business not incorporated" or "own business incorporated," then this occupation should be coded "075."

Coding Industry from Occupation Returns. In some cases, blank industry returns can be coded from the occupation return. In other cases, industry codes must be changed to be consistent with the occupation return.

> (1)   A middle numerical entry in parentheses:
> Parking attendant . . . .(749)   711

This entry means that, if the industry item was blank, then, based on the occupation, you can code the industry. In the example, if industry was blank and occupation was "parking attendant," then you would code industry "749."

It also means that, if you do not have enough information to correctly classify the proper industrial category, you would code the industry listed in parentheses.

For example, a chemist may indicate that he works for a chemical firm. This may seem specific enough, but it is not. There are many different kinds of chemical firms listed under different industrial categories. Normally, this man could not be placed in a single industrial category, since "firm" is so vague. But the occupation entry in the *Alphabetical Index* reads as follows:

Chemist . . . . (897) 045

This means that, in this instance, the chemist could be assigned to industrial category 897.

> (2)   A middle entry of a *"boldface"* number:
> Foster mother **879** 942

This entry means that we will permit this occupation to occur only in the boldface industry. If the industry code box has any other code in it, it should be changed to the boldface code. In the example, if industry was anything but 879 and the occupation was "foster mother," then you would change the industry code to "879." Of course, if industry was blank, it should also be coded "879."

The Classified Index

The *Classified Index* is similar to the *Alphabetical Index*. The only difference is that the *Classified Index* lists all the industries and occupations by the category they are included under. However, this can be very valuable information at times.

Occasionally, you might tentatively classify a man in a certain industrial or occupational category but wish to be sure that he really belongs in this category. If reference to the Industrial Classification System or the Occupation Classification System (both are found in the introductory section of both the *Alphabetical Index* and the *Classified Index*) is not adequate, then it is advisable to check the listings under categories, as given by the *Classified Index*. In this way, it is sometimes possible to determine the proper classification by looking at the other industries or occupations listed under a category.

The Dictionary of Occupational Titles

Finally, there is also the *Dictionary of Occupational Titles (DOT)*. The *DOT* recognizes 35,550 job titles; for each job title recognized, the *DOT* either describes the job or refers you to another title for the same job.

This is then an invaluable reference for several reasons. Sometimes a job title cannot be found in the *Alphabetical Index;* however, it well may be listed in the *DOT*. The *DOT* will also list other titles for the same occupation; this allows you to go back to the *Alphabetical Index,* find the appropriate job title, and properly classify the occupation.

For example, a respondent might indicate that he is an "oven unloader." The *Alphabetical Index* has listings for oven bakers, oven builders, oven dumpers, oven heaters, oven laborers, oven loaders, oven operators, oven tenders, oven workers, and ovenmen. There is no entry for oven unloaders. Turning to the *DOT,* we find an entry for oven unloaders. The entry refers the coder to the entry for material handlers. Since material handlers are listed in the *Alphabetical Index,* the oven unloader can be assigned the code "753." In this instance, he can be assigned this code whether or not an industrial category has been coded; this occupation is not specific to any industrial category.

There is also a second reason the *DOT* is an invaluable source of information. It includes a listing of the activities and duties associated with each job listed; thus, the survey information obtained on job activities and duties can be matched against the activities and duties listed in the *DOT*. For example, a respondent might indicate that he is a data-processing clerk in the radio broadcasting and television industry. The description of activities and duties might indicate that he compiles and tabulates statistics. Turning to the *Alphabetical Index,* we find three immediate possibilities. These are:

Clerical technician	055
Clerk analyst	375
Clerk, n.s.	395

At this point, we cannot tell in which of the three occupational categories the respondent belongs. Furthermore, reference to the Occupational Classification System and to the *Classified Index* is no great help, though it does tell us that occupational category 375 is for statistical clerks.

Turning to the *DOT,* we find that a clerical technician "studies clerical and statistical methods in commercial or industrial establishments to develop improved and standardized procedures . . . makes recommendations for improvements by introduction of new forms, modifications of existing procedures, or some other method." A statistical clerk "compiles and tabulates statistics for use in statistical studies . . . assembles and classifies statistics, following prescribed procedures . . . operates adding machine and calculator to compute statistical formulas." Noting the qualitative difference between the two entries, we can now assign the respondent to occupational category 375. We need not worry about the third possibility, for it is a residual category to use when the respondent cannot be properly classified elsewhere.

There are three important things to note from the example above. First, it may be very difficult to assign properly an occupational category—to do so may require the use of all the information given, as well as great resourcefulness on the coder's part. Second, note that without the *DOT* and without the description of the job's activities and duties, as recorded in the survey, it would have been impossible to classify this respondent. Third, note the importance of taking the time to classify this respondent properly. Occupational category 375 comes under the occupational group *"clerical and kindred workers,"* whereas occupational category 055 comes under the occupational group *"professional, technical and kindred workers."* The distinction between these two groups is qualitative and substantial; in this instance, only attention to minute detail prevented misclassification.

What to Do When All Else Fails

Although it should not occur frequently, it is sometimes impossible to make an assignment to an industrial or occupational category that will be anything other than arbitrary. The main reason this happens is because the survey information about the industrial or occupational category is not detailed enough. For example, a man might indicate that he is a sales manager in the air conditioning industry. Upon turning to the *Alphabetical Index*, we find the following possibilities for industrial category:

Air conditioners, room(ret.)	668
Air conditioning	
Contracting	B
Equipment, commercial(whsl.)	537
Equipment, household(whsl.)	529
Equipment(ret.)	607
Units(mfg.)	197

In this particular instance, not only is the given information insufficient to allow the proper coding of industry: Because coding of the occupation "sales manager" depends on the industrial code, even this information cannot be coded. For example, in this instance, there are two possible occupational categories listed in the *Alphabetical Index* under the key word "manager." These are:

Sales..........E, F, G, 607–698	231
Sales..........Exc. E, F, G, 607–698	233

Thus, if the respondent were employed in the air conditioning retail equipment industry, or in the retail room air conditioning business, he would be coded "231." If he were employed in any of the other categories, he would be coded "233."

This example illustrates several things. First, it is imperative that respondents be probed in detail concerning the industry they are in; of course, the same is true for occupation. We must know whether or not the industry is a manufacturing concern, or whether it is a retailing or wholesaling concern, for example.

Second—this is the most important thing to note about the above example—where we do not know how to assign industrial and/or occupational categories properly, coders should fill out a card for this respondent, listing *all* industrial and/or occupational categories that are possible. The card itself can be much like the listings given in the foregoing example. This card should then be turned over to the supervisor, who will make the final judgment by using census techniques. In fact, whenever a coder feels incapable of making a good decision, a card should be filled out and turned over to the supervisor (see Figure 2.1).

Sometimes the coder might feel that it is possible to classify a respondent properly if information in a previous or later part of the survey is used. This procedure is unacceptable because the use of this information would build biases into the survey results. For this reason, in surveys in which occupational data are collected on the same person at various times in his life, coders are generally asked to code the appropriate information for one point in time only and to then continue with the next questionnaire. That is, coders *should not* code an entire questionnaire at once, but they should code one set of questions for a single job for *every* assigned questionnaire before going on to a second set of job questions.

Finally, a coder might come across a questionnaire in which a name of a company or organization is listed for the industry or business. Since many companies and organizations fulfill multiple purposes and activities, this information is inadequate. In these cases, the coder will have to fill out a card for the supervisor, and the interview schedule will be sent back to the interviewer to follow up.

Steps in Coding

Step 1: Code the industry described in interview schedule using Alphabetical Index *listings of industries.*

Coder No.

Interview No.

Interview Question No(s).

1. R's occupation _____

    _____

2. R's activities and duties _____

    _____

3. R's industry _____

    _____

4. R's class of worker _____

    _____

- -

Why can't code R: _____

    _____

    _____

All industrial, occupational, and (or) class-of-worker possibilities _____

    _____

    _____

Any other problems _____

    _____

    _____

Figure 2.1 Illustration of card.

A. Industry titles are listed in several ways in front of the *Alphabetical Index:*

    1. Listings without restrictive qualifications:

        e.g., Academy ....   K
            Lead drawing   149

    2. Listing with restrictions and qualifications:

        e.g., Radio (ret.)   668

Industry code is 668 only if in retail sales rather than wholesale (whsl.), manufacturing (mfg.), etc. Note further abbreviations like "const." for construction, building, excavating, etc., and "ext." for extraction, mining, mine, well, quarry, etc.

Textile finishing, exc. knit and wool 308

Except for those listed, all textile finishing industries are 308.
B. For those questionnaire items not listing industry:
   1. Use industry code in parentheses, if available, in the middle of *occupation title line;*

e.g., Excavating contractor . . . .(B) 245

   2. Use industry code in boldface letters, if available, in the middle of *occupational title line;*

e.g., Hair boiler **259** 690

   3. If no help is available from the occupation code information, *code all unknown industries as "999."*
Step 2: *Code the job described or the job title using the* Alphabetical Index *listings of occupation titles.*
   A. Occupation titles appear in the *Alphabetical Index* in several forms:
      1. Titles with no restrictions on industry in which it is found or on the class of worker (whether or not self-employed) who has the title; for example:

Title	Occ. Code
Animal trainer	194
Inspector, die	561

   2. Titles with restrictions on industry:

e.g., Fruit receiver 278 374

This person receives occupation code 374 *only* if he is in an industry coded "278."

e.g., Fruit vendor. 619 264

If occupation code is 264 but industry code other than code in *boldface* type has been assigned, change to industry code in boldface.

e.g., Marbelizer 159, 167, 168 644
Matrix-bath man . . . .:. .199–209 635

These men are given codes 644 or 635 only when they are employed in specific industries listed in middle of line or in the range of industries indicated in middle of line.

e.g., Matron....exc. city police department M ... 933

All matrons coded "933," except those in listed industries.

e.g., Selector........any not listed above........ 610

If selector is not employed in industries covered by previous selector listings, use occupation code 610.

3. Titles with restrictions on class of worker. *Note:* Following each question about type of work a person is in, there is an interview item asking if person works for himself or someone else. This is a *class-of-worker* question. The census uses the following class-of-worker distinctions:

Abbrev.	*Class of Worker*
Pr	Working for a private company, business, or individual for wages, salary, or commission.
Gov	Working for federal, state, or local government.
Inc	Self-employed in own *incorporated* business, or *incorporated* professional practice.
Own	Self-employed in own *unincorporated* business, *unincorporated* professional practice, or any farm.
WP	Works without pay in a family business or farm.

e.g., Service-station attendant .....PR or WP, G, 648 623

Use occupation code 623 only if PR, G, or 648 is indicated by the questionnaire.

B. If occupation title is codable but no industry is listed:
1. Occupation title may suggest an industry; if so, and no industry is given on schedule, use industry code in parentheses:

e.g., Factory representative........(398)......... 280

Here, occupation code is 280 with no restrictions; but use industry 398 if none given on interview schedule. This would, of course, also apply if the industry were listed in boldface letters, because this means that the occupation must be in that industry.
2. If occupation title appears without industry suggestion and none appears in questionnaire, then code occupation, and leave industry coded "999."

C. If occupation title must be in a specific industry:
1. If an occupation title must be in a certain industry, as evidenced by boldface letters for the industry title, check to see

whether or not the industry has been coded properly. If there is a conflict between the *Alphabetical Index* and the code you have assigned for industry, change the industry code to that given in the *Alphabetical Index*.

D. If no occupation is listed on interview schedule, code occupation "995."

Step 3: Code class of worker from interview schedule.

A. Essentially, we will use the census class-of-worker distinctions.

B. Code these by the following digits (far right):

Abbrev.	Class of Worker	Numer. Code
Pr	Working for a private company, business, or individual for wages, salary, or commission.	1
Gov	Working for federal, state, or local government.	2
Inc	Self-employed in own *incorporated* business, or *incorporated* professional practice.	3
Own	Self-employed in own *unincorporated* business, *unincorporated* professional practice, or any farm.	4
WP	Works without pay in a family business or farm.	5
DK	R didn't know what class of worker applied to him.	8
NA	Information not ascertained, due to omission or inapplicability.	9

Examples and Practice Examples

Study the following examples closely; then, try to code the practice examples at the end of this section.

1. R says he is an assistant manager in a paint and wallpaper store. His main activity is selling, and he works for a private company.

Step 1: We assume that, by "store," the "retail" classification is intended. In the *Alphabetical Index*, the code for "paint (ret.)" is 607. Though the code for "wallpaper (ret.)" is also 607, we don't need to use this information. In cases like these, we always take the first alternative (paint). This is because the first alternative is more likely to be the most important. So, R is coded "607."

Step 2: Turning now to the keyword "manager," we use the job activity information; consequently, two possibilities for sales managers are found. These are:

```
Manager
  Sales..........E, F, G, 607–698 .........  231
  Sales........Exc. E, F, G, 607–698.......  233
```

Since R is employed in industry category 607, his occupation code is 231.

Step 3: Finally, because R works for a private company, he is coded "1" for the class-of-worker item.

2. R says he is a tool-and-die maker in the special machines and automotive industry. His main activities are the making and repairing of metal-working dies. Further, R works for a business.

Step 1: In the *Alphabetical Index,* there are no industry listings for "special machines," "special machinery," "machinery, special," or "machines, special." Furthermore, there is no entry for either "automotive machinery" or "machinery, automotive." In this instance, the respondent can at least be placed in the "automobile (mfg.)" industry. Thus, we assign him code 219.

Step 2: In this case, the *Alphabetical Index* lists only one entry, which is not specific to certain industries. The proper code to assign a tool-and-die maker is 561.

Step 3: Since R works for a business code him "1."

3. R says he is an electrical substation engineer in an electrical utilities consulting firm. His main activity is to coordinate the operation of facilities for the transmission of power from distribution points to consumers. Finally, R is self-employed in his own incorporated firm.

Step 1: There are several immediate possibilities for industrial category. These are:

> Electric
> Power company 467
> Power plant 467
> Power, public utility 467
> Power, utility 467
> Engineering company, consulting 888
> Engineering consultants 888

We code R as "888" because he specifically works for a consulting firm; he does not work for a power company or a power plant, for example.

Step 2: Turning to occupation section of the *Alphabetical Index,* we find no entry for "substation enginner." Turning now to the keyword "engineer," we find that an electrical engineer is coded "012" regardless of the industry he is in. One would think the job finished now. However, there are still other possibilities. In the *DOT,* under the entry "Electrical engineer, power," "distribution engineers" are included. The activities associated with that type of employment are exactly those duties reported by R. Furthermore, the *DOT* lists a substation engineer as one type of distribution engineer. Having used to full advantage our information on job activities, we turn back to the keyword "engineer" in the *Alphabetical Index*. There are several industry-specific possibilities for a distribution engineer. In this case, the appropriate choice is the following:

> Engineer
> Distribution . . . . .Exc. 467, 469   023

Thus, R is coded "023."

Step 3: Because R is self-employed, we want to code him as an owner, or "1." But remember that R's business is incorporated, making him technically an employee of that corporation. Therefore, R is coded "Inc.," or "3."

4. R says he works on a diary farm for his father. His main activity was farming, and he is in the farming industry. As class of worker, R says he is in partnership with his father.

Step 1: In the industry section of the *Alphabetical Index*, there is no entry for "dairy farms." Turning to "farm," we find no entry for "farm, dairy." Therefore R's industry is coded as:

> Farm . . . . .any not listed above . . . .   A

Code A is 017, so R's industry is coded "017."

Step 2: In this case, R's occupation category depends upon the class of worker. So Step 3 must be completed before the occupation category can be assigned.

Step 3: Although R says he works for his father, he then says this is a partnership. In cases like this, the specific class-of-worker question overrides the previous information. So, for this example, R is coded "own," or "4."

Step 4: Now it is possible to return to R's occupation and assign his occupation category. Since R is in the category "own," he is coded as:

> Farmer, dryland . . . . .A . . . .   W

W is equivalent to occupation code 801. Therefore, R is coded "801."

5. R says he is a laborer in the brick and tile industry. His specific task is the making of tiles, and he works for a private company.

Step 1: In the industry section of the *Alphabetical Index,* there are numerous possibilities listed under bricks. Unfortunately, we do not know which is most applicable. However, rather than first filling out a card, we might want to check R's occupation; this may settle the industry question. So, for the time being, we continue on.

Step 2: From the description of activities and duties, R can be called a "tile maker," as opposed to a "laborer," as he originally classified himself. In the occupation section of the *Alphabetical Index,* we find the following entry:

Tile maker . . . .(128) 694

Therefore, R's occupation can be coded "694." Also, we now go back and code R's industry as "128."

Step 3: Finally, since R works for a private company, he is coded "1."

6. R says he is a messenger in the grain elevator business. His activities consist of delivering messages and running errands. R works for a private firm.

Step 1: The *Alphabetical Index* lists three possibilities for industrial code. These are:

Grain elevator (const.) 067
Grain elevator warehouse 418
Grain elevators (whsl.) 528

Unfortunately, from the information given, we have no idea as to which of these three industries R works in. Therefore, we turn to Step 2; this may decide the matter.

Step 2: In the *Alphabetical Index,* there is no occupation entry for "grain elevator messenger." There is, however the following entry:

Grain elevator man 205

Following up this possibility in the *DOT,* we find that a grain elevator man operates a conveyor. Clearly, this is inapplicable. Therefore, we try under the listing for messengers. In this instance, R fits the following occupation listing:

Messenger . . . . . .Any not listed above 333

R is coded "333" for his occupation; this is only because the other industries listed for messengers were not the same as listed for the possible industrial entries for the grain elevator industry. If any of these entries had been appropriate to a different listing for messenger, we could not have coded R's occupation.

Step 3: Since R works for a private company, he is coded "1."
Step 4: Remember that it was impossible to code R's industry.
In these cases, coders should turn in a card to their supervisor (see
Figure 2.1). In this particular case, the card should appear as follows:

Coder No.

Interview No.

Interview Question(s) No(s).

1. Kind of work: messenger

2. Activities and duties: delivers messages and runs errands

3. Industry: grain elevator industry

4. Class of worker: not self-employed

- -

Couldn't code R as to his industry. Possibilities are:

Grain elevator 067
Grain elevator (warehouse) 418
Grain elevators (whsl.) 528

Encountered no other problems.

Here we provide several examples for practice coding:

1. R says he is principal of a trade school. His activities include the
handling of the school's administrative functions. R is an employee of
the county.

2. R says he is a safety inspector in an industry that manufactures
cables for cars. His main activities include checking on the safe operation of machines, and he works for a private company.

3. R says he is a marketing specialist in the electrical appliance
industry. His main activities include the forecasting of the state of
affairs of the national market. R works for a private firm.

4. R says he is a helper in a machine shop. His main activities
include setting up materials and tools for others. He works for a private company.

5. R is a supervisor in a factory that makes seat belts for cars. R's main activities include coordinating the activities of those who work under him. The interviewer forgot to ask the class-of-worker question.

6. R says he is a lift-truck operator in a factory that makes refrigerators. His main activities include the operation of equipment that facilitates the loading and unloading of refrigerators. R did not understand the class-of-worker question and thus this information was not obtained.

Answers: 1. 867/245/2; 2. 149/452/1; 3. card—199, 668, 529/091/1; 4. 197/694/1; 5. 441/327/9; 6. 197/706/9.

II

TRENDS IN MOBILITY AND ACHIEVEMENT

3

Trends in the Occupational Mobility of U.S. Men, 1962–1972

Only in the past decade have satisfactory data on the rate or volume of social mobility in the United States become available. Sociologists and other observers of the American scene had long engaged in pessimistic speculation about the trend of occupational mobility (Sibley, 1942; Havighurst, 1947; Hertzler, 1952; Hollingshead, 1952) which was later countered by critical discussions (Sjoberg, 1951; Chinoy, 1955; Lenski, 1958) and by a comparison of national surveys carried out between 1945 and 1957 (Jackson and Crockett, 1964). The later evidence suggested "that no striking changes have occurred in mobility patterns and rates since World War II. . . . What movement has occurred, however, is in the direction of increasing rates of movement" (Jackson and Crockett, 1964:15).

The 1962 Occupational Changes in a Generation survey yielded the first definitive measurements of patterns and trends in occupational mobility among U.S. males. Analyses of the OCG survey established that there had been substantial upward mobility in the occupational hierarchy between generations, and by an ingenious arrangement of OCG, Current Population Survey (CPS), and census data it was possible to show that more recent cohorts enjoyed greater opportunities for movement into high-status occupations than their predeces-

This chapter was prepared by Robert M. Hauser and David L. Featherman. Under their authorship, it appeared by the same title in the *American Sociological Review*, Vol. 38 (June 1973), pp. 302–310.

sors (Blau and Duncan, 1967: 90–111; O. D. Duncan, 1965). Further
analyses of the 1962 data by means of age-constant intercohort comparisons have suggested that improvements in occupational opportunities in the aggregate have not been accompanied by substantial
changes in the rigidity of the occupational structure (Duncan, 1968d).
That is, there has been no appreciable tightening or loosening of the
regime connecting the occupations of men with those of their fathers.

In the past decade, there has probably been as much concern about
trends toward "rigidification" in American society as in any earlier
period. Thus, efforts to obtain a new reading on trends in occupational
mobility are surely in order. Definitive measurements of trend over
the decade await the completion of analyses of a replicate OCG survey, carried out in connection with the March 1973 CPS (Featherman
and Hauser, 1975). However, by adaptation of a procedure used earlier by O. D. Duncan (1965), it is possible to obtain indirect evidence
of changes in occupational mobility in the past decade.

With an early replication of the OCG in prospect, one may ask
whether an assessment of trend by indirect methods is worthwhile at
this time. We think it is. Published analyses from the 1973 OCG replicate will not be available until late 1976. Moreover, the discussion of
recent mobility trends has begun already (Lipset, 1972; Lasswell and
Benbrook, 1974; Dietrick, 1974; Boudon, 1974; Miller, 1975). We
think it desirable that the inevitable anticipations and conjectures
about trends in occupational mobility be given some basis in fact.
Moreover, we think our present effort has immediate methodological
value in demonstrating how a continuous, if limited, monitoring of
trends in occupational mobility over several decades may be based on
a single baseline survey.

METHOD

Following O. D. Duncan's notation, we let $P = (p_{ij})$ be the transition
matrix of an intergenerational occupational mobility table. Then, its
elements represent the probability of a son's movement from the ith
category of father's occupation to a current occupation in the jth category. Clearly, $\Sigma_j p_{ij} = 1.0$. Let $A = (a_i)$ be the origin vector of the mobility table, a row vector which gives the proportion of men who originate
in the ith occupation class, $\Sigma_i a_i = 1.0$; and let $C = (c_j)$ be the vector
which gives the proportionate distribution of men over destination
categories, $\Sigma_j c_j = 1.0$. Thus, we have the identity, $C = AP$. Likewise,
we may also write $C = BQ$, where C is defined as before; while B is
the vector of occupations of men in their first full-time jobs, and Q

represents the matrix of transition probabilities from first to current jobs.

We use functional notation to identify the vectors and matrices of men in a given cohort observed in a particular year. Thus, $C(r, s)$ is the occupation distribution of men in the rth cohort in the sth year, and so on. For a selected cohort and year, then, the transition from fathers' to current occupation distributions takes the form $C(r, s) = A(r, s)P(r, s)$. From the OCG survey, we have estimates of C, A, P, B, and Q for cohorts within ages 20–64 in 1962. First full-time civilian occupation and father's occupation at son's age 16 were ascertained in the OCG supplement, while current occupation was ascertained in the regular March CPS interview. In order to make inferences about changes over time in P and Q, we make the following assumptions: that within the prime working ages, the occupation distributions and mobility patterns of U.S. males are random with respect to mortality, net migration, and movement into and out of the experienced civilian labor force and that the quality of data on current occupation, father's occupation, and first job does not vary with age or time.[1] These assumptions have two pertinent consequences. First, for men born in year r, $A(r, s + t) = A(r, s)$ and $B(r, s + t) = B(r, s)$, where t may be greater or less than zero. This says that we may use the 1962 survey to estimate the origin vectors (fathers' occupations or first jobs) observed in any year for cohorts covered in the 1962 survey. Second, the assumptions imply that it is legitimate to compare observed destination distributions across years. Thus, we can make the age-constant intercohort comparison, $C(r, s)$ with $C(r + t, s + t)$, or the intracohort comparison $C(r, s)$ with $C(r, s + t)$. Obviously, our assumptions are not perfectly met, either as to population coverage or response quality, and our inferences are subject to substantial risks of measurement error.

Granting our assumptions, it becomes possible to make inferences about intercohort change in a mobility matrix. Consider the null hypothesis $P(r, 1962) = P(r + t, 1962 + t)$, where we have observed only $P(r, 1962)$. This says that the mobility matrix for men aged $(1962 - r)$ is unchanged t years later (or earlier). Under the null hypothesis, we may write

$$C(r + t, 1962 + t) = A(r + t, 1962 + t) \times P(r + t, 1962 + t)$$
$$= A(r + t, 1962 + t) \times P(r, 1962),$$

[1]The assumption of randomness with regard to labor force entry and exit may be relaxed if we change the population referent to all men in the civilian noninstitutional population, rather than men in the experienced civilian labor force. We have replicated our analyses with this change in definition, and it does not affect our results. The present definition permits direct comparison of our results with those of O. D. Duncan (1965).

which we can estimate by $\hat{C}_P(r + t, 1962 + t) = A(r + t, 1962)P(r, 1962)$, since $A(r + t, 1962 + t) = A(r + t, 1962)$ by assumption. We denote our estimate of the expected distribution here by $\hat{C}_P(r, s)$ in order to differentiate it from $\hat{C}_Q(r, s)$, the estimate based on the first job vector and the transition from first to current occupation. For example, we can estimate the 1972 occupation distribution (at age 35–44) of men born in 1927–1936 (aged 25–34 in 1962) by applying the 1962 intergeneration transition matrix of men born in 1917–1926 (aged 35–44 in 1962) to the origin vector of the younger cohort. The same logic applies to hypotheses about intercohort change in the intragenerational mobility matrix. Of course, this procedure is simply an application of the common demographic technique of indirect standardization based on the 1962 occupational mobility rates.

Comparisons among expected and observed distribution for recent years permit us to make limited inferences about change in mobility matrices in the past decade. While identity of destination vectors does not imply identity of transition matrices, differences between destination vectors clearly imply rejection of the null hypothesis (subject to the possibility that internal changes in the matrix are due solely to changes in the marginals and not at all to changes in interactions between rows and columns of the matrix).

In his 1965 paper, O. D. Duncan used this procedure to measure trends from 1932 through 1962. That is, he applied the 1962 matrix for a younger cohort to the origin distribution of a cohort 10, 20, or 30 years older to obtain an expected occupation distribution of the older cohort when it was 10, 20, or 30 years younger. Following Duncan's proposal (1965: 493–494) that his procedure also be used projectively, we have applied transition matrices for older cohorts to the origin vectors of younger cohorts to obtain expected destination vectors for them in later years.

Using the destination vectors estimated from inter- and intragenerational mobility, it is possible to partition the net intercohort differences in occupation distributions for men of the same age into components attributable to intercohort changes in occupational origins, in the transition from father's occupation to first job, and in the transition from first job to current occupation. The necessary identity is

$$C(r + t, s + t) - C(r, s) = [C(r + t, s + t) - \hat{C}_Q(r + t, s + t)]$$
$$+ [\hat{C}_Q(r + t, s + t) - \hat{C}_P(r + t, s + t)] + [\hat{C}_P(r + t, s + t) - C(r, s)].$$

The two terms in the first bracket on the right differ only because of intercohort differences in the transition matrix from first job to current occupation. That is,

$$C(r + t, s + t) = B(r + t, s + t)Q(r + t, s + t),$$

while

$$\hat{C}_Q(r + t, s + t) = B(r + t, s)Q(r, s).$$

Thus, since $B(r + t, s) = B(r + t, s + t)$ by assumption, the difference between $C(r + t, s + t)$ and $\hat{C}_Q(r + t, s + t)$ is the effect of intercohort change in the transition from first job to current occupation on the net intercohort difference. To interpret the difference in the second bracket, denote the transition matrix from father's occupation to first job as $M(r, s)$. Then

$$P(r, s) = M(r, s)Q(r, s),$$

so

$$\hat{C}_P(r + t, s + t) = A(r + t, s) M(r, s)Q(r, s).$$

Also,

$$\hat{C}_Q(r + t, s + t) = A(r + t, s)M(r + t, s + t)Q(r, s)$$

since

$$B(r + t, s) = A(r + t, s) M(r + t, s + t)$$

by assumption. Thus, $\hat{C}_P(r + t, s + t)$ and $\hat{C}_Q(r + t, s + t)$ differ only because of intercohort change in the transition from father's occupation to first job, and their difference represents the effect of that change on the net intercohort difference.

Finally, $C(r, s) = A(r, s)P(r, s)$, while $\hat{C}_P(r + t, s + t) = A(r + t, s)P(r, s)$, which differs from the first expression only by virtue of changes between cohorts in the vector of occupational origins. Thus, the difference between the terms in the third bracket is the effect on the net intercohort difference of the intercohort shift in the distribution of sons by their fathers' occupations.

Had we been limited to tabulations by standard 10-year age breaks, our efforts would have been stymied by the fact that 1972 occupation distributions were not available when these analyses were carried out. However, since we have access to unit record tapes of the OCG survey, we have proceeded to make trend comparisons over a shorter period by varying the age breaks in our origin vectors. Specifically, we have applied the transition matrices for those aged 35–44, 45–54, and 55–64 in 1962 to the origin vectors of those aged 27–36, 37–46, and 47–56 in March 1962 in order to generate expected distributions for men aged 35–44, 45–54, and 55–64 in March 1970. We obtained observed distributions in 1970 from the March 1970 Current Population Survey person tape. In passing, we should note that with freedom to vary age breaks in both the OCG and CPS tabulations, it is possible to make annual trend measurements at any desired ages.

NET INTERCOHORT SHIFTS, 1962–1970

The occupation distributions of men aged 35–44, 45–54, and 55–64 in 1962 and 1970 are compared in Table 3.1. The net intercohort shifts from 1962 to 1970 may be summarized as a fairly smooth continuation of the trends of earlier decades (Duncan, 1966b). There were substantial intercohort shifts toward employment as salaried professionals and managers and smaller shifts toward employment as craftsmen, foremen, and kindred workers. The former were largest at the two younger ages and the latter at the oldest age. Within the professional category, there was no net shift toward self-employment; all of the net change was attributable to increases in salaried professionals. The growth among salaried managers was almost perfectly offset at each age by a substantial decline in the proportion of proprietors.[2] A similar, but weaker pattern can be ascertained in net inter- and intra-generational shifts from 1952 to 1962 at younger ages in Duncan's 1965 paper on mobility trends (Table 4, p. 497). Only the decline in the percentage of farmers rivals that among self-employed managers, but the decline in the percentage of nonfarm laborers is also fairly large. The remaining categories show small downward shifts in their share of the occupation distribution.

It should be kept in mind that small percentage point shifts in the total occupation distribution imply rapid growth or decline of smaller occupational groups. For example, the decline of 2.5 percentage points in the share of men who are farmers or farm managers at ages 35–44 represents a fall of 50% in the proportion of men in that category.

While the March 1970 CPS estimated there were 7,151,000 men aged 55–64 in the experienced civilian labor force, the number of men 47–56 in March 1962 estimated from the OCG survey was 9,104,000.

---

[2]Friendly critics have suggested to us that the complementary net shifts between salaried and self-employed managers, officials, and proprietors may be an artifact of a 1967 procedural change in the Current Population Survey which improved the quality of self-employment reports. We estimate this change of procedure could account for a shift of no more than 1% of the male occupation distribution from self-employed to salaried status within the category of managers, officials and propieters. While our conclusions about the pattern of shifts within that category are unaffected, our numerical results probably do overstate the extent of the shifts.

TABLE 3.1

Percentage Distribution by Occupation and Net Change, 1962–1970, by Age: U.S. Men in the Experienced Civilian Labor Force, March 1962 and March 1970

Occupation	35-44			45-54			55-64		
	1962	1970	Change	1962	1970	Change	1962	1970	Change
Professional, technical, and kindred workers									
Self-employed	1.91	1.85	-0.06	1.51	1.59	0.08	1.71	1.55	-0.16
Salaried	10.89	14.45	3.56	7.66	10.38	2.72	7.37	8.77	1.40
Managers, officials and proprietors, except farm									
Salaried	9.59	13.50	3.91	8.36	13.56	5.20	9.60	11.70	2.10
Self-employed	7.62	4.15	-3.47	9.94	5.42	-4.52	10.05	5.51	-4.54
Sales workers	5.14	4.93	-0.21	5.00	4.87	-0.13	3.99	5.63	1.64
Clerical and kindred workers	6.47	6.06	-0.41	6.66	6.78	0.12	5.92	6.47	0.55
Craftsmen, foremen and kindred workers	21.16	22.77	1.61	22.56	23.45	0.89	19.51	22.53	3.02
Operatives and kindred workers	19.10	18.93	-0.17	17.68	18.84	1.16	16.10	16.82	0.72
Service workers, including private household	4.86	4.69	-0.17	6.28	5.16	-1.12	7.91	7.57	-0.34
Laborers, except farm and mine	6.96	5.25	-1.71	6.53	5.24	-1.29	6.51	5.80	-0.71
Farmers and farm managers	4.92	2.46	-2.46	6.41	3.85	-2.56	9.22	6.05	-3.17
Farm laborers and foremen	1.39	0.96	-0.43	1.41	0.87	-0.54	2.11	1.60	-0.51
Total	100.00	100.00		100.00	100.00		100.00	100.00	
Number	11,085	10,513		9,594	10,423		6,563	7,151	

SOURCE: March 1962 OCG survey and March 1970 Current Population Survey (person tapes).

89

The net loss of nearly 22% of the cohort, due in about equal measure to retirement and mortality, is an obvious threat to our assumption of closure. Specifically, the validity of our findings for 55–64-year-olds is reduced (*a*) insofar as labor force exits between 1962 and 1970 occurred differentially with respect to occupational origins (*not* occupations at the survey date) and (*b*) insofar as changes from 1962 to 1970 in occupational mobility matrices for men in the labor force at ages 55–64 were effected by changing patterns of occupation-specific exit from the labor force. We do not think that either of these sources of invalidity could be very large, but our findings for men aged 55–64 should be interpreted with caution. In the two younger cohorts, there is no *prima facie* evidence of severe violation of our closure assumption; the 1962 and 1970 estimated population totals differ by only 2.8% and 5.0%, respectively, for those aged 27–36 and 37–46 in 1962.

COMPONENTS OF INTERCOHORT SHIFTS

The components of intercohort change in the occupation distribution between 1962 and 1970 are shown in Table 3.2. The most striking feature of the table is the fact that virtually all of the net intercohort shifts in the occupation distribution are attributable to changes in the matrix of transitions from first jobs to current occupations. In no occupation group at any age is the effect of change in occupational origins or in the transition from origin to first job as large as one percentage point.

With but one exception, intercohort shifts in occupational origins at each age increase the chances that a man will become a professional, salaried manager, salesman, or clerical worker; and they decrease the chances of his becoming a laborer or farmer. Shifting occupational origins have virtually no impact on the likelihood that a man will become a proprietor or a service worker. Since the occupation categories are listed in an order that approximates the socioeconomic ranking of major occupation groups from top to bottom, it is fair to conclude that the overall effect of intercohort shifts in occupational origins is to produce a slight upgrading of the occupation structure. That is, the historical upgrading of the occupational structure implies a modest intercohort shift of employment from lower- to higher-status occupations. If recent expectations of mobility between generations are to be met in the future, there will have to be a continuing expansion of opportunities for employment in higher-status occupations.

The transition from occupational origins to first jobs takes place over

TABLE 3.2

Components of Intercohort Change in Occupation Distributions Due to Social Origins and Transitions from Father's Occupation to First Occupation and from First Occupation to Current Occupation: U.S. Men in the Experienced Civilian Labor Force, March 1962 and March 1970

Occupation	35-44			45-54			55-64		
	Origins	Father's Occ to First Job	First Job to Current Job	Origins	Father's Occ to First Job	First Job to Current Job	Origins	Father's Occ to First Job	First Job to Current Job
Professional, technical, and kindred workers									
Self-employed	0.13	0.36	-0.55	0.02	-0.05	0.11	-0.02	-0.05	-0.09
Salaried	0.75	0.56	2.25	0.29	0.46	1.97	0.16	-0.32	1.56
Managers, officials and proprietors, except farm									
Salaried	0.27	0.17	3.47	0.18	-0.16	5.18	0.19	-0.09	2.00
Self-employed	0.01	0.01	-3.49	0.00	0.41	-4.93	0.10	0.28	-4.92
Sales workers	0.21	-0.21	-0.21	0.08	-0.13	-0.08	0.17	0.15	1.62
Clerical and kindred workers	0.21	-0.30	-0.32	0.12	-0.23	0.23	0.10	-0.23	0.68
Craftsmen, foremen and kindred workers	-0.03	-0.35	1.99	-0.01	0.39	0.50	0.21	0.29	2.52
Operatives and kindred workers	-0.30	-0.28	0.41	-0.04	-0.14	1.33	0.20	0.19	0.33
Service workers including private household	0.00	0.03	-0.20	0.07	-0.05	-1.14	0.05	0.11	-0.50
Laborers, except farm and mine	-0.28	0.07	-1.50	-0.06	-0.11	-1.12	-0.11	0.11	-0.71
Farmers and farm managers	-0.82	0.03	-1.67	-0.58	-0.27	-1.71	-0.87	-0.18	-2.12
Farm laborers and foremen	-0.17	-0.08	-0.18	-0.08	-0.11	-0.35	-0.18	0.04	-0.37

SOURCE: March 1962 OCG survey and March 1970 Current Population Survey (person tapes).

an interval in the life cycle which is roughly invariant with respect to calendar time. Thus, comparisons across ages of intercohort shifts due to changes in that transition matrix represent intertemporal change. At ages 35–44, changes in the origin–first job transition matrix place more men in professional and salaried managerial jobs and fewer as salesmen, clerical workers, craftsmen, or operatives, while there are virtually no effects on the proportions of proprietors, service workers, laborers, or farmers. At ages 45–54, changes in the same transition matrix place more men as salaried professionals, proprietors, and craftsmen; and fewer are placed as salaried managers, salesmen, clerical workers, operatives, and farmers; while the remaining groups are virtually unaffected. At age 55–64, shifts in the origin–first job transition matrix lead to the placement of more men as proprietors, craftsmen, and operatives, and fewer as salaried professionals, salesmen, clerical workers, and farmers. In light of these observations and the modest size of the observed shifts, we conclude that there are no consistent trends in the influence on the occupational structure of change in the transition matrices from occupational origins to first jobs.

Following the pattern of earlier decades (O. D. Duncan, 1965:497), net intercohort shifts in the occupation distribution are largely attributable to changes in the transition matrix from first full-time jobs to current occupations. The components due to shifts in the transition matrix are similar across the age groups; and, of course, they are much like the net intercohort shifts described above. There are substantial positive shifts toward employment as salaried professionals and managers and as craftsmen; and there is a smaller positive shift into the operative category. There is a large shift away from proprietorship; and there are small, but consistent shifts out of the four lowest categories: service workers, farm and nonfarm laborers, and farmers. Finally, shifts involving self-employed professionals, salesmen, and clerical workers are generally small and form no consistent pattern across the age groups.

Overall, the components of intercohort change in the occupation distribution due to changes in the first job–current occupation transition matrix can be said to have increased opportunities for upward mobility. The seeming exception to this generalization, net movement out of the category of self-employed managers, may not be as much a contradiction as it appears. Proprietors are typically small businessmen, not the heads of large firms or corporations; and they have less education and lower incomes than do salaried managers. If one takes self-employment as a self-evident virtue, then he may be less sanguine about this development. The overall pattern of shifts due to change in the intracohort mobility matrices might be described as an upgrading of the occupational structure within both the manual and nonmanual sectors, accompanied by a smaller shift from manual to nonmanual occupations.

The differences between occupation distributions we have compared to form components of intercohort change are summarized using indexes of dissimilarity in Table 3.3. The index of dissimilarity is equal to the sum of positive percentage point differences between two distributions. It represents the percentage of cases in one distribution which would have to be shifted to a different category in order to make it identical to a second distribution. The relative sizes of the indexes on the first three lines in each row confirm our earlier observation that changes in occupational opportunities between cohorts are due primarily to changes in the transition matrix from first jobs to current occupations. The indexes for that transition are nearly as large as the indexes for the total intercohort comparisons, shown on the fourth line of Table 3.3.

By 1970, the groups at the bottom of the occupation hierarchy from which there was net out movement during 1962–1970 contained 13.4%, 15.1%, and 21.0% of the experienced civilian labor force at ages 35–44, 45–54, and 55–64, respectively, compared to 18.1%, 20.6%, and 25.8% in 1962. By 1970, farm occupations included only

TABLE 3.3

Indexes of Dissimilarity Representing Components of Intercohort Change in Occupation Distributions at Selected Ages: U.S. Men in the Experienced Civilian Labor Force, March 1962 and March 1970

Component of Intercohort Change	Age		
	35–44	45–54	55–64
Occupational origin	1.59	0.76	1.18
Transition from father's occupation to first job	1.22	1,26	1.02
Transition from first job to current occupation	8.12	9.32	8.71
Total intercohort change 1962–1970	9.08	10.16	9.43

SOURCE: Tables 3.1 and 3.2.

3.4%, 4.7%, and 7.6% of the labor force at those ages. Thus, the possibilities for continued upward mobility are limited unless there appear new patterns of movement out of occupations in the middle of the hierarchy.

LONG-TERM TRENDS

In Table 3.4, we present our estimates of components of intercohort occupational shifts during 1962–1970 due to changes in intergenerational and intragenerational mobility matrices along with O. D. Duncan's (1965) estimates for men aged 35–44 and 45–54 in earlier periods. Note that the intergenerational effects shown here include the effects of changes in both the occupational origin–first job and first job–current occupation transition matrices. Unfortunately, we are unable to separate self-employed from salaried professionals prior to 1952.

The indexes of dissimilarity, shown at the base of each column, suggest that net changes in the mobility matrices had a larger effect on the occupational distribution during 1942–1952 than in 1952–1962 or 1962–1970. Because the professional and managerial categories are collapsed, we have obviously underestimated the decline in net occupational redistribution from 1942–1952 to the present; but the decline, if real, is surely not monotonic. Shifts in the occupation distribution due to changing mobility patterns are clearly larger during 1962–1970 than in 1952–1962 both at ages 35–44 and 45–54.

At age 35–44, changing mobility matrices produced more movement into professional employment during 1952–1962 than in either 1942–1952 or 1962–1970. At age 45–54, there was no clear pattern of change between 1952–1962 and 1962–1970. There has been a clear shift away from the category of managers, officials, and proprietors in the past three decades. At age 35–44, there was a net shift of 3.4% due to changes in intragenerational mobility during 1942–1952, but no net shift during 1962–1970. The apparent explanation is a continuing net movement into the ranks of salaried managers, compensated by net movement away from proprietorship, where both sorts of changes occurred more rapidly during 1962–1970 than in the preceding decade. There have been essentially no net movements into or out of sales or clerical occupations during the period covered by Table 3.4.

At age 35–44, there was substantial net movement into the ranks of craftsmen and operatives in 1942–1952, and there were small net shifts away from and into those categories in 1952–1962 and 1962–

TABLE 3.4

Differences, in Percentage Points, Between Occupation Distributions for Men of Specified Ages Produced by 1962 Intergeneration and Intrageneration Mobility Matrices and by Matrices for Earlier and Later Years

| | Intergeneration Mobility | | | | | Intrageneration Mobility | | | | |
| | 35-44 | | | 45-54 | | 35-44 | | | 45-54 | |
Occupation	1952 -1942	1962 -1952	1970 -1962	1962 -1952	1970 -1962	1952 -1942	1962 -1952	1970 -1962	1962 -1952	1970 -1962
Professional, technical, and kindred workers	0.9					1.7				
Self-employed		0.3	-0.2	-0.1	0.1		0.3	-0.6	0.0	0.1
Salaried		3.5	2.8	1.5	2.4		2.8	2.2	1.9	2.0
Managers, officials and proprietors, except farm	3.1					3.4				
Salaried		2.4	3.6	0.7	5.0		2.4	3.5	0.9	5.2
Self-employed		0.0	-3.5	1.0	-4.5		-0.4	-3.5	0.5	-4.9
Sales workers	-1.5	0.1	-0.4	0.3	-0.2	-1.3	0.3	-0.2	0.3	-0.1
Clerical and kindred workers	0.2	0.4	-0.6	0.6	0.0	0.5	0.7	-0.3	0.9	0.2
Craftsmen, foremen and kindred workers	3.7	-0.8	1.6	0.1	0.9	3.3	-1.0	2.0	0.2	0.5
Operatives and kindred workers	3.3	-2.0	0.1	0.0	1.2	2.7	-1.8	0.4	-0.4	1.3
Service workers, including private household	-1.1	-0.3	-0.2	-0.3	-1.2	-1.4	-0.3	-0.2	-0.2	-1.1
Laborers, except farm and mine	-3.1	-0.5	-1.4	-1.0	-1.2	-3.3	-0.4	-1.5	-1.1	-1.1
Farmers and farm managers	-3.5	-2.6	-1.6	-2.3	-2.0	-3.5	-2.3	-1.7	-2.5	-1.7
Farm laborers and foremen	-2.0	-0.5	-0.3	-0.5	-0.5	-2.1	-0.3	-0.2	-0.5	-0.4
Index of dissimilarity	(11.2)	(6.7)	(8.2)	(4.2)	(9.6)	(11.6)	(6.5)	(8.1)	(4.7)	(9.3)

SOURCE: March 1962 OCG survey and March 1970 Current Population Survey (person tapes) and O. D. Duncan, "The Trend of Occupational Mobility in the United States," *American Sociological Review* 30 (August, 1965): Table 4, p. 497.

1970, respectively. At age 45–54, there were essentially no shifts in the craft and operative categories due to changing mobility regimes between 1952–1962 and 1962–1970. There is a consistent pattern of net movement out of the four lowest manual occupation categories. The net shift away from the two farm categories appears to have declined continuously (along with the relative numbers in those categories) over the three decades. Shifts away from services and nonfarm labor were smaller in 1952–1962 than in the preceding decade, but the net out movement may have increased again from 1962 to 1970.

SUMMARY

Intercohort net shifts in the male occupation distribution between 1962 and 1970 are similar to those observed over the past several decades. There were shifts toward employment as salaried professionals and managers and as craftsmen, foremen, and kindred workers and shifts away from employment as self-employed managers, as laborers, and in farm occupations. In terms of the status hierarchy of occupations, these changes consist of a shift from manual to nonmanual occupations combined with shifts from lower to higher status occupations within both the manual and nonmanual groups.

For men aged 35–44, 45–54, and 55–64, we have decomposed the sources of intercohort shifts into three components: (a) changes in the distribution of occupational origins (fathers' occupations) between cohorts, (b) changes in mobility between occupational origins and first full-time occupations, and (c) changes in mobility between first jobs and current occupations. At each age, we find that changing occupational origins account for a modest upgrading of the occupation distribution, while changes in mobility to first jobs produce small and unsystematic shifts in the distribution. The largest component of intercohort shifts in the occupation distribution is change in mobility patterns from first to current occupations. While the first two components each account for net shifts of .75% to 1.60% of the occupation distribution, changed patterns of intragenerational mobility account for net shifts of 8% to 9% of the occupation distribution. Thus, the total intercohort shifts in the occupation distribution are essentially reflections of those shifts produced by changing patterns of intragenerational mobility.

While the experience of the period 1962–1970 continues the historical tendency toward upward mobility among U.S. men, that tendency is neither uniform nor inevitable. For example, there appears to have been more change in occupational mobility patterns in 1962–1970 than in 1952–1962, but less than in 1942–1952. The continuation of historical trends of occupational mobility is strictly limited by the depletion of occupation groups—service workers, laborers, and farmers—which have earlier served as sources of recruitment into higher-status occupations.

4

Trends in Occupational Mobility by Sex and Race in the United States, 1962–1972

Despite substantial popular commentary on role differentiation and socioeconomic inequalities between the sexes in the United States, it is only recently that empirical research has documented their extent and details (DeJong, Brawer, and Robin, 1971; Carter, 1972; Suter and Miller, 1973; Tyree and Treas, 1974; Treiman and Terrell, 1975a, 1975c; Featherman and Hauser, 1976c; see also Chapter 8 of this volume.) This lacuna between speculation and fact arose from a lack of reliable data for broad cross-sections of men and women in comparable social circumstances (e.g., marital status, age, color), coupled with a probable lack of interest in the socioeconomic plight of females. For whatever reasons, far more is known about the process of social stratification and the conditions of unequal opportunities for men than for women.

As part of the 1962 Occupational Changes in a Generation (OCG) survey, married male respondents reported on the occupations of their fathers-in-law. Together with reports of the present spouses' current (last week) occupations to the March Current Population Survey (CPS), these OCG proxy reports on paternal origins provide the bivariate data for a comparison of occupational stratification (or occu-

This chapter was prepared by David L. Featherman and Robert M. Hauser. A version of this analysis was presented at a Mathematical Social Sciences Board seminar, "Measurement and Models in Stratification and Mobility Research," Toronto, August 14–16, 1974.

pational mobility) for the sexes. Given recent analyses (Tyree and Treas, 1974; Chase, 1975; see also Chapter 8 of this volume) of these intergenerational data for the 1962 period, we inquire here about trends in the sexual patterns of mobility in the decade 1962–1972.

To accomplish this exercise we employ the same techniques of indirect standardization which we borrowed from O. D. Duncan (1965) and which we applied to the analysis of male trends in Chapter 3. In brief, we apply the March 1962 rates (i.e., matrices of outflow probabilities) for older cohorts of men and women to the 1962 compositions (i.e., origin vectors, paternal occupation) of younger cohorts to calculate the expected distribution of current occupations for the younger cohort 10 years later, March 1972. By comparing the observed vectors of current occupation from the March 1972 CPS with those vectors expected on the null hypothesis (viz, no intercohort change in age-specific mobility matrices, 1962–1972), we gain indirect evidence about the presence or absence of age-specific shifts in mobility patterns (in the absence of our new OCG data for 1973). These techniques can be employed with color and/or sex controls, which we have done below.

Furthermore, we take advantage of our ability to decompose each age-constant intercohort comparison (by color and /or sex) of observed occupation distributions into two components of net shift. The first component indicates the shifts stemming from intercohort differences in paternal occupation; a second reflects changes derivative from intercohort differentials in intergenerational mobility (i.e., outflow probabilities from paternal to current occupation). (Among men analyzed in Chapter 3, we identified a significant third component— mobility from first job to current job—which comprised the largest source of total shifts between 1962 and 1972. Since no first job was reported by or for the females covered in the OCG–CPS overlap, we cannot estimate this component here.)

COVERAGE OF POPULATION

As with our prior analyses, the validity of this one rests upon several assumptions: namely, that within the prime working ages, mortality and net migration are random with respect to occupational mobility and that the quality of data on current occupation and father's occupation does not vary with age or time. In order to maintain coverage of the male and female elements of the civilian noninstitutional population, we introduce "no occupation reported" and "unmarried" as categories in the origin vectors, and "unemployed" and "not in the labor force" as classes in the destination vectors. Hence, each destination vector contains categories of occupation for employed men and women, a combined category of experienced and inexperienced unemployed, and a category for those neither at work nor looking for work. Problems in reconciling the 1960- and 1970-basis U.S. census classifications of occupations are reported and resolved in earlier work (cf. Hauser and Featherman, 1974b).

In the month of March, the CPS adds to its sample of the civilian noninstitutional population those households containing members of the armed forces living in families on military posts or off posts in civilian quarters. For our analysis here, we have eliminated all armed forces personnel from the 1962 and 1972 data, leaving only elements of the civilian noninstitutional populations in those years. Table 4.1 reports the frequencies of men and women by color and age, as given in the March 1972 CPS and as expected from the projection of the 1962 (younger) cohorts into 1972. If our previously discussed assumptions are valid, then the signed values in the third line of each color–sex panel bespeak real intercohort changes in the size of each subpopulation. Our methods of projection come closest to approximating the nonblack (hereafter, white) subpopulation of women, with a small

TABLE 4.1

Estimated Number (1,000s) of Men and Women in Selected Cohorts by Color: U.S. Persons in the Civilian Noninstitutional Population, March 1962 and March 1972

	Age in 1972			Age in 1972		
Date	35-44	45-54	55-64	35-44	35-54	55-64
	Nonblack Men			Nonblack Women		
March 1962	9,217	10,374	9,227	10,059	11,137	9,643
March 1972	9,710	10,170	8,121	10,303	10,964	9,106
Percent change, 1962-1972	+5.1	-2.0	-12.0	+2.4	-1.6	-5.6
	Black Men			Black Women		
March 1962	968	1,030	881	1,241	1,230	981
March 1972	1,023	975	719	1,304	1,166	868
Percent change, 1962-1972	+5.4	-5.3	-18.4	+4.8	-5.2	-11.5

SOURCES: March 1962 and 1972 Current Population Surveys and Occupational Changes in a Generation Survey (person tapes).

net gain in size over the decade for women aged 35–44 and small, increasing losses at the two oldest ages. Differences as small as 2% may reflect sampling and rounding errors, while larger positive values likely indicate gains between 1962 and 1972 in the civilian population at the expense of elements of a cohort within the armed forces. Larger negative values probably denote the invalidity of our assumption of randomness among mortality, age, and time. That the negative percent changes reflect mortality is suggested by larger (age-constant) values for men than for women, for blacks than for whites, and for older ages within each sex–color panel. Clearly, our results are less secure for blacks than for whites and are least valid for the oldest age category.

NET INTERCOHORT SHIFTS, 1962–1972

Table 4.2 presents the age-constant 1962 and 1972 occupational distributions for men and women by color. As reported elsewhere (Hauser and Featherman, 1974b, and Chapter 3 of this volume), there are four major net shifts, or intercohort shifts, for men of both races (although the black shifts are somewhat attenuated). First, we observe a shift from self-employment to salaried status within both of the highest white-collar classes. (We have arranged the occupation categories in rank order based on Duncan's (1961) socioeconomic index; no order is implied, however, in the positioning of "unemployed" and "not in the labor force.") Whether these net shifts are connected, such that entrepreneurs and self-employed professionals become salaried managers and professionals, respectively, we cannot say without our new 1973 data. We can concede, however, that such shifts are consistent with declines in self-employment and the growth in the consolidation of business and professional enterprises over several decades (Lebergott, 1968). Moreover, such trends incorporate the second major shift in our male data, namely, the movement out of farming.

Third, the period 1962–1972 marks a net shift upward in the percentages of white and black men holding higher- (versus lower-) status white-collar and blue-collar jobs. Fourth, among the oldest white men and, to a lesser extent, among the oldest black men, there appears to be a recent shift out of the labor force. Whether such changes signify the greater availability of social security benefits or other means toward earlier retirement is not clear from our data. However, the removal of larger percentages of young black men from the 1972 labor force vis-à-vis the prior decade cannot foster a sanguine interpretation, despite intercohort gains in status among the employed. Finally, there is a minor shift toward greater employment among blacks.

Among women, the intercohort shifts in Table 4.2 are more striking for blacks than for whites. Black women of all ages have experienced substantial declines in service work in private households, with concomitant gains in other service occupations. (Again, the connectedness of these net shifts are obscure here, although the growth of enterprises offering contractual maid and janitorial services to businesses and homes may provide such a connection.) Second, black women have enlarged their share of non-secretarial–stenographic jobs as clerks in recent years. Third, higher percentages of black females now work as salaried professionals, especially at ages 35–44, although we note no decrease in self-employment (except in proprietorships, especially for the oldest women). Fourth, young black women in 1972 are more likely to be at work, despite the slight opposing tendency at the older ages.

White women in 1972 undertake clerical employment (both categories) to a greater extent than in 1962; this is the dominant shift at all ages among the employed. Like blacks, white females are less likely to be in private household service and somewhat more likely to be employed in other service, although these shifts are less distinctive than among blacks. Here, too, we observe small increases in salaried professions. But the most noticeable shift for white females is into the labor force as employed workers, especially at the youngest ages.

We conclude from these intercohort shifts that female changes in occupation are more localized than for males, probably associated with the longstanding allocation of women to clerical and service work and to positions outside the ordinary labor force (e.g., housewifery). While there is evidence for a decline in private household service employment for blacks, it may be offset by gains in other service jobs. Certainly there is no apparent decline in the recruitment of women, especially whites, to clerical work, although the gain in this category for black females might be interpreted as a net upward status shift (see below). Table 4.2 foreshadows comparisons which follow: Namely, females have experienced quite similar intercohort shifts over the decade, and they are more alike in this regard than are white men and women, on the one hand, or black men and women, on the other. In addition, color differences in female shifts reveal lingering historical patterns (by race) in labor force participation, fertility and marital status, and employment.

TABLE 4.2

Percentage Distribution of Employed Persons by Occupation and Net Change, 1962-1972, by Age, Sex, and Color: U.S. Persons in the Civilian Noninstitutional Population, March 1962 and March 1972

Occupation	Nonblack Men 35-44 1962	1972	Change	Nonblack Men 45-54 1962	1972	Change	Nonblack Men 55-64 1962	1972	Change	Nonblack Women 35-44 1962	1972	Change	Nonblack Women 45-54 1962	1972	Change	Nonblack Women 55-64 1962	1972	Change
Professional, technical and kindred																		
Self-employed	1.9	1.9	0.0	1.6	1.9	0.3	1.7	1.8	0.1	0.4	0.5	0.1	0.4	3.8	3.4	0.6	0.5	-0.1
Salaried	11.3	15.0	3.7	7.4	10.9	3.5	7.0	7.2	0.2	5.6	7.6	2.0	6.5	7.4	0.9	5.2	5.5	0.3
Managers, officials, proprietors																		
Salaried	9.9	12.7	2.8	8.7	11.9	3.2	8.4	9.5	1.1	1.4	1.9	0.5	2.1	2.4	0.3	1.6	2.3	0.7
Self-employed	7.1	3.4	-3.7	9.8	3.2	-6.6	8.9	3.7	-5.2	0.8	0.5	-0.3	1.7	0.8	-0.9	1.7	0.8	-0.9
Sales, other	4.0	4.8	0.8	3.3	4.3	1.0	2.4	3.2	0.8	0.4	0.5	0.1	0.6	0.8	0.2	0.3	0.6	0.3
Clerical and kindred																		
Stenographers and secretaries	0.3	0.1	-0.2	0.2	0.1	-0.1	0.1	0.1	0.0	4.5	6.2	1.7	4.0	6.2	2.2	2.3	3.8	1.5
Other	6.0	5.3	-0.7	6.1	5.8	-0.3	5.1	5.1	0.0	9.8	11.3	1.5	9.4	11.4	2.0	6.3	7.5	1.2
Sales, retail	1.5	1.3	-0.2	1.7	1.8	0.1	1.5	2.0	0.5	2.9	2.8	-0.1	4.5	3.5	-1.0	3.0	3.0	0.0
Craftsmen																		
Foremen	3.0	3.2	0.2	3.7	3.9	0.2	2.6	2.7	0.1	0.2	0.4	0.2	0.3	0.3	0.0	0.2	0.2	0.0
Other	17.2	18.2	1.0	17.0	19.0	2.0	13.4	14.9	1.5	0.4	0.5	0.1	0.3	0.5	0.2	0.3	0.4	0.1
Operatives																		
Other	9.2	9.2	0.0	7.8	9.0	1.2	7.7	7.6	-0.1	5.7	6.3	0.6	6.0	6.6	0.6	3.6	5.0	1.4
Manufacturing	8.3	6.6	-1.7	7.8	6.5	-1.3	5.6	5.1	-0.5	1.1	1.6	0.5	1.3	1.3	0.0	1.5	1.2	-0.3
Service																		
Other	4.0	4.7	0.7	5.0	5.4	0.4	5.6	6.4	0.8	5.1	7.4	2.3	6.6	7.9	1.3	5.5	7.0	1.5
Private household	0.0	0.0	0.0	0.1	0.0	-0.1	0.2	0.1	-0.1	0.9	0.7	-0.2	2.0	1.0	-1.0	2.9	1.7	-1.2
Laborers, except farm	3.9	3.6	-0.3	4.0	3.9	-0.1	4.0	3.7	-0.3	0.1	0.3	0.2	0.3	0.3	0.0	0.2	0.3	0.1
Farmers, farm managers	4.8	2.7	-2.1	6.3	3.5	-2.8	7.7	4.5	-3.2	0.1	0.1	0.0	0.3	0.2	-0.1	0.7	0.3	-0.4
Farm laborers	1.2	0.8	-0.4	1.2	0.6	-0.6	1.5	1.1	-0.4	0.1	0.1	0.0	0.3	0.2	-0.1	0.7	0.3	-0.4
Unemployed	3.9	3.3	-0.6	4.3	2.9	-1.4	4.0	3.4	-0.6	2.0	2.5	0.5	2.0	2.2	0.2	1.3	1.4	0.1
Not in labor force	2.4	3.1	0.7	4.3	5.4	1.1	12.7	18.1	5.4	57.4	48.1	-9.3	51.0	46.0	-5.0	61.9	58.1	-3.8
Total	100.0	100.0		100.0	100.0		100.0	100.0		100.0	100.0		100.0	100.0		100.0	100.0	
Number	10,374	9,710		9,227	10,170		6,939	8,120		11,137	10,303		9,642	10,964		7,500	9,106	

104

TABLE 4.2 (continued)

| | Black Men | | | | | | | | | Black Women | | | | | | | | |
| | 35–44 | | | 45–54 | | | 55–64 | | | 35–44 | | | 45–54 | | | 55–64 | | |
Occupation	1962	1972	Change	1962	1972	Change	1962	1972	Change	1962	1972	Change	1962	1972	Change	1962	1972	Change
Professional, technical and kindred																		
Self-employed	0.4	1.0	0.6	0.0	0.1	0.1	0.8	0.2	-0.6	0.3	0.1	-0.2	0.0	0.2	0.2	0.5	0.4	-0.1
Salaried	2.5	5.9	3.4	1.5	3.9	2.4	1.2	3.2	2.0	4.5	7.6	3.1	4.1	5.1	1.0	2.1	3.0	0.9
Managers, officials, proprietors																		
Salaried	1.2	1.9	0.7	1.2	1.7	0.5	1.1	1.0	-0.1	0.3	0.8	0.5	0.5	0.8	0.3	0.5	1.3	0.8
Self-employed	1.8	1.6	-0.2	2.2	1.2	-1.0	1.1	1.0	-0.1	0.5	0.4	-0.1	0.7	0.1	-0.6	1.3	0.0	-1.3
Sales, Other	0.3	0.3	0.0	0.6	0.3	-0.3	0.0	0.2	0.2	0.3	0.1	-0.2	0.2	0.0	-0.2	0.0	0.3	0.3
Clerical and kindred																		
Stenographers and secretaries	0.0	0.0	0.0	0.0	0.4	0.4	0.0	0.0	0.0	1.2	2.1	0.9	0.7	0.7	0.0	0.3	0.2	-0.1
Other	5.9	6.3	0.4	4.7	6.6	1.9	1.1	4.2	3.1	2.7	6.5	3.8	2.9	3.9	1.0	0.8	3.3	2.5
Sales, retail	0.7	0.5	-0.2	0.0	0.3	0.3	0.0	0.7	0.7	0.6	1.1	0.5	0.4	1.4	1.0	0.6	0.2	-0.4
Craftsmen																		
Foremen	0.3	1.2	0.9	0.9	1.5	0.6	0.2	0.7	0.5	0.2	0.1	-0.1	0.0	0.6	0.6	0.0	0.0	0.0
Other	10.3	12.8	2.5	7.6	11.0	3.4	6.6	10.0	3.4	0.0	0.2	0.2	0.0	0.3	0.3	0.3	0.2	-0.1
Operatives																		
Other	11.9	14.9	3.0	7.4	13.6	6.2	9.1	7.5	-1.6	5.8	6.7	0.9	3.9	6.0	2.1	1.5	2.1	0.6
Manufacturing	9.0	12.8	3.8	13.1	10.3	-2.8	8.3	8.3	0.0	2.9	2.3	-0.6	2.2	2.7	0.5	2.6	3.0	0.4
Service																		
Other	9.7	11.4	1.7	13.6	12.9	-0.7	16.7	16.0	-0.7	12.1	18.9	6.8	14.5	20.3	5.8	9.0	12.2	3.2
Private household	0.2	0.0	-0.2	1.4	0.3	-1.1	0.5	0.0	-0.5	19.9	8.7	-11.2	23.5	12.9	-10.6	24.2	16.2	-8.0
Laborers, except farm	21.3	12.1	-9.2	19.8	15.3	-4.5	16.9	14.6	-2.3	0.1	0.7	0.6	0.0	0.5	0.5	0.2	0.5	0.3
Farmers, farm managers	3.2	0.0	-3.2	3.7	0.5	-3.2	2.8	2.0	-0.8	0.0	0.0	0.0	0.2	0.3	0.1	0.7	0.0	-0.7
Farm laborers	3.7	2.1	-1.6	4.4	2.6	-1.8	4.6	2.8	-1.8	1.1	0.1	-1.0	1.0	0.3	-0.7	0.7	0.4	-0.3
Unemployed	12.2	6.8	-5.4	10.3	4.0	-6.3	11.2	4.4	-6.8	5.3	4.9	-0.4	4.7	3.0	-1.7	1.8	1.9	0.1
Not in labor force	5.5	8.4	2.9	7.7	13.6	5.9	17.9	23.3	5.4	42.3	38.6	-3.7	40.7	41.0	0.3	53.1	55.0	1.9
Total	100.0	100.0		100.0	100.0		100.0	100.0		100.0	100.0		100.0	100.0		100.0	100.0	
Number (1,000)	1,030	1,023		881	975		627	719		1,230	1,304		908	1,166		691	868	

SOURCES: March 1962 Current Population Survey and March 1962 and March 1972 Current Population Surveys (person tapes).

105

TABLE 4.3

Components[a] of Intercohort Change in Occupation Distribution by Age, Sex, and Color: U.S. Persons in the Civilian Noninstitutional Population, March 1962 and March 1972

| | Nonblack Men | | | | | | Nonblack Women | | | | | |
| | 35-44 | | 45-54 | | 55-64 | | 35-44 | | 45-54 | | 55-64 | |
Occupation	(1)	(2)	(1)	(2)	(1)	(2)	(1)	(2)	(1)	(2)	(1)	(2)
Professional, technical and kindred												
Self-employed	0.1	-0.1	0.0	0.3	-0.1	0.2	0.0	0.2	0.0	0.0	-0.1	0.0
Salaried	0.6	3.1	0.2	3.3	0.2	-0.1	0.2	1.7	-0.6	1.5	-0.1	0.4
Managers, officials proprietors												
Salaried	-0.1	2.9	0.4	2.8	0.3	0.8	0.0	0.5	-0.1	0.4	-0.1	0.8
Self-employed	-0.4	-3.4	0.0	-6.6	0.0	-5.2	0.0	-0.3	-0.1	-0.8	-0.2	-0.7
Sales, other	0.0	0.8	0.1	0.9	0.1	0.7	0.1	0.0	-0.1	0.3	-0.1	0.4
Clerical and kindred												
Stenographers and secretaries	0.0	-0.2	0.0	-0.1	0.0	-0.1	0.3	1.4	-0.3	2.5	-0.3	1.8
Other	0.3	-1.0	0.1	-0.4	0.1	-0.1	0.2	1.3	-0.4	2.4	-0.5	1.7
Sales, retail	0.0	-0.2	0.0	0.1	0.0	0.5	-0.1	0.0	0.0	-1.0	-0.1	0.1
Craftsmen and kindred												
Foremen	-0.1	0.3	0.2	0.0	0.1	0.0	-0.1	0.2	0.0	0.0	0.0	0.0
Other	-0.6	1.6	0.1	1.9	0.2	1.3	0.0	0.1	0.0	0.2	0.0	0.1
Operatives												
Other	-0.1	0.1	0.1	1.1	0.1	-0.2	-0.1	0.9	-0.3	0.9	-0.3	1.7
Manufacturing	-0.3	-1.4	-0.1	-1.2	0.1	-0.6	0.1	0.4	-0.1	0.1	-0.1	-0.3
Service												
Other	0.2	0.5	0.0	0.4	0.0	0.8	-0.1	2.4	-0.4	1.7	-0.7	2.3
Private household	0.0	0.0	0.0	-0.1	0.0	-0.1	0.0	-0.2	-0.3	-0.7	-0.5	-0.7
Laborers, except farm	0.3	-0.6	-0.1	0.0	0.0	-0.3	0.0	0.2	0.0	0.0	0.0	0.1
Farmers, farm managers	-0.7	-1.4	-0.6	-2.2	-0.8	-2.4	0.0	0.1	-0.1	0.0	-0.2	-0.2
Farm laborers	0.3	-0.7	-0.1	-0.5	-0.1	-0.3	0.0	-0.1	-0.1	0.1	0.1	-0.7
Unemployed	0.0	-0.6	-0.2	-1.2	-0.1	-0.5	0.0	0.5	-0.1	0.3	0.0	0.1
Not in labor force	0.5	0.2	-0.3	1.4	-0.2	5.7	-0.4	-8.9	2.9	-7.9	3.0	-6.9

TABLE 4.3 (continued)

| | Black Men | | | | | | Black Women | | | | | |
| | 35-44 | | 45-54 | | 55-64 | | 35-44 | | 45-54 | | 55-64 | |
Occupation	(1)	(2)	(1)	(2)	(1)	(2)	(1)	(2)	(1)	(2)	(1)	(2)
Professional, technical and kindred												
Self-employed	0.0	0.6	0.0	0.1	0.0	-0.6	0.0	-0.2	0.0	0.2	-0.1	0.0
Salaried	0.4	3.0	0.1	2.3	-0.1	2.1	0.1	3.0	0.0	1.0	0.0	0.9
Managers, officials, proprietors												
Salaried	0.2	0.5	0.0	0.5	0.2	-0.3	0.0	0.5	-0.1	0.4	-0.2	1.0
Self-employed	-0.1	-0.1	0.0	-1.0	0.1	-0.2	0.0	-0.1	0.0	-0.6	0.2	-1.4
Sales, other	0.0	0.0	0.0	-0.3	0.0	0.2	0.0	-0.2	0.0	-0.2	0.0	0.3
Clerical and kindred												
Stenographers and secretaries	0.0	0.0	0.0	0.4	0.0	0.0	0.2	0.7	0.0	0.0	0.0	-0.1
Other	0.1	0.3	0.3	1.6	-0.1	3.3	0.1	3.7	0.7	0.3	-0.2	2.7
Sales, retail	0.0	-0.2	0.0	0.3	0.0	0.7	-0.1	0.6	0.3	0.7	-0.1	-0.3
Craftsmen and kindred												
Foremen	0.0	0.9	-0.1	0.7	0.0	0.5	-0.1	0.0	0.0	0.6	0.0	0.0
Other	0.5	2.0	-0.5	3.9	0.2	3.2	0.0	0.2	0.0	0.3	0.0	0.0
Operatives												
Other	0.1	2.9	-0.1	6.3	0.8	-2.4	0.3	0.6	-0.3	2.4	-0.3	0.9
Manufacturing	-0.4	4.2	-0.3	-2.5	0.3	-0.3	-0.3	-0.3	-0.1	0.6	-0.6	0.9
Service												
Other	-0.2	1.9	0.7	-1.4	0.4	-1.1	0.1	6.7	0.2	5.6	-0.1	3.3
Private household	0.0	-0.2	0.1	-1.2	-0.1	-0.4	0.2	-11.4	-1.0	-9.6	-1.1	-7.0
Laborers, except farm	-0.7	-8.5	-0.1	-4.4	-0.3	-2.1	0.0	0.6	0.0	0.5	-0.1	0.4
Farmers, farm managers	-0.8	-2.4	-0.4	-2.8	-0.1	-0.7	0.0	0.0	0.0	0.1	-0.1	-0.6
Farm laborers	-0.1	-1.5	-0.3	-1.5	-0.1	-1.7	-0.1	-0.9	0.0	-0.7	-0.3	0.0
Unemployed	0.6	-6.0	0.3	-6.6	0.1	-6.9	-0.3	-0.1	-0.4	-1.3	-0.4	-0.6
Not in labor force	0.3	2.6	0.3	5.6	-1.3	6.7	0.0	-3.7	0.5	-0.2	3.3	-1.4

SOURCES: March 1962 Occupational Changes in a Generation Survey and the March 1962 and March 1972 Current Population Surveys (person tapes).

[a] Components are (1) net intercohort changes in occupational origins, and (2) net intercohort changes in the transition from father's occupation to current occupation.

COMPONENTS OF INTERCOHORT SHIFTS

Net shifts as revealed in Table 4.2 are decomposed into the two orthogonal components of intercohort change in Table 4.3. Without dwelling on the impact of these components, we conclude for men (both white and black) that intercohort improvements in social origins (e.g., the average SEI score for father's occupation has risen at each son's age over the period 1962–1972 (Chapter 5 of this volume)) stimulate but modest alterations (also, status upgrading) in the occupational destinations of same-aged men in the two periods. Changes in Component (1) for females (black and white) imply few systematic shifts in women's current occupations. Component (2), intercohort change in age-specific mobility patterns, in all four sex-color subgroups marks the occupation destinations more distinctly, with effects by race and sex as described from Table 4.2. In summary of these components of net change between 1962–1972, Table 4.4 gives indexes of dissimilarity which underscore the small impact of intercohort changes in occupational origin and the larger bearing of changing intergenerational tran-

TABLE 4.4

Indexes of Dissimilarity Representing Components of Intercohort Change in Occupation Distributions by Age, Sex, and Color: U.S. Persons in the Civilian Noninstitutional Population, March 1962 and March 1972

Component of Intercohort Change	35–44	45–54	55–64	35–44	45–54	55–64
	Nonblack Men			Nonblack Women		
Occupational origin	2.3	1.4	1.3	0.8	3.0	3.1
Transition from father's occupation to current occupation	9.5	12.3	9.9	9.5	10.4	9.5
Sum of components	11.8	13.7	11.2	10.3	13.4	12.6
Total intercohort change, 1962–1972	9.9	13.3	10.4	9.9	8.0	7.3
	Black Men			Black Women		
Occupational origin	2.3	1.8	2.0	1.0	1.9	3.6
Transition from father's occupation to current occupation	18.9	21.7	16.7	16.6	12.7	11.0
Sum of components	21.2	23.5	18.7	17.6	14.6	14.6
Total intercohort change, 1962–1972	20.0	21.7	15.3	17.3	13.8	11.0

SOURCES: TABLES 4.2 and 4.3.

sition probabilities. If there is a sexual pattern in the coefficients for Component (1), it suggests that older cohorts of women benefit from shifting occupational origins to a greater degree than younger women; among men, perhaps the reverse relationship with age obtains, especially for whites. Component (2) clearly accounts for substantial intercohort change in current occupation and, in some comparisons, is equivalent to or larger than the total net intercohort differences. In all subgroups, the oldest cohorts experience the greatest inefficiency in effecting the total intercohort changes (1962–1972), since the sums of their components exceed these total changes.

SEX DIFFERENTIALS IN NET SHIFTS

We obtain our first direct comparison of male–female trends by color in Table 4.5 by subtracting the female columns of Table 4.2 from the same-color, same-age male columns. Hence, positive values represent excesses of male vis-à-vis female percentages. For whites in both years, employed females are disproportionately clustered in clerical and service work, and relative to males they are less likely to be in the labor force. White men tend to dominate the crafts and salaried managerial categories.

Between 1962 and 1972, white women have enlarged their concentration in both types of clerical work, and young women experience a modest increase in percentages employed in other services. Outside these traditional roles, white females have gained in employment in proprietorships, as manufacturing operatives (among the two youngest cohorts) and in farming. While white women have increased their chances of being in the labor force, relative to men, they also suffer a greater vulnerability to unemployment vis-à-vis men over this period. On the other hand, white men gain in percentages allocated into salaried positions as both professionals and managers (especially among the two youngest cohorts). Among whites, therefore, males may be "preferred workers" to females in that they have shifted into the "growth" occupations (salaried, high-status white-collar categories), while females either enlarge their allocations to "traditional" work as clerks and service employees or experience gains in those "decline" occupations which males are abandoning—farming, manufacturing operatives, and proprietorships. This interpretation (rather speculative in the absence of corroborating intracohort comparisons) of the relationship between white men and women is consistent with that advanced earlier with respect to white and black men (Hauser and

TABLE 4.5

Percentage-Point Differences between Male and Female Occupation Distributions by Age and Color: U.S. Persons in the Civilian Noninstitutional Population, March 1962 and March 1972

| | Nonblacks | | | | | | | | | Blacks | | | | | | | | |
| | 35-44 | | | 45-54 | | | 55-64 | | | 35-44 | | | 45-54 | | | 55-64 | | |
Occupation	1962	1972	Change	1962	1972	Change	1962	1972	Change	1962	1972	Change	1962	1972	Change	1962	1972	Change
Professional, technical and kindred																		
Self-employed	1.5	1.4	-0.1	1.2	-1.9	-3.1	1.1	1.3	0.2	0.1	0.9	0.8	0.0	-0.1	-0.1	0.3	-0.2	-0.5
Salaried	5.7	7.4	1.7	0.9	3.5	2.6	1.8	1.7	-0.1	-2.0	-1.7	0.3	-2.6	-1.2	1.4	-0.9	0.2	1.1
Managers, officials, proprietors																		
Salaried	8.5	10.8	2.3	6.6	9.5	2.9	6.8	7.2	0.4	0.9	1.1	0.2	0.7	0.9	0.2	0.6	-0.3	-0.9
Self-employed	6.3	2.9	-3.4	8.1	2.4	-5.7	7.2	2.9	-4.3	1.3	1.2	-0.1	1.5	1.1	-0.4	-0.2	1.0	1.2
Sales, other	3.6	4.3	0.7	2.7	3.5	0.8	2.1	2.6	0.5	0.0	0.2	0.2	0.4	0.3	-0.1	0.0	-0.1	-0.1
Clerical and kindred																		
Stenographers and secretaries	-4.2	-6.1	-1.9	-3.8	-6.1	-2.3	-2.2	-3.7	-1.5	-1.2	-2.1	-0.9	-0.7	-0.3	0.4	-0.3	-0.2	0.1
Other	-3.8	-6.0	-2.2	-3.3	-5.6	-2.3	-1.2	-2.4	-1.2	3.2	-0.2	-3.4	1.8	2.7	0.9	0.3	0.9	0.6
Sales, retail	-1.4	-1.5	-0.1	-2.8	-1.7	1.1	-1.5	-1.0	0.5	0.1	-0.6	-0.7	-0.4	-1.1	-0.7	-0.6	0.5	1.1
Craftsmen																		
Foremen	2.8	2.8	0.0	3.4	3.6	0.2	2.4	2.5	0.1	0.1	1.1	1.0	0.9	0.9	0.0	0.2	0.7	0.5
Other	16.8	17.7	0.9	16.7	18.5	1.8	13.1	14.5	1.4	10.3	12.6	2.3	7.6	10.7	3.1	6.3	9.8	3.5
Operatives																		
Other	3.5	2.9	-0.6	1.8	2.4	0.6	4.1	2.6	-1.5	6.1	8.2	2.1	3.5	7.6	4.1	7.6	5.4	-2.2
Manufacturing	7.2	5.0	-2.2	6.5	5.2	-1.3	4.1	3.9	-0.2	6.1	10.5	4.4	10.9	7.6	-3.3	5.7	5.3	-0.4
Service																		
Other	-1.1	-2.7	-1.6	-1.6	-2.5	-0.9	0.1	-0.6	-0.7	-2.4	-7.5	-5.1	-0.9	-7.4	-6.5	7.7	3.8	-3.9
Private household	-0.9	-0.7	0.2	-1.9	-1.0	0.9	-2.7	-1.6	1.1	-19.7	-8.7	11.0	-22.1	-12.6	9.5	-23.7	-16.2	7.5
Laborers, except farm	3.8	3.3	-0.5	3.7	3.6	-0.1	3.8	3.4	-0.4	21.2	11.4	-9.8	19.8	14.8	-5.0	16.7	14.1	-2.6
Farmers, farm managers	4.7	2.6	-2.1	6.0	3.3	-2.7	7.0	4.2	-2.8	3.2	0.0	-3.2	3.5	0.2	-3.3	2.1	2.0	-0.1
Farm laborers	0.3	0.1	-0.2	0.4	-0.2	-0.6	0.4	0.6	0.2	2.6	2.0	-0.6	3.4	2.3	-1.1	3.9	2.4	-1.5
Unemployed	1.9	0.8	-1.1	2.3	0.7	-1.6	2.7	2.0	-0.7	6.9	1.9	-5.0	5.6	1.0	-4.6	9.4	2.5	-6.9
Not in labor force	-55.0	-45.0	10.0	-46.7	-40.6	6.1	-49.2	-40.0	9.2	-36.8	-30.2	6.6	-33.0	-27.4	5.6	-35.2	-31.7	3.5
Index of Dissimilarity	66.4	62.0	16.0	60.1	59.6	17.0	56.8	49.3	13.4	62.1	51.0	28.9	59.7	50.1	25.1	60.9	48.7	19.1

SOURCE: TABLE 4.2.

Featherman, 1974b) and with historical trends in the sexual division of labor since 1940 (Treiman and Terrell, 1975c).

Within the black subpopulation, men dominate the other crafts and nonfarm labor, relative to women, in both years. Black females cluster in private household service, although, in relation to men, they enjoy a somewhat larger percentage employed as salaried professionals; women are less likely to be in the labor force than men in both years.

In the years between 1962 and 1972, black women have increased their percentages employed in nonfarm labor (especially among the youngest cohort), as nonmanufacturing operatives (among the oldest cohort). They have supplanted males in proportions working in non-secretarial–stenographic clerking (mainly for the youngest cohort), and they are recently more vulnerable to unemployment vis-à-vis men. Yet in addition to these trends toward incursion into occupational roles commonly held by black men (e.g., other clerical, nonfarm labor), black females have consolidated their prominence in service work outside private households. At the same time, black males generally strengthen their high percentages as craftsmen (other) and as operatives, as which black men rather than women have typically gained employment, while experiencing increases in percentages working in the "female" category of private household work and in roles outside the regular labor force.

We venture the speculation, based on Tables 4.5 and 4.2, that job competition between the sexes is somewhat more prevalent among blacks than among whites. Age-constant intercohort changes in Table 4.5 portray an erosion of black female employment, vis-à-vis black men, although this may have more to do with increases in female (versus male) percentages looking for work than with displacements of employed women by men; we cannot tell from these data. In the salaried profession, especially among older cohorts, black men are gaining in an area where the percentages of employed black women have been larger than for employed men; while the reverse pattern is observed for nonfarm labor and the other clerical category (youngest cohort only). As black women reallocate percentages employed in private households and other services, the percentages of black men engaged in private household service increase.

For whites, we advanced the notion that men constitute "preferred" workers over women, relative to the "growth" occupation categories. Among black men and women, a similar but lesser pattern might be observed. Black men have strengthened their percentages in high-status blue-collar jobs (e.g., crafts) or "growth" categories and have experienced increases in salaried professions. Some "decline" categories (e.g., nonfarm labor) show decreases among employed men, but increases among women. Thus, subject to larger errors of interpretation stemming from greater sampling errors in the black data, we find a dual relationship between black male and female roles: first, a slight "preference" for men over women, and, second, greater competition (than for whites) between the sexes for jobs to which blacks are recruited.

Additional evidence for the competition interpretation lies in the coefficients of dissimilarity in Table 4.5. Generally, blacks display more sexual equality (i.e., lower coefficients of dissimilarity) in role allocation and experience more recent intercohort changes toward equality at each age than do whites. For both races, sexual inequality has declined over the decade, at all ages. However, we do not want to miss the importance of the magnitude of sexual inequality within *both* races; pertinent coefficients of sexual dissimilarity range from .5 to .6. From Table 4.2, we compute the racial dissimilarity coefficients to range between .3 and .4 for men and between .2 and .3 for women.

Of course, the major source of dissimilarity in sexual patterns of role allocation is the differential probability of being in the regular labor force. While larger percentages of women are at work or seeking employment outside the home than in recent decades, and even though women constitute a larger proportion of the labor force than in the recent past (Sweet, 1973), being out of the labor force typifies a central role-set for large minorities or small majorities of black and white women in the economically active ages of the last decade. Housewifery, mothering, and unpaid public service are activities not included in the regular labor force, although undoubtedly these roles constitute the occupations of large percentages of women, and surely they still differentiate the life cycles of mature women of both races from those of men.

SEXUAL PATTERNS OF ROLE ALLOCATION

We cannot fathom here the basis for this role differentiation—be it social, biological, psychological, or whatever. Neither do we here speak fully to the bearing of this differentiation on sexual inequality of status or on inequalities of socioeconomic opportunity. What little we can say is found in Tables 4.6 through 4.8. Tables 4.6 and 4.7 imply that the intercohort, age-specific shifts in the proportions of females versus males allocated to occupation roles in and out of the labor force cannot be attributed to factors associated directly with intercohort

TABLE 4.6

Percentage-Point Differences between Male and Female Components[a] of Intercohort Change in Occupation Distributions by Age and Color: U.S. Persons in the Civilian Noninstitutional Population, March 1962 and March 1972

| | Nonblacks | | | | | | Blacks | | | | | |
| | 35-44 | | 45-54 | | 55-64 | | 35-44 | | 45-54 | | 55-64 | |
Occupation	(1)	(2)	(1)	(2)	(1)	(2)	(1)	(2)	(1)	(2)	(1)	(2)
Professional, technical, and kindred												
Self-employed	0.1	-0.3	0.0	0.3	0.0	0.2	0.0	0.8	0.0	-0.1	0.1	-0.6
Salaried	0.4	1.4	0.8	1.8	0.3	-0.5	0.3	0.0	0.1	1.3	-0.1	1.2
Managers, officials, proprietors												
Salaried	-0.1	2.4	0.5	2.4	0.4	0.0	0.2	0.0	0.1	0.1	0.4	-1.3
Self-employed	-0.4	3.1	0.1	-5.8	0.2	-4.5	-0.1	0.0	0.0	-0.4	-0.1	1.2
Sales, other	-0.1	0.8	0.2	0.6	0.2	0.3	0.0	0.2	0.0	-0.1	0.0	-0.1
Clerical and kindred												
Stenographers and secretaries	-0.3	-1.6	0.3	-2.6	0.3	-1.9	-0.2	-0.7	0.0	0.4	0.0	0.1
Other	0.1	-2.3	0.5	-2.8	0.6	-1.8	0.0	-3.4	-0.4	1.3	0.1	0.6
Sales, retail	0.1	-0.2	0.0	1.1	0.1	0.4	0.1	-0.8	-0.3	-0.4	0.1	1.0
Craftsmen and kindred												
Foremen	0.0	0.1	0.2	0.0	0.1	0.0	2.0	0.9	-0.1	0.1	0.0	0.5
Other	-0.6	1.5	0.1	1.7	0.2	1.2	0.5	1.8	-0.5	3.6	0.2	3.2
Operatives												
Other	0.0	-0.8	0.4	0.2	0.4	-1.9	-0.2	2.3	0.2	3.9	1.1	-3.3
Manufacturing	-0.4	1.5	0.0	-1.3	0.2	-0.3	-0.1	4.5	-0.2	-3.1	0.9	-.2
Service												
Other	0.3	-1.9	0.4	-1.3	0.7	-1.5	-0.3	-4.8	0.5	-7.0	0.5	-4.4
Private household	0.0	0.2	0.3	0.6	0.5	0.6	-0.2	11.3	1.1	8.4	1.0	6.6
Laborers, except farm	0.3	-0.8	-0.1	0.0	0.0	-0.4	-0.7	-9.1	-0.1	-4.9	-0.2	-1.5
Farmers, farm managers	-0.7	-1.5	0.5	-2.2	-0.6	-2.2	-0.8	-2.4	-0.4	-2.9	0.0	-0.1
Farm laborers	0.3	-0.6	0.0	-0.6	-0.2	0.4	0.0	-0.6	-0.3	-0.8	0.2	-1.7
Unemployed	0.0	-1.1	-0.1	-1.5	-0.1	-0.6	0.9	-5.9	0.7	-5.3	0.5	-7.5
Not in labor force	0.9	9.1	-3.2	9.3	-3.2	12.6	0.3	6.3	-0.2	5.8	-4.6	8.1

SOURCE: TABLE 4.3.

[a]Components are (1) net intercohort changes in occupational origins of men and women; (2) net intercohort changes in transitions of men and women from their respective paternal occupation origins to their own respective current occupations.

113

TABLE 4.7

Sums of Positive Percentage-Point Differences between Male and Female Components of Change in Occupation Distributions by Age and Color: U.S. Persons in the Civilian Noninstitutional Population, March 1962 and March 1972

Component of Intercohort Change	35-44	45-54	55-64	35-44	45-54	55-64
	Nonblacks			Blacks		
Occupational origin	2.6	3.4	4.1	2.4	2.7	5.1
Transition from father's occupation to current occupation	15.5	18.1	15.6	28.1	24.9	22.5
Sum of components	18.1	21.5	19.7	33.1	27.6	27.6
Total intercohort change, 1962-1972	16.2	17.0	13.4	28.8	25.1	19.1

SOURCES: TABLES 4.5 and 4.6.

changes in the sex composition of social origins (Component (1)) in either race. (This is a somewhat trivial observation, since no one would argue that sex and origin occupation should be related systematically in either 1962 or 1972.) However, changes between 1962 and 1972 in sex differences involving origin statuses have affected (modestly) the probabilities of men versus women being out of the labor force at ages 45–64 for whites and 55–64 for blacks. This has occurred as improvements in the socioeconomic origins of older white and black women have encouraged them to withdraw from the labor force and as similar changes or improvements in origins redistribute the oldest black men into the labor force (cf. Table 4.3).

Aside from these rather minor sources of age-constant intercohort shifts in sexual role differentiation, which stem from Component (1), the more major source of sexual shifts derives from intercohort changes in intergenerational mobility (Component (2)). The most striking feature of Component (2) in Table 4.6 is the reallocation of same-aged black and white women into the labor force of 1972 (vis-à-vis men), relative to the 1962 period; these changes more than offset any countereffects arising from changes in Component (1) at all ages and in each race. Otherwise, the impact of altered mobility matrices for females versus males on the occupation distributions of whites and blacks follows the discussion of the intercohort shifts by color and age in Table 4.5.

We hasten to add this caveat. Although in both Table 4.4 and Table 4.7, we find that changes in mobility matrices comprise the larger component of age-constant intercohort shifts over occupational roles, one should not assume that the origin-to-current mobility relationships themselves have changed, apart from changes in outflow probabilities in these matrices which follow from "structural" (i.e., the margins of mobility tables) shifts in (1) the labor force of 1962 to that of 1972 and in (2) the origin statuses of the 1962 and 1972 age cohorts (see Chapters 6, 7, and 8 of this volume).

Table 4.8 underscores much of the analysis of male–female trends in mobility contained in Tables 4.6 and 4.7. We collapse our data over

TABLE 4.8

Hypothetical Components[a] of Change, 1962-1972 in the Female Occupation Distribution by Age, Based on Transition Matrices of Males in the Civilian Noninstitutional Population in March 1962

Occupation	35-44		45-54		55-64	
	(1)	(2)	(1)	(2)	(1)	(2)
Professional, technical, and kindred						
Self-employed	1.5	-1.4	1.4	-1.4	1.1	-1.2
Salaried	5.3	-3.2	4.1	-3.2	5.3	-5.0
Managers, officials, proprietors						
Salaried	8.0	-7.4	6.9	-6.6	7.0	-6.3
Self-employed	5.8	-6.0	4.9	-5.8	4.8	-5.6
Sales, other	3.3	-3.2	3.0	-2.7	3.2	-2.8
Clerical and kindred						
Stenographers and secretaries	-3.9	5.4	-3.4	5.3	-1.8	3.2
Other	-3.0	4.7	-2.8	4.7	0.0	1.2
Sales, retail	-1.1	1.1	-2.7	1.9	-1.4	1.3
Craftsmen and kindred						
Foremen	2.5	-2.3	2.4	-2.3	2.3	-2.3
Other	15.7	-15.6	16.1	-15.9	15.6	-15.5
Operatives						
Other	3.7	-3.1	3.8	-3.1	6.1	-4.7
Manufacturing	6.9	-6.5	7.1	-6.9	6.7	-7.0
Service						
Other	-1.1	3.9	-2.6	4.3	-1.1	3.0
Private household	-2.8	1.6	-4.0	2.2	-4.7	2.9
Laborers, except farm	5.6	-5.4	5.5	-5.4	6.0	-5.9
Farmers, farm managers	3.8	-3.8	4.1	-4.2	4.2	-4.6
Farm laborers	0.6	-0.8	0.7	-0.8	0.8	-1.3
Unemployed	2.5	-2.0	2.6	-2.6	3.5	-3.3
Not in labor force	-52.8	43.9	-47.1	42.6	-57.6	54.3
Index of dissimilarity	64.6	60.7	62.6	60.9	66.6	65.9

SOURCES: March 1962 Occupational Changes in a Generation Survey and March 1972 Current Population Survey (person tape).

[a]Components are (1) changes in occupation origin; (2) changes in the transition from father's occupation to current occupation.

race to compare men with women, and we apply the 1962 male mobility rates to the origin distributions of appropriately aged women. In
doing so, we inquire about the hypothetical occupational consequences in 1972 of permitting cohorts of women to experience the
outflow probabilities of men which obtained 10 years earlier.

At each age, the intercohort shifts in the social origins of women,
coupled with the male mobility patterns, would have entered massive
percentages of women into the labor force; they would have reallo-
cated employed women *into* crafts, managerial posts, operative jobs,
and the professions and *out of* clerical, service, and retail sales. The
substantial redistributional impact of the male matrices, relative to the
force of changing female origins, is apparent in the comparison of
Table 4.3 (black and white female Component (1)) and Table 4.4 (coefficient of dissimilarity for black and white female Component (1))
with corresponding values in Table 4.8.

Hypothetical consequences on female roles in 1972 of changing
male mobility between 1962 and 1972 (Component (2)) would have
stimulated, at all ages, parallel redistributions of women as just discussed for Component (1); the coefficients of dissimilarity for the two
components are nearly identical as well. The results of this hypothetical exercise are clear. If females had experienced the outflow relationships of men circa 1962, their 1972 occupational roles (including the
role-set encompassed by "out of the labor force") would have more
closely approximated those of men in the same cohorts. In addition,
the ensuing hypothetical redistribution would have yielded a far more
equivalent sexual division of labor than has emerged as a result either
of the relative improvements for females (versus males) in social origins or, more importantly, of the actual relative shifts in women's
(versus men's) intergenerational mobility (cf. Table 4.5). Therefore, we
can document the presence of sexual inequality of opportunity (viz,
sex-specific outflow probabilities), even if we cannot explain it with
our data. Were we able to decompose net intercohort changes into
three components, using information on women's first jobs to differentiate intergenerational from career mobility, we would have a better
grasp on explanations. For example, one might be able to examine the
relative merits of sex socialization versus sex discrimination arguments
including, here, differential life cycle patterns.

RACIAL INEQUALITY AMONG WOMEN

We turn from sex differences in mobility trends to racial trends
among females, an analysis which complements that for males in

Chapter 3 of this volume. Table 4.9 depicts a racial differentiation of the occupation structure among women which is quite different from the racial differentiation for men (cf. Hauser and Featherman, 1974b), despite the obvious prevalence, among females as well as males, of socioeconomic inequality by race. At all ages and in both 1962 and 1972, black women are more likely than whites to hold service jobs in private households and outside households. At the youngest ages in both years, blacks suffer higher unemployment. Although lower percentages of white women participate in the labor force than among blacks, employed whites more frequently take up clerical work (especially other clerical) and the salaried professions (at older ages).

TABLE 4.9

Percentage-Point Differences between the Black and Nonblack Occupation Distributions by Age: U.S. Women in the Civilian Noninstitutional Population, March 1962 and March 1972

Occupation	35-44			45-54			55-64		
	1962	1972	Change	1962	1972	Change	1962	1972	Change
Professional, technical and kindred									
Self-employed	0.1	0.4	0.3	0.4	3.6	3.2	0.1	0.1	0.0
Salaried	1.1	0.0	-1.1	2.4	2.3	-0.1	3.1	2.5	-0.6
Managers, officials, proprietors									
Salaried	1.1	1.1	0.0	1.6	1.6	0.0	1.1	1.0	-0.1
Self-employed	0.3	0.1	-0.2	1.0	0.7	-0.3	0.4	0.8	0.4
Sales, Other	0.1	0.4	0.3	0.4	0.8	0.4	0.3	0.3	0.0
Clerical and kindred									
Stenographers and secretaries	3.3	4.1	0.8	3.3	5.5	2.2	2.0	3.6	1.6
Other	7.1	4.8	-2.3	6.5	7.5	-1.0	5.5	4.2	-1.3
Sales, retail	2.3	1.7	-0.6	4.1	2.1	-2.0	2.4	2.8	0.4
Craftsmen and kindred									
Foremen	0.0	0.3	0.3	0.3	-0.3	-0.6	0.2	0.2	0.0
Other	0.4	0.3	-0.1	0.3	0.2	-0.1	0.0	0.2	0.2
Operatives									
Other	-0.1	-0.4	-0.3	2.1	0.6	-1.5	2.1	2.9	0.8
Manufacturing	-1.8	-0.7	1.1	-0.9	-1.4	-0.5	-1.1	-1.8	-0.7
Service									
Other	-7.0	-11.5	-4.5	-7.9	-12.4	-4.5	-3.5	-5.2	-1.7
Private household	-19.0	-8.0	11.0	-21.5	-11.9	9.6	-21.3	-14.5	6.8
Laborers, except farm	0.0	-0.4	-0.4	0.3	-0.2	-0.5	0.0	-0.2	-0.2
Farmers, farm managers	0.1	0.1	0.0	0.1	-0.1	-0.2	0.0	0.3	0.3
Farm laborers	-0.2	0.6	0.8	-0.2	0.5	0.7	0.4	0.1	-0.3
Unemployed	-3.3	-2.4	0.9	-2.7	-0.8	1.9	-0.5	-0.5	0.0
Not in labor force	15.1	9.5	-5.6	10.3	5.0	-5.3	8.8	3.1	-5.7
Index of Dissimilarity	31.4	23.4	15.1	33.2	27.1	15.6	26.4	22.2	10.6

SOURCE: Table 4.2.

The pattern of signs in the years columns of Table 4.9 (at all ages, positive values indicate surplus of whites relative to blacks) clarify the dominance of white women in white-collar, higher-status occupations. However, the overall differences by race are few, save for the prevalence of blacks in service work and the advantage of white women in clerking and in roles outside the labor force. Coefficients of dissimilarity decline between 1962 and 1972 at all ages, and, at each age, the role differentiation and socioeconomic inequality by race are less among women than among men (compare Table 4.9 with Hauser and Featherman, 1974b: Table 5).

Between 1962 and 1972, black women enlarged the percentage working in service outside private households (relative to whites), but they also have increased their relative percentages in roles heretofore largely dominated by white women—namely other clerical work and roles outside the regular labor force. The major shift, however, has involved the substantial exit of black women of all ages from private household service, increasing thereby the relative percentage of whites in this category.

The foregoing intercohort shifts of blacks and whites are decomposed in Table 4.10 and summarized in Table 4.11 by coefficients of dissimilarity. Changing racial patterns of the social origins of women account for quite small proportions of total intercohort changes over the decade; this reproduces the findings for men by race. Table 4.10 provides little insight into the impact of these reallocations arising from Component (1), as the values are small and unsystematic. On the other hand, racial differences in changing mobility matrices (Component (2)) have had a considerable bearing on intercohort shifts. For example, among the women aged 35–44, blacks gain in the salaried professions, other clerical work, and other service. In addition to this modest upgrading of the socioeconomic profile of black employees (vis-à-vis whites) over the decade, black women of all ages are more likely (relative to whites) to be occupied outside the 1972 labor force than a decade earlier. Again, this result parallels that for men, although absence from the regular labor force may have different significance within the ordinary role-sets of women and those of men. For white women, changes in the racial occupation distribution stemming from Component (2) follow the pattern described in Table 4.9.

Although the patterns are a bit irregular by age, we find a modest socioeconomic upgrading for employed black females vis-à-vis whites, together with increasing relative percentages outside the labor force, even among the young. Intercohort shifts for employed black women, especially the youngest ages, indicate their ability to compete successfully for jobs in those occupations which recruit women and which

TABLE 4.10

Percentage-Point Differences between Black and Nonblack Components[a] of Intercohort Change in Occupation Distributions by Age: U.S. Women in the Civilian Noninstitutional Population, March 1962 and March 1972

Occupation	35-44 (1)	35-44 (2)	45-54 (1)	45-54 (2)	55-64 (1)	55-64 (2)
Professional, technical and kindred						
Self-employed	0.0	0.4	0.0	-0.2	0.0	0.0
Salaried	0.1	-1.3	-0.6	0.5	-0.1	-0.5
Managers, officials, proprietors						
Salaried	0.0	0.0	0.0	0.0	0.1	-0.2
Self-employed	0.0	-0.2	-0.1	-0.2	-0.4	0.7
Sales, other	0.1	0.2	-0.1	0.5	-0.1	0.1
Clerical and kindred						
Stenographers and secretaries	0.1	0.7	-0.3	2.5	-0.3	1.9
Other	0.1	-2.4	-1.1	2.1	-0.3	-1.0
Sales, retail	0.0	-0.6	-0.3	-1.7	0.0	0.4
Craftsmen and kindred						
Foremen	0.0	0.2	0.0	-0.6	0.0	0.0
Other	0.0	-0.1	0.0	-0.1	0.0	0.1
Operatives						
Other	-0.4	0.3	0.0	-1.5	0.0	0.8
Manufacturing	0.4	0.7	0.0	-0.5	0.5	-1.2
Service						
Other	0.0	-4.3	-0.6	-3.9	-0.6	-1.0
Private household	-0.2	11.2	0.7	8.9	0.6	6.3
Laborers, except farm	0.0	-0.4	0.0	-0.5	-0.1	-0.3
Farmers, farm managers	0.0	0.1	-0.1	-0.1	-0.1	0.4
Farm laborers	0.1	0.8	-0.1	0.8	0.4	-0.7
Unemployed	0.3	0.6	0.3	1.6	0.4	-0.5
Not in labor force	-0.4	-5.2	2.4	-7.7	-0.3	-5.5

SOURCE: TABLE 4.3.

[a] Components are (1) net intercohort changes in occupational origins of blacks and nonblacks; (2) net intercohort changes in transitions of blacks and nonblacks from their respective paternal origins to their own respective current occupations.

have expanded in size over the decade (e.g., salaried professionals, clerical). This pattern, albeit weak, is consistent with our assessment that the female labor force may be less sensitive to racial characteristics than the male labor force. We are loathe to advance a firm interpretation of rising black withdrawals from the labor force (relative to changing white percentages between 1962 and 1972). We cannot say whether or not white women constitute "preferred" workers for "female" jobs such that an increasing supply of white women for the labor force displaces black women. However, the data on unemployment are

TABLE 4.11

Sums of Positive Percentage-Point Differences between Black and Nonblack Components of Change in Occupation Distributions by Age: U.S. Women in the Civilian Noninstitutional Population, March 1962 and March 1972

Components of Intercohort Change	35–44	45–54	55–64
Occupational origin	1.2	3.3	2.3
Transition from father's occupation to current occupation	15.2	17.0	10.7
Sum of components	16.4	20.3	13.0
Total intercohort change, 1962–1972	15.1	15.6	10.6

SOURCES: Tables 4.9 and 4.10.

not consistent with this interpretation; neither is the intercohort increase in labor force participation for young black women. Interpretations having to do with "discouraged workers," evolution toward a white female role-set, and withdrawals contingent upon improvments in employment opportunities for black men remain as some unanalyzed possibilities.

While racial differences in role allocation are fewer for women than for men, despite modest intercohort advances on the socioeconomic dimension, we might inquire about the hypothetical consequences of applying the 1962 white mobility matrices to black female origins. Table 4.12 displays the occupational redistribution which would ensue had such relationships obtained; it can be compared to actual components in black intercohort shifts in Table 4.3.

Both Components (1) and (2) would have stimulated a massive socioeconomic upgrading of black females between 1962 and 1972 had they experienced the white 1962 mobility regime. Relative to actual intercohort shifts, there would be large exits from service employment (especially in private households) and substantial entrances into clerical work (especially other clerical) and into salaried professions and managerial posts; at the older ages, percentages in nonmanufacturing operatives would increase. Overall, these hypothetical reallocations would provide status upgrading for black females within both the blue- and white-collar sectors in excess of actual changes. White matrices would decrease percentages of unemployed blacks, especially among the younger women, but they also would transfer larger percentages out of the labor force.

Coefficients of dissimilarity in Table 4.12, when compared to corresponding values in Table 4.3, emphasize that any intercohort reductions in unequal role allocation by race among women are most modest when compared to the reorganizations of black female occupation distributions which would result from equal intergenerational opportunities for both races of women. In that sense, racial discrimination is a clear burden on both black sexes, despite the unique manifestations of that discrimination within the different sexual role-sets of black men and women.

TABLE 4.12

Hypothetical Components[a] of Change, 1962-1972, in the Black and Nonblack Female Occupation Distributions by Age, Based on Transition Matrices of Nonblack Women in the Civilian Noninstitutional Population in March 1962

Occupation	35-44 (1)	35-44 (2)	45-54 (1)	45-54 (2)	55-64 (1)	55-64 (2)
Professional, technical and kindred						
Self-employed	0.1	-0.3	0.4	-0.2	-0.1	0.0
Salaried	1.9	-1.2	2.4	-1.4	4.7	-3.8
Managers, officials, proprietors						
Salaried	1.4	-0.9	1.2	-0.9	1.3	-0.5
Self-employed	0.6	-0.7	0.4	-1.0	-0.1	-1.1
Sales, other	0.3	-0.5	0.4	-0.6	0.6	-0.3
Clerical and kindred						
Stenographers and secretaries	4.9	-4.0	5.3	-5.3	5.9	-6.0
Other	8.8	-5.0	8.7	-7.7	11.1	-8.6
Sales, retail	2.3	-1.8	2.5	-1.5	2.4	-2.8
Craftsmen and kindred						
Foremen	0.1	-0.2	0.3	0.3	0.3	-0.3
Other	0.5	-0.3	0.5	-0.2	0.3	-0.3
Operatives						
Other	1.3	-0.4	3.1	-1.1	5.8	-5.2
Manufacturing	-1.3	0.7	-0.6	1.1	-1.0	1.4
Service						
Other	-6.0	12.8	-8.4	14.2	-2.8	6.0
Private household	-18.4	7.2	-22.1	11.4	-22.7	14.7
Laborers, except farm	0.0	0.6	0.1	0.4	-0.1	0.3
Farmers, farm managers	0.3	-0.3	0.0	0.1	-0.4	-0.3
Farm laborers	-0.2	-0.8	-0.1	-0.6	0.3	-0.6
Unemployed	-2.4	2.0	-1.8	0.0	1.2	-1.1
Not in labor force	5.9	-10.2	7.3	-7.0	-6.8	8.7
Index of dissimilarity	28.4	25.4	32.6	27.5	33.9	31.1

SOURCES: March 1962 Occupational Changes in a Generation Survey and March 1972 Current Population Survey (person tape).

[a]Components are (1) changes in occupational origin; (2) changes in the transition from father's occupation to current occupation.

5

Socioeconomic Achievements of American Men, 1962–1972

Only within the past decade has it become possible to characterize the distribution of education, occupational status, and income using an explicit, quantitive model of the process of socioeconomic achievement (Duncan and Hodge, 1963; Blau and Duncan, 1967; Duncan, Featherman, and Duncan, 1972; Jencks *et al.*, 1972). The development of causal models of stratification has greatly increased the possibilities for cumulative scientific investigation of the persistence of social inequality from one generation to the next. Among the important possibilities are the elaboration of models of achievement which elucidate the social and psychological mechanisms of stratification (Duncan and Featherman, 1972; Sewell, 1971; Hauser, 1972; Featherman, 1971, Sewell and Hauser, 1975; Duncan, Featherman, and Duncan, 1972) and the pursuit of comparative study, as among population subgroups in one society, among societies (Featherman, Hauser, and Sewell, 1974) or between points in time. Our present interest is in the last of these possibilities, the comparison of processes of socioeconomic achievement across time. Specifically, we report trends from 1962 to 1972 in the educational attainment, occupational status, and income of black and white men in the United States, and we analyze and interpret those trends in light of a structural equation model of socioeconomic achievement.

This chapter was prepared by Robert M. Hauser and David L. Featherman. An earlier version of this work appeared in *Science*, Vol. 185 (July 1974), pp. 325–331.

Analyses of the 1962 Occupational Changes in a Generation (OCG) survey established that there had been substantial upward mobility in the educational and occupational hierarchies between generations, and by rearrangement of OCG, CPS (Current Population Survey), and census data it was possible to show that more recent cohorts enjoyed greater opportunities for movement into higher status occupations than their predecessors (Blau and Duncan, 1967:90–111; O. D. Duncan, 1965). Further analyses of the 1962 data by means of age-constant intercohort comparisons suggested that improvements in educational and occupational opportunities in the aggregate have not been accompanied by substantial changes in the rigidity of the stratification system. That is, there has been no appreciable tightening or loosening of the regime connecting the achievements of men with those of their fathers (Duncan, 1968d).

In Chapter 2 of this volume, we looked at trends in occupational mobility of U.S. men at ages 35 to 64 during 1962 to 1970. We found there had been net intercohort shifts toward employment as salaried professionals and managers and as skilled manual workers and away from employment as self-employed managers, as farmers, and as nonfarm laborers. These changes may be described as a shift from manual to nonmanual occupations combined with shifts from lower- to higher-status occupations within both the manual and nonmanual groups. Changing occupational origins (fathers' occupations) account for a modest upgrading of the occupation distribution, while changes in mobility to first jobs have no systematic effect. The largest component of intercohort shifts in the occupation distribution is change in mobility patterns from first to current occupations. The historical trend of upward occupational mobility among U.S. men is neither uniform nor inevitable. There was more change in occupational mobility patterns from 1962 to 1970 than from 1952 to 1962, but less than from 1942 to 1952. A continuation of historical trends of occupational mobility is strictly limited by the depletion of occupational groups—service workers, laborers, and farmers—which have earlier served as sources of recruitment into higher status occupations.

In another study, we compared white and nonwhite trends in occupational mobility at ages 35 to 64 during 1962 to 1972 (Hauser and Featherman, 1974b). Both white and nonwhite occupation distributions were upgraded over the decade, but, among nonwhites, the shifts away from the lower status occupations were expressed partly by increasing rates of absence from the labor force. There were indications of especially rapid shifts in the occupation distributions of nonwhite men at ages 35 to 44. Among men of both racial groups, intercohort shifts in the occupation distribution were effected primarily by changing patterns of movement from first jobs to current occupations.

The white and nonwhite occupation distributions did not show a clear pattern of convergence over the decade. They became less similar at ages 35 to 44 and more similar at older ages. White and nonwhite distributions were most likely to converge in those occupation groups where the share of whites was stable or declining, rather than in groups whose share of the occupation distribution was increasing. Recent cohorts of nonwhites would have a much more favorable occupation distribution if they had enjoyed the mobility chances of whites in earlier cohorts. In 1972, as in 1962, the inferior occupational chances of nonwhites were due primarily to their disadvantageous patterns of occupational mobility, rather than to impoverished social origins.

In this chapter, we extend our analyses of trends in achievement to the educational attainment and income of U.S. men, and, in addition, we express occupational status in Duncan's (1961) scale of the socioeconomic status of occupations, rather than in major occupation groups. By treating socioeconomic achievements as interval variables and adopting a regression-standardization method, we can interpret intercohort shifts in achievement in terms of predetermined differences in socioeconomic background and family size and in terms of prior socioeconomic achievements.

DATA AND METHODS

The logic of our analysis is straightforward. Using 1962 OCG data, we estimate a simple three-equation model of socioeconomic achievement for black and nonblack men at ages 35–44, 45–54, and 55–65. (Since almost all nonblack persons are white, hereafter we refer to nonblacks as whites.) If we substitute the means of cohorts 10 years younger in each of these equations, we obtain expected levels of achievement in 1972, when the younger cohorts are as old as those for whom the equations were estimated. If there were no intercohort shifts in achievement other than changes in the means of variables entering the equations, the expected levels of achievement would agree (except for sampling error) with the actual levels of achievement observed in the March 1972 CPS. Differences between actual and expected achievements can be attributed to changes in the process of achievement or in variables other than those entering the equations. Further, by substituting intercohort shifts in the means of variables entering the equations, we obtain components of change in achievement attributable to each variable in turn.

The important assumption of our analysis is that the younger men, for whom we ascertain means of the regressors entering each equation from the 1962 OCG survey, are drawn from the same population as those 10 years older for whom we ascertain achievements in 1972 from the CPS. Since our analysis must of necessity pertain to men in the experienced civilian labor force, our comparisons are vulnerable to changes in coverage occasioned by death, migration, and entry into and exit from the labor force. Death and retirement substantially reduce a cohort's participation in the labor force between ages 45–54 and 55–64; many men complete military service and enter the civilian labor force between ages 25–34 and 35–44; and increasing numbers of nonwhites are outside of the labor force at ages 35–54 (Hauser and Featherman, 1974b). For these reasons, it should be borne in mind that our analyses pertain to men of a given age who occupy a particular labor force status, not to all men of that age.

A MODEL OF SOCIOECONOMIC ACHIEVEMENT

Our model of socioeconomic achievement is displayed as a path diagram in Figure 5.1. The straight, single-headed arrows represent assumptions of unidirectional causation, and the curved, two-headed arrows represent correlations that we have not interpreted in causal terms (Duncan, 1966c). The model takes educational attainment in

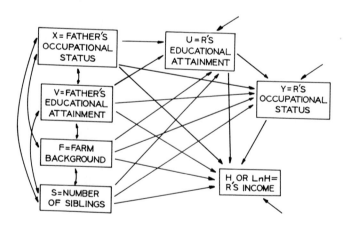

Figure 5.1 A model of socioeconomic achievement among the United States men.

years of schooling (U) to depend on father's occupational status in units of Duncan's (1961) scale (X), father's educational attainment (V), respondent's farm background (F), and respondent's number of siblings (S). Respondent's current occupational status (Y) depends on the four background varaibles and on educational attainment. Finally, the respondent's income $(H \text{ or } lnH)$ depends on the background variables, educational attainment, and occupational status. Formally, the model is given by the recursive linear equations

$$U = \beta_{US}S + \beta_{UF}F + \beta_{UV}V + \beta_{UX}X + \epsilon_U$$
$$Y = \beta_{YU}U + \beta_{YS}S + \beta_{YF}F + \beta_{YV}V + \beta_{YX}X + \epsilon_Y$$

and

$$H = \beta_{HY}Y + \beta_{HU}U + \beta_{HF}F + \beta_{HV}V + \beta_{HX}X + \epsilon_H$$

where the disturbances $(\epsilon_U, \epsilon_Y, \epsilon_H)$ are not correlated with one another or with variables on the right-hand side of the equation in which they appear, and where we have suppressed notation for race–age cohorts and for individuals within cohorts.

We have modified the basic Blau–Duncan model by entering farm background as a predetermined variable because it has been suggested that the social status of farming is not accurately represented by its position on the Duncan scale and also because there have been large intercohort shifts out of farming in the recent past. In estimating the model, we have run two equations for income, one in real (1961) dollars and the other in semi-log form. In the first functional form, the regression coefficients are interpretable as dollar shifts in income, and, in the second, they are interpretable as approximate proportionate shifts in income. (Tables of the coefficients of the equations for each age–race cohort and their standard errors are in Appendix C.) Similar estimates have been analyzed extensively elsewhere (Blau and Duncan, 1967; Duncan, Featherman, and Duncan, 1972), and we have no interest in these estimates beyond their implications for our analysis of intercohort change.

INTERCOHORT SHIFTS IN BACKGROUND
AND ACHIEVEMENT

Table 5.1 gives the arithmetic means of background and achievement variables by age and race as ascertained in the March 1962 CPS and OCG surveys or in the March 1972 CPS. For example, if we look at white men aged 35 to 44 (see the upper left panel of the table), all of the means reported for 1962 were ascertained in the March 1962 CPS or

TABLE 5.1

Means of Achievement Variables at Selected Ages by Race: U.S. Men in the Experienced Civilian Labor Force, March 1962 and March 1972

Variable	Age 35-44 in		Age 45-54 in		Age 55-64 in	
	1962	1972	1962	1972	1962	1972
Nonblack men						
X	28.63	30.23	26.47	28.63	25.86	26.47
V	7.99	8.73	7.55	7.99	7.40	7.55
F	.2616	.1980	.3017	.2616	.3568	.3017
S	4.11	3.72	4.55	4.11	4.95	4.55
U	11.36	11.98	10.55	11.36	9.65	10.55
Y	40.67	42.94	38.08	40.65	36.93	38.42
H	6873.	8327.	6765.	8214.	5930.	7375.
lnH	8.565	8.821	8.520	8.792	8.303	8.602
Black men						
X	14.79	17.41	16.33	14.79	16.35	16.33
V	6.09	7.06	5.69	6.09	4.00	5.69
F	.3748	.2965	.4398	.3748	.4855	.4398
S	5.31	5.30	6.02	5.31	6.02	6.02
U	8.37	9.70	7.43	8.37	5.68	7.43
Y	19.31	25.16	17.20	22.66	14.73	20.80
H	3118.	5132.	3020.	5093.	2711.	4475.
lnH	7.537	8.367	7.711	8.334	7.522	8.100

NOTE: Sources are March 1962 and March 1972 Current Population Surveys and March 1962 CPS supplement, "Occupational Changes in a Generation." Variables are X = father's occupational status (Duncan SEI scale), V = father's educational attainment in single years, F = farm background, S = number of siblings, U = educational attainment in single years, Y = occupational status (Duncan scale), H = income (1961 dollars).

the OCG supplement. The reports of X, V, F, S, and U for men aged 35 to 44 in 1972 were ascertained from men aged 25 to 34 in 1962 in the March CPS or OCG supplement, and the reports of Y and of H for men aged 35 to 44 in 1972 were ascertained in the March 1972 CPS. As a consequence of these procedures, the means of X, V, F, S, and U for the cohort aged 35 to 44 in 1962 appear again as entries for the cohort aged 45 to 54 in 1972, and the means of X, V, F, S, and U for the cohort aged 45 to 54 in 1962 appear again as entries for the cohort aged 55 to 64 in 1972.

In the case of educational attainment (U), we actually have two reports for each cohort, one from the March 1962 CPS and one from the March 1972 CPS. Since little schooling is completed after age 25, if there were no time-dependent biases in reports of schooling, comparisons of these reports might indicate changes in coverage between 1962 and 1972. However, there is a tendency for men to inflate reports of their educational attainment with age (Farley, 1968: 5–6), so the education data could not be used to assess changes in population coverage. Throughout our analyses, we used reports of educational attainment from the March 1962 CPS. Had we used same-age rather than same-year reports of schooling, we would have estimated slightly larger intercohort shifts in educational attainment and attributed correspondingly larger shares of the shifts in occupational status and income to changes in educational attainment between cohorts.

With a few small exceptions, the intercohort shifts in socioeconomic background and numbers of siblings all tended to improve the socioeconomic chances of more recent cohorts of U.S. men. That is, in younger cohorts men were generally reared in smaller families and were less likely to be reared on farms, or in families headed by a poorly educated father or one with an occupation of low status. Consequently, if the process of socioeconomic achievement were unchanged, we would expect younger cohorts to obtain more education, hold higher-status jobs, and earn more money than their predecessors. The exceptions to this pattern occur among the older blacks. In 1962, 45- to 54-year-old black men reported fathers with higher occupational status than did men of the same age in 1972, and, among black men aged 55 to 64 years old, there were essentially no changes in father's occupational status and in numbers of siblings between 1962 and 1972.

Every age-constant intercohort comparison in Table 5.1 shows increasing educational attainment, occupational status, and real income between 1962 and 1972. In educational attainment, the shifts range from .6 to .9 year among whites and from .9 to 1.8 years among blacks. At each age, the intercohort shift is larger for blacks than for whites. The intercohort shifts in occupational status range from 1.5 to 2.5 points on the Duncan scale among whites and from 5.5 to 6.1 points among black men. At each age, the intercohort shifts in occupational status are between two and four times larger among blacks than among whites. The increases in real dollar income are substantial for men of both racial groups, and again the shifts are larger among blacks than whites. The intercohort shifts in real income were each about $1450 for white men and ranged from $1800 to $2100 among black men. In proportionate terms, the intercohort increases in real income were much larger for black than for white men because blacks had lower incomes in 1962 than whites. Thus, the shifts in ln(income) ranged from .25 to .30 among whites and from .58 to .83 among blacks.

Evidently, white and black members of the civilian labor force have experienced substantial improvements in their socioeconomic standing in recent years, and the increments have been greater for black than for white men. However, it should be kept in mind that these estimated intercohort shifts in status do not apply to the substantial numbers of black men in the prime working ages who are not in the labor force. Further, in 1972, as in 1962, black men have lower levels of educational attainment, occupational status, and income than their white age-peers; we shall return in a later section to the persistence of racial differentials in achievement. We turn next to an interpretation of intercohort shifts in achievement within each racial group.

INTERPRETATION OF INTERCOHORT SHIFTS

Table 5.2 gives the components of intercohort shifts in achievement among white and black men which were generated by our regression–standardization technique. For example, there is a total difference in educational attainment of .62 year between white men aged 35 to 44 in 1962 and in 1972. Of this shift, .25 year or 40% can be attributed to intercohort changes in socioeconomic background (father's occupa-

TABLE 5.2

Components of Intercohort Change in Educational Attainment, Occupational Status, and Income, 1962-1972, by Race and Age: U.S. Men in the Experienced Civilian Labor Force

Component	Nonblack				Black			
	U	Y	H	lnH	U	Y	H	lnH
Men aged 35-44								
X, V and F	.25	.52	131.	.0180	.55	.66	-20.	.0256
S	.08	.07	18.	.0039	.00	.00	0.	.0001
U	.29	2.47	141.	.0215	.78	1.76	287.	.1117
Y		-.79	116.	.0193		3.43	181.	.0515
H or lnH			1048.	.1933			1566.	.6411
Total	.62	2.27	1454.	.2560	1.33	5.85	2014.	.8300
Men aged 45-54								
X, V and F	.20	.46	84.	.0091	.24	-.16	43.	.0291
S	.08	.09	7.	.0036	.11	.06	24.	.0087
U	.53	2.80	167.	.0331	.59	1.25	74.	.0253
Y		-.78	203.	.0278		4.31	137.	.0437
H or lnH			988.	.1984			1795.	.5162
Total	.81	2.57	1449.	.2720	.94	5.46	2073.	.6230
Men aged 55-64								
X, V and F	.08	.37	44.	.0166	.30	.21	-84.	-.0684
S	.06	.13	6.	-.0037	.00	.00	0.	.0000
U	.76	2.75	192.	.0444	1.45	2.59	380.	.2082
Y		-1.76	98.	.0179		3.27	130.	.0437
H or lnH			1105.	.2238			1338.	.3945
Total	.90	1.49	1445.	.2990	1.75	6.07	1764.	.5780

NOTE: Source, see Table 5.1.   Variables are X = father's occupational status (Duncan SEI scale), V = father's educational attainment in single years, F = farm background, S = number of siblings, U = educational attainment in single years, Y = occupational status (Duncan scale), H = income (1961 dollars).

tional status, farm background, and father's education), and another .08 year or 13% is explained by the smaller families of younger men. The remaining .29 year or 47% of the intercohort shift in educational attainment must be attributed to other changes in the social structure between the times when these two cohorts completed their schooling. Of the net shift in occupational status of 2.27 points on the Duncan scale between the cohorts aged 35 to 44 in 1962 and in 1972, .52 point or 23% is due to the intercohort shift in social background, .07 point or 3% to the reduction of family size, and 2.47 points or 109% of the observed shift is due to increases in educational attainment. Since the sum of these components is larger than the observed intercohort shift in occupational status, the net shift in status between 1962 and 1972 is a negative .79 point on the Duncan scale. That is, 35- to 44-year-old white men with given "qualifications" of social background and education held lower-status jobs in 1972 than in 1962, primarily because of the increased supply of men who were educationally qualified by 1962 standards.

Of the $1454 shift in real income of 35- to 44-year-old white men between 1962 and 1972, $131 or 9% was due to changing socioeconomic background, $18 or 1% to changing family size, $141 or 10% to increased educational attainment, and $116 or 8% to increased occupational status. The remaining $1048 or 72% of the increase in real income could not be explained by intercohort shifts in social background, educational attainment, or occupational status. Expressing the same components in semi-log form, we find a total increase in income between the two cohorts of about 26% of which less than 1% is due to smaller families, about 2% each to the shifts in socioeconomic background, educational attainment, and occupational status, and about 20% to other differences between the cohorts.

The components of intercohort shifts in educational attainment, occupational status, and income among white men at the two older ages are generally similar to those of white men at ages 35 to 44. Changes in socioeconomic background, as well as the secular increase in schooling, contribute to rising levels of educational attainment, but the secular increase is more important at the older ages. Intercohort shifts in socioeconomic background account for about a fifth of the change in occupational status between cohorts of white men, but changes in family size explain little of the increase in status. At every age, the intercohort shifts in educational attainment are more than large enough to explain the observed increases in occupational status. Consequently, the net or structural shift in occupational status between 1962 and 1972 is negative for whites at every age. Changes in socioeconomic background, educational attainment, and occupational status each make modest contributions to the observed intercohort growth of real income among whites, but changes in family size have a negligible direct effect on income shifts, and two-thirds to three-quarters of the growth of income at each age must be attributed to social changes other than those expressed in our model of achievement.

While the intercohort shifts in educational attainment are larger for blacks than for whites at every age, the components of shifts in educational attainment are, proportionately, similar for black and white men at the same age. In the case of occupational status, the black and white components are quite different. For blacks, as for whites, changes in socioeconomic background make a modest contribution to the inter-cohort increase in occupational status. Shifts in educational attainment contribute an increment of 1.25 to 2.59 points of occupational status to the black intercohort shifts. While these are not trivial, they are smaller than the corresponding components of change in status among whites of the same age. Since the shifts in mean educational attainment are larger for blacks than whites, the smaller effect of changing educational attainments must be attributed to the lower returns to schooling of blacks relative to whites (Hauser, 1973; also, see Appendix Table C.2 of this volume). This finding provides powerful evidence of the obstacles faced by blacks in attempting to achieve socioeconomic parity with whites through the educational system. Not only do blacks obtain fewer years of schooling than whites, but they need to increase their schooling by a larger amount than whites to effect a given increase in occupational status.

The major difference between the black and white intercohort shifts in occupational status is not in the effect of schooling, but the effect of changes in the social structure that are not specified explicitly in our model of achievement. We think it is appropriate to refer to these changes as shifts in opportunity. While the occupational opportunities of white men were reduced by .75 to 1.75 points on the Duncan scale between 1962 and 1972, the occupational opportunities of black men increased by 3.25 to 4.25 points. Over the decade 1962 to 1972, increases in occupational status among whites were more than accounted for by the changes in social origins and educational attainments between cohorts, but black men between the ages of 35 and 64 experienced an improvement in occupational status which could not be explained by intercohort shifts in social origins or in schooling. Again, the restriction of our analysis to men in the labor force should be kept in mind.

The components of intercohort shifts in real income are generally similar for black and white men of each age. There are some anomalous results among blacks at ages 55 to 64 which we are inclined to attribute to the limited number of observations on those two cohorts. Elsewhere, our finding is that shifts in socioeconomic background, schooling, and occupational status each contribute modestly to the growth in real income between cohorts, but the largest component of change is changing opportunity, that is, factors not specified explicitly in our model. Just as the growth of opportunity for schooling and for occupational achievement was greater for black than for white men in the labor force at every age from 35 to 64, so was the growth in income opportunities greater for black than for white men. Among whites, the net intercohort shifts in real income were about $1000, but, among blacks, the net increases in real dollar income ranged from $1300 to $1800, or 50% to 60% of income in 1962.

RACIAL DIFFERENTIALS IN ACHIEVEMENT

Table 5.3 shows components of black–white differences in educational attainment, occupational status, and income at ages 35 to 44, 45 to 54, and 55 to 64 in 1962 and in 1972. To generate these interpretations of racial differentials in achievement, we took the 1962 regressions for whites as the standard and substituted differences of means between black and white men in 1962 and in 1972. Given the predominant pattern of interaction (differences in slope) between the white and black regressions in 1962, the choice of regressions for whites as the standard yields lower-bound estimates of racial differentials in achievement which are not attributable to social background or prior achievements (Duncan, 1967; 1968b). Following Duncan's usage, we think it appropriate to refer to such residual racial differentials as effects of discrimination.

Our procedure may be clarified by an example. At ages 35 to 44 in 1962, white men obtained 3 years more of schooling than blacks. Think of a group of white men with the same social origins as the average black man. From the white regressions in 1962, we would expect this disadvantaged group's educational attainment to fall .98 years below the mean for all whites because of its poorer socioeconomic background and to fall another .25 years below the mean for all whites because of its members' larger numbers of siblings. In fact, the mean educational attainment of 35- to 44-year-old blacks falls still another 1.76 years below the mean for whites, and we attribute this last component to racial discrimination.

In carrying out similar calculations for men in 1972, we make the additional assumption that the slopes of the regressions for white men

TABLE 5.3

Components of Black-Nonblack Differences in Educational Attainment, Occupational Status, and Income by Age: U.S. Men in the Experienced Civilian Labor Force, March 1962 and March 1972

Component	1962				1972			
	U	Y	H	lnH	U	Y	H	lnH
Men aged 35-44								
X, V and F	.98	2.70	501.	.0296	.88	2.47	454.	.0255
S	.25	.22	54.	.0120	.33	.29	72.	.0158
U	1.76	11.90	681.	.1034	1.07	9.07	519.	.0789
Y		6.54	1090.	.1816		5.95	907.	.1511
H or lnH			1429.	.7014			1243.	.1827
Total	2.99	21.36	3755.	1.0280	2.28	17.78	3195.	.4540
Men aged 45-54								
X, V and F	.88	2.05	398.	.0349	1.05	2.68	553.	.0354
S	.27	.29	23.	.0119	.22	.24	18.	.0097
U	1.97	10.78	644.	.1276	1.72	10.33	617.	.1223
Y		7.76	1650.	.2255		4.74	1421.	.1943
H or lnH			1030.	.4091			512.	.0963
Total	3.12	20.88	3745.	.8090	2.99	17.99	3121.	.4580
Men aged 55-64								
X, V and F	1.23	2.38	148.	.0293	.89	2.42	186.	.0333
S	.16	.35	17.	-.0098	.22	.48	23.	-.0135
U	2.58	12.14	848.	.1957	2.01	9.54	666.	.1538
Y		7.33	1463.	.2664		5.18	1162.	.2114
H or lnH			743.	.2994			863.	.1170
Total	3.97	22.20	3219.	.7810	3.12	17.62	2900.	.5020

NOTE: Source, see Table 5.1. Variables are X = father's occupational status (Duncan SEI scale), V = father's educational attainment in single years, F = farm background, S = number of siblings, U = educational attainment in single years, Y = occupational status (Duncan scale), H = income (1961 dollars).

of a given age are the same in 1972 as in 1962. For example, among 35- to 44-year-old men in 1972, the racial differential in educational attainment is 2.28 years. If the white regressions at age 35 to 44 in 1962 were valid for men of the same age in 1972, we would conclude that .88 years of the 1972 differential is explained by the inferior socioeconomic origins of black men, .33 years by the larger families in which black men are raised, and the remaining 1.07 years by the residue of discrimination. The critical assumptions affecting the validity of these calculations are those of population coverage, to which we referred earlier, and the constancy of the white regressions. Further, the status of our discrimination components as lower-bound estimates is vulnerable to the possibility that changes in the regression lines for blacks have altered this result. We think it unlikely that intercohort changes in regression slopes for blacks or whites at the ages in question could be large enough to affect the outcome of our analyses in any important respect.

If black men in the labor force have experienced greater increases in educational attainment, occupational status, and income than whites of the same age over the past decade, these gains have not been great enough to offset the discriminatory obstacles faced by black men. In 1972, as in 1962, there are large differences in the educational attainment, occupational status, and income of black and white men in each of the age groups 35 to 44, 45 to 54, and 55 to 64. In 1962, the racial differential in educational attainment ranged from 3 to 4 years of schooling, and, in 1972, it ranged from 2.25 to 3 years. In 1962, the occupational differential between the races was 21 or 22 points on the Duncan scale at every age, and, in 1972, it was about 18 points. In 1962, the income differential between the races ranged from $3200 to $3800, and, in 1972, it ranged from $2900 to $3200. In ln(income) the differentials ranged from .78 to 1.03 in 1962 and from .45 to .50 in 1972.

Not only the total differences between the races, but also the discriminatory components of those differentials, persisted from 1962 to 1972. In 1962, the net racial difference in educational attainment ranged from 1.75 to 2.6 years of schooling, and, in 1972, it was 1.1 to 2.0 years. In 1962, the discriminatory component of the racial differential in occupational status was between 6.5 and 7.8 points on the Duncan scale, and, in 1972, it was between 4.7 and 6.0 points. In 1962, the discriminatory component of the difference in income between the races ranged from $740 to $1430, and, in 1972, it ranged from $510 to $1240.

While the differences in socioeconomic achievement between black and white men persisted from 1962 to 1972, they were also smaller at the later point in time. Of the total racial differentials in education, occupational status, and income, and their discriminatory components, only one was larger in 1972 than in 1962. That exception was the discriminatory component in the black–white income difference at ages 55 to 64, which increased from $743 to $863; in the corresponding semi-log decomposition, this mild reversal did not occur. If the discriminatory components of the black–white differentials were absolutely smaller in 1972 than in 1962, so also were the components explained by social background and prior achievements. That is, the discriminatory differentials between the races in educational attainment, occupational status, and income were as large a proportion of the total racial differentials in 1972 as they were in 1962 (cf. Milner, 1973).

At every age, and in both 1962 and 1972, a substantial component of the educational differential between the races could be explained by differences in socioeconomic background. These components were between .9 years and 1.2 years of schooling, and they accounted for 28% to 39% of the black–white difference in years of schooling. A smaller component of the differential, from .16 to .33 years of schooling or 4%

to 15% of the total, could be explained by the larger families in which black men were reared. The remaining 47% to 65% of the racial differentials in schooling was not explained by the variables in our model, and, in this sense, they are attributable to discrimination. (A substantial share of the residual difference in schooling between blacks and whites may be attributable to racial differences in academic ability; see Duncan, 1968b; Jencks *et al.*, 1972.)

Components of 2.0 to 2.7 points on the Duncan scale or 10% to 15% of the racial differentials in occupational status were attributable to differences of socioeconomic background between black and white cohorts in 1962 and in 1972. The larger number of siblings in black families contributed little to the observed differences in occupational status between blacks and whites, only .22 to .48 points on the Duncan scale or 1.0% to 2.7% of the total racial difference in status. Black–white differences in years of schooling accounted for the largest component of the racial gap in occupational status. These components ranged from 9 to 12 points on the Duncan scale and accounted for 51% to 57% of the black–white difference in occupational status. Discrimination was the second largest component of the racial differential in occupational status; it accounted for differences between the races of 4.7 to 7.8 points on the Duncan scale or 26% to 37% of the total black–white differential.

In 1962 and in 1972, at every age, socioeconomic background differences between the races accounted for a small share of the black–white income differential. These shares ranged from 5% to 18% of the dollar gap, or between $150 and $550 in 1961 dollars. Only a negligible share of the racial gap in incomes could be explained by the direct effects of the larger families in which black men were reared. Black–white differentials in educational attainment accounted for $500 to $850 of the racial gap in income; this was 16% to 26% of the total black–white difference. Black–white differences in occupational status accounted directly for 28% to 46% of the racial gap in income: Those components of the dollar gap ranged from $900 to $1650. The remaining 16% to 38% or $500 to $1400 of the racial gap in income was attributable to racial discrimination in incomes which occurred independently of racial differences in socioeconomic background, numbers of siblings, educational attainment, or occupational achievement.

DISCUSSION

In the present analysis, we have tried to address two questions: "What has been the trend of socioeconomic opportunity for black and white men in the U.S. during the past decade?" and "What has been the trend of racial discrimination in the socioeconomic achievements of black men?" We have found that the socioeconomic opportunities of all men in the labor force, and especially of blacks, have increased in the past decade, but the opportunities for white men to hold high-status jobs may have leveled off. Black–white differences in educational attainment, occupational status, and income have been reduced substantially, but there remain large residues of discrimination against blacks in all three areas of achievement. These made up as large a proportion of the total racial gap in schooling, occupational status, and income in 1972 as they did in 1962. In 1972, as in 1962, the source of black–white differentials in achievement is not primarily the greater prevalence of poverty origins among blacks, but the cumulative effects of discrimination by race at every stage of the socioeconomic life cycle.

We hasten to add that our analyses are tentative and incomplete, and it would be inappropriate for us to conclude without mentioning some of their limitations. We wish to repeat that our analyses pertain to men in the experienced civilian labor force, and not to all men. This is particularly relevant to our findings for black men. In earlier work, we found that the upgrading of the nonwhite occupation distribution between 1962 and 1972 was accomplished partly by shifts out of lower-status occupations and into higher-status occupations and partly by increased rates of absence from the labor force. Among nonwhite men at ages 35 to 44, 5.8% were not in the experienced civilian labor force in 1962, and 8.2% were not in the experienced civilian labor force in 1972. At ages 45 to 54, 10.8% of nonwhite men were out of the labor force in 1962, and 14.1% were out of the labor force in 1972. These figures may be compared with rates of absence from the labor force among whites of 3% to 6% in the same age ranges and during the same years (Hauser and Featherman, 1974b). It would be misleading to note the apparently improved socioeconomic life chances of black men who are in the labor force without adding that growing numbers of black men in the prime working ages simply do not participate in ordinary economic activities.

Further, our operational definitions of "opportunity" and "discrimination" deserve elaboration. We have defined changes in opportunity as intercohort shifts in the distribution of education, occupation, or income, to the extent that they are not explained by shifts in the distributions of their measured causes in our model of socioeconomic achievement. Likewise, we have defined discrimination as racial differences in the distribution of educational attainment, occupational status, or income to the extent that they are not explained by differences between the races in their measured causes in our model of achievement. These definitions are invalid insofar as the specification of our model of achievement is in error. The omission of relevant causal factors which vary between cohorts and between the races is one important source of error, and a second is error of measurement in variables entering our model of achievement as regressors. For example, we have already noted that measured differences in academic ability between black and white men may account for a substantial share of the black–white difference in years of schooling not otherwise explained by our model. Also, measurement errors in retrospective reports of socioeconomic background could lead to serious downward biases in the estimated effects of background variables in the OCG data (Bowles, 1972). We think the best available data show that the biases are not large (Bielby, Hauser, and Featherman, 1976; Kerckhoff, Mason, and Poss, 1973; Jencks *et al.*, 1972; also, see Chapter 3 of this volume). The likely effect of either sort of error would probably be to make our estimates of opportunity and of discrimination too large (algebraically, not in absolute value).

Because of the recursive property of our model of achievement, the components of changing opportunity or of discrimination do not express the full impact of changes in opportunity or of racial discrimination on occupational status and income. For example, the educational component of racial differentials in occupational status represents discrimination by race to the extent that the racial differential in educational attainment is based on discrimination. The same holds for the educational and occupational components of the racial differential in income. Thus, the components of change in each measure of socioeconomic achievement which we have attributed to discrimination or to changing opportunities represent those factors to the extent that they operate independently of the measured causes of achievement in the model.

While we do not regard our estimates of trends in opportunity and in discrimination as definitive, we do think they provide some answers to important questions that have been raised about changing opportunities in the United States. For example, Jencks *et al.* (1972:191) speculate:

> Unfortunately, we do not have good data on developments since 1962. One thing is clear, however. If the occupational status of blacks has improved, this has been because of direct efforts to eliminate discrimination and compensate for past discrimination. It has not been because black's test scores have risen or because they have appreciably more educational credentials than they did a decade ago.

From our analysis, we can suggest that Jencks *et al.* are both right and wrong on this point. From the right-hand panel of Table 5.2, we can see that there has been a substantial improvement in the occupational opportunities of black men, although we are unable to say whether this is due to "direct efforts to eliminate discrimination and compensate for past discrimination." At the same time, our analysis shows that shifts in educational attainment between black cohorts do account for a substantial share of their intercohort increases in occupational status.

We would caution against efforts to interpret our estimates of changes in socioeconomic opportunities and in discrimination in terms of programmatic efforts at social melioration carried out during the 1960s. The cohorts we have investigated are far too old to have been affected by programs aimed at children and youth in the past decade. Their educational attainments and, to some degree, their occupational distributions were determined 15 or more years ago. While we have analyzed intercohort shifts of the past decade, to a large extent, the outcomes of our analyses were determined much earlier in the lives of these cohorts. Some men who were already in the prime working ages at the beginning of the 1960s were undoubtedly touched by public interventions in the job market, but we doubt that such interventions have been extensive or successful enough to have effected many of the changes we have measured.

Finally, we note some of the questions on which the present analysis has not touched at all. One important issue is that of intercohort change in opportunity and in discrimination at the younger ages. Since our method of analysis can be applied only to cohorts covered in the 1962 survey, we have not been able to say anything about trends in the socioeconomic achievements of cohorts who entered the prime working ages after 1962. Since these are the cohorts most likely to have been affected by public policies directed to equalizing opportunities, it is at the younger ages that we might expect to find changing patterns of inequality and opportunity. Second, throughout our analysis, we have assumed the constancy of the coefficients of our model of socioeconomic achievement, but changes in these coefficients would reflect important trends in stratification and mobility. Is the effect of educational attainment on jobs and income rising or falling? Are there different trends in returns to education for white and for black men? Is there a greater or lesser tendency for statuses to persist across generations? Have there been changes in the mechanisms by which socioeconomic background affects the achievements of U.S. men? We cannot begin to answer these and other important questions about trends in stratification in this volume, but we are hopeful of doing so as we complete analyses of the 1973 OCG survey.

6

Temporal Change in Occupational Mobility: Evidence for Men in the United States

Trends in intergenerational occupational mobility or stratification have long been subjects of interest and controversy among sociologists. There are numerous reasons for an interest in mobility trends: a concern with the prospects for social equality or equality of opportunity, efforts to understand the transformation of the labor force in economic development, attempts to analyze the rise and fall of groups competing for power. Research and writing about mobility trends have often suffered from conceptual or analytic failures to separate the several aspects of stratification and mobility. Our purpose is to provide empirical estimates of mobility trends among American men which avoid this confusion.

Variations in professional opinion about occupational mobility trends in the U.S. have probably been greater than any well-documented trends (Duncan, 1968d: 675–680). Indeed, students of social mobility have reached no greater consensus on the matter than has the society they have sought to enlighten. Relying on the few available

This chapter was prepared by Robert M. Hauser, John N. Koffel, Harry P. Travis, and Peter J. Dickinson. It appeared originally in the *American Sociological Review*, Vol. 40 (June 1975), pp. 279–297. An earlier version was read before the Research Committee on Social Stratification, International Sociological Association in Warsaw, Poland, March 1974.

data, or in some cases on no data, mobility analysts have concluded that American society is becoming more rigid, that it is not becoming more rigid, that there has been no change in rates of mobility, or that we are moving toward a situation of full equality of opportunity. That observers have reached disparate conclusions from the same statistics is a problem in the sociology of knowledge (see Koffel, 1974). In other cases, it may be possible to trace differences in conclusions about mobility trends to differences among data and statistical measures applied to them. We shall explore the latter possibility.

Relatively few facts are available about trends in intergenerational occupational mobility among U.S. men. Opportunities to enter high-status occupations appear to have improved in successive cohorts of U.S. men for at least the last 40 years, irrespective of those men's occupational origins (see Chapter 5 of this volume).

There is less evidence about changes in the ease of movement among occupational positions from one generation to the next, but a serious and comprehensive effort to assess trend from available data has suggested that the dependence of son's on father's occupation has been remarkably stable for more than half a centruy (Duncan, 1968d; but see Duncan, 1966a; Jackson and Crockett, 1964; Blau and Duncan, 1967; Tully, Jackson, and Curtis 1970). For related evidence of occupational mobility trends among U.S. women, see Chapters 4 and 8 of this volume.

In this chapter, we reexamine trend data on occupational mobility among men in the U.S. Our analysis of temporal change follows the traditional interest of social mobility analysts in separating parameters of the occupational structure from the process of occupational mobility. This long-standing concern is well expressed by Raymond Boudon (1973) in his exhaustive review of mobility measures: "A good mobility index should make a distinction between the amount of mobility generated by the changes in the social structure and the amount of mobility generated by other factors. Indeed, the former should be eliminated." Andrea Tyree (1973) has ably documented the parallel arguments by which several authors mistakenly hit upon the ratios of actual frequencies in a mobility table to those expected under independence as indices of "social distance mobility." These ratios are defective because the index for each cell in a mobility table varies inversely with the marginal proportion in its row and column and because the set of such ratios in a table determines both the row and column marginal distributions up to a constant of proportionality (Duncan, 1966a; also see Goodman, 1969b). Thus, social distance mobility ratios are intimately related to the marginal distributions of the mobility table from whose influence they were supposedly freed.

Applying the work of Leo Goodman (1969a, 1969b, 1970, 1972a, 1972b) and Otis Dudley Duncan (1966a), we shall define particular ways in which the pattern of movement among occupation groups across generations might be constant even when the occupational structure is changing. (Also see Haberman, 1974a: 215–227.) We then reanalyze most (but not all) of the existing trend data on father-to-son occupational mobility in the U.S., and our analysis suggests that no change has taken place in occupational mobility (as specified by our definition). That is, there is minimal evidence of change in the process of occupational mobility beyond that induced by the changing occupational structure and the succession of cohorts. This suggests a possible redirection of comparative studies of occupational mobility. It is no longer possible to assume that the underlying process of mobility is problematic in comparative analysis, while variations in the occupation distribution are a nuisance factor or disturbance. Rather, attention should be directed both to the causes of shifts in the occupation distribution and to their consequences in rates and patterns of mobility. We will take up the latter issue in Chapter 7 of this volume.

A MULTIPLICATIVE MODEL

Suppose we observe tables of son's occupation by father's occupation at several different times. Denote the categories of father's occupation by $P(i = 1, \ldots, I)$, those of son's occupation by $S(j = 1, \ldots, J)$, and those of time by $T(k = 1, \ldots, K)$. We may specify the observed frequencies, f_{ijk}, in the three-way classification of P by S by T by the multiplicative identity,

$$f_{ijk} = \eta \tau_i^P \tau_j^S \tau_k^T \tau_{ij}^{PS} \tau_{ik}^{PT} \tau_{jk}^{ST} \tau_{ijk}^{PST}. \tag{1}$$

Here, η is the geometric mean of the f_{ijk}, and the τ-parameters pertain to the probability that an observation appears in the subscripted cell of the superscripted univariate or joint distribution (Goodman, 1972a). Thus, the parameters τ_i^P, τ_j^S, τ_k^T pertain to the respective probabilities that an observation appears in the ith, jth, or kth cell of the marginal distributions of father's occupation, son's occupation, or time, relative to the grand mean. The parameters τ_{ij}^{PS}, τ_{ik}^{PT}, and τ_{jk}^{ST} pertain to the respective chances that an observation appears in the ijth, ikth, or jkth cell of the marginal classifications of father's occupation by son's occupation, father's occupation by time, or son's occupation by time, relative to the probabilities given by the products of lower-order parameters. Finally, the parameters $\tau_{ijk}{}^{PST}$ pertain to the probability that an observation appears in the ijkth cell of the complete three-way classification, relative to the probability given by products of lower-order parameters. (For an introductory discussion of multiplicative models for contingency tables, see Ku and Kullback, 1974.)

We are not especially interested in the complete or saturated model given by Equation 1, but rather with the possibility that a more parsimonious model will accurately reproduce the observed cross-classification. According to our first alternative,

$$F_{ijk} = \eta \tau_i{}^P \tau_j{}^S \tau_k{}^T \tau_{ik}{}^{PT} \tau_{jk}{}^{ST}, \tag{2}$$

where F_{ijk} is the expected frequency in the ijkth cell. The hypothesis expressed by the model is that the distributions of father's and son's occupations are determined exogenously at each time, and father's and son's occupations are conditionally independent. That is, Equation 2 gives the same model as Equation 1, except $\tau_{ij}{}^{PS} = \tau_{ijk}{}^{PST} = 1$ for all i, j, and k. Using Leo Goodman's computer program, ECTA, or other available programs, it is a routine matter to obtain maximum-likelihood estimates of the F_{ijk} and to run a likelihood-ratio (LR) χ^2 test of the departure of the F_{ijk} from the f_{ijk}. A large value of χ_{LR}^2 indicates that net of change in occupational structure there is association between father's occupation and son's occupation, or that association varies over time, or both. (For a lucid account of statistical inference in log-linear models, see Davis, 1974.) We do not believe the model of Equation 2, since it postulates the statistical independence of father's and son's occupation at each time. (The χ_{LR}^2 for this test may be written as the sum over time periods of the χ_{LR}^2 for the test of independence between father's and son's occupations at each time.) Rather, it represents a set of baseline conditions of temporal change in the marginal distributions of father's and son's occupation against which we may assess and compare the associations between father's and son's occupations net of shifting occupation distributions.

We can also supplement the model of Equation 2 to reflect temporally constant associations between son's and father's occupations:

$$F_{ijk} = \eta \tau_i{}^P \tau_j{}^S \tau_k{}^T \tau_{ij}{}^{PS} \tau_{ik}{}^{PT} \tau_{jk}{}^{ST}. \tag{3}$$

This differs from the model of Equation 1 in that $\tau_{ijk}{}^{PST} = 1$ for all i, j, and k, and it differs from the model of Equation 2, because the $\tau_{ij}{}^{PS}$ are not constrained to equal one. Equation 3 corresponds to a substantively interesting null hypothesis: There are changes over time in the marginal distributions of father's and son's occupations, but the latter associations are invariant with respect to time. Again, we may obtain maximum-likelihood estimates of the frequencies under the model of Equation 3 and run a χ_{LR}^2 test of goodness of fit. Here, a large value of χ_{LR}^2 indicates the association between father's occupation and son's occupation is not constant across time (after controlling change over time in the occupational structure). Moreover, because the model in Equation 3 includes all of the parameters of the model in Equation 2, plus the parameters of the father–son association, the difference between the χ_{LR}^2 for the model of Equation 2 and that of Equation 3 gives a test of the null hypothesis that there is no temporally constant association between father's occupation and son's occupation (after controlling change over time in the occupational structure).

While our analyses are not limited to the models specified in Equations 2 and 3, all of our analysis does follow the same pattern. That is, in looking at a mobility table (or some aspect of it) we take change in the distributions of father's occupation and of son's occupation as a baseline condition. Then we measure the extent of temporally constant and of temporally variable association between father's occupation and son's occupation.

An illustration may clarify the implications of the model in Equation 3. Suppose at time k, the observed frequencies in the sub-table classifying a pair of categories of father's occupation by a pair of categories of son's occupation are as follows:

	Son's	
Father's occupation	occupation	
	1	2
1	f_{11k}	f_{12k}
2	f_{21k}	f_{22k}

The model of Equation 3 specifies that the odds-ratio

$$\frac{(f_{11k}/f_{12k})}{(f_{21k}/f_{22k})} = \frac{(f_{11k}/f_{21k})}{(f_{12k}/f_{22k})} = \frac{f_{11k}f_{22k}}{f_{12k}f_{21k}} \tag{4}$$

is the same for all k within the limits of sampling error. For example, Expression 4 might describe the chance that the son of a white-collar worker became a white-collar worker rather than a blue-collar worker relative to the chance that the son of a blue-collar worker became a white-collar worker rather than a blue-collar worker. The model of Equation 3 says that odds-ratio does not vary across time. Moreover, the model says this invariance over time in the odds-ratios holds for any pair of categories of father's occupation and for any pair of categories of son's occupation, which need not be the same pair of father's and son's occupations. In general, the models investigated here may be described in terms of odds-ratios or certain functions of them, which may or may not vary across time. An implication of the model with temporally constant odds-ratios is that, if we observe a table of father's occupation by son's occupation at any one time, and if we know the marginal distributions of son's occupation and of father's occupation at a second time, we can estimate the frequencies in the cross-classification of father's occupation by son's occupation at the second time by a simple iterative procedure (for example, see Deming, 1943; Mosteller, 1968).

In the following section, we apply the models given by Equations 2 and 3 and other instructive models in a reanalysis of available data on trends in occupational mobility among U.S. men. We shall see that models which are similar to Equation 3 fit the data rather well. It should be noted that our choice of years, ages, or time periods forms a part of the null hypothesis. That is, aggregation in the temporal dimension of our three-way classification may affect the association between father's occupation and son's occupation within time periods and its variation over time periods. However, our major empirical result does appear to stand up under alternative representations of the temporal dimension.

1962 OCG: MOBILITY TO FIRST JOB

Figure 6.1 gives the names of 12 major occupation groups which combine detailed titles in the 1960 classification system of the U.S. Bureau of the Census. The groups are arrayed in descending order of the socioeconomic status of constituent occupations on the Duncan scale (1961), but much of our analysis requires no assumptions about hierarchy in the occupational structure. Using the classification scheme of Figure 6.1, we have tabulated son's first full-time civilian occupation after leaving school for the last time by father's occupation when the son was about 16 years old in each of nine 5-year cohorts covered in the Occupational Changes in a Generation (OCG) survey. Our analyses pertain to 17,200 male OCG respondents who reported father's occupation and own first occupation. Since father's occupation refers to the sixteenth birthday of the son, while the son's first occupation refers to a fixed point in the son's career (even though son's age at first job varies), comparisons of the nine mobility tables for men of

Occupation group	Duncan SEI
Professional, technical, and kindred workers, self-employed	84
Professional, technical, and kindred workers, salaried and others	73
Managers, officials, and proprietors, excluding farm, salaried	68
Sales workers	49
Managers, officials, and proprietors, excluding farm, self-employed	47
Clerical and kindred workers	45
Craftsmen, foremen, and kindred workers	31
Operatives and kindred workers	18
Service workers, including private household	17
Farmers and farm managers	14
Farm laborers and foremen	9
Laborers, except farm and mine	7

Figure 6.1 Twelve-category occupation distribution, United States data from 1962 "Occupational Changes in a Generation" survey.

different ages in 1962 represent true intercohort comparisons, flawed only by the possibilities of differential mortality and recall.

We have proportionately adjusted values of χ^2_{LR} for the OCG data downward by a factor of .62 to reflect the efficiency of the Current Population Survey (CPS) sample design relative to simple random sampling. This design factor is based on published standard errors of percentages (Blau and Duncan, 1967: 477), but the efficiency of the CPS design may be greater for more complex statistics like those used here (Kish and Frankel, 1974). Thus, our selection of a design factor may incorrectly reduce the likelihood of our rejecting the null hypothesis when it is false. This potential bias may be offset because we have not made an adjustment for simultaneous inference. The effect of this adjustment on our analysis could be large. For example, Table 6.1 reports 16 tests of significance (specified without looking at the data). Thus, if we wished to maintain an overall significance level of $p = .05$ in the set of analyses reported in Table 6.1, we should reach a nominal probability level of .05/16 = .003 in any one test before rejecting the null hypothesis in that test (Goodman, 1969a: 8–10). Moreover, even after the application of our design factor, the OCG sample is so large that we run a substantial risk of rejecting null hypotheses in favor of trivial alternatives at conventional levels of statistical significance.

Table 6.1 summarizes our analyses of the classification of father's occupation by son's first occupation by age in the 1962 OCG data.

TABLE 6.1

Analyses of Temporal Homogeneity in Mobility from Father's Occupation to Son's First Full-Time Occupation: U.S. Men Aged 20–64 in 1962 by 5-Year Cohorts (N = 17,200)

Null Hypothesis	χ^2_{LR}	df	p	Δ	χ^2_H/χ^2_T
A. Marginal Trends					
1. Constant distribution of father's occupation	432.22	88	.000	--	--
2. Constant distribution of son's first occupation	429.95	88	.000	--	--
B. Full Matrix (12 × 12)					
1. Margins vary with time (age)	5344.57	1089	.000	26.31	100.0%
2. Margins vary with time (age), constant father-son interactions	854.19	968	>0.5	8.56	16.0
3. No father-son interactions (B2 vs. B1)	4490.38	121	.000	17.75	84.0
C. Main Diagonal Blocked					
1. Margins vary with time (age)	3512.87	981	.000	18.94	65.7
2. Margins vary with time (age), constant father-son interactions	739.99	872	>0.5	7.03	13.8
3. No father-son interactions (C2 vs. C1)	2772.88	109	.000	11.91	51.9
D. Five Broad Groups Blocked					
1. Margins vary with time (age)	1213.48	801	.000	8.71	22.7
2. Margins vary with time (age), constant father-son interactions	593.93	712	>0.5	5.56	11.1
3. No father-son interactions (D2 vs. D1)	619.55	89	.000	3.15	11.6
E. Selected Tests for Trend					
1. Constant occupational inheritance (C2 vs. B2)	114.20	96	>0.1	1.53	2.2
2. Constant interactions within major groups off the main diagonal (C2 vs. D2)	146.06	160	>0.5	1.47	2.7
3. Constant mobility	18.12	8	.022	0.24	0.3
4. Constant upward and downward mobility	25.54	16	.064	0.28	0.5
5. Constant occupation-specific inheritance	96.09	88	.271	1.29	1.8

There is a line in the table for each model or comparison among models. The left-hand column gives a verbal statement of the null hypothesis, and the columns to the right report a goodness-of-fit test and other descriptive results. In reading this and subsequent tables, it will be helpful to recall that χ^2 with ν degrees of freedom has expectation ν and variance 2ν and $\chi^2(\nu)$ is distributed normally when ν is large. It is also helpful to look at the ratio, $\chi^2(\nu)/\nu$, in assessing the size of a component of association relative to others based on the same number of observations (Goodman, 1972a: 1058; Haberman, 1974b: 592–593).

Panel A of Table 6.1 reports the analysis of change over time in the occupational distributions of fathers and sons. Clearly, those distributions have changed over the half-century represented in the OCG data. Against the null hypothesis of temporally constant occupation distributions, we obtain χ^2_{LR} of 432.22 in the case of father's occupation and 429.95 in the case of son's first occupation. The marginal tables of occupation by time each have 88 degrees of freedom, so the changes over time in the occupation distributions are statistically significant. (We thank Keith Hope for recommending these two calculations. See Hope, 1974, for an elegant analysis of mobility trends in British society.)

In line B1, we estimate the baseline model of Equation 2. This model makes the temporal changes in the occupation distributions of fathers and sons a part of the null hypothesis, but it also attempts to account for all of the frequencies in the three-way classification of father's occupation by son's first occupation by age. Against the baseline model, we obtain χ^2_{LR} of 5344.57 with 1089 degress of freedom, which is obviously statistically significant at any of the conventional levels. We reject the model with temporally variable marginals but no association between father's occupation and son's first occupation.

The column labeled Δ gives the index of dissimilarity between the distributions of observed frequencies and the maximum-likelihood estimates. (See Taeuber and Taeuber, 1965: 195–245, for a discussion of Δ and related measures, and Goodman, 1965, for a related application.) In contrasts between models and in tests for trend, the value of Δ measures the improvement in fit between expected and observed distributions. Values of Δ may legitimately be compared within Table 6.1 and within later tables, but not between tables, because the index is sensitive to differing levels of aggregation. The model of line B1 misclassifies 26.31% of the distribution. This is the percentage of cases which would be shifted to another cell of the classification by a proper specification of the relationship between father's occupation and son's first occupation and changes in it over time.

Finally, the entry of 100.0% in the column labeled χ_H^2/χ_T^2 indicates that we take $\chi_{LR}^2 = 5344.57$ to represent all of the variation or association in the data which we might wish to explain by subsequent complications of our baseline model. That is, we shall treat the baseline χ_{LR}^2 just like the total sum of squares in a conventional analysis of variance. This analogy is developed extensively by Goodman (1970, 1971, 1972a). However, in the present context, explaining all of the variance does not imply accounting for interunit variability, but fitting a joint frequency distribution. Thus, the present effort has more in common with the testing of overidentifying restrictions in a path model than with increasing the size of a multiple correlation.

When we estimate the model of Equation 3, we obtain the results shown in line B2 of Table 6.1. Under the hypothesis of temporally constant father's-occupation–son's-first-occupation interactions, we obtain $\chi_{LR}^2 = 854.19$ with $df = 968$. (By "interactions" in this context, we refer to the multiplicative parameters of association between father's occupation and son's first occupation.) Our test statistic is well below its expected value, so clearly we do not reject the null hypothesis. The model of temporally constant father–son interactions accounts for all but 16% of the variation in the baseline model, and it misclassifies only 8.56% of the distribution.

It is instructive to compare lines A1 and A2 of Table 6.1 with line B2, for these, respectively, represent change over time in father's occupation, in son's occupation, and in their association. The χ_{LR}^2 in line B2 is almost as large as the sum of the corresponding entries in lines A1 and A2, but this is misleading because the χ_{LR}^2 in line B2 uses many more degrees of freedom. Note the χ_{LR}^2 in line A1 and in line A2 is each about five times larger than its expectation, while the χ_{LR}^2 in line B2 is less than its expected vlaue. (Adjusting components of χ_{LR}^2 for their differing degrees of freedom is similar to adjusting R^2, the coefficient of determination, for loss of degrees of freedom.) Thus, we conclude that changes over time in the distributions of father's occupation and of son's first occupation are far more important than changes over time in the association between father's occupation and son's first occupation.

In line B3, we report the differences between corresponding entries in lines B1 and B2. This gives us a test of the hypothesis of no father's-occupation–son's-first-occupation interactions, given son's birth cohort. As might be expected, we obtain a large and statistically significant χ_{LR}^2 which accounts fo 84% of the variation in the baseline model and correctly classifies an additional 17.75% of the distribution.

While we have not detected any changes in father–son occupation interactions in the analysis of panel B, we are not yet content to conclude that no change has occurred. The failure to reject null in a global test does not imply that a more narrowly specified hypothesis will not be rejected. For this reason, we have specified and tested a series of hypotheses about changes in the relationship between father's and son's occupation which involve occupational mobility and/or occupational inheritance or disinheritance. It should be kept in mind that "inheritance" does not here refer to job inheritance in the strict sense, but only to the possibility that a son may enter the same major occupation group as his father (Goodman, 1969a: 14).

In panel C of Table 6.1, we test a series of models following the same logic as in panel B, but we block the entries along the main diagonal of each father–son mobility table. That is, we constrain the entries involving occupational inheritance, forcing each frequency on the main diagonal to take on its observed value. In this way, the null hypothesis presumes the observed pattern of occupational inheritance in each time period. Thus, entries in panel C of Table 6.1 differ from corresponding entries in panel B by excluding the effects of departures from the null hypothesis where father and son are in the same major occupation group. By comparing entries in panels B and C, we will be able to isolate the effects of occupational mobility and changes therein from the effects of differential occupational inheritance and changes therein (Goodman, 1969a: 29–39).

In line C1, we fit the model of temporally variable margins with no father–son interactions off the main diagonal. Clearly, this model can be rejected, although the main diagonals do account for about 35% of the association in the tables (compare lines B1 and C1). In line C2, we fit the model with observed frequencies in the main diagonals and a temporally constant set of father–son interactions off the diagonal. Goodman (1969a: 29–30) uses the term "quasi-homogeneity" to refer to models in which two (or more) cross-classifications are specified to be alike in some interactions but not in others. In the model of line C2, patterns of occupational mobility, but not of occupational inheritance, are assumed stable across time. Here, χ^2_{LR} is much less than its expectation, and we are unable to reject the model of quasi-homogeneity, in other words, temporally constant father–son interactions off the main diagonal. Line C3 contrasts the models of lines C1 and C2, and from it we conclude that there is a significant set of father–son interactions off the main diagonal. Thus, while the cross-classification is quasi-homogeneous in respect to patterns of occupational mobility, it does not fit the model of quasi-perfect mobility or quasi-independence (White, 1963; Goodman, 1965, 1968, 1969a), at least in respect to the distinction between occupational inheritance and occupational mobility as defined by the 12 major occupational groups. Indeed, the temporally constant, off-diagonal interactions account for more of the variation from the baseline model than do the observed frequencies in the main diagonals. (Compare line C3 with the difference between lines B1 and C1.) However, we shall take up this hypothesis again.

In line E1 of Table 6.1, we contrast the models of line B2 and line C2. Since the former model posits a temporally constant pattern of association between father's and son's occupations, and the latter differs only in permitting occupational inheritance to fluctuate with time, the comparison in line E1 tells whether the pattern of occupational inheritance has changed over time. Changes in occupational inheritance account for only 2.2% of the association in the table, and they reclassify only 1.5% of the distribution. Effects this small might have occurred by chance more than 10% of the time. Thus, we may specify our earlier finding of no significant changes in father–son interactions to say there have been no changes of association in the aggregate of cells involving occupational inheritance or in the aggregate of cells involving occupational mobility.

In the analyses of panel D of Table 6.1, we again block the main diagonal entries of each father–son mobility table, and additionally we block cells off the main diagonal of the tables which pertain to movement within five very broad occupation groups. The broad occupation groups are upper white-collar (professional, technical, and kindred workers; managers, officials, and proprietors, except farm), lower white-collar (sales workers; clerical and kindred workers), upper blue-collar (craftsmen, foremen, and kindred workers; operatives and kindred workers), lower blue-colar (service workers, including private household; laborers, except farm and mine), and farm (farmers and farm managers; farm laborers and foremen). As before, when we block cells within the five broad groups (including the main diagonal), we are constraining the model to reproduce exactly the observed frequencies in those cells in each time period. Thus, the null hypotheses in panel D presume the observed patterns of association within the five broad groups and changes in them over time. Looking at panel D, we can assess the amount of association between father's occupation and son's occupation outside the five broad groups; the null hypothesis here (line D3) is quasi-perfect mobility, but in a smaller subset of cells then in the analysis of panel C. Also, we can assess changes over time in association outside the five broad groups, testing the null hypothesis of quasi-homogeneity (line D2), but in a smaller subset of cells than in the analyses of panel C. Finally, by comparing corresponding entries in panels D and C, we can assess the amount and changes in the amount of association between father's occupation and son's first occupation which involves sons in the same broad group, but not the same major group as their fathers.

As shown in line D1, even when we block all of the cells within these very broad occupation groups, there remains a statistically significant and substantial amount of association in the tables, about a quarter of the association in the complete tables. In line D2, we estimate a model which contains temporally constant father–son occupation interactions outside the five broad occupation groups, and χ^2_{LR} is less than its expected value. We are unable to reject this model of quasi-homogeneity, which misclassifies only 5.56% of the distribution and accounts for almost 89% of the association in the baseline model. As reported in line D3, the temporally constant interactions outside the five broad groups account for a statistically significant 11.6% of the association in the baseline model, thus permitting us to reject this weaker statement of the hypothesis of quasi-perfect mobility. Finally, in line E2, we contrast the models of lines C2 and D2, which differ only in that the latter permits temporal variation in the association between father's and son's occupation in cells which are off the main diagonal but within the five broad groups defined above. The χ^2_{LR} in line E2 is well below its expected value, so we are unable to reject the hypothesis of temporal homogeneity in the association between father's occupation and son's occupation off the main diagonal, but within the five broad occupation groups. Thus, our analysis continues to support the hypothesis of temporal homogeneity in occupational mobility between generations, and at the same time, it fails to support the hypothesis of quasi-perfect mobility outside the five broad groups.

Panel E of Table 6.1 reports other tests for trend in mobility which are related to, but distinct from, the earlier ones. Line E3 tests the hypothesis that the pattern of mobility from father's occupation to son's first occupation is the same in every cohort, except the rate of mobility, in other words, the propensity to move versus stay, has changed over time. This model differs from the model of line E1 in introducing time-varying parameters for occupational mobility per se, rather than the several occupation-specific parameters of the model in line E1. Our mobility parameter is a special case of the "triangles" parameters described by Goodman (1972b), but our model under the null hypothesis is not a triangles model, but the model of Equation 3. If the alternative hypothesis were true, the model of Equation 3 would have to be supplemented by time-varying mobility parameters. The addition of the time-varying parameters is nominally significant at the .022 level. The changing mobility parameters account for only .3% of the association in the baseline model, and they allocate only .24% of the distribution to a different cell in the classification. We regard this effect as substantively trivial and possibly random for the reasons given earlier.

Under the alternative hypothesis just discussed, the mobility parameter only makes the distinction between movers and stayers, thus neglecting the possibility that propensities to move upward and downward may change over time in different directions. That is, offsetting changes in upward and downward mobility rates may yield no change in overall mobility rates. In line E4 of Table 6.1, we test the hypothesis that rates of upward or downward mobility have changed (as well as rates of stability). To define "upward" or "downward" mobility (a distinction not used in any earlier model), we ordered the major occupation groups by Duncan scores (see Figure 6.1) and we introduced separate time-varying parameters for the triangular aggregates of cells pertaining to upward and to downward mobility. However, the model under the null hypothesis is not a triangles model, but that of Equation 3. In line E4, the χ^2_{LR} for changes in upward and downward mobility is not even significant at a nominal .05 level. Moreover, there is no significant difference between the changes over time in upward and in downward mobility. Changes over time in rates of upward relative to downward mobility account for a χ^2_{LR} of only 7.42 with 8 degrees of freedom, and they account for only .2 percent of the association in the baseline model (compare lines E3 and E4 of Table 6.1).

Finally, in line E5 of Table 6.1, we report a test of changes across time in occupation-specific inheritance. That is, we ask whether there are any changes over time in propensities to inherit specific occupations aside from possible trends in propensity toward mobility per se (tested in line E3). The reader will note this test contrasts the model of line E1 with that of line E3. That is, changing occupational inheritance permits changes both in general and occupation-specific propensities to move. Again, as shown in line E5, we fail to reject the null hypothesis of temporal homogeneity in occupation-specific inheritance. By an extension of the methods used here, it would be possible to assess changes over time in occupational inheritance in each major occupation group, but we have not done so.

It may be useful to summarize our analyses of mobility from father's occupation to son's first occupation by cohort in the 1962 OCG data. First, we have found substantial change in the occupational structure over time, as evidenced by change in the distributions of father's occupation and of son's occupation. Second, we have found strong patterns of association between father's occupation and son's occupation. Considering only the temporally constant association between father's occupation and son's first occupation, the ratios of χ^2_{LR} to its degrees of freedom are 143.13 for the aggregate of cells on the main diagonal, 107.67 for the aggregate of cells off the main diagonal but within the five broad occupation groups, and 6.96 for the aggregate of cells outside the five broad occupation groups. While much of the association in the tables is attributable to occupational inheritance or to movement between closely related occupation groups, there appears to be association throughout most, if not all, of the mobility table. Thus, the OCG data on mobility to first occupations do not appear to conform to the pattern of quasi-perfect mobility which Goodman (1965, 1969a, 1969b) has observed in British and Danish mobility tables. This may partly be a consequence of the larger number of occupation groups employed in the present analysis (Haberman, 1974a: 216), or perhaps we have not located the subset of cells in which quasi-perfect mobility holds.

Third, we have found remarkable homogeneity in the patterns of association between father's occupation and son's first occupation when changes in the occupational structure have been controlled. There appear to be negligible differences among cohorts in the propensity to move versus stay; in the propensities to move up, move down, or stay; in the propensity to move up relative to the propensity to move down; in the propensity to inherit one's father's occupation; in patterns of movement among similar occupation groups; and in patterns of movement among dissimilar occupation groups.

Blau and Duncan (1967: 107–111) have preceded us in attempting to measure mobility trends by comparing tables of mobility from father's occupation to son's first occupation among men of different ages in the 1962 OCG survey. They compared four 10-year age cohorts using a 3-category occupation classification (manual, nonmanual, farm), a 10-category classification and scores of detailed titles on Duncan's scale (1961). From standard mobility indexes and contingency measures in the 3-by-3 and 10-by-10 classifications, Blau and Duncan (1967: 109) concluded, "the extent of association between origin and destination has been less recently than at an earlier date." However, the product–moment correlations between status scores of fathers and sons are virtually the same in each cohort. We shall see that at least the first of these results may be consistent with the hypothesis of temporal invariance which we have advanced (Chapter 7 of this volume).

FIVE NATIONAL SURVEYS: 1947 TO 1972

Much of the recent analysis of trends in occupational mobility in the U.S. rests on comparisons among four national surveys in which both father's occupation and son's current occupation were ascertained. These are a 1947 survey by the National Opinion Research Center (NORC), 1952 to 1957 surveys by the Survey Research Center (SRC) at the University of Michigan, and the 1962 OCG survey carried out by the U.S. Bureau of the Census. The first three surveys were compared by Jackson and Crockett (1964), and the last was added to the series by Blau and Duncan (1967: 97–105). We have added a fifth observation to the series of mobility tables for all U.S. men. This is a table for about 500 adult men in 1972 obtained from an NORC (1972) survey.

Jackson and Crockett emphasized the lack of evidence of increasing rigidity in the stratification system and suggested there may have been some lessening of the dependence of son's on father's occupation. They conclude (Jackson and Crockett, 1964: 15), "The data suggest, however, that the rate of occupational mobility in the United States has increased somewhat since the end of World War II. At the least, we found scant evidence that the system of occupational inheritance is growing more rigid." Blau and Duncan (1967: 105) reached a similar conclusion.

There are serious questions about the comparability of data across years, since there was some variation in the items used to ascertain occupation, and the five surveys were carried out by three different agencies (Jackson and Crockett, 1964: 11; Blau and Duncan, 1967: 98–103). In particular, there are peculiarities in the marginal distributions of father's and of son's occupations in the 1947 NORC data. These were recognized by Jackson and Crockett and by Blau and Duncan, but still leave their conclusions in doubt (Koffel, 1974). Unfortunately, the four mobility tables were rendered comparable only in respect to a division among manual, nonmanual, and farm occupations.

Our analyses of the 3-by-3 tables from five national surveys are summarized in Table 6.2. We shall not recapitulate the logic of our analysis, which follows that of Table 6.1. In panel A, we report the likelihood-ratio χ^2 for the variation across surveys of father's occupation and of son's current occupation. Each of these is large, relative to its degrees of freedom, but the variation in the occupation distributions across surveys may reflect methodological factors as well as change over time. (We caution the reader against comparison of χ^2_{LR} and our other measures across tables, because of their differing levels of aggregation and numbers of observations.) In the baseline model of

TABLE 6.2

Analyses of Temporal Homogeneity in Mobility from Father's Occupation to Son's Current Occupation: U.S. Men in 1947 (NORC), 1952 (SRC), 1957 (SRC), 1962 (OCG), and 1972 (NORC) by 3 Major Occupation Groups

Null Hypothesis	χ^2_{LR}	df	p	Δ	χ^2_H/χ^2_T
A. Marginal Trends					
1. Constant distribution of father's occupation	118.40	8	.000	--	--
2. Constant distribution of son's occupation	140.05	8	.000	--	--
B. Full Matrix (3 × 3)					
1. Margins vary with time	3268.18	20	.000	17.74	100.0%
2. Margins vary with time, constant father-son interactions	19.52	16	.242	1.02	0.6
3. No father-son interactions	3248.66	4	.000	16.72	99.4
C. Main Diagonal Blocked					
1. Margins vary with time	30.87	5	.000	0.61	0.9
2. Margins vary with time, constant father-son interactions	1.00	4	> 0.5	0.06	0.0
3. No father-son interactions	29.87	1	.000	0.55	0.9
D. Selected Tests for Trend					
1. Constant occupational inheritance (C2 vs. B2)	18.52	12	.100	0.96	0.6
2. Constant mobility	2.95	4	> 0.5	0.16	0.1
3. Constant upward and downward mobility	11.10	8	> 0.1	0.64	0.3
4. Constant occupation-specific inheritance	15.57	8	.050	0.80	0.5

NOTE: N's are NORC-1947, 1153; SRC-1952, 747; SRC-1957, 1023; OCG-1962, 17,615; NORC-1972, 483.

line B1, the margins are free to vary across time, but there is no association between father's occupation and son's occupation. The baseline
model yields a large and statistically significant χ^2_{LR}, and it misclassifies 17.74% of the distribution. As shown in line B2, when we introduce a set of time-constant parameters for the interactions between
father's and son's occupations, we account for 99.4% of the association
in the baseline model. The observed results might easily have occurred by chance if the model of time-constant interactions were correct, and the model misclassifies only 1% of the cases. As shown in line
B3, the time-constant interactions are large and statistically significant.

In panel C of Table 6.2, we report analyses in which the three main
diagonal cells of each mobility table have been blocked to permit
occupational inheritance to vary freely over time. (Recall that occupational inheritance is defined by our occupation categories, which are
very broad.) When the margins are fixed and the main diagonals are
blocked, there remains a very small but statistically significant association in the tables (line C1). Slightly more than 1% of the distribution is
misclassified, and less than 1% of the association in the baseline model
remains. Thus, the five-survey data come very close to fitting a model
of quasi-perfect mobility, when they are analyzed in a 3-by-3 mobility table. As shown in lines C2 and C3 of the table, virtually all
of the remaining association may be explained by temporally constant
interaction between father's occupation and son's occupation off the
main diagonal. When that association is entered into the model, a virtually perfect fit of the data is obtained.

Line D1 of Table 6.2 contrasts the models of lines C2 and B2, which
differ only with respect to the possibility of changes in occupational
inheritance over time. The χ^2_{LR} for this contrast is not significant at
even the .05 level, so we fail to reject the hypothesis of no change in
occupational inheritance. Changes over time in father–son interactions
on the main diagonal of the five-survey tables account for less than 1%
of the association in the baseline model and reclassify less than 1% of
the distribution. We next consider the possibility that there is a changing propensity to move versus stay, but there is no support for this in
the data (line D2). There is no support for the hypothesis that propensities toward upward mobility, downward mobility, and stability have
changed across surveys (line D3), nor is there any support for the
hypothesis that propensities toward upward relative to downward
mobility have changed across surveys (compare lines D2 and D3).
Finally, a test for temporal changes in occupation-specific inheritance
reaches a nominal .05 level of significance, but such changes account
for a negligible share of the association in the five-survey mobility

tables. Thus, our analysis of the 25-year time series of mobility tables for U.S. men supports the analyses of other researchers insofar as they have emphasized a lack of change in the association between father's occupation and son's occupation.

INDIANAPOLIS: 1910 AND 1940

The original and classic study of mobility trends in the U.S. was that of Natalie Rogoff (1953a, 1953b), who analyzed occupation reports of men about themselves and their fathers obtained from marriage license applications in Indianapolis in years centered around 1910 and 1940. About 10,000 reports were obtained in each period. Rogoff's analyses of these data were based primarily on comparisons of the flawed "social distance mobility ratio" (Duncan, 1966a; Blau and Duncan, 1967; Tyree, 1973). Depending on where one looks in Rogoff's writings, her conclusions are discrepant with regard to changes in the dependence of son's on father's occupation. In her monograph, Rogoff (1953a: 106) writes: "The processes by which men selected and were selected for occupations were more closely related to social origins in 1940 than they had been in 1910." However, in a summary of her work (Rogoff, 1953b: 451), she concludes, "No great change has taken place in recent times in the extent to which men may move from the occupational origins represented by their fathers' positions. The channels to social mobility afforded by the contemporary occupational structure are about as easily traversed now as they were at the beginning of the century."

Otis Dudley Duncan's (1966a) reanalysis of Rogoff's data was primarily methodological in intent. With the possible exception of the analyses most closely resembling our own, his results suggested that the 1910 and 1940 mobility tables were very similar with regard to the dependence of son's on father's occupations. For example, after running regression analyses of the 1910 and 1940 data from Rogoff's detailed tables using several alternative scales of occupational status, Duncan (1966a: 69–70) writes, "The socioeconomic status of occupations held by white Indianapolis men marrying in 1940 was no more closely related to the socioeconomic status of their occupational origins than had been the case for white men marrying in 1910."

Another of Duncan's reanalyses of Rogoff's data was a major stimulus to our thinking about change in mobility tables, though with somewhat different empirical results. After verifying that the 1910 and 1940 outflow matrices produce different destination vectors when multiplied by the same origin vector, and that the two matrices have correspondingly different fixed point distributions, Duncan (1966a: 73) asks,

> Is it possible that differences in the 1910 and 1940 mobility patterns are due solely to shifts in the distribution of job opportunities open to young men? . . . Can we, in other words, contrive a comparison between the two mobility tables putting the change in occupation structure in the role of an exogenously determined factor, which then induces a change in mobility patterns? The starting point of the comparison is to test the null hypothesis that all changes in the mobility table are due to proportional adjustments occasioned by changes, 1910 to 1940, in the two marginal distributions–the distribution of sons by their fathers' occupations, and the distribution of sons by their own occupations.

In order to test this hypothesis, Duncan used a least-square procedure suggested by Deming (1943) to estimate the frequencies in the 1940 table by proportional adjustment of rows and columns of the 1910 table. This null hypothesis is exactly the same as that of our Equation 3, namely that the father's and son's occupation distributions vary over time, and there is a temporally constant set of father–son interactions. However, Duncan's statistical analysis differs from our own, in that Duncan fitted the 1940 margins to the 1910 table, while we have obtained maximum-likelihood estimates of the frequencies using the data for both periods.

Figure 6.2 gives the titles of the 10 major occupation groups into which the Indianapolis data were aggregated, listed in order of socioeconomic standing on the Duncan scale. Our analyses of the Indianapolis data (Rogoff, 1953a: 44–45) are summarized in Table 6.3. Again, the logic of our analysis is the same as in Table 6.1, but the reader should not compare components of variation or indexes of dissimilarity across tables. Between 1910 and 1940, there were large shifts in the distributions of father's occupation and of son's occupation in Indianapolis (lines A1 and A2). Obviously, we reject the baseline model of changes in the occupational structure, but no association between father's occupation and son's occupation (line B1), which misclassifies 17.68% of the distribution. As shown on lines B2 and B3, when we also specify a temporally constant set of father–son interactions, we correctly classify an additional 15.04% of the distribution, leaving only 2.64% wrongly classified. The model of temporally constant interactions accounts for 97.5% of the association in the baseline model. As in the OCG data on mobility to first occupations, changes over time in the marginal distributions of the mobility table for Indianapolis are much larger relative to their degrees of freedom than

Professional
Semi-professional
Proprietors, managers, officials
Clerks and salesmen
Skilled
Semi-skilled
Protective service
Farming
Personal service
Unskilled

Figure 6.2   Ten-category occupation distribution, Indianapolis data from Rogoff's *Recent Trends in Occupational Mobility* (1953a).

are changes over time in the association between father's occupation and son's occupation.

Since the Indianapolis data are not from a probability sample, it is not clear how seriously we should take the probability levels associated with our goodness-of-fit tests. At conventional levels, we would reject the hypothesis of temporally constant interactions, for $p = .003$ in line B2. However, given the very large number of observations and the very small amount of association attributable to changes in the father–son interactions, our analyses of the Indianapolis data lead us to the same conclusion as our analyses of the OCG data on mobility to first job and the five national surveys. There has been little if any change in the association between father's occupation and son's occupation. We have also analyzed the 5-by-4 tables of mobility for men in Indianapolis with urban occupations in 1910, 1940, and 1967 with similar results (Tully, Jackson, and Curtis, 1970: 192). There are nominally significant differences in father–son interactions between years, but these account for only 1.7% of the association in the baseline model. We have given less attention to the 1967 Indianapolis data than to the 1910 and 1940 data because of the different methods used in the 1967 survey.

In panel C of Table 6.3, we report analyses in which the main diagonals of the 1910 and 1940 tables have been blocked, permitting occupational inheritance to vary over time. When the margins are fixed and the main diagonal is blocked, there is still substantial association between father's and son's occupations (line C1), but three-quarters of the association in the baseline model for Indianapolis data may be attributed to occupational inheritance (compare lines B1 and C1).

TABLE 6.3

Analyses of Temporal Homogeneity in Mobility from Father's Occupation to Son's Current Occupation: Men Married in Indianapolis in 1910 and 1940 by 10 Major Occupation Groups (N = 20,146)

Null Hypothesis	χ^2_{LR}	df	p	Δ	χ^2_H/χ^2_T
A. Marginal Trends					
1. Constant distribution of father's occupation	686.06	9	.000	--	--
2. Constant distribution of son's occupation	848.55	9	.000	--	--
B. Full Matrix (10 × 10)					
1. Margins vary with time	4794.62	162	.000	17.68	100.0%
2. Margins vary with time, constant father-son interactions	121.73	81	.003	2.64	2.5
3. No father-son interactions	4672.89	81	.000	15.04	97.5
C. Main Diagonal Blocked					
1. Margins vary with time	1201.19	142	.000	7.56	25.1
2. Margins vary with time, constant father-son interactions	96.71	71	.046	1.93	2.0
3. No father-son interactions	1104.48	71	.000	5.63	23.0
D. Selected Tests for Trend					
1. Constant occupational inheritance (C2 vs. B2)	25.02	10	.008	0.71	0.5
2. Constant mobility	4.98	1	.013	0.23	0.1
3. Constant upward and downward mobility	5.13	2	.081	0.26	0.1
4. Constant occupation-specific inheritance	20.03	9	.019	0.48	0.4

When we estimate frequencies based on temporally constant father–son interactions off the main diagonal (line C2), we account for all but 2% of the association in the baseline model, and we misclassify less than 2% of the distribution. The temporally homogeneous father–son interactions off the main diagonal are overwhelmingly significant (line C3).

When we contrast the models with and without changes over time in occupational inheritance (line D1), we find the temporal shifts to be extremely small, though they would be statistically significant at conventional probability levels. Changes over time in occupational inheritance account for only .5% of the association in the baseline model, and they reclassify only .71% of the distribution. The test for changes in the propensity to move between 1910 and 1940 is not even nominally significant at the .01 level (line D2), and it accounts for only .1% of the variation in the baseline model. Even less substantial results are obtained when we test for possible changes both in upward and downward mobility (line D3), and there is virtually no change over time in the propensity toward upward relative to downward mobility (compare lines D2 and D3). Finally, there is little evidence of change in occupation-specific inheritance in Indianapolis (line D4). Considering the strict comparability of measurement in the Indianapolis data, the 30-year separation between the two measurements and the very large samples in the two years, the stability of occupational mobility patterns is remarkable.

It is instructive to compare our results with those in Duncan's test of proportional change in the Indianapolis data (Duncan, 1966a: 74–77). Taking the 1910 matrix as the standard, Duncan's model misclassifies 7% of the distribution under the model of proportional change, while we misclassify 2.64% of the distribution under the same model. Duncan reports a decomposition of the sum of squares of ratios of 1940 to 1910 frequencies whose interpretation parallels that of the components of association in our baseline model. In Duncan's analysis, 76% of the sum of squares is attributable to proportional change in the row or column marginals. There are no corresponding figures in our decomposition since our baseline model incorporates change in the marginal distributions; however, we did note the substantial shifts in the occupational structure from 1910 to 1940. Duncan reports that 7% of the sum of squares is "due to proportional change in both distributions, reflecting the initial correlation between son's and father's occupation," and 17% is "due to nonproportional change, or interaction" (1966a: 74). In our analysis, 97.5% of the association in the baseline model is due to temporally constant patterns of association between father's and son's occupations. In our view, this gives a stronger basis to Duncan's conclusion (1966a: 96) that

> some considerable modifications of the mobility *pattern* (emphasis in the original) . . . occurred in consequence of the change in 'structure' represented by alterations of the frequency distributions of origin and destination classes.

OTHER DATA ON MOBILITY TRENDS

The analyses reported above do not exhaust the possibilities for measuring trend in occupational mobility among U.S. men. For example, the Johns Hopkins University sample of men aged 30 to 39 in 1968 might be compared with the cohort of that age in the 1962 OCG survey (Coleman *et al.*, 1972). Data from the Six-City Survey of Labor Mobility might be used to contrast mobility patterns in 1940 and 1950, and it may be possible to construct a time series of data from the Detroit Area Study (Duncan, 1968d: 697–703). Comparisons might be made between certain male OCG respondents and those in the two male panels of Herbert Parnes' National Longitudinal Surveys (Parnes, Miljus, and Spitz, 1970; Parnes, Fleisher, Miljus, and Spitz, 1970). These examples probably do not exhaust the resources presently available, and another important test of our hypothesis will become possible when the 1973 OCG data are analyzed (Featherman and Hauser, 1975).

While the data listed above are available in published or machine-readable form, we have not exploited any of them in the present analysis. Rather, we made two other comparisons, neither of which pertains strictly to temporal change, but both of which bear on the extension of our finding of invariant mobility patterns. First, we compared mobility of (OCG) men in the U.S. in 1962 to the mobility of Wisconsin men in 1973, using data from a statewide survey commissioned by Featherman and Hauser (1975). Second, we compared the mobility of U.S. men in 1962 from father's occupation to son's current occupation, using the same nine 5-year cohorts as in our earlier analysis of mobility to first full-time occupations. While both of these comparisons are sound with regard to survey method, the first confounds time and place, and the second confounds time (cohort) with chronological age. We carried out these two comparisons using the same methods as in the analysis of Table 6.1, with the same results. That is, once controlling for change in the occupational structure, we found no change in occupational mobility.

DISCUSSION

The foregoing analyses apply an appropriate solution to the standard problem in comparative mobility analysis—how to separate the effects of changes of occupational structure, given by shifting marginal distributions, from those of the process of mobility, given by associations between occupational origins and destinations, for the purpose of measuring change in the latter. Analytically, the solution is to adopt the multiplicative or log-linear specification of the frequencies, which posits separate parameters for the marginal distributions and changes therein and for the underlying associations and changes therein. In several large bodies of data on U.S. men, we have observed that the pattern of association between father's occupation and son's occupation is largely invariant with respect to time.

It is always a logically difficult matter to maintain the null hypothesis, but we think we have offered sufficient evidence of temporal invariance to challenge the ingenuity of other researchers who would offer a more plausible alternative hypothesis and supporting data. One simple model of change we have not treated explicitly is linear trend; but in scanning reams of computer output, we have seen little evidence of order in deviations from the model of temporal homogeneity. We did locate one trend across OCG cohorts to increase the ratio of actual to expected chances of mobility from father's occupation to son's first full-time occupation. This trend accounts for about half the variation in mobility propensity across nine OCG cohorts, but the total of that variation represents less than a third of 1% of the association in the baseline model (see line E3 of Table 6.1). Other models may capture systematic patterns of change in mobility with relatively few parameters, but the explanatory potential of such models is necessarily limited.

We have used our imagination in specifying models of change in mobility, but beyond noting that the OCG data do not conform to the hypothesis of quasi-perfect mobility, the present analysis says little about the pattern of occupational mobility at any one time. That is an important, but distinct, problem. For alternative models of the mobility table, see Goodman (1972b) and Haberman (1974a).

Among serious students of mobility in the U.S. there has been agreement of late that trends, if any, have been slight. Thus, one might ask what motivates so long and tedious an effort to sustain the hypothesis of no trend. We think the present essay is amply justified by the variety of hypotheses about trend which we have been able to test. However, we believe it equally important that we have eliminated trends in the occupational structure from our measurements of trend in mobility.

Sociologists have long recognized that the occupational structure and changes in it affect mobility patterns. This recognition has generally taken the form of injunctions to control variation in the occupational structure before venturing comparisons between mobility tables and of efforts to construct mobility indexes which would make this possible. However, once trends in the occupational structure are controlled, there are no trends in the occupational mobility of U.S. men. This suggests an inversion of the traditional problem of comparative mobility analysis.

Rather than treating shifts in the occupational structure as a nuisance factor, to be set aside before undertaking comparative mobility analysis, we suggest that shifts in the occupational structure may be both the driving force and the problematic issue in comparative mobility studies. We ought to be asking what changes in observed mobility chances may be induced by transformations of the occupational structure, such as occur in the processes of urbanization and industrialization. That is, even when the relative chances of men (as defined by our model) do not change, it is possible for other interesting properties of the mobility tables to vary systematically with changes in the marginal distributions (Duncan, 1966a: 76–77). Moreover, if changing occupational mixes affect mobility patterns, students of mobility will want to take more than a casual interest in the sources of occupational transformations. We believe our analysis adds force to Wilbert E. Moore's (1966: 196) observation:

> the analytical separation of mobility accounted for by changes in the distribution of occupation within the socioeconomic structure from that accounted for by change in the distribution of opportunity or accessibility is a perfectly legitimate procedure. But there is no reason to say that only the second datum is interesting.

In the next chapter, we shall attack the first of the problems just posed. Given a fixed pattern of mobility from father's occupation to son's current occupation, we shall ask what the implications are of changes in the marginal distributions of father's and of son's occupations. In discussing his analysis of proportional change in the Indianapolis data, Duncan wrote (1966a: 75), "Had only the 1910 table been available, plus the 1940 marginals, the assumption of proportional changes would have been a reasonable basis for estimating the 1940 table." Applying a well-known technique of proportional adjustment (Mosteller, 1968), we have taken tables of U.S. men's mobility from father's occupation to current occupation for certain cohorts in

1962, and we have projected them backward and forward in time to fit earlier and later occupation distributions, while preserving the underlying patterns of association in the mobility tables. Several properties of the resulting hypothetical mobility tables vary systematically across years both within and between cohorts. Changes in the occupational structure and the succession of cohorts have led to increased rates of mobility and of upward mobility, even though the underlying process of mobility has not changed over time.

7

Structural Changes in Occupational Mobility among Men in the United States

In this century, there has been essentially no trend in the relative mobility chances of American men whose fathers held differing occupations. To put the matter crudely, but correctly, there has been no change in the odds that a man of low-status origin will achieve high rather than low occupational standing relative to the odds that a man of high-status origin will achieve high rather than low occupational standing. This striking lack of trend has been documented in log-linear analyses of intergenerational occupational mobility tables for the period from about 1910 to 1970 (see Chapter 6 of this volume). The same result holds throughout men's work careers, and it holds whether occupations are classified in as few as 3 or as many as 12 categories. Findings from the 1962 Occupational Changes in a Generation (OCG) survey might be applied to all of the available trend data:

> We have found remarkable homogeneity in the patterns of association between father's occupation and son's first occupation when changes in the occupational structure have been controlled. There appear to be negligible differences among cohorts in the propensity to move vs. stay; in the propensities to move up, move down, or stay; in the propensity to move up relative to the propensity to move down; in the propensity to inherit one's father's occupation; in patterns of move-

This chapter was prepared by Robert M. Hauser, Peter J. Dickinson, Harry P. Travis and John N. Koffel. Original publication was in the *American Sociological Review*, Vol. 40 (October 1975), pp. 585–598.

ment among similar occupation groups; and in patterns of movement among dissimilar occupation groups.

Regression and correlation analyses of status variables have led to
parallel conclusions (Duncan, 1966a, 1968d). While traditional contingency table analyses suggest a possible increase in occupational mobility across time (Jackson and Crockett, 1964; Blau and Duncan,
1967: 109), we shall offer an explanation of this seemingly exceptional
finding.

In the same period that the relative mobility chances of American
men have been virtually constant, the occupational structure has completed the transformation from that of a rural and industrializing society to that of a metropolitan and technological society (Duncan, 1966c;
P. M. Hauser, 1969). Of middle-aged men who were in the labor force
when the last quarter of the twentieth century began, more than 1 in 5
were in salaried professional or managerial occupations, and fewer
than 1 in 25 were in farm occupations. Yet, when these men were
teenagers, one in 12 of their fathers were salaried professionals or
managers, and 1 in 4 were farmers. Temporal shifts in the occupation
distribution have sustained the chances of American men for upward
occupational mobility between generations (see Chapter 3 of this
volume). In the detailed intergenerational occupational mobility table
of Blau and Duncan (1967: 28), upward mobility exceeded downward
mobility between the great majority of pairs of occupations.

Together, the constancy of relative mobility chances and the secular
shifts in the occupational division of labor imply that the changing
occupational distribution is the major factor effecting trends in the
intergenerational flow of manpower among occupations. Sociologists
have long recognized that changes in the occupational structure affect
mobility patterns. This recognition has generally taken the form of
injunctions to control variation in the occupational structure before
venturing comparisons between mobility tables and of efforts to construct mobility indexes which would make such comparisons possible.
However, once trends in the occupational structure are controlled,
there are no trends in the occupational mobility of United States men.

This suggests an inversion of the traditional problem in comparative
mobility analysis. Rather than treating the underlying process of mobility as a variable in comparative research (across time or across
societies) and variation in the distribution of occupations as a disturbance, we suggest that shifts in the occupational structure are both the
driving force and the problematic issue in comparative mobility
studies. That is, we ask what changes in observed mobility chances

are induced by transformations of the occupational structure, such as occur in the processes of urbanization and industrialization. Even though the relative mobility chances of men do not change, it is possible for other important properties of a mobility table to vary systematically with changes in the occupational structure. There is no paradox here; as O. D. Duncan (1966a: 76–77) has observed, "It is well to bear in mind the fact that invariance with respect to some aspects of the mobility process is compatible with variation in other aspects."

In this chapter, we shall document trends in the intergenerational occupational mobility of American men which have been induced by temporal changes in the occupational distribution. That is, given a fixed pattern of association between father's occupation and son's current occupation, we shall ask what the implications are of changes over time in the marginal distributions of father's and of son's occupations. Our procedure follows a logic similar to indirect standardization or regression standardization (Duncan, 1965; Chapter 5 of this volume). We have applied constant patterns of association between father's and son's occupations (analogous to fixed regression coefficients) to populations of men who differ in the distribution of their own and their father's occupations. The one conceptual difference between our method and these other methods of standardization is that we vary composition both in respect to the distributions of origin and destination occupations; these other methods are usually applied to assess the implications of changes in occupational origins for the distribution of destination occupations. Applying a well-known technique of proportional adjustment (Mosteller, 1968; Deming, 1943), we have taken tables of U.S. men's mobility from father's occupation to current occupation for certain cohorts covered in the 1962 OCG survey, and we have projected them backward and forward in time to fit occupation distributions of fathers and sons in 1952 and 1972, while preserving the underlying patterns of association in the tables. This procedure is often used by economists to adjust tables of input–output coefficients for short-term changes in supply and demand (Theil, 1972: 131–143).

Since we currently are analyzing a new set of occupational mobility data for the U.S. (Featherman and Hauser, 1975), our effort to predict or project the entries in occupational mobility tables for U.S. men in 1972 might be viewed more as an exercise in quantitative hypothesis construction than one of finding new social facts. While we think our work is justifiable on the former ground alone, our indirect methods may prove useful for measuring mobility in future decades, particularly if resources should diminish for monitoring social change.

TECHNIQUE OF PROPORTIONAL ADJUSTMENT

The technique of proportional adjustment can be illustrated in a straightforward way. Consider the hypothetical mobility data in Table 7.1, where f_{ij} is the frequency of men from origin i in destination j. The association between occupational origins and destinations is given by the odds-ratio,

$$\frac{f_{11}/f_{12}}{f_{21}/f_{22}} = \frac{f_{11}/f_{21}}{f_{12}/f_{22}} = \frac{f_{11}f_{22}}{f_{21}f_{12}}. \tag{1}$$

Odds-ratios like that in Equation (1) appear to be invariant across time for U.S. men (see Chapter 6 of this volume). Suppose the frequencies in interior rows 1 and 2 of the table are multiplied by arbitrary non-zero constants, say, a and b, respectively; likewise, the frequencies in the interior columns of the table are multiplied by non-zero constants c and d. The resulting proportionately adjusted frequencies are shown in Table 7.2. In general, when both row and column frequencies are adjusted, neither the original row nor column percentage distributions will be preserved. However, this transformation does not affect the odds-ratio,

$$\frac{(acf_{11})(bdf_{22})}{(adf_{12})(bcf_{21})} = \frac{f_{11}f_{22}}{f_{12}f_{21}}. \tag{2}$$

This illustrates the way in which proportional adjustment preserves the association in a frequency table.

As a practical matter, a frequency table may be adjusted to desired row and column marginal distributions by an iterative method. Each row entry is multiplied by the ratio of the desired row sum to the actual row sum, and then each column entry is multiplied by the ratio of the desired column sum to the actual column sum. By alternating adjustments of this kind, convergence of the adjusted cell frequencies

TABLE 7.1

A Hypothetical Occupational Mobility Table

Father's Occupation	Son's Occupation		
	1	2	Total
1	f_{11}	f_{12}	$f_{1.}$
2	f_{21}	f_{22}	$f_{2.}$
Total	$f_{.1}$	$f_{.2}$	$f_{..}$

TABLE 7.2

Proportional Adjustment of a Hypothetical Occupational Mobility Table

Father's Occupation	Son's Occupation		
	1	2	Total
1	acf_{11}	adf_{12}	$a(cf_{11} + df_{12})$
2	bcf_{21}	bdf_{22}	$b(cf_{21} + df_{22})$
Total	$c(af_{11} + bf_{21})$	$d(af_{12} + bf_{22})$	$acf_{11} + adf_{12} +$ $bcf_{21} + bdf_{22}$

to both the desired row and column totals is usually obtained within a few iterations.

Whether or not the model of proportional change is correct, we think it is instructive to estimate the 1952 and 1972 mobility tables from the associations in the 1962 tables for the following reason. The process of proportional adjustment preserves the odds-ratios in the table which is taken as the standard. Thus, when we compare a table adjusted to 1972 (or 1952) marginals with the original table, we know that none of the observed differences may be attributed to change in the underlying pattern of association in the table. All must be attributable to changes in the occupational structure. In discussing proportional adjustment, Mosteller notes (1968: 10):

> Making the assumption that when a subgroup is formed from the parent population the multiplicative invariance is preserved does not make it true (as a vehicle for getting an estimate in ignorance, it has the same status as the use of linear regression in the absence of knowledge of the shape of the function).

In the present case, the forward and backward projection of 1962 mobility tables is especially compelling because there is a fair amount of evidence that the tables so projected will be substantially correct (Chapter 6 of this volume).

The empirical problem in adjusting mobility tables to reflect the occupational structure at earlier or later times is to obtain the marginal distributions of father's and son's occupations. Our solution is to assume that cohorts covered in the 1962 OCG survey are represented equally well in the U.S. census and in the Current Population Survey (CPS) in earlier and later years. For example, we take the reports of current occupation of men aged 25 to 34 in the 1952 CPS and of men aged 45 to 54 in the March 1972 CPS to pertain to the same cohort of men as reports of father's occupation and of current occupation of men aged 35 to 44 and covered in the March 1962 OCG survey.

We have reviewed (in Chapters 3 and 5 of this volume) the threats to the validity of these assumptions, which include differentials in survey coverage, mortality, immigration and entrances into and exits from the experienced civilian labor force.

Assuming temporally invariant association between father's and son's occupations, we have estimated the frequencies in father–son mobility tables in 1952 and 1972 for 10-year age groups of men aged 25 to 64 in 1962 who were not outside that age range 10 years earlier or later. Our estimated mobility tables are based on the 12-category major occupation group classification displayed in Figure 6.1. Our assignment of off-diagonal cells to "upward" or "downward" mobility is based on the rank positions of the major groups on the Duncan (1961) scale.

Because the marginal occupation distributions in the March 1972 CPS were based on the occupation classification system of the 1970 Census of Population, while the occupation distributions in the 1962 OCG were based on the 1960 classification system, we have adjusted the observed 1972 occupation distributions for men of different ages to a 1960 basis (Priebe *et al.*, 1972). We did not think changes in occupational classifications between 1950 and 1960 were large enough to warrant adjustment of the 1952 data (Priebe, 1968). However, occupation distributions from the 1952 CPS were not tabulated by age, so we adjusted the 1950 census table of men's occupations by age to the 1952 marginal distributions of age and occupation (U.S. Bureau of the Census, 1953, 1956). This same procedure was used earlier by Duncan (1965: 492–493).

SHIFTS IN COHORT DISTRIBUTIONS

The distributions of son's current occupation by age and year which were used in our analysis are shown in Table 7.3. The columns of the table are arranged to facilitate age-constant intercohort comparisons, for example, among men aged 35 to 44 in 1952, 1962 and 1972. However, it is also legitimate to follow the experience of a single cohort through the life cycle. For example, men born in 1917 to 1926 were 25 to 34 in 1952, 35 to 44 in 1962 and 45 to 54 in 1972. Both within and

TABLE 7.3

Occupation by Age: U.S. Men in the Experienced Civilian Labor Force at Selected Ages in 1952, 1962 and 1972[a]

Occupation	25 to 34		35 to 44			45 to 54			55 to 64	
	1952	1962	1952	1962	1972	1952	1962	1972	1962	1972
Professional, tech., & kindred, self-employed	0.9%	1.0%	1.6%	2.0%	2.8%	1.6%	1.5%	2.0%	1.9%	1.6%
Professional, tech., & kindred, salaried & other	7.8	17.2	6.2	11.1	15.4	5.1	7.9	11.2	7.6	9.0
Mgrs., officials, & prop., excl. farm, salaried	4.5	7.1	6.4	9.6	9.9	6.9	8.5	9.6	9.7	9.9
Sales workers	6.1	5.9	5.2	5.3	5.8	5.0	5.2	6.0	3.9	6.1
Mgrs., officials, & prop., excl. farm, self-employed	3.8	3.4	6.5	7.6	5.8	7.7	10.1	5.7	10.3	5.8
Clerical & kindred workers	7.8	7.4	6.1	6.4	6.0	6.1	6.9	6.8	5.8	6.7
Craftsmen, foremen & kindred workers	19.2	19.1	20.3	21.5	21.9	20.7	22.2	23.7	19.5	21.8
Operatives & kindred workers	24.8	20.9	21.8	19.0	19.0	18.1	17.8	18.9	15.6	17.7
Service workers, incl. private household	4.6	5.1	5.4	4.3	5.2	6.8	5.7	6.3	7.5	8.6
Farmers & farm managers	6.5	3.3	8.3	5.2	2.5	9.6	6.8	3.5	9.7	5.2
Farm laborers & foremen	5.0	2.5	3.9	1.4	1.0	3.7	1.4	0.8	2.3	1.6
Laborers, excl. farm & mine	9.1	7.2	8.5	6.6	4.9	8.6	6.0	5.6	6.3	6.1
Total	100.0%	100.0%	100.0%	100.0%	100.0%	100.0%	100.0%	100.0%	100.0%	100.0%

[a]In 1962, men who did not report their father's occupation in the OCG survey are excluded. Rounded percentages may not add to 100 percent. See text for sources of data.

between cohorts the occupation distributions in Table 7.3 reflect the historic pattern of change in the U.S. labor force: net shifts out of occupations at the base of the status hierarchy and net shifts into occupations near the top of the hierarchy. Even in the relatively recent period represented by the table, the shifts out of farming and laboring occupations and into professional and salaried managerial occupations are noteworthy. (For further evidence and discussion of net occupational trends, see Duncan, 1965, 1966b; and Chapters 3, 4, and 5 of this volume.)

Intercohort shifts among the occupation distributions in Table 7.3 are summarized by indexes of dissimilarity in the right-hand panel of Table 7.4. The index of dissimilarity gives the percentage of observa-

TABLE 7.4

Indexes of Dissimilarity Between Cohorts in Distributions of Father's Occupation and of Son's Current Occupation: U.S. Men at Selected Ages in 1952, 1962 and 1972.

Age	Year	Father's Occupation		Son's Current Occupation	
		1962	1972	1962	1972
25 to 34	1952	8.6	--	12.6	--
35 to 44	1952	5.0	12.1	11.3	16.0
	1962	--	8.6	--	7.0
45 to 54	1952	7.7	12.2	9.2	14.6
	1962	--	5.0	--	8.7
55 to 64	1962	--	7.7	--	10.0

tions in one distribution which would have to be shifted to other categories to render that distribution identical to a second distribution. Obviously, there are substantial net occupational shifts between cohorts. Even over a single decade, the net shift is 7% or more of the occupation distribution in all of the six possible intercohort comparisons. Table 7.4 also gives indexes of dissimilarity between the distributions of father's occupation in successive cohorts. Because there is substantial variability in the age at which fathers have sons, the net shifts are in most cases less between the distributions of father's occupation than between those of son's, but they are not negligible. (For further evidence of intercohort shifts in the distributions of father's and son's occupations, see Chapter 6 of this volume.)

TRENDS IN GROSS MOBILITY

In Table 7.5 we display measures of gross mobility by age and year in the observed and adjusted mobility tables. For example, 79.5% of men in the observed 12-by-12 table for men aged 35 to 44 in 1962 were mobile, compared to 76.6% mobile in the same table adjusted to the 1952 marginal distributions for men aged 35 to 44, and 80.4% mobile in the same table adjusted to the 1972 marginal distributions for men aged 35 to 44. Thus, at ages 35 to 44, intercohort shifts in the occupation distributions of fathers and sons induced an increase in the total rate of mobility. At ages 35 to 44 in 1962, 57.4% of men were upwardly mobile, but, of men at that age in 1952, we estimate 48.5% were upwardly mobile, and, in 1972, we estimate 59.3% were upwardly mobile. Finally, 22.0% of men aged 35 to 44 in 1962 were downwardly mobile, but, in our adjusted table for men of that age in 1952, 28.1% were downwardly mobile, and 21.1% were downwardly mobile in 1972. Not only did shifts in the occupational distribution induce a higher rate of mobility among 35- to 44-year-old men in more recent years, but they increased the rate of upward mobility and decreased the rate of downward mobility. Moreover, these intercohort trends among 35- to 44-year-olds are replicated with only one exception among men at other ages; the percentage downwardly mobile at ages 55 to 64 in 1972 is inconsistently large, 22.7% compared with the observed 22.3% at the same ages in 1962.

With the exception just noted, there are similar intracohort increases in total and upward mobility and decreases in downward mobility. These may be observed by reading the diagonal entries of Table 7.5 from upper left to lower right. For example, in the cohort of 1917 to

TABLE 7.5

Gross Measures of Occupational Mobility from Father's Occupation to Son's Current Occupation for U.S. Men by Age: from Mobility Tables Observed in 1962 and Adjusted to 1952 and 1972 Marginal Distributions

Age	Total Mobile			Upwardly Mobile			Downwardly Mobile		
	1952	1962	1972	1952	1962	1972	1952	1962	1972
25 to 34	77.1	79.6	--	45.7	53.8	--	31.4	25.8	--
35 to 44	76.6	79.5	80.4	48.5	57.4	59.3	28.1	22.0	21.1
45 to 54	78.2	79.9	82.1	50.6	57.6	60.4	27.5	22.3	21.7
55 to 64	--	78.3	81.0	--	56.0	58.3	--	22.3	22.7

1926 (aged 25 to 34 in 1952), 77.1% were mobile in the estimated 1952 table, 79.5% were mobile in the observed 1962 table, and 82.1% were mobile in the estimated 1972 table. In the same cohort, 45.7% were upwardly mobile in 1952, 57.4% were upwardly mobile in 1962, and 60.4% were upwardly mobile in 1972. Further, in that cohort, 31.4% were downwardly mobile in 1952, 22.0% in 1962, and 21.7% in 1972.

While these intracohort comparisons are strictly correct, it should be kept in mind they do not have the same logical status as the intercohort comparisons, relative to the distinction between structure (marginals) and process (association) in the mobility table. That is, in making intercohort comparisons, we look at two tables which share the same underlying pattern of association but have differing origin and destination marginals. In making intracohort comparisons, we look at two tables which share the same origin distribution but differ in respect to both patterns of association and destination distributions. As shown in Chapter 6, the differences among age groups in the association of father's occupation and son's occupation are not very great, but any such differences will enter intracohort comparisons. Both intercohort and intracohort comparisons are of substantive interest, but only the former unequivocally represent our interest in measuring the effects of changes in the occupational structure.

The structurally induced changes in mobility rates within and between cohorts are not very large. Only two of the 10-year intracohort shifts in occupational mobility are as large as 10 percentage points, and many of the changes between adjacent years or cohorts are only 1 or 2 percentage points. At the same time, the pattern and consistency of the estimated changes in mobility rates convince us that we have located a real and substantial trend.

One might easily be misled in attempting to infer trend in Table 7.5 from cross-sectional age comparisons within any one year. For example, in 1952, the rate of upward mobility varied directly with age, and the rate of downward mobility varied inversely with age. Thus, by identifying the experience of older cohorts with the past and that of younger cohorts with the present, one would reach precisely the wrong conclusions about trend.

INDEXING TREND IN MOBILITY

In one sense, there is no need for a more refined analysis of our data. The proportional adjustment method guarantees that changes in the occupational structure are the only source of variability between cohorts for men of any given age. Thus, even the gross mobility rates in Table 7.4 have been purged of extraneous variation in the mobility process. At the same time, we thought there were substantive and methodological reasons for carrying our analysis further. For example, an intergenerational occupational mobility table is not a transformation of the labor force from one period to another, and differences between the marginal distributions of fathers and sons reflect rates and age-variations in nuptuality, fertility, mortality, and labor force participation, as well as interperiod changes in the occupational structure. Thus, our results might simply reflect changes in the disjuncture between the occupation distributions of fathers and sons. Also, we thought it would be instructive to see whether some descriptively interesting mobility indexes would display the insensitivity to changes in the occupational structure which have been claimed for them.

The first panel of Table 7.6 gives percentages of *structural* (or minimum) *mobility* for each cohort–year combination. These are indexes of dissimilarity between the occupation distributions of sons and their fathers. They indicate the percentage of sons who could not possibly have entered their fathers' occupations, but in no other way do they describe the actual distribution of long- and short-distance mobility. Of course, the measurement of structural mobility is unrelated to our adjustment procedure, since it involves only the marginal distributions of the mobility tables for each cohort and year. However, the interpretation of the indexes does depend on our assumptions about survey coverage of 1962 OCG men in earlier and later years.

Neither within nor between cohorts is there a consistent temporal pattern of variation in the volume of structural mobility. For some ages or cohorts, structural mobility increases with time; for others, it decreases; and in still others, there is no consistent trend. Indeed, the only reasonably clear pattern is a tendency for structural mobility to vary directly with age within years. Clearly, no systematic trends in structural mobility are responsible for the pattern in the data of Table 7.5.

The second panel of Table 7.6 gives percentages of *circulation mobility* in the observed and estimated tables. Circulation mobility is the excess of total mobility over structural mobility; that is, it tells what percentage of men moved whose moves were not dictated by the transformation of the marginal distributions between generations. These coefficients come closer than those of structural mobility to displaying the pattern of total and upward mobility rates in Table 7.5, but there are several exceptions to the temporal increase in circulation mobility.

TABLE 7.6

Net Measures and Indexes of Occupational Mobility from Father's Occupation to Son's Current Occupation for U.S. Men by Age: from Mobility Tables Observed in 1962 and Adjusted to 1952 and 1972 Marginal Distributions

Age	Structural Mobility			Circulation Mobility			Yasuda Index[a]			Boudon Index[a]		
	1952	1962	1972	1952	1962	1972	1952	1962	1972	1952	1962	1972
25 to 34	24.6	23.1	--	52.5	56.4	--	.821	.857	--	.696	.734	--
35 to 44	24.4	24.2	23.6	52.3	55.3	56.7	.817	.852	.896	.691	.730	.743
45 to 54	29.0	26.0	28.7	49.1	53.9	53.3	.826	.858	.881	.692	.728	.748
55 to 64	--	28.5	29.4	--	49.8	51.6	--	.826	.859	--	.696	.731

[a]See text for explanation of Yasuda's and Boudon's indexes.

At ages 45 to 54, there was a slight decrease in circulation mobility between 1962 and 1972. Also, in the cohorts of 1907 to 1916 and of 1917 to 1926, there were declines of circulation mobility between 1962 and 1972.

Numerous indexes have been proposed to eliminate the effects of changes in the occupational structure in the measurement of mobility. Given the construction of our data, an index with this desirable property would not vary across years for men of any given age. Two of the proposed mobility indexes are formed as the ratio of circulation mobility to a hypothetical maximum value. Yasuda (1964; also see U.S. Bureau of the Census, 1964a; Durbin, 1955; Jones, 1975) suggests that the difference between mobility under the hypothesis of statistical independence and structural mobility be placed in the denominator of the index. Thus, the index says how close observed circulation mobility would be to circulation mobility if there were no relationship between father's and son's occupations, conditional on the observed marginal distributions.

Boudon (1972, 1973) has proposed a modification of Yasuda's index in which maximum mobility is substituted for mobility under independence in the denominator of the ratio. For mobility tables based on more than two occupational categories and where the marginal distributions are not highly skewed, maximum mobility is always unity. That is, it would be possible for no son to remain in his father's occupation. Jones (1975) has characterized the Yasuda and Boudon indexes as based on "liberal" and "radical" normative criteria, respectively; the former takes chance association between father's occupation and son's occupation as the standard, and the latter takes maximum dissociation as the standard.

The Yasuda and Boudon indexes are based in common on the notion that subtracting structural mobility from observed and from ideal mobility (under independence or dissociation) controls or eliminates the influence of the occupational structure. However, as shown in the last two panels of Table 7.6, both the Yasuda and Boudon indexes show virtually the same pattern of variation across ages and years as do the gross measures of total mobility and upward mobility in Table 7.5. As indexed by these two measures, by "liberal" or "radical" criteria of evaluation, the mobility of American men has increased in the past 20 years. While these two indexes obviously do not eliminate the effects of changes in the occupational structure, we would not thereby disregard the results of Table 7.6. Despite their methodological defects, these indexes do have descriptive value, and we believe their empirical variation reflects substantively important consequences of change in the occupational structure.

Are these trends peculiar in some sense to the measures of mobility we have thus far reported? In order to be sure this was not the case, we reanalyzed our data using several of the better-known indexes of mobility, including some which pertain to individual cells or occupational categories in a mobility table. Among the measures we looked at were the social distance mobility ratio (Rogoff, 1953a; Glass, 1954) and the "percentage determinations" suggested by Hope (1972). These additional analyses were consistent with those we have already reported, but we shall not detail them for reasons of economy. We did carry out three additional analyses which we think are instructive and which can be summarized briefly.

Recently, Klatzky and Hodge (1971) and Hope (1972) have suggested that *canonical correlation* analysis be used to describe the strength of association in a mobility table. The canonical correlation is determined by assigning that set of scale values to origin and destination categories which yields the largest product–moment correlation between father's and son's occupations. Additional canonical correlations may be extracted if one set of scores is insufficient to represent all of the association in the table, and the evidence suggests that at least two canonical correlations are needed to describe the association in occupational mobility tables. The sum of squares of all possible canonical correlations in a table is equal to the mean square contingency, formed as the ratio of χ^2/N, where χ^2 is the usual Pearson Chi-square and N is the number of observations on which the table is based.

The first and second canonical correlations and the mean square contingencies of our observed and adjusted mobility tables are reported in Table 7.7. Without exception, these three measures of association decline with the passage of time both within and between cohorts. In some cases, these declines are substantial. For example, among 35- to 44-year-old men, the first canonical variate in father's occupation accounted for 24.5% of the variance in the first canonical variate in son's occupation in 1952. Twenty years later among men of the same age, the first canonical variate in father's occupation accounted for but 19.4% of the variance in the first variate of son's occupation. Thus, these correlational measures suggest a tendency for the mobility of U.S. men to increase in recent years simply because of the pattern of change in occupational structure.

McFarland (1969) has advocated an *index of uncertainty* (information or entropy) to measure the "permeability" of occupational struc-

TABLE 7.7

Canonical Correlations and Mean Square Contingency in Matrices of Mobility from Father's
Occupation to Son's Current Occupation for U. S. Men by Age: from Mobility Tables
Observed in 1962 and Adjusted to 1952 and 1972 Marginal Distributions

Age	First Canonical Correlation			Second Canonical Correlation			Mean Square Contingency		
	1952	1962	1972	1952	1962	1972	1952	1962	1972
25 to 34	.491	.451	--	.300	.275	--	.446	.382	--
35 to 44	.495	.459	.441	.313	.281	.252	.445	.382	.355
45 to 54	.467	.434	.430	.300	.280	.243	.373	.329	.308
55 to 64	--	.441	.409	--	.259	.232	--	.366	.324

tures, which we take to be the converse of the dependence of son's on
father's occupation. Entropy is defined as

$$H = -\Sigma p_i \log(p_i) \tag{3}$$

where p_i is the relative frequency of observations in the ith category of
a distribution, so $\Sigma p_i = 1$. If we adopt the convention $0 \log 0 = 0$, H is
always positive or zero, and it takes on the maximum $\log K$ when there
is a uniform distribution of observations across K categories. That is,
the more uniform or heterogeneous a distribution, the more closely H
approaches its maximum value.

In Table 7.8, we show the uncertainty in the marginal distribution of
son's occupation for each year and cohort covered in our analysis, and
we also show an average measure of the conditional uncertainty in
son's occupation. That is, the latter measure is the expected value
(weighted by the marginal distribution of father's occupation) of the
uncertainty of the distribution of son's occupation for each category of
father's occupation. In calculating H, we have taken natural logs, so
the maximum of each entry in Table 7.8 is $\log_e 12 = 2.48$. Between
cohorts, but not within them, uncertainty in the distribution of men's
occupations has declined. That is, the occupation distribution has become less heterogeneous. There is less consistent evidence of trend in
the conditional uncertainty measures. These coefficients vary directly
with age in each year, and excepting the estimate for 45- to 54-year-old
men in 1972, conditional uncertainty increases with age within
cohorts. However, there is no consistent pattern of variation in conditional uncertainty in the age-constant intercohort comparisons. In the
right-hand panel of Table 7.8, we give the percentage reduction in

TABLE 7.8

Marginal and Conditional Uncertainty in the Occupation Distributions of U. S. Men by Age:
from Mobility Tables Observed in 1962 and Adjusted to 1952 and 1972 Marginal Distributions

Age	Uncertainty in destination			Conditional uncertainty in destination			Percentage reduction in uncertainty		
	1952	1962	1972	1952	1962	1972	1952	1962	1972
25 to 34	2.222	2.208	--	2.030	2.035	--	8.6	7.4	--
35 to 44	2.268	2.248	2.201	2.074	2.080	2.047	8.6	7.5	7.0
45 to 54	2.298	2.259	2.210	2.125	2.109	2.069	7.5	6.7	6.3
55 to 64	--	2.311	2.267	--	2.146	2.124	--	7.2	6.3

uncertainty when father's occupation is known. This is 100% minus conditional uncertainty as a percentage of total uncertainty. The larger the percentage reduction in uncertainty, the greater is the dependence of son's on father's occupation. Taken in combination, the declining total uncertainty between cohorts and declining conditional uncertainty within cohorts produce a consistent pattern of decline in the percentage reductions both within and between cohorts. That is, knowledge of father's occupation gives us relatively less information about son's occupational position more recently than in the past.

Suppose we think of occupational mobility as a probability process (Hodge, 1966), and specifically as a *Markov process,* so the occupation distribution k generations hence may be obtained by multiplying the vector of father's occupations by the kth power of the matrix of row (outflow) probabilities estimated from a mobility table. Of course, an intergenerational mobility table does not literally represent an inter-period population transformation because of differential fertility and the variance in ages at which fathers have sons, and fathers and sons enter and leave the labor force. See Duncan (1966a) for an elaboration of these observations.

The equilibrium vector or fixed point distribution of an outflow matrix is obtained by forming the matrix of relative frequencies of son's occupation within categories of father's occupation and raising that matrix to a high power. The distribution of relative frequencies across any row of the resulting matrix is the equilibrium vector. An equilibrium vector may be thought of as the end-state of a Markov process, an origin vector which would be transformed back into itself by another step in the process. If one chooses not to take the Markovian assumptions seriously, the equilibrium vector may be taken as a convenient summary of tendencies in the mobility table.

TABLE 7.9

Indexes of Dissimilarity Between Cohorts in Equilibrium Vectors of the Age-Specific Occupation Distribution of U.S. Men by Age: from Mobility Tables Observed in 1962 and Adjusted to 1952 and 1972 Marginal Distributions

Age	Year	1962	1972
25 to 34	1952	19.5	--
35 to 44	1952	16.5	23.2
	1962	--	7.6
45 to 54	1952	11.4	14.4
	1962	--	7.6
55 to 64	1962	--	8.2

In Table 7.9, we give indexes of dissimilarity between cohorts in the equilibrium vectors of the outflow tables which were observed in 1962 and estimated for 1952 and 1972. Detailed comparisons of the equilibrium vectors within and between cohorts would lead to conclusions similar to those which might be drawn from direct examination of the changing destination vectors of the mobility tables. However, the important conclusion to be drawn from these projections is adequately documented by the indexes of dissimilarity in Table 7.9. That is, the equilibrium vectors do change substantially between cohorts because the distribution of occupational destinations changes. That result dramatically illustrates the difference between the assumption of constant transition probabilities in the Markov model, and the assumption of constant odds-ratios which is supported by the analysis of Chapter 6 and has been applied throughout this chapter. It is implicit in the changing equilibrium vectors that the observed intergenerational mobility tables could not have been generated by a single Markov process.

Our analysis carries implications for efforts to estimate future occupation distributions with projections based on an observed occupational mobility matrix. Even if the relative mobility chances of men with differing occupational origins were constant over time, the distribution of outflow probabilities would be subject to change so long as the occupational structure is changing. We cannot expect transition probabilities to remain constant over time. However, only by making the assumption of constant outflow probabilities can future occupation distributions be projected from a mobility table. Thus, the invariance of relative mobility chances is insufficient to permit estimation of future occupation distributions by projection of observed mobility tables.

One might use other methods to forecast future occupation distributions. For example, one can project future industrial growth and then aggregate industry-specific occupation distributions across industries. Once projections of the occupation distribution were obtained, it would be possible to estimate all of the entries in a future mobility table using the method applied here. Were there published forecasts of the distribution of occupation by age, we could forecast the future of occupational mobility.

DISCUSSION

We began with the finding of Chapter 6 that there has been no trend whatever in the relative mobility chances of American men whose fathers held different occupations. Taking that finding as an assumption, we used the observed intergenerational occupational mobility tables for men at several ages in 1962 to estimate the frequencies in similar tables which might have been observed in 1952 and 1972. In fact, less detailed mobility tables based on small samples are available for both those years (NORC, 1972; Jackson and Crockett, 1964), and the assumptions underlying our estimation procedure are consistent with comparisons among the observed 1952, 1962, and 1972 tables (Chapter 6).

Using our observed and constructed mobility tables, we carried out an analysis of mobility trends between and within cohorts of U.S. men which have been induced by changes in the occupational structure. Our analysis pertains to the period since World War II, so the processes of industrialization and urbanization must be regarded as essentially complete throughout our series of observations. Despite the limited temporal scope of our inquiry, there appeared a remarkably consistent set of trends in occupational mobility both within and between cohorts. In our time series, with few exceptions, the total rate of occupational mobility increased, upward mobility increased, downward mobility decreased, and, by several measures, the relationship between the occupational positions of fathers and sons became less strong. Recall, however, that each of these results presumes a fundamental invariance in the relative mobility chances of American men.

How seriously shall we take these findings? Are they established social facts or reasonably well-grounded hypotheses, or do they merely illustrate a tendency in the occupational structure? Obviously, each reader must judge that from the available evidence. We think the present results are of more than theoretical or analytic interest, and fortunately they may soon be disconfirmed or substantiated by data from the 1973 replicate of the 1962 OCG survey (Featherman and Hauser, 1975).

At the very least, we think our analysis seriously calls into question the thesis of Boudon's (1974) monograph on mobility in Western societies that the rigidity of occupational structures has led inexorably to constant rates of mobility and to a predominance of downward mobility. On the contrary, at least in the United States, the occupational structure has changed continually between and within cohorts, and, in consequence of these structural shifts, upward intergenerational mobility appears to have increased and downward mobility to have decreased over time.

It is sobering that the trends toward greater occupational mobility which we have documented presume a fundamental invariance in processes of occupational mobility. Despite the many social changes in the United States in the last two decades, it is a more favorable occupational structure, and only that, which has sustained or improved the mobility opportunities of American men. In light of this finding, it may be discomforting to ponder the social consequences of economic, technological, or demographic impediments to further upgrading of the occupational structure.

Whether or not our specific findings are ultimately found valid, we think our analysis carries important implications for the conduct of comparative mobility research. Students of occupational mobility may have placed disproportionate emphasis on differences in mobility processes across time and space. Important and systematic variations in mobility rates may be induced by changes in the occupational structure. These tendencies may be measured even with rather primitive analytic tools, such as those employed herein, and their causes and consequences seem worthy of further study.

III

STUDIES IN STATUS
ALLOCATION

8

Sex in the Structure of Occupational Mobility in the United States, 1962

Within the past few years, there has been a tremendous growth of sociological interest in sexual inequalities of social position in the United States. This growth was surely late in coming (Watson and Barth, 1964), and no doubt it was induced in part by the development of a diffuse but ubiquitous women's movement (Acker, 1973; Steinmetz, 1974). There has been a virtual explosion of researches into the socioeconomic careers of women, which has increased our understanding of the labor force participation of women, economic and occupational segregation and discrimination in the labor market, and conflicts between the familial and nonfamilial roles of women and men.

Only a few researches have attempted to relate the sexual division of labor in American society to the intergenerational stratification of occupational roles. We detect three related themes in this work: (1) describing basic patterns of intergenerational occupational mobility (father to daughter) of women and contrasting these with male patterns of mobility, (2) describing patterns of women's intergenerational occupational mobility through marriage (father to husband) and contrasting these with men's or women's mobility to own occupations, and (3) constructing and contrasting structural equation models of the process of socioeconomic achievement among women and men.

This chapter was prepared by Robert M. Hauser, David L. Featherman, and Dennis P. Hogan. A preliminary version of this paper was presented at the 8th World Congress of Sociology in Toronto, August 19–23, 1974.

STRUCTURAL EQUATION MODELS OF
SEXUAL STRATIFICATION

The structural equation approach attempts to model social psychological, educational, or other career processes directly, rather than merely mapping the interactions between social origins and destinations. At the same time, structural equation models have thus far revealed little difference between the sexes in the process of stratification. Models of educational attainment and the achievement of occupational status among working men and women have displayed few or none of the expected sexual inequalities in a statewide sample of Wisconsin youth (Sewell, 1971; Carter, 1972), in comparisons of Occupational Changes in a Generation (OCG) men in 1962 with middle-aged women in the later National Longitudinal Surveys (Wang, 1972; Treiman and Terrell, 1975a), in comparisons of married OCG men in 1962 with their wives (Featherman and Hauser, 1976c), or in comparisons based on the annual social surveys of the National Opinion Research Center (NORC) (McClendon, 1976). Only in respect to the determination of income are there substantial differences between the sexes (Featherman and Hauser, 1976c; Treiman and Terrell, 1975a). For example, other things being equal married women earn substantially less than married men, and the earnings of married women reflect their educational and occupational standing less than do the earnings of men (Featherman and Hauser, 1976c).

One need not look far to comprehend the limitations of structural equation models in elucidating sexual inequalities in the world of work. Sexual segregation among occupations does not follow socioeconomic lines as closely as does, say, racial segregation. Consequently, analyses of stratification or mobility which represent occupations by indexes of their socioeconomic standing or their prestige cannot be expected to represent sexual inequalities in the occupational distribution or the causes of those inequalities. Tyree and Treas (1974: 294) report an index of dissimilarity, $\Delta = 41$, between the occupation distributions (over 10 major groups) of OCG men in 1962 and women who ever worked in a series of NORC surveys, and they report an index of 44 between OCG men and wives. However, over 20 5-point intervals of the Duncan SEI scale (Duncan, 1961), the Δ is only 25.4 between the distributions of men in the 1962 OCG survey and women in the experienced civilian labor force (ECLF) at the time of the 1960 census.

The index of dissimilarity tells what percentage of one distribution would have to be shifted into another category to match a second percentage distribution. The index must remain the same or increase in size as a classification is subdivided. Thus, one may guess that Tyree and Treas understated the difference between socioeconomic and nominal representations of sexual inequality in the occupational distribution.

Another set of contrasts may reveal more of the difference between dimensions of sexual and racial segregation in work. Among nonblack OCG men in the ECLF at ages 35 to 44 in 1962, the mean occupational status (Duncan SEI) was 40.7 ($s = 24.7$), but it was 19.2 ($s = 16.0$) in the comparable group of black men (Featherman and Hauser, 1976a: Tables 1, 2). In the same year, the index of dissimilarity between 18-category occupation distributions of white and black men in the ECLF at ages 35 to 44 was 40.7 (treating "unemployed" as an occupation. See Chapter 4: Table 4.2). In March 1962, the mean occupational status of married, spouse-present OCG men aged 20 to 64 was 37.9 ($s = 22.5$), and among their wives who worked, it was very nearly the same: 38.9 ($s = 21.4$) (Featherman and Hauser, 1976c: Table 1). Yet, among nonblack working men and women aged 35 to 44 in 1962, the Δ between 18-category occupation distributions was 49.8, and it was similarly large throughout the working ages (Chapter 4 of this volume: Table 4.2). Thus, among working persons, occupational segregation between the sexes was greater than that between black and white working men. However, racial segregation across occupations was largely socioeconomic in character, while there was little overall difference in the socioeconomic level of occupations held by men and women. Moreover, these measures of occupational segregation among working men and women vastly understate the role segregation of adult men and women, since they are conditional on participation in the labor force.

SOCIAL MOBILITY THROUGH MARITAL MOBILITY

Recent research on the "occupational" mobility of women through marriage is partly a reflection of current interest in stratification processes among women (Glenn, Ross, and Tully, 1974; Chase, 1975), and marital mobility may fruitfully be contrasted with patterns of intergenerational mobility to own occupations among both men and women (Tyree and Treas, 1974). However, the novelty of these studies may be exaggerated, since they continue a tradition of research into the extent of assortative mating (and nonmating) (Blau and Duncan, 1967: 346–359) and the prevalence of upward or downward mobility through marriage (see Rubin, 1968, and references cited therein. Also, see Scott, 1969; Rubin, 1969; Martin, 1970.). As an aside, we observe that research into sex diffentials in hypergamy (marrying up) and hypogamy (marrying down) has been sustained in large part by the inability of researchers to agree on a question. The major dimensions of the issue are (1) whether one takes account of nonmarriage, as well as intermarriage patterns among those who marry, (2) whether one defines marital mobility with reference to parental statuses alone or cross-generationally to one or another stage in the occupational career of the younger generation, or (3) whether one wishes to ignore issues of selection into marriage and generational or period shifts in the occupational distribution and define the problem as one of asymmetry in intermarriage patterns between social classes.

Whatever the possibilities of resolving long-standing controversies about class intermarriage, our present interest is in a comparison of men's and women's mobility from father's (or other head's) occupation to own occupation. Lest there be any misapprehension, we believe marital and career (own) mobility patterns are important and distinct (but not necessarily independent) objects of study. That is, we disagree both with those who believe that a woman's social standing is solely determined by her choice of mate and with those who believe that such status attributions are necessarily misleading and inappropriate. We think the notion that the family is a "solidary unit of equivalent evaluation" (Watson and Barth, 1964: 10) in the contemporary United States is no more naive than the countersuggestion that gross errors are generated by the attribution of husband's statuses to wives (Acker, 1973; Haug, 1973; Steinmetz, 1974). In American families, status variables (education, occupation, and income) are moderately associated within household members and between them. The choice of one or two convenient status measurements is in most cases likely to give an imperfect, but not wildly inaccurate, characterization of the social standing of a family and its members (for example, see Blau and Duncan, 1967: 188–194; Sewell and Hauser, 1975: 51–88). Further, we doubt the existence of some unitary "status" of a family—with or without reference to status characteristics of female household members—which applies equally to all household members and to all social situations. Were we to measure a full array of status variables for each member of a household, we expect the import of those status attributes would vary significantly among household members and social situations. Global status indexes are useful heuristically, but we can think of few sociological enterprises more sterile than attempting to define *the* status of a woman, a man, or a household.

SEXUAL PATTERNS OF INTERGENERATIONAL OCCUPATIONAL MOBILITY

This chapter follows the first theme mentioned above—the study of male and female patterns of intergenerational occupational mobility. To place it in context, we shall recapitulate briefly two other comparisons of the intergenerational occupational mobility of men and women in the U.S. (We are indebted to Tyree and Treas, 1974, for their lucid exposition of these same matters.) In their innovative paper, DeJong, Brawer, and Robin (1971) compared 10-by-10 tables of mobility from father to son among OCG men in 1962 with a composite table of occupational mobility from father to daughter. They aggregated the women's table across six national surveys carried out by NORC between 1955 and 1965, classifying women who had ever been in the labor force by their current or last occupation. Thus there was both conceptual and temporal variance between the measurements of men's and women's occupations. DeJong, Brawer, and Robin analyzed the women's matrix following the exposition of Blau and Duncan (1967: Chapter 2), and they found patterns of occupational inheritance, short distance mobility, recruitment, and selection, which paralleled those among U.S. men observed by Blau and Duncan. Moreover, they compared social distance mobility ratios across the male and female mobility tables, and concluded that there were "essentially no differences between female and male patterns of mobility in the American occupational structure" (DeJong, Brawer, and Robin, 1971: 1033). DeJong, Brawer, and Robin found these results puzzling in light of their expectations that conflict between the work and familial roles of women would lead to distinct intergenerational mobility patterns.

Havens and Tully (1972) raised several pertinent criticisms of the paper by DeJong, Brawer, and Robin. First, there is an insufficient connection between the microsocial theory of role conflict developed by DeJong, Brawer, and Robin and the gross patterns of mobility which they investigated. Had the expected differences between the sexes emerged, no conclusions about role conflict would have been warranted. We emphasize our concurrence in this criticism. Global comparisons of male and female mobility describe phenomena which may need to be explained. In no sense do they "model" the mobility process or bear on the validity of particular theories of it. Second, DeJong, Brawer, and Robin ignored the important differences in the occupational positions held by men and women. They neither presented nor discussed the distributions of occupation by sex. The omission is mitigated by the fuzzy temporal referent of the woman's own occupation in the composite NORC table, for it is not clear how to compare the distribution of those occupations—referring to diverse points in the life cycle and aggregated across years—with the distribution of current occupations of men in one year. Further, the attempt made by DeJong, Brawer, and Robin to control the occupation distributions in their comparison of male and female mobility patterns was defective. The several flaws of social distance mobility ratios are so amply demonstrated that it is difficult to comprehend their continued use by social researchers (Duncan, 1966a; Blau and Duncan, 1967; Goodman, 1969b; Tyree, 1973). Finally, Havens and Tully noted that broad occupation categories mask the extent of sex segregation in work and, perhaps, also in occupational mobility.

In a later comment, Ramsøy (1973) seconded some of the earlier criticisms, and she emphasized the dangers of ignoring sex differences in occupation among the employed. In addition, she argued that the conditional nature of women's participation in the labor force was another important aspect of women's "status biographies" which DeJong, Brawer, and Robin had neglected.

In a reanalysis of the several NORC surveys and the 1962 OCG data, Tyree and Treas (1974) demonstrated that DeJong, Brawer, and Robin had overstated the similarity in mobility patterns between working men and women. Unlike the earlier researchers, Tyree and Treas eliminated marginal sex differences in occupational origins and destinations by adjusting entries in both the male and female tables to conform with equiproportional marginals (Tyree and Treas, 1974: 295; also, see Chapter 7 of this volume for an exposition of this procedure). There were several sex differences in the adjusted tables. The correlation between the sexes in adjusted entries was .69 over all cells in a 9-by-9 table and .84 over cells in which there were at least five women (in the original table). Among nonfarm men, occupational origins did not affect the chance of moving into farming, but among women of nonfarm origin, only the daughters of laborers and service workers went into farming. Daughters of professionals were more likely than sons of professionals to enter white-collar occupations. Also, farm daughters were more likely than farm sons to enter white-collar occupations, and they were less likely to enter blue-collar occupations (Tyree and Treas, 1974: 296). These differences might be partly attributable to some women not entering the labor force unless a suitable job were available.

Recognizing that judgments of similarity or its absence are partly subjective, Tyree and Treas adduced a second male–female mobility comparison which showed far fewer differences between the sexes.

Here, they compared father-to-son mobility among working men with father-to-spouse mobility among the nonworking wives of OCG men. The adjusted entries in the latter table of marital mobility of women were highly correlated ($r = .93$) with entries in the adjusted intergenerational mobility table for men. Thus, women's patterns of mobility through marriage approximate those of men in the world of work, while male mobility diverges from that among working women (Tyree and Treas, 1974: 297–299). Tyree and Treas buttressed these conclusions by showing that similar results were obtained when OCG men were compared with working women in the National Longitudinal Survey of women aged 30 to 44 in 1967 (U.S. Department of Labor, 1970), and when more realistic origin and destination distributions were taken as the standard (rather than uniform distributions).

The present analysis is very much in the spirit of that undertaken by Tyree and Treas, but we have used more powerful statistical methods based on the log-linear model. Like them and DeJong, Brawer, and Robin, we use 1962 OCG data to measure intergenerational occupational mobility among men. Within the OCG sample, our population definitions differ from those in the earlier studies, but we have been able to ascertain the own 1962 occupations of wives of OCG men as well as their father's occupations. By using data for women in the 1962 OCG survey, we have been able to minimize conceptual differences between the sexes in the measurement of labor force status and of occupations of origin and destination. Also, we have a much larger sample of working (and of nonworking) men and women than has previously been available. Consequently, we have been able to use a more detailed occupational classification, which captures more of the differences between the sexes than do the census major groups. We have looked at sex differences in labor force participation as well as in occupational mobility per se in their intergenerational aspect, and, in addition, we have looked at sex differences in mobility by age and by race. Thus, without attempting to minimize the contribution of Tyree and Treas, we believe that our analysis extends their work in several important ways.

AVAILABILITY OF SPOUSE DATA
IN THE OCG SURVEY

The OCG supplement to the March 1962 Current Population Survey (CPS) asked that each married, spouse-present male aged 20–64 describe his wife's father's occupation when she was about 16 years old (Blau and Duncan, 1967: Appendix B). Men were encouraged to seek their wives' help in answering this item. The variable, wife's father's occupation, was used in analyses of assortative mating and of its effects and in an analysis of social mobility and fertility, but Blau and Duncan did not undertake a separate investigation of the occupational or social mobility of women.

The original OCG data file constructed by the U.S. Bureau of the Census contained little of the March CPS data for women, so we commissioned the bureau to prepare a new merger of the March 1962 CPS and OCG records which would contain a more extensive set of women's social characteristics. Of necessity, our analysis of intergenerational mobility among women must be restricted to the wives of married, spouse-present OCG respondents, so our results do not pertain to the important subgroups of never-married, separated, divorced, and widowed women. To maintain comparability, we have also excluded the corresponding subgroups of men from the present analysis. In addition, we have restricted some parts of our analysis to married, spouse-present men and women who were employed in the civilian labor force, thus excluding persons who were in the armed forces, unemployed, or out of the labor force. Most importantly, this excludes the plurality of housewives who are not in the labor force under the U.S. definition. As we shall demonstrate, being in or out of the labor force is a major component of sexual inequality in allocations to adult roles in the United States (also, see Chapter 4 of this volume).

In connection with the 1973 replicate and extension of the OCG survey, we have obtained a more extensive set of measurements of the social background of OCG wives. These have been merged with the March 1973 CPS record for women, enabling us to carry out more extensive analyses of the achievements of married women and of changes in them over time. Featherman and Hauser (1976c) have reported a preliminary analysis of these data.

Our analysis pertains to about 15,500 married couples in which the husband was a 1962 OCG respondent and both husband and wife were aged 20 to 64 in March 1962. Of the husbands, all but 500 were in the experienced civilian labor force (ECLF), that is, employed currently or unemployed with previous work experience. Only 5600 wives were in the ECLF. We look first at descriptive statistics of the cross-classification of father's occupation by own occupation by sex, and then we take up a series of hypotheses concerning the interactions of sex with this classification and with subclassifications by age or race.

Our analysis is based on a 17-category classification of census occupation titles which adds selected industrial, class of worker, and occupational distinctions to the conventional breaks among major groups.

There is one additional category of origin for fathers (or other house-hold heads) who did not work or for whom no occupation was reported, and there is an additional destination category for men and women outside the ECLF. The unemployed were assigned to the category of their last job, and the employed persons for whom no occupation was ascertained were allocated across occupation groups following the standard procedures of the CPS. The basic mobility data for men and women appear in Appendix D. The entries are weighted estimated population frequencies, scaled down to cumulate to the observed number of sample cases.

GROSS DIFFERENCES IN THE OCCUPATIONAL ORIGINS AND DESTINATIONS OF THE SEXES

Table 8.1 shows indexes of dissimilarity (Δ) between men and women in the total mobility tables and in outflow (selection) and inflow (recruitment) distributions. In the full 18-by-18 tables, the index of dissimilarity between male and female distributions is 69.6; that is, nearly 70% of men (or women) would have to be in a different origin–destination combination to render the male and female tables identical. Interestingly, this is only slightly higher than the Δ between the sexes in the total outflow distribution, that is, the difference between men and women in current occupations (counting not in the labor force as an occupation). Moreover, excepting the origin (father's occupation) categories in which there were virtually no men or women (because they are occupied almost exclusively by women), the indexes of dissimilarity between the sexes are very close to 70 in every category of origin. Women of high-status origins are no more advantaged relative to men than those of lowly origin. Of course, Δ tends to be larger when one or both of the distributions compared is subject to substantial sampling variability, as well as when the two distributions differ in the population. In contrast, the index of dissimilarity between the occupational origins of married men and women is only 5, and the Δ between male and female inflow distributions is never as large as 20 in any of the destination categories in which there are substantial numbers of men and women.

One other comparison of the male and female mobility tables sheds some light on the differences between occupational origins and destinations and their role in mobility differences between the sexes. The Δ between the male origin and destination distributions is 26.1. This index of differences between occupational origins and destinations,

TABLE 8.1

Indexes of Dissimilarity Between Occupational Inflow and Outflow Distributions of Married, Spouse-Present Women Aged 20 to 64, March 1962

Occupation	Inflow	Outflow
All origin-destination combinations		69.6
Father's occupation	5.0	--
Own occupation	--	68.9
Professional, technical, and kindred		
Self-employed	19.2[a]	73.7[b]
Salaried	13.4	69.9
Managers, officials, proprietors		
Salaried	19.6[a]	74.8
Self-employed	18.7[a]	69.3
Sales, other	39.2[a]	72.1
Clerical and kindred, stenographers and Secretaries	36.9[a]	91.6[a,b]
Clerical and kindred, other	5.4	72.2
Sales, retail	17.9	70.0
Craftsmen, foremen	39.4[b]	69.0
Craftsmen, other	27.8[a]	70.7
Operatives, other	10.0	71.9
Operatives, manufacturing	6.4	68.5
Service, other	11.2	69.6
Service, private household	35.7[b]	91.0[a,b]
Laborers, except farm	36.1[a]	68.7
Farmers, farm managers	39.1[a]	68.2
Farm laborers	19.8[a]	70.0
Not in labor force, not ascertained	13.5	67.9

[a]Fewer than 200 observations on women.
[b]Fewer than 200 observations on men.

sometimes termed "structural mobility," tells the minimum percentage of entries off the main diagonal, that is, mobile, which is consistent with the observed marginal distributions. Among men, the index of structural mobility reflects temporal changes in the occupational distribution of the labor force as well as differential fertility and the disjuncture between cohorts and generations (Duncan, 1966a). Among women, the index of structural mobility is a much larger 68.3, for it represents both the disjuncture between generations and that between the sexes.

Clearly, the current occupation distributions of married men and women are very different, and these differences may be strongly implicated in observable mobility differences between the sexes. The first panel of Table 8.2 shows the distributions of men and women over

TABLE 8.2

Current Occupation by Sex: Married, Spouse-Present Persons Aged 20 to 64, March 1962

Occupation	All persons		Experienced Civilian Labor Force	
	Male	Female	Male	Female
Prof., tech. & kindred				
Self-employed	1.5	0.4	1.5	1.2
Salaried	10.2	4.7	10.6	13.1
Mgrs., officials, prop.				
Salaried	8.8	1.0	9.2	2.8
Self-employed	7.5	0.7	7.8	2.0
Sales, other	3.3	0.3	3.5	0.8
Clerical and kindred, stenog. and secretaries	0.2	3.6	0.2	10.0
Clerical, other	6.0	7.7	6.2	21.5
Sales, retail	1.5	2.8	1.6	7.6
Craftsmen, foremen	3.2	0.3	3.3	0.8
Craftsmen, other	18.0	0.2	18.6	0.6
Operatives, other	9.4	1.0	9.8	2.9
Operatives, manufacturing	9.6	5.1	10.0	14.3
Service, other	4.9	5.1	5.1	14.2
Service, private household	0.0	1.8	0.0	5.0
Laborers, except farm	5.8	0.2	6.0	0.5
Farmers, farm managers	5.3	0.1	5.5	0.3
Farm laborers	1.3	0.9	1.3	2.4
Not in labor force, not ascertained	3.5	64.0	--	--
Total	100.0	100.0	100.0	100.0

all 18 destination categories, and the second panel gives the occupational distributions of persons in the experienced civilian labor force (ECLF), excluding the inexperienced unemployed and those not in the labor force. The concentration of women in clerical, sales, and service occupations is so great that the proportions of women in those categories exceed those of men even when the two-thirds of women outside the labor force are included in the distribution. Other occupational differences between men and women become clearer when those outside the labor force are excluded from the distribution. Clearly, the large indexes of dissimilarity in Table 8.1 are not merely a consequence of the lower labor-force participation rates of women. The index of dissimilarity between the occupation distributions of married men and women in the ECLF was $\Delta = 53.2$, compared to $\Delta = 68.9$ for all husbands and wives. Men were far more likely than

women to be managers (salaried or self-employed), nonretail salesmen, craftsmen or foremen, nonmanufacturing operatives, nonfarm
laborers, and farmers. Women were more likely than men to be
salaried professional or technical workers, secretarial or clerical workers, retail sales workers, manufacturing operatives, service workers,
and farm laborers. (For further comparisons of male and female occupation distributions, see Chapter 4 of this volume.)

At least as reflected in fathers' occupations, the "status biographies"
of men and women are not strongly implicated in their presence or
absence from the labor force. Rather, the major factor affecting labor
force participation of married persons is sex. For example, we looked at
the three-way classification of sex by father's occupation by labor force
participation, ignoring occupational distinctions within the ECLF.
Taking the joint distribution of father's occupation by sex as given,
there was a great deal of association in the table ($\chi^2(33) = 8412.57$).
The index of dissimilarity was $\Delta = 30.3$ between the observed classification and that under the null hypothesis of no association between sex
and labor force participation or between father's occupation and labor
force participation. However, the greater proportion of men in the
labor force accounted for virtually all (99.4%) of this association
($\chi^2(1) = 8366.11$). Even with more than 28,000 cases in which father's
occupation was reported, the remaining association between father's
occupation and labor force participation was barely statistically significant at the .05 level ($\chi^2(32) = 46.46$), and the model with a main
effect of sex on labor force participation misclassified only 1.4% of the
distribution. There was no association between father's occupation and
labor force participation ($\chi^2(16) = 12.79, p > .5$), and only a very small
three-way interaction among sex, father's occupation, and labor force
participation ($\chi^2(16) = 33.67, p < .01$). Thus, father's occupation did
not affect the labor force participation either of men or of women, nor
were there substantial differences between the sexes in the classification of father's occupation by labor force participation. For these reasons, we limit our later examination of sex differentials in mobility to
those married men and women who were in the experienced civilian
labor force.

MOBILITY DIFFERENTIALS STEMMING FROM
OCCUPATIONAL DISTRIBUTIONS

Most but not all of the differences between the intergenerational
occupational mobility patterns of men and women may be attributed

to the different occupational distributions of the sexes. To illustrate this, we adjusted the mobility matrix for men to conform with the female origin and destination distributions, and then we compared the adjusted male matrix with the observed female matrix (see Chapter 7 of this volume; Tyree and Treas, 1974; Tyree, 1973; Levine, 1967; Deming, 1943). In this comparison, the index of dissimilarity between the sexes was only 11.3 over all origin–destination combinations (including those with "not in the labor force"), compared with 69.6 in the unadjusted comparison between the sexes. (The results of these calculations would be similar if we limited the analysis to members of the experienced civilian labor force.) Table 8.3 presents indexes of

TABLE 8.3

Indexes of Dissimilarity Between Adjusted Male and Observed Female Occupational Inflow and Outflow Distributions: Married, Spouse-Present Men and Women Aged 20 to 64, March 1962[a]

Occupation	Inflow	Outflow
All origin-destination combinations	11.3	
Professional, technical, and kindred		
Self-employed	25.1[b]	14.2[c]
Salaried	20.0	27.7
Managers, officials, proprietors		
Salaried	23.8[b]	8.5
Self-employed	18.8[b]	6.9
Sales, other	41.7[b]	17.0
Clerical and kindred, stenographers and Secretaries	37.5[c]	81.0[b,c]
Clerical, other	11.5	21.2
Sales, retail	22.2	12.6
Craftsmen, foremen	43.4[b]	17.0
Craftsmen, other	27.7[b]	7.3
Operatives, other	15.7[b]	6.3
Operatives, manufacturing	10.1	7.5
Service, other	17.1	21.5
Service, private household	40.7[c]	52.4[b,c]
Laborers, except farm	29.7[b]	7.4
Farmers, farm managers	31.9[b]	14.5
Farm laborers	25.3[b]	13.4
Not in labor force, not ascertained	6.5	4.9

[a]Male matrix was adjusted to female marginal distributions and compared with observed female matrix.

[b]Fewer than 200 observations on women.

[c]Fewer than 200 observations on men.

dissimilarity which summarize the adjusted sex differences in each inflow and outflow distribution. Comparisons between inflow distributions are changed very little by the adjustment; this is to be expected because the occupational origin distributions scarcely differ between the sexes. At the same time, the adjustment markedly reduces the difference between the sexes in every outflow distribution in which there is a large number of observations. The indexes of dissimilarity were about 70 in all of the comparisons between observed outflow distributions, but, in the adjusted comparisons, most of the indexes were less than 20 and several were less than 10. The deviations between entries in the observed women's matrix and the adjusted men's matrix are presented in Table. 8.4. There appear to be some patterned differences between the mobility of men and of women which persist after the marginal distributions have been standardized. For example, all but three of the elements of Table 8.4 along the main diagonal are negative, indicating that women are less likely than men to enter the occupation of their fathers, even after controlling sex differences in the occupation distribution. Similarly, most of the entries near the main diagonal are negative; that is, men are more likely than women to enter occupations whose social standing is close to that of their father. These results may appear to be an artifact of the inclusion of "not in the labor force" as a destination category; note the positive deviations in the last column of the table. This is not the case, for similar results are obtained when the analysis is limited to members of the ECLF. Rather than pursuing hypotheses about sex differences in mobility by inspection or intuition, we turn to an analysis of the two mobility tables under the loglinear specification.

TESTING MOBILITY HYPOTHESES

Table 8.5 reports a series of statistical tests of hypotheses about occupational mobility and sex differences in mobility in the 17-by-17-by-2 classification of father's occupation by own 1962 occupation by sex among members of the ECLF reporting father's occupation. We denote these three variables by the letters F, O, and S, respectively, and we describe null hypotheses using letters or combinations of letters in brackets to indicate which marginal or joint distributions have been fitted in each model (see Goodman, 1972a, for further explanation and examples). In line A1 of Table 8.5, we fit the model of complete independence among father's occupation, own occupation, and sex, which we obviously reject. (Following Chapter 6 in this

TABLE 8.4

Deviations of Observed Frequencies in Female Mobility Table from Frequencies in Male Mobility Table Adjusted to Female Marginal Distributions: Married, Spouse-Present Men and Women Aged 20 to 64, March 1962

Father's Occupation	March 1962 Occupation																		Total
	(1)	(2)	(3)	(4)	(5)	(6)	(7)	(8)	(9)	(10)	(11)	(12)	(13)	(14)	(15)	(16)	(17)	(18)	
(1) Prof., tech., & kind., self-employed	-7	-4	-2	1	-2	20	5	-7	0	0	5	2	-3	3	0	0	-1	-9	71
(2) Prof., tech., & kind., salaried	-4	-53	-7	-3	3	33	-38	-15	-2	1	-2	-14	-21	4	0	0	0	120	320
(3) Mgrs., officials, prop., salaried	-3	-10	-6	-2	-2	-1	-3	-10	-2	-1	2	-1	9	4	0	0	1	27	84
(4) Mgrs., officials, prop., self-employed	2	15	-7	-2	-2	24	-5	-17	0	-1	-2	-4	4	-29	0	1	6	18	139
(5) Sales, other	2	-5	5	3	-3	-42	8	-2	0	0	0	-1	2	1	0	0	0	33	107
(6) Clerical & kindred, stenog & secretaries	0	-9	-2	0	0	1	1	-4	0	0	0	0	0	0	0	0	0	15	32
(7) Clerical, other	0	-19	0	-2	-1	-18	-16	-6	-2	1	-3	-9	-14	1	1	0	3	85	181
(8) Sales, retail	0	-6	-4	1	-2	16	-7	-8	-1	0	-1	5	-6	2	0	1	0	9	69
(9) Craftsmen, foremen	2	15	-1	-1	1	23	13	0	-1	-1	-1	-4	1	3	1	0	0	-48	116
(10) Craftsmen, other	-2	-27	-1	3	2	-118	4	-3	-4	-3	1	-1	-15	-8	3	2	3	165	365
(11) Operatives, other	0	-7	0	-5	-2	-6	-15	15	-3	-2	-6	-20	-10	20	-1	0	-1	43	156
(12) Operatives, mfg.	0	5	6	5	5	7	28	16	-2	1	-3	-14	5	15	2	1	2	-81	198
(13) Service, other	0	-5	-4	-4	-3	28	-31	-8	-2	4	-4	-10	-49	3	-1	1	-1	86	244
(14) Service, private household	0	2	0	0	0	0	-2	-3	0	0	-1	-2	-4	4	0	0	0	7	25
(15) Laborers, except farm	0	-2	0	3	1	28	-14	-4	-1	-1	-2	9	-2	-42	4	2	-3	26	144
(16) Farmers, farm mgrs.	9	95	25	1	2	-23	72	63	5	5	12	46	113	39	-3	-5	17	-473	1008
(17) Farm laborers	0	2	2	-1	5	1	4	-2	0	0	3	11	5	15	-1	0	-20	-23	95
(18) Not in labor force, not ascertained	2	14	-3	3	-1	29	-1	-5	14	0	1	10	-12	-34	-3	0	-8	-3	143
Total	33	295	75	40	37	418	267	188	39	21	49	163	275	227	20	13	66	127	3497

205

TABLE 8.5

Analyses of Sexual Homogeneity in Mobility from Father's Occupation to Own 1962 Occupation: Married, Spouse-Present Men and Women Aged 20 to 64 in the Experienced Civilian Labor Force

Model (null hypothesis)	χ^2_{LR}	df	p	Δ	χ^2_H/χ^2_T
A. Full mobility matrix (17 X 17)					
1. [F][O][S]	7077.32	544	.000	18.1	--
2. [FS][O]	7052.01	528	.000	18.1	--
3. [OS][F]	3139.99	528	.000	11.0	--
4. [FS][OS]	3114.69	512	.000	11.0	100.0
5. A4 vs. A2	3937.32	16	.000	7.1	--
6. A4 vs. A3	25.30	16	.068	0.0	--
7. [FS][OS][FO]	218.19	256	>0.5	1.9	7.0
8. A7 vs. A4	2896.50	256	.000	9.1	93.0
B. Main diagonal blocked					
1. [FS][OS]	1852.50	478	.000	8.1	59.5
2. [FS][OS][FO]	175.90	239	>0.5	1.6	5.6
3. B2 vs. B1	1676.60	239	.000	6.5	53.9
C. Five major groups blocked					
1. [FS][OS]	1147.67	390	.000	5.6	36.8
2. [FS][OS][FO]	146.43	195	>0.5	1.3	4.7
3. C2 vs. C1	1001.24	195	.000	4.3	32.1
D. Hierarchical decomposition					
1. B2 vs. A7	42.29	17	<.001	0.3	1.4
2. C2 vs. B2	29.47	44	> 0.5	0.3	0.9

NOTE: S = sex, F = father's occupation, O = own 1962 occupation.

volume, χ^2_{LR} values have been adjusted downward to reflect a sampling design factor of .62.) Model A2 fits the joint distribution of F and S, but O is taken to be independent of that joint distribution. Clearly, Model A2 gives little improvement over Model A1. Model A3 posits independence of F from the joint OS distribution. This model, too, is readily rejected, but, at the same time, it is clear that variation in own occupation by sex explains more than half of the association under full independence. Moder A4 fits both the sex by occupation distributions, and the results are similar to those under Model A3. In lines A5 and A6, we measure the net association of S with O and F, respectively; clearly, variations in own occupations with sex, but not those of fathers' occupations with sex, explain much of the association in the three-way classification. This is obviously congruent with our descriptive analyses of observed and adjusted mobility tables.

We treat Model A4, where sex interacts with own and fathers' occupations, as a baseline against which to assess the associations between fathers' and own occupations and sex differences in those associations. Model A7 fits all two-way joint distributions, and, clearly, it cannot be rejected, since χ^2_{LR} is less than its expectation (degrees of freedom). That is, there is no great need to posit different relationships between fathers' and own occupations by sex in order to account for the observed data. However, this result is based on a global test (note $df = 256$), and we consider more specific sex interactions below. Line A8 contrasts Models A7 and A4, demonstrating that the FO interactions account for about three-fourths as much association as the main effect of sex on own occupation (compare line A5), and the FO interactions explain fully 93% of the association in the baseline model.

In panel B of Table 8.5, we fit models analogous to those of lines A4, A7, and A8, except we exactly fit (block) observations along the main diagonals of the mobility tables. The models in panel B pertain to association off the main diagonals of the tables, that is, not involving occupational inheritance in terms of the 17-category classification. Model B1 (no FO association) can be rejected; there is a great deal of association between fathers' and sons' or daughters' occupations which does not involve the "inheritance" of the father's occupational category. Moreover, as in the full table, a global test detects no sex differences in the FO associations (line B2) away from the main diagonal. Indeed, such sex interactions with mobility could account for no more than 5.6% of the association in the baseline model, whereas FO interactions off the main diagonal and regardless of sex account for 53.9% of the association in the baseline model (line B3).

In Panel C of Table 8.5, we report another parallel analysis in which all of the frequencies within each of five major occupation groups have been fitted exactly. (The groups are upper white collar, lower white collar, upper blue collar, lower blue collar, and farm). In effect, we broaden our definition of occupational inheritance to include anyone who remained within one of the five broad categories. As before, we find substantial associations between fathers' and own occupations outside the major groups, but we do not detect any differences in these associations by sex. While 32.1% of the association in the baseline model occurs outside the five broad groups, at most 4.7% of the association under the baseline model may be associated with sex differences in mobility.

At this point, one might be tempted to reach a strongly negative conclusion about interactions between sex and occupational mobility, perhaps one more in line with that of DeJong, Brawer, and Robin than that of Tyree and Treas. Yet this would be premature. In Panel D of Table 8.5, we undertake a hierarchical decomposition of earlier tests with the hope of locating sex interactions in specific parts of the mobility table. Line D1 contrasts the models of lines B2 and A7. Since the former tests sex interactions in the full table, and the latter tests them off the main diagonal, the contrast in line D1 tests sex differences in occupational inheritance, namely, differences on the main diagonal. While the sex interaction with inheritance accounts for less than half a percent of the association in the baseline model, it also uses only 17 degrees of freedom and is clearly statistically significant at any of the conventional levels. This is consistent with our earlier suggestion that women are more mobile than men. Line D2 reports a parallel contrast between Models C2 and B2, which attempts to detect sex differences in mobility (that is, noninheritance) within the five broad groups. In this case, the test yields negative results.

In one additional test (not reported in Table 8.5), we fitted (blocked) all of the outflows from farm occupations as well as all movements within each of the five broad groups. There were no significant sex interactions outside the five broad groups and the farm outflows, but there were barely significant interactions between sex and mobility out of farm occupations ($\chi^2(32) = 46.08, p = .039$). From Table 8.4 (and a similar table for the ECLF), we believe these interactions represent an accentuation among the sons and daughters of farmers of typical sex differences in the current occupational distribution. Relative to farm sons, farm daughters are especially likely to become salaried professionals, clerks (other than secretaries), retail sales workers, and service workers. These interactions appear to be consistent with the previously cited findings of Tyree and Treas (1974).

To summarize, we believe that we have located small but significant interactions between sex and the process of occupational mobility. Women appear to be more mobile than men, and sex differentials in the occupational distribution appear to be accentuated among the sons and daughters of farmers. At the same time, we think it would be misleading to ignore the preponderant evidence of similarity in the mobility regimes to which married men and women are subjected. Women differ greatly from men in their propensity to be in the labor force and in their occupations, if they are in the labor force. Yet, once these factors are taken into account, more than 90% of the association between the occupations of persons and their fathers may be explained by a mobility regime which does not differ at all between the sexes.

INTERGENERATIONAL MOBILITY BY SEX AND AGE
AND BY SEX AND RACE

In addition to the classification of father's occupation by own occupation by sex, we have also analyzed four-way tables of mobility by sex by age and of mobility by sex by race. Age is represented by five categories (20 to 24, 25 to 34, 35 to 44, 45 to 54, and 55 to 64), while race is a dichotomous variable, black versus nonblack. Our purpose in introducing the factors of age and race is twofold. First, we wish to see whether sex differences in the mobility process are in any way confounded with mobility differences by race or age. For example, we know that occupation distributions vary by age in cross-section and that married women differ substantially from married men in the age pattern of their participation in the labor force. Further, it is conceivable that sex differences in mobility might appear at some ages, but not at other ages; that is, there are four-way interactions among father's occupation, own occupation, sex, and age. Similarly, in the case of race, relatively fewer black men than white men are in the labor force, while relatively more black women than white women are in the labor force, and there may be interactions among mobility, sex, and race. Second, we think that comparison of the interactions between occupational mobility and age or race will help to put our findings about sex and mobility into proper context. That is, we think it is appropriate to assess variations in mobility by sex relative to those by age and race.

Table 8.6 presents our analyses of the table of father's occupation by own 1962 occupation by sex by age. In Model A1, we take as given the observed variations in father's occupation in own occupation by age and sex. Obviously we reject this baseline model, which misclassifies almost 13% of the observations. Model A2 is the same as Model A1, except we fit one set of interactions (or associations) between father's occupation and own occupation which is assumed to be the same over all combinations of age and sex. While the χ^2_{LR} is still very large for this model, it is still much less than its degrees of freedom. Thus, we cannot reject Model A2, which accounts for almost two-thirds of the association in the baseline model (A1). As shown in line A3, the improvement of fit in Model A2 relative to Model A1 is quite substantial and statistically significant. Models A4 and A5 permit the classification of father's occupation by own occupation to vary by age and by sex, respectively, and Model A6 permits variations in mobility both by age and by sex, though not within the joint distribution of age by sex. As we might expect from the results of Model A2, we cannot reject any of Models A4, A5, and A6. The last of these results is particularly impor-

TABLE 8.6

Analyses of Age and Sex Variations in Mobility from Father's Occupation to Own 1962 Occupation: Married, Spouse-Present Men and Women Aged 20 to 64 in the Experienced Civilian Labor Force

Model (null hypothesis)	χ^2_{LR}	df	p	Δ	χ^2_H/χ^2_T
A. Full mobility matrix (17 X 17)					
1. [OAS][FAS]	4323.08	2560	.000	12.98	100.0
2. [OAS][FAS][FO]	1494.45	2304	>0.5	6.31	34.6
3. A2 vs. A1	2828.63	256	.000	6.67	65.4
4. [OAS][FAS][FOA]	677.36	1280	>0.5	3.27	15.7
5. [OAS][FAS][FOS]	1270.48	2048	>0.5	5.87	29.4
6. [OAS][FAS][FOA][FOS]	459.56	1024	>0.5	2.59	10.6
7. A6 vs. A4	217.80	256	>0.5	0.68	5.0
8. A6 vs. A5	810.92	1024	>0.5	3.28	18.8
B. Main diagonal blocked					
1. [OAS][FAS]	3015.24	2390	.000	9.98	69.7
2. [OAS][FAS][FO]	1355.70	2151	>0.5	5.73	31.4
3. B2 vs. B1	1659.54	239	.000	4.25	38.4
4. [OAS][FAS][FOA]	598.22	1195	>0.5	2.93	13.8
5. [OAS][FAS][FOS]	1174.97	1912	>0.5	5.35	27.2
6. [OHS][FAS][FOA][FOS]	420.28	956	>0.5	2.33	9.7
7. B6 vs. B4	177.94	239	>0.5	0.60	4.1
8. B6 vs. B5	754.69	956	>0.5	3.02	17.5
C. Five major groups blocked					
1. [OAS][FAS]	2068.83	1950	.029	7.16	47.9
2. [OAS][FAS][FO]	1090.05	1755	>0.5	4.54	25.2
3. B2 vs. B1	978.78	195	.000	2.62	22.6
4. [OAS][FAS][FOA]	477.63	975	>0.5	2.36	11.0
5. [OAS][FAS][FOS]	941.15	1560	>0.5	4.19	21.8
6. [OAS][FAS][FOS][FOS]	330.51	780	>0.5	1.80	7.6
7. C6 vs. C4	147.12	195	>0.5	0.56	3.4
8. C6 vs. C5	610.64	780	>0.5	2.39	14.1
D. Hierarchical decompositions					
1. B7 vs. A7	39.86	17	.000	0.08	0.9
2. C7 vs. B7	30.82	44	>0.5	0.04	0.7
3. B8 vs. A8	56.23	68	>0.5	0.26	1.3
4. C8 vs. B8	144.05	176	>0.5	0.63	3.4
5. B6 vs. A6	39.28	68	>0.5	0.26	0.9
6. C6 vs. B6	89.77	176	>0.5	0.53	2.1

NOTE: F = father's occupation, O = own occupation, A = age, S = sex.

tant, since it says that there are no four-way interactions among the factors in the classification. That is, at least at the global level, there is no age variation in sex differences in mobility. Models A4, A5, and A6 are most important in permitting us to test for three-way interactions among father's occupation, own occupation, and age and among father's occupation, own occupation, and sex. We do this by constrasting Model A6 with Models A4 and A5, respectively, as reported in lines A7 and A8. In both of these cases, the χ^2_{LR} values are smaller than their expected values under the null hypothesis, and we are unable to detect any sex or age differences in mobility at the global level. Given our earlier results with regard to sex and mobility and the findings of Chapter 6 on age and time variations in mobility, this should come as no surprise.

Panels B and C of Table 8.6 report analyses which parallel those in Panel A, except the analyses in Panel B are restricted to off-diagonal entries in the mobility tables, and those in Panel C are restricted to entries lying outside the five major occupation groups. The results in Panels B and C are similar to one another and to those already reported in Panel A. That is, a model which explains association between father's and own occupations must be rejected, but there is no need to posit changes in the father's-occupation–own-occupation relationships across categories of age, of sex, or of the joint distribution of age and sex in order to obtain a satisfactory fit of the observed data.

In Panel D of Table 8.6, we report several contrasts among models in Panels A, B, and C which might help us to test interactions between sex or age and the mobility process. Line D1 contrasts Models B7 and A7. Since Model A7 measures the extent of variation in mobility processes by sex in the full matrix and Model B7 measures the extent of variation in mobility processes by sex off the main diagonal, the contrast between them tells us whether there are variations in the extent of occupational inheritance by sex. As in the case of the analyses in Table 8.5, this contrast accounts for a small but statistically significant component of association. Controlling variations in occupation of fathers and married persons by age and sex, and also controlling variations in occupational inheritance by age, there are still some differences between the sexes in the extent of occupational inheritance. This result is more impressive when we realize that there are no similar variations in occupational inheritance by age (see line D3 of Table 8.6). At the same time, as shown in lines D2 and D4 of the table, there are no statistically significant variations in the mobility process by sex or by age within each of the five major occupational groups. Finally, we partition the four-way interactions among father's occupation, own occupation, sex, and age into components involving occupational inheritance (line D5) and movement outside of the father's occupation but within the same major group (line D6). Here, too, there are no statistically significant four-way interactions. Thus, while we are still impressed with the homogeneity of the mobility process across age and sex groups, the previously noted sex difference in occupational inheritance stands up under controls for age and its possible interactions with the mobility process.

Table 8.7 reports parallel analyses of the classification of father's occupation by own occupation by sex by race, and the results are very similar to those reported above in the case of age. Once the variations in father's occupation and in own occupation by race and sex are taken into account, a common set of relationships between categories of father's occupation and of own occupation is sufficient to fit the data rather well. Indeed, such a set of interactions, which are invariant with respect to race and sex, accounts for almost 85% of the association in the baseline model. As before, a sex differential in occupational inheritance does appear, but elsewhere, the mobility process appears to be homogeneous with regard to sex. Last, there do not appear to be any variations in the mobility process with race or among combinations of race and sex.

DISCUSSION

With but one exception, the intergenerational occupational mobility process appears to be homogeneous with respect to sex, age, and race. One may reasonably ask whether this apparent homogeneity is not an artifact. Have we used such a detailed occupational classification that observations are too sparse for us to detect statistically significant interactions? We think not. Except in the fine age classification, we do fit the data rather well, in other words, without a lot of noise. Moreover, we have reported on a rather detailed mobility classification because of the several suggestions in the literature that one cannot properly assess sexual differences in occupations or in mobility using broad occupational groups; however, we have replicated virtually all of the present analyses using a 12-category occupational classification, and our conclusions are the same. We still find sex differences in occupational inheritance, but not in occupational mobility, and we find the mobility process to be homogeneous with regard to age and race.

Our finding of racial homogeneity in the mobility process is particularly striking because racial differences in relationships among status

TABLE 8.7

Analyses of Race and Sex Variations in Mobility from Father's Occupation to Own 1962 Occupation: Married, Spouse-Present Men and Women Aged 20 to 64 in the Experienced Civilian Labor Force

Model (null hypothesis)	χ^2_{LR}	df	p	Δ	χ^2_H/χ^2_T
A. Full mobility matrix (17 X 17)					
1. [ORS][FRS]	3205.47	1024	.000	10.94	100.0
2. [ORS][FRS][FO]	504.66	768	>0.5	2.72	15.7
3. A2 vs. A1	2700.81	256	.000	8.22	84.3
4. [ORS][FRS][FOR]	283.42	512	>0.5	2.09	8.8
5. [ORS][FRS][FOS]	295.46	512	>0.5	1.45	9.2
6. [ORS][FRS][FOR][FOS]	78.47	256	>0.5	2.29	2.4
7. A6 vs. A4	204.95	256	>0.5	1.53	6.4
8. A6 vs. A5	216.99	256	>0.5	0.89	6.8
B. Main diagonal blocked					
1. [ORS][FRS]	1953.28	956	.000	8.09	60.9
2. [ORS][FRS][FO]	439.13	717	>0.5	2.42	13.7
3. B2 vs. B1	1514.15	239	.000	5.67	47.2
4. [ORS][FRS][FOR]	235.60	478	>0.5	1.84	7.3
5. [ORS][FRS][FOS]	273.16	478	>0.5	1.33	8.5
6. [ORS][FRS][FOR][FOS]	72.78	239	>0.5	0.52	2.3
7. B6 vs. B4	162.82	239	>0.5	1.32	5.1
8. B6 vs. B5	200.38	239	>0.5	0.80	6.3
C. Five major groups blocked					
1. [ORS][FRS]	1241.67	780	.000	5.65	38.7
2. [ORS][FRS][FO]	346.02	585	>0.5	1.89	10.8
3. B2 vs. B1	895.65	195	.000	3.76	27.9
4. [ORS][FRS][FOR]	197.91	390	>0.5	1.51	6.2
5. [ORS][FRS][FOS]	207.50	390	>0.5	0.99	6.5
6. [ORS][FRS][FOR][FOS]	61.55	195	>0.5	0.44	1.9
7. C6 vs. C4	136.36	195	>0.5	1.07	4.3
8. C6 vs. C5	145.95	195	>0.5	0.55	4.6
D. Hierarchical decompositions					
1. B7 vs. A7	42.13	17	.001	0.21	1.3
2. C7 vs. B7	26.46	44	>0.5	0.25	0.8
3. B8 vs. A8	16.61	17	>0.5	0.09	0.5
4. C8 vs. B8	54.43	44	.134	0.25	1.7
5. B6 vs. A6	5.69	17	>0.5	1.77	0.2
6. C6 vs. B6	11.23	44	>0.5	0.08	0.4

NOTE: F = father's occupation, O = own occupation, R = race, S = sex .

variables are typically found in studies of social stratification and inequality. The repeated finding is that blacks are subjected to a per-
verse form of equality of opportunity, in which they are less able than
whites to transmit status positions across generations.

In order to describe the extent to which differences in occupational
origins and destinations bring about the differing observed mobility
patterns of blacks and whites, we undertook additional comparisons of
the mobility of black and white men, using a more aggregated 12-
category occupation distribution. As in our initial description of sex
differences in mobility, we first compared the outflow distributions
between black and white mobility tables, and then we compared the
outflow distributions in the observed black mobility table and the
white mobility table adjusted to the marginal distributions of the black
table. Some of the differences are quite striking. For example, consider
the four occupation groups from which black men were most likely to
have come: craftsmen, foremen, and kindred workers; operatives and
kindred workers; farmers and farm managers; and nonfarm laborers. In
these respective groups, the indexes of dissimilarity between outflow
distributions were 39.6, 27.7, 43.4, and 43.8; however, when adjusted
for differences in the marginal distributions of the white and black
men's mobility tables, these differences were reduced to 13.1, 12.3,
4.6, and 17.4, respectively.

As Duncan (1968c: 11) has described the difference between occupational mobility patterns of white and black men: "Negro men who
originated at the lower levels were likely to remain there; white men
were likely to move up. Negro men who originated at the higher levels
were likely to move down; white men were likely to stay there." Our
finding of racial homogeneity in the mobility process adds force to this
observation. If the mobility process itself is homogeneous with regard
to race, it is the differing occupational origins and destinations of
blacks and whites which account for apparent differences in mobility
between the races. Other things being equal, as the occupational
chances of blacks improve, we may expect the gross patterns of occupational mobility among blacks to converge with those among whites.

With respect to sexual differences in intergenerational mobility, the
future of equality of opportunity also depends upon improvements in
the occupational chances, but sexual inequalities may prove to be
more obdurate than strictly racial ones. Analyses of this chapter have
demonstrated that gross mobility patterns which distinguish men from
women and whites from blacks are, in the main, reflections of the
differential occupations into which blacks and women are recruited,
relative to white men. Unlike women, however, black males suffer the

additional disadvantage in mobility of lower social origins, as indexed by the distributions of paternal occupations of the races. Yet, there the similarities of race and sex in occupational stratification end. Whereas the disadvantages of occupational segregation by race are largely socioeconomic, such is not the case for occupational segregation by sex (although there is ample evidence of economic discrimination by sex and by race within occupations). If sexual disadvantages were solely or primarily socioeconomic, we might expect affirmative action in hiring and advancement within business and industry to have a major impact on the current differences in gross intergeneration mobility for the sexes. Instead, women face a more fundamental handicap to their occupational chances in the subtle normative practices of sex socialization and the current institutions of childrearing and homemaking.

Analyses in this and Chapter 4 suggest that the primary (but not exclusive) source of sexual difference in occupational mobility is in the preponderant allocation of women to roles outside the regular labor force, irrespective of a woman's social origins or color. In that sense, the future of sexual equality of opportunity for intergenerational mobility may call for far more fundamental rearrangements of institutional life in the United States than does equality between the races. Irrespective of one's philosophical position on sexual equality, the prospects for redesigning the family seem limited, although putative shifts in sex-role attitudes may augur a more flexible future. Meanwhile, we are impressed by the virtual invariance in the relationship between the occupational origins and destinations of men in this century, once the impacts of changing occupation distributions on mobility are considered (cf. Chapters 6 and 7). While it is incorrect to attribute to family process all of this constancy, surely the role of the family in creating stocks of human capital for social mobility is quite important, if not central, to the connection of social destinations and origins. In view of this evidence, we speculate that the task of altering now normative family processes may be most difficult, especially as an issue of public policy.

9

Situs and Status Dimensions of Occupational Stratification: An Examination of Interindustry and Interoccupational Mobility

SITUS AND STATUS DISTINGUISHED

Students of social mobility have long recognized that the movement of an individual in social space can result from either a horizontal shift in group memberships or in function, or from a vertical shift within a heirarchically ordered dimension (Sorokin, 1959; Benoit-Smullyan, 1944; Morris and Murphy, 1959; Horan, 1972). Benoit-Smullyan (1944) categorizes these patterns of social movement into three types: a horizontal shift in group membership is a *situs* movement, a horizontal shift in function is a shift of *locus*, and a vertical shift along a hierarchically ordered social dimension is classified as a *status* shift. In a somewhat different typology, Sorokin (1959: 7) suggests a two-category classification which combines situs and locus into a single horizontal dimension, retaining the distinction between the horizontal and vertical dimensions.

As with most typologies, the real-world situation is not quite so

This chapter was prepared by Dennis P. Hogan and is based on his 1973 unpublished Master's thesis, "Industrial mobility in the situs effect of industry," written in the Department of Sociology, University of Wisconsin, Madison.

clear-cut. Though it need not necessarily do so, an intermixing of the situs and status dimensions can occur. As Benoit-Smullyan succinctly states: "A distinction between two groups as such is a distinction of situs, but when the members of one group have on the average a higher status than members of another group, situs ascription is connotative of status as well" (1944: 154). Defining occupational situs as "categories of work which are differentiated in some way but are not invidiously compared," Morris and Murphy (1959: 233) have attempted to draw a clearer distinction between the situs and status concepts. They insist that although each situs category may differ in the range of occupations or in the prestige dimension over time, the situses must remain equally valued *as categories* (Morris and Murphy, 1959: 233–234).

This restriction of the situs concept to a situation in which situses are not "connotative of status" is one of limited utility. What empirical evidence is available suggests that the approaches of Sorokin and Benoit-Smullyan, in which situs can be "connotative of status" but need not be, is the more realistic formulation (Hatt, 1950; Reiss, 1961: 97–99; Horan, 1972). It will be this conception of situs as a separate dimension of social space having possible, but not necessary, connections with the status dimension which will be the conceptual basis of this paper.

One early empirical study which documented a situs dimension was that of Hatt (1950). Using Guttman scaling techniques on a 100-case subsample from the data file on which the National Opinion Research Center (NORC) prestige scores are based, Hatt tried to determine whether situs groupings could be identified. The occupational prestige scores in such situs groupings would be more scalable and item-reproducible than a single prestige scale for all occupations, but without reference to any situs distinction (Hatt, 1950: 533–543). Hatt's findings are suggestive of the existence of a horizontal (situs) dimension of stratification within which prestige scores with different means, variances, and ranges were evident. A subsequent test of this hypothesis by Reiss (1961: 97–99) produced equivocal results.

So we are left to consider the implications of a possible, though not certain, situs effect on the occupational prestige scale. Hatt (1950: 542–543) suggests that the theoretical implications of situs effects are potentially quite important: "The difference between inter- and intra-situs mobility is considerable. Inter-situs movement is characterized by increased risk and intra-situs movement by increased security. In addition, there probably are differences between the two with reference to the potential distance which may be moved." He goes on to suggest that these intersitus and intrasitus differences may be important intergenerationally.

Have situs categories been identified? In what ways, if any, do situs categories have influence on a person's occupational status, and how do these situs categories assert this influence? The industry or industrial sector in which one is employed is often equated with a situs. Reiss, for example, suggests: "The U.S. Bureau of Census provides detailed occupation by industry tabulations. . . . These tabulations should be very helpful in determining the distribution of occupations within a situs, since there is considerable overlap between 'situs' and 'industry' definitions" (1961: 45–46, Footnote 10). Horan (1972: 27) claims that situs effects on occupational mobility will be indicated if "there exists a set of discrete groupings of occupations (situses) which are important for mobility in the sense that intergenerational movement between these groupings is more difficult than within them." Blau and Duncan (1967: 37) report precisely this phenomenon when certain major occupation groups are separated by industry and the occupational mobility tables based on the resultant classification examined: "Hence another distinctive pattern to which the tables call attention is that industrial lines constitute stronger barriers to mobility than do skill levels within an industry."

Palmer (1954) reports that differences in mobility of industrial groups is less than that of the occupation groups, though the industry classification is perhaps too broad to display the full extent of mobility patterns. She suggests that the industrial barriers to mobility seem less dependent on the types of goods and services produced by the industry than on the skills and knowledge required for specific *jobs* and on the wages, working conditions, and usual length of job tenure characteristic of an industry. Spilerman (1968, 1969) and Alexander (1970) emphasize the importance of the labor market and tenure characteristics of specific industries, particularly with regard to black employment. Spilerman (1968) also stresses the importance of industry differentials with regard to working conditions, the control of the worker over his work situation, and external rewards. Alexander (1970) focuses on the "firm" or "company" effects indicated by industries. He maintains that technology, size, and organization of complex processes are factors characteristic of the firms within the industries—it being, after all, the firms rather than the industry which make employment-relevant decisions.

Lane (1968) suggests that the city effects on occupational mobility in the "Six City" data (Palmer, 1954) may be attributable to the industrial mix of the cities in 1950. But Mueller (1974), using the 1962 Occupational Changes in a Generation (OCG) data, does not find any consistent city effects for the Standard Metropolitan Statistical Areas (SMSA) he examines. However, he does note industry differences in mean occupational prestige (measured by Duncan's socioeconomic index scores), independent of many basic socioeconomic background factors. (See Chapter 10 of this volume.)

Thus, the existence of the industrial structure has given rise to both speculative and empirical research concerning its relationship to the position one occupies in social space. The available evidence suggests that systematic, nonrandom factors operate to place an individual in a given industry. Furthermore, it appears that one's position on this *horizontal* dimension of the labor market bears a relationship to one's position on the *vertical* (occupational status) dimension. Therefore, there are both theoretical and empirical reasons to expect industrial mobility matrices to display systematic regularities and to expect these industrial associations to play some part in intergenerational and intragenerational occupational mobility. The evidence reviewed here is certainly extensive enough and strong enough to render worthwhile the testing of such an hypothesis.

ANALYTIC STRATEGY AND SUBSAMPLING

In order to facilitate the analysis of industrial mobility and the relation of industrial situs to occupational status, it is useful to deal with a subsample of the 20,700 men in the 1962 OCG survey. Men of farm background (viz., men whose fathers were farmers, farm managers, farm laborers, or farm foremen) or of foreign birth are not included in the analysis of this chapter, since it would be difficult to classify unambiguously the industries of their fathers into the industry categories of interest here—those most germane to the employment characteristics of an urban–industrial society.[1] To ensure a more accurate occupational and industrial classification, those men who are not members of the experienced civilian labor force and all men aged 20–24 (who are at an early point in their work careers) are dropped from analysis. This leaves a sample of 11,330 cases representing the population of native-born American males, aged 25–64, of nonfarm backgrounds and in the experienced civilian labor force.

[1] The 14-category industry distribution on which this analysis is based is shown in Figure 9.1.

This population will be divided into three control groups based on the findings and suggestions of previous researchers who have discerned differential situs effects for certain classes of people. Blacks ($N = 672$) will be considered separately. There is extensive evidence, particularly in Spilerman (1968, 1969) and Alexander (1970), that industrial situs effects do differ substantially by race since many salient industry characteristics (e.g., hiring practices, average length of job tenure) exert a differing impact by race. The nonblacks (hereafter, whites) will be divided into two analytic groups: those of native parentage ($N = 7431$) and those of nonnative (including mixed native–foreign) parentage ($N = 3227$). This is an attempt to index any ethnic effects—ethnics being operationally defined here as second-generation Americans. The distinction of ethnic status is suggested by Reiss (1961: 88). Spilerman (1968: Chapter 1) notes that ethnics tend not only to be occupation-specific, but industry-specific, these industries relating to later occupational mobility.[2]

In order to enable the reader to more readily understand the analysis which follows, we offer a brief overview of the precise research questions to be addressed and of the methods used. Defining situs operationally as industry, we examine separately the mobility matrices for father's industry to son's first industry, father's to son's current industry, and son's first to current industry for each of the three control groups. The examination of the first two mobility matrices aids in determining whether industrial position is transmitted intergenerationally from father to son at either the point of son's first job or at some point in his later career. The first to current industry matrix is pertinent to the intragenerational, or career, transmission of situs.[3] The separate analysis of the mobility tables also allows us to answer questions as to whether the two types of intergenerational mobility differ from each other and/or from the career mobility patterns.

The interest here goes further than just determining whether the associations in the industrial mobility matrices are statistically sig-

[2] It should be observed, however, that the distinction made here actually relates to nativity rather than to ethnicity. The cross-classificatory analysis to be pursued prohibits any separate examination by ethnic subgroups due to inadequate sample size.

[3] Because of the small sample size, no age controls or separate analyses by cohort are attempted. This means that the industry at first job is reported for men of all ages at the time of survey for roughly comparable points in their work careers (i.e., for roughly similar ages and thus at different periods of time), whereas the report of current industry is for an identical period (March 1962) but different points (ages) in the life cycle. The models in this paper thus implicitly assume that the transmission of situs is unaffected by age, period, or cohort.

nificant. Questions as to the importance of the industrial structure (i.e., the margins of the matrices) in the formation of the observed patterns, whether the industrial associations are due solely to "inheritance" (i.e., the tendency of sons to be employed in the same broad industry as their fathers) or include a component of noninherited association, and whether the structure underlying each mobility matrix is linear in nature, will also be answered. The different control groups into which the population has been divided are compared for differentials with regard to each of these issues.

Three major methods will be used to answer these various questions. The mobility matrices will first be characterized as to minimum, expected, and observed mobility, using traditional summary indexes. Applying log-linear models to the matrices, the statistical significance and relative strength of the industrial associations will be ascertained. The relative size of the inheritance and noninheritance components of the total associations will likewise be determined. A series of Chi-square tests for differences in industrial association by nativity and by race are also included as part of this second method. Finally, the techniques of canonical analysis will be applied to the industry matrices. This phase of the analysis is intended to supplement the first two phases by asking whether the associations that are observed can be characterized as linear. Differentials in the emergent linear dimensions will then be characterized and compared with the results of the first two methods.

At this point, the issues raised concerning the existence and characteristics of occupational situses will have been resolved as fully as possible. The final issue to be explicated is the relationship of the situs to the status dimension. Again making use of the log-linear modeling techniques, the association in the four-way occupation by industry matrices for each of the three intertemporal transitions will be partitioned. This partition is intended to accomplish several goals. First, it will establish whether the association between industry at two points in time exists, net of any relationship due to the association of occupations or of industry with occupation. Second, the utility of viewing the social organization of the labor market as composed of separate situs and status dimensions will be demonstrated. Third, the relationship, if any, between the situs and status dimensions will be adduced.

STRUCTURE OF INDUSTRIAL MOBILITY

As described in the overview, the first portion of the analysis concerns the examination of the industrial matrices for each population control group in order to demonstrate the existence of an intertemporal situs dimension, characterize the form of this dimension, and check for differentials in this form by type of transition and/or by control group. As a first step in this analysis, we compute several summary measures for these tables (Table 9.1).[4] These summary measures deal with industrial mobility viewed as a phenomenon characterized by inheritance or noninheritance; noninherited industrial association is not evidenced by these summary measures.

In Table 9.1, patterning of minimum (structural) mobility is of interest since it is indicative of the net changes in the industrial distribution over time. Extensive black mobility is required to effect parity in the industry of father's and son's first industry distributions (32.3%), whereas both white subgroups require about 18% to be mobile. The shifts into the durable manufacturing and retail trade industries and out of the personal service industry is the key factor in these greater shifts among the blacks (Hogan, 1973: 29).

The first-industry-to-1962-industry movement also shows the blacks as experiencing the most minimum mobility (23.6%), with the whites of native parentage experiencing the least structural shifting (12.9%). Among the blacks, movement occurs *out* of the agriculture, forestry, fisheries, retail trade, and personal services and into construction, the professional and related services, and public administration. This indicates some movement back into a distribution like that of the fathers (e.g., the movement out of retail trade). This describes why the least structural shifting of industrial employment among blacks (21.0%) is in the industry-of-father-to-1962-industry movement. For that transition, the whites of foreign parentage display a similar level of structural mobility (20.6%) to the blacks, though it is due to movement out of mining and construction and into public administration and the professional and related services. The whites of native parentage display relatively little (13.0%) structural change (Hogan, 1973: 29).

The levels of mobility observed are roughly similar within each subgroup for the industry-of-father-to-first-industry and first-industry-to-1962-industry transitions. The white subgroups are similar on the levels of observed mobility for these two transitions, ranging from 68.0% to 72.1%. The blacks show consistently greater movement (8–10% more) on these transitions than either of the other groups. In contrast, the industry-of-father-to-1962-industry transition displays considerably more observed mobility for each group than in the other

[4] For illustrative purposes, the three-industry outflow matrices for total population appear in Appendix E. The reader interested in examining the outflow percentage tables for each population subgroup should consult Hogan (1973: Tables 1–12).

TABLE 9.1

Summary of Mobility Between Industry Groups: Experienced Civilian Labor Force, Nonfarm Background, Native-Born, Aged 25-64, March 1962

Type of Mobility and Group	Percent Changing Industry Groups			Mobility Index[d]
	Minimum[a]	Observed[b]	Expected[c]	
Father's Industry to First Industry				
Total	18.44	72.07	89.11	75.89
Nonblacks, native parentage	18.09	72.02	89.39	75.64
Nonblacks, non-native parentage	17.95	70.39	87.91	74.96
Blacks	32.27	80.10	89.59	83.44
Father's Industry to Current Industry				
Total	15.34	78.14	89.53	84.65
Nonblacks, native parentage	12.99	77.99	89.62	84.82
Nonblacks, non-native parentage	20.62	77.51	88.97	83.23
Blacks	20.95	82.40	89.96	89.05
First Industry to Current Industry				
Total	14.39	68.91	88.88	73.19
Nonblacks, native parentage	12.94	67.97	88.92	72.43
Nonblacks, Non-native parentage	16.67	68.95	88.60	72.78
Blacks	23.59	77.32	89.26	81.82

[a] Net mobility; coefficient of dissimilarity comparing row and column marginals.

[b] Percentage off main diagonal.

[c] Percentages off the main diagonal under model of independence of rows and columns.

[d] Mobility Index = $\left(\dfrac{\text{Observed} - \text{Minimum}}{\text{Expected} - \text{Minimum}}\right) \times 100$.

transitions. The blacks again display more movement than the whites, although, in this case, the difference is somewhat less.

The difference between the observed and structural mobility provides a measure of "circulation" mobility. The ratio of this observed circulation mobility to the circulation mobility expected under a model of independence of origin and destination industries provides a mobility index by which the various tables may be compared.[5] For each matrix, the two white groups display quite similar mobility indices. For these groups, the highest mobility indices are found in the industry-of-father-to-1962-industry transition. The index value is slightly higher for the father's-industry-to-first-industry transition than for the first-industry-to-1962-industry move for these white groups, but the differences are not large. The blacks display similar patterning of the mobility index for the three transitions, but in each case the level of the mobility index among the blacks is higher (by 6–9%) than among the whites. The mobility index for blacks in the industry-of-father-to-current-industry transition is extremely high (89.1%), indicating that most of the distance between minimum mobility and the expected mobility is accounted for by the difference between the miminum and the observed mobility.

One way in which to evaluate these summary measures with respect to the importance and prevalence of industrial inheritance is to compare them with corresponding values for occupational inheritance (Hogan, 1973: 31–32). The mobility indices computed over the combined groups (total population) for the comparable occupation and industry transitions are quite similar as are the levels of expected mobility. Some caution is in order in drawing this comparison, since the levels of observed mobility are slightly different and the levels of minimum mobility quite different. (Structural occupational mobility is 8–26 points higher than industrial mobility for the same transition.) Nevertheless, it does seem reasonable to conclude that industrial inheritance in the United States circa 1962 was a real phenomenon characterizing the social mobility of men.

The analysis to this point indicates that, while the levels of inheritance do not differ greatly by nativity among the whites, they do differ importantly by race. The three transitions examined show distinctive patterns for all of the subgroups, with fathers more successfully transmitting their industry to their sons at the time of first job

[5] This index does not provide a basis of comparison that is free of the influences of structural (i.e., marginal distribution) differences. For a discussion of this point, see Chapter 7 of this volume.

than at the later 1962 observation. For each subgroup, the level of immobility observed is about the same for the father-to-first-industry matrix as for the career (viz., first-job-to-current-occupation) matrix.

This discussion of summary measures of the mobility tables is unsatisfactory in several regards. It fails to adequately control for the effects of differences in the industrial structure. Also, only the inheritance of industry and no other type of industrial association is reflected in these summary measures. Besides these problems, no statistical test of the relationship in the industrial tables is provided. To circumvent these deficiencies, the application of the log-linear modeling techniques explicated in recent years by Goodman (1970, 1971, 1972a) is appropriate. (For a related application of log-linear models, see Chapter 6 of this volume.)

The association in each matrix that is independent of variations in the marginal distributions is presented in Table 9.2.[6] The Chi-square statistic and its level of significance for the association in the complete table is shown in the columns labeled "Including Industrial Inheritance." This total association for each industry matrix is then partitioned into components due to (1) industrial inheritance, and (2) excluding industrial inheritance. We partition by blocking the main diagonal, and we compute the Chi-square statistic for a matrix which is reduced in size through the exclusion of the blocked cells. This yields a test statistic for the association in each table that is independent of the margins and excludes the effects of industrial inheritance. It is thus a test of significance for noninherited industrial association. By comparing the association in the tables with and without the inclusion of industrial inheritance (comparing the Chi-square for the complete table with the Chi-square for the table with the main diagonal blocked), the relative strength of the association due to strict inheritance and to noninherited industrial association can be readily evaluated. Table 9.2 also presents the index of dissimilarity (Δ) between observed and expected cell frequencies for each fitted model, permitting a comparison between population groups. This index may be interpreted as the percentage of cases misallocated by the model being evaluated.

From Table 9.2, we see that the total association (the association including industrial inheritance) for each matrix is quite significant for

---

[6] For all log-linear models presented in this paper, the sample cases have been weighted to reflect true population proportions. The likelihood-ratio Chi-square values presented are adjusted to reflect deviations from simple random sampling. For the models presented in Tables 9.2–9.3, a value of .01 was added to each cell of each matrix.

TABLE 9.2

Chi-Square Test of Association for Each Industrial Mobility Matrix[a] by Population Group, With and Without the Inclusion of Industrial Inheritance

Type of Mobility and Group	Including Industrial Inheritance			Excluding Industrial Inheritance			Association Due to Inheritance			
	X^2_{LR}	p (169 df)	Δ[b]	X^2_{LR}	p (155 df)	Δ	X^2_{LR}	p (14 df)	Δ	X^2_H/X^2_T
Father's Industry to First Industry										
Total	2080.0	.000	20.0	258.6	.000	5.7	1821.4	.000	14.3	87.6
Nonblacks, native parentage	1420.1	.000	20.4	212.4	.001	6.2	1207.7	.000	14.2	85.0
Nonblacks, non-native parentage	762.2	.000	23.4	213.2	.001	10.3	549.0	.000	13.1	72.0
Blacks	219.3	.003	26.5	141.5	>.5	18.6	77.8	.000	7.9	35.5
Father's Industry to Current Industry										
Total	1117.0	.000	14.9	196.9	.009	6.5	920.1	.000	8.4	82.4
Nonblacks, native parentage	769.3	.000	15.0	204.8	.002	6.9	564.5	.000	8.1	73.4
Nonblacks, non-native parentage	458.1	.000	17.6	194.1	.013	9.5	264.0	.000	8.1	57.6
Blacks	202.7	.033	25.2	160.4	.380	20.3	42.3	.000	4.9	20.9
First Industry to Current Industry										
Total	2994.3	.000	22.5	388.6	.000	6.8	2605.7	.000	15.7	87.0
Nonblacks, native parentage	2110.8	.000	23.9	298.0	.000	7.1	1812.8	.000	16.8	85.9
Nonblacks, non-native parentage	984.2	.000	24.8	267.0	.000	9.7	717.2	.000	15.1	72.9
Blacks	277.7	.000	26.1	170.1	.196	18.1	107.6	.000	8.0	38.7

[a] The null hypothesis tested by each model is that of no association between origin and destination industry other than that due to marginal variations.

[b] Index of dissimilarity.

the two white groups, with less than one chance in a thousand of being an artifact of sampling. For the blacks, the association between industries net of any structural effects is also significant, but more marginally so (especially for the father to current matrix). The partition of this total association into components attributable to inheritance and to noninherited association is also of interest. For the whites, both components of the total association are significant, but the major component is clearly industrial inheritance. A relatively small number of cases (6.2% to 10.3%) is misclassified by a model in which the main diagonal is blocked.

For the blacks, the picture is quite different. The association due to inheritance is the only significant component of the total association; it is quite possible that the noninherited association observed for each black matrix is an artifact of sampling. This is especially problematic since the inheritance component accounts for such a small proportion (between 20.9% and 38.7%) of the total association. The model with this inheritance component blocked is clearly not satisfactory in that between 18.1% and 20.3% of the blacks are misallocated in each matrix. Yet, this misallocation could be an artifact of sampling, as the small black sample ($N = 672$) renders a conclusive interpretation impossible.

Comparing the indexes of dissimilarity for the different population groups on the tables of total association, the whites of native parentage consistently form the lower extreme and blacks the upper. The dissimilarity index value of the whites of foreign parentage falls between these groups, but it is invariably closer to the other whites. This pattern is more pronounced in the model with inheritance blocked. A racial distinction certainly seems to be the crucial one when comparing the relative importance of the components of the partition between the different population groups. The relative absence of inheritance among the blacks is really not surprising, however, in light of the earlier discussion of inheritance based on the data in Table 9.1. The problem is that the sizable racial differences in partitioning total association observed here may be due to sampling variability among the blacks. This possibility is further explored in Table 9.3.

Table 9.3 tests for racial and for nativity differences in industrial association overall and in the components of such association involving inheritance and noninheritance. In these models, the whites of native parentage are used as the standard for comparison. The whites of foreign parentage are contrasted with this standard population to test for interactions of nativity with industrial association. This comparison

TABLE 9.3

A Chi-Square Test for Differences in Industrial Association by Nativity and by Race for Each Industrial Mobility Matrix

Type of Mobility

Comparison Groups and Partition of Association	Father to First				Father to Current				First to Current			
	χ^2_{LR}	df	p	χ^2_H/χ^2_T	χ^2_{LR}	df	p	χ^2_H/χ^2_T	χ^2_{LR}	df	p	χ^2_H/χ^2_T
A. Nonblacks, native parentage and nonblacks, non-native parentage												
Marginal variation (Baseline model)	2349.6	364	.000	100.0	1395.9	364	.000	100.0	3202.3	364	.000	100.0
Association of industry margins with nativity	167.4	26	.000	7.1	168.5	26	.000	12.1	107.3	26	.000	3.4
Association of industries	2015.4	169	.000	85.8	1075.3	169	.000	77.0	2880.9	169	.000	89.9
Interaction of industrial association with nativity	166.8	169	> .5	7.1	152.1	169	> .5	10.9	214.1	169	.007	6.7
Due to difference in inheritance	7.3	14	> .5	0.3	19.0	14	.172	1.4	17.2	14	.273	0.6
Due to difference in non-inheritance	159.5	155	.399	6.8	133.1	155	> .5	9.5	196.9	155	.009	6.1
B. Nonblacks, native parentage and blacks												
Marginal variation (Baseline model)	1935.4	364	.000	100.0	1165.3	364	.000	100.0	2587.0	364	.000	100.0
Association of industry margins with race	296.0	26	.000	15.3	193.2	26	.000	16.6	198.5	26	.000	7.7
Association of industries	1455.3	169	.000	75.2	796.3	169	.000	68.3	2206.9	169	.000	85.3
Interaction of industrial association with race	184.1	169	.206	9.5	175.8	169	.356	15.1	181.6	169	.247	7.0
Due to difference in inheritance	28.6	14	.011	1.5	13.6	14	> .5	1.2	23.7	14	.050	0.9
Due to difference in non-inheritance	155.5	155	.488	8.0	162.2	155	.341	13.9	157.9	155	.435	6.1

produces only one statistically significant interaction—the noninheritance component of the career matrix. In any case, the percentage of the total association due to such interaction is relatively minor; for each matrix, the association of industries accounts for the major portion of the total association. The marginal variation of industry by nativity status is a relatively small component of the total association except for the father to current matrix (where it accounts for 12.1% of the baseline Chi-square).

For the racial comparison, the association of industries is again the major component of the total association, although, for the intergenerational transitions, it accounts for about 10% less of the baseline Chi-square than was the case for the nativity comparisons. This is partly due to the greater importance of racial differences in the industry margins and partly to a somewhat larger interaction component. These racial interactions are barely significant for only two contrasts—the father to first and career matrices inheritance component. This is somewhat at variance with the sizable interactions one might have expected on the basis of Table 9.2, where it appears that the inheritance component of the association is much larger for the whites than for the blacks. The earlier suggestion that the observed differences could be a result of sampling variability is confirmed. That significant interactions were found at all is probably surprising, given the small black sample.

In summary, the log-linear analysis has provided us with a good deal of information concerning the situs dimension. Industrial mobility associations are statistically significant and independent of the influences of variation in industrial structure. This association of industries arises from both an inheritance and a noninheritance component. For every transition and for every group, there is a statistically significant and prevalent inheritance of industry. For both white groups, there is also a statistically significant noninherited component of somewhat lesser prevalence. Thus, a white male entering the labor force can realistically expect the industry he enters to depend on the industry of his father. He can expect his industry at a later point in his career to depend on his own industry at time of entry into the labor force as well as on the industry of his father. The major way in which this dependence is manifested is through a greater likelihood of direct inheritance. This characterization is true for all whites regardless of the parental nativity.

For blacks, the conclusions to be drawn are somewhat less clear-cut. The inheritance component is statistically significant for each transition. But inheritance appears less prevalent for blacks than for whites.

Conversely, the noninherited component is somewhat more pronounced for the blacks, but it is not significant statistically. Tables 9.1 and 9.2 thus suggest a substantial racial difference in the industrial situs dimension, whereas Table 9.3 discounts such a differential. It seems safest to remark that sizable differences may in fact occur between the races, but the small black sample confounds the separation of such real differences from differences that are an artifact of sampling.

Additional evidence on these same points regarding the structure of industrial situses, comes from an examination of the major *linear* dimensions underlying the total association in each interindustry table. Whereas the previous analysis dealt with general questions of association in the structure of the different matrices and looked for differentials in the overall association, the analysis to follow deals with the more specific question of the linear structures of the mobility matrices and differentials in the linear structures by ethnic subpopulation and by transition. These issues are most readily approached by the application of the techniques of canonical analysis.[7]

In canonical analysis, no assumptions are made concerning either the structure of association in the table or the ordering of the row and column categories. Such a structure is allowed to emerge in the unique solution which provides the maximum linear correlation between the row and column variables (Duncan-Jones, 1972: 195). This technique has been used with considerable success by other researchers interested in the analysis of occupational mobility tables (Klatzky and Hodge, 1971; also see Chapters 1 and 7 of this volume).

Two orthogonal dimensions of substantive size were extracted by the canonical technique for each interindustry mobility matrix. The canonical correlations among the derived industry variates in both dimensions are arrayed in Table 9.8, and they reflect the canonical weights assigned to individuals in their respective origin and destination industry categories (see Tables 9.4–9.7). A comparison of these correlations among the first canonical variates indicates that the maximum correlation for the industry-of-father-to-1962-industry table is consistently smaller for each of the groups than is that for their other moves. Looking at the differences among the groups within each tran-

---

[7] These same questions could be answered through further elaboration of the earlier log-linear analysis. A canonical analytic strategy was chosen instead in order to provide evidence on the situs structure from a variety of methods. For a discussion of the advantages of the use of multiple methods, specifically on the use of both log-linear and canonical methods, see Campbell and Evers (1974).

TABLE 9.4

Canonical Weights on First and Second Variates of 14 Industry Categories, Based on Intergenerational and Intragenerational Mobility Matrices, Nonblacks of Native Parentage

Industry	First Variate						Second Variate					
	Father's Industry		First Industry		Current Industry		Father's Industry		First Industry		Current Industry	
	A[a]	B	C	D	E	F	A	B	C	D	E	F
Agriculture, forestry and fisheries	0.18	-0.19	-0.02	-0.45	-0.55	-0.51	0.11	0.21	0.03	1.04	-0.16	1.48
Mining	-4.39	-4.08	-6.03	-0.22	-6.56	-0.28	0.12	1.42	0.25	2.64	2.59	3.12
Construction	0.08	-0.06	-0.04	0.02	-0.26	-0.24	-0.26	-1.42	-0.53	0.96	-1.64	0.90
Manufacturing, durable goods	0.22	-0.38	0.16	-0.32	-0.39	-0.43	-2.07	-1.11	-1.79	0.65	-1.03	0.67
Manufacturing, non-durable goods	0.32	0.35	0.19	-0.33	0.35	-0.36	0.94	-0.40	0.82	-0.30	-0.09	-0.31
Transportation, communication, other public utilities	0.28	0.19	0.15	-0.32	0.03	-0.40	0.01	-0.07	0.16	0.00	0.07	0.05
Wholesale trade	0.25	0.66	0.33	-0.04	0.54	-0.27	1.18	0.80	0.93	-0.73	0.70	-0.84
Retail trade	0.27	0.42	0.13	-0.33	0.16	-0.52	0.77	1.06	0.56	-0.68	0.51	-0.55
Finance, insurance, and real estate	0.35	0.92	0.44	0.39	0.80	0.19	1.22	2.19	1.36	-3.40	2.18	-3.26
Business and repair services	0.09	-0.51	0.08	-0.30	-0.21	-0.35	0.47	-0.14	0.52	0.06	-0.55	0.06
Personal services	0.08	0.38	0.28	-0.15	0.65	-0.42	0.26	0.31	0.46	-0.66	0.22	-0.29
Entertainment and recreation services	-0.01	0.63	0.43	-0.63	0.82	-0.05	0.07	-0.71	1.60	-0.51	-0.64	0.06
Professional and related services	0.29	0.81	0.32	3.92	0.76	3.01	0.36	1.16	0.40	0.37	1.03	0.31
Public administration	0.22	0.59	0.17	0.43	0.40	0.12	0.13	0.40	0.08	-1.48	0.66	-0.91

[a]Column: From:
A   Father to first matrix
B   Father to current matrix
C   Father to first matrix

Column: From:
D   First to current matrix
E   Father to current matrix
F   First to current matrix

TABLE 9.5

Canonical Weights on First and Second Variates of 14 Industry Categories, Based on Intergenerational and Intragenerational Mobility Matrices, Nonblacks of Non-native Parentage

Industry	First Variate						Second Variate					
	Father's Industry		First Industry		Current Industry		Father's Industry		First Industry		Current Industry	
	A[a]	B	C	D	E	F	A	B	C	D	E	F
Agriculture, forestry and fisheries	0.28	0.74	0.16	-0.72	0.19	-0.80	1.48	0.20	0.59	0.20	0.37	0.29
Mining	-3.99	-2.47	-5.77	-0.45	-5.54	-0.82	0.19	2.98	0.49	5.36	7.23	8.56
Construction	0.34	0.39	0.31	-0.16	0.51	-0.33	-0.04	-0.41	0.17	0.65	0.18	0.69
Manufacturing, durable goods	0.10	-1.24	-0.05	-0.44	-1.24	-0.51	-1.49	-0.97	-1.36	0.37	-0.67	0.37
Manufacturing, non-durable goods	0.34	-0.14	0.27	-0.21	-0.28	-0.30	-0.81	-0.58	-0.84	-0.57	-0.68	-0.62
Transportation, communication, other public utilities	0.15	0.42	0.04	-0.07	0.25	-0.37	0.50	0.34	0.45	-0.15	0.49	-0.18
Wholesale trade	0.39	0.26	0.27	-0.33	0.10	-0.10	2.01	-0.38	1.55	-0.83	-0.22	-0.38
Retail trade	0.27	0.88	0.16	-0.16	0.57	-0.29	1.11	0.19	0.63	-0.38	0.28	-0.26
Finance, insurance, and real estate	0.39	0.96	0.45	0.65	1.42	0.23	1.37	-0.07	0.45	-0.92	-0.04	-0.78
Business and repair services	0.26	0.11	0.06	-0.36	0.16	-0.15	0.75	-0.78	1.19	-0.25	-0.57	-0.34
Personal services	0.14	1.29	0.08	-0.57	1.06	-0.44	0.38	1.52	0.08	-0.64	1.52	-1.10
Entertainment and recreation services	0.48	2.12	0.27	0.18	2.63	0.75	0.63	2.37	0.73	-0.24	3.48	-1.02
Professional and related services	0.42	0.80	0.38	4.11	0.36	3.29	1.50	-0.07	1.86	0.37	-0.18	0.37
Public administration	0.35	0.16	0.49	1.11	0.25	0.11	-0.10	-0.38	0.92	-0.21	-0.22	-0.14

[a]Column: From:
A   Father to first matrix
B   Father to current matrix
C   Father to first matrix

Column: From:
D   First to current matrix
E   Father to current matrix
F   First to current matrix

233

TABLE 9.6

Canonical Weights on First and Second Variates on 14 Industry Categories, Based on Intergenerational and Intragenerational Mobility Matrices, Blacks

Industry	First Variate						Second Variate					
	Father's Industry		First Industry		Current Industry		Father's Industry		First Industry		Current Industry	
	A[a]	B	C	D	E	F	A	B	C	D	E	F
Agriculture, forestry and fisheries	0.44	-1.38	0.33	-0.51	0.53	-0.72	2.68	0.05	2.03	2.41	1.46	4.32
Mining	-7.57	-1.65	-7.87	5.60	-1.28	7.80	0.71	3.73	1.11	0.48	5.81	0.33
Construction	0.02	1.44	0.10	-0.52	1.77	-0.42	-0.80	-0.29	-1.00	-0.31	0.56	-0.28
Manufacturing, durable goods	0.15	-0.99	0.09	0.37	-0.74	0.15	-0.36	-0.37	-0.81	-0.21	0.22	0.29
Manufacturing, non-durable goods	0.37	-0.12	0.34	-0.11	0.17	0.61	2.09	1.87	1.74	-0.32	0.03	-0.29
Transportation, communication, other public utilities	0.06	-0.35	-0.10	0.10	-0.19	-0.27	0.35	-0.36	-0.14	0.90	-0.27	0.47
Wholesale trade	0.21	-0.37	0.11	-0.12	-0.96	-0.50	-0.44	-0.69	0.27	-0.27	0.55	-0.35
Retail trade	-0.17	0.50	0.21	-0.30	-1.07	-0.42	0.14	0.89	0.04	-0.42	-0.09	0.17
Finance, insurance, and real estate	0.18	1.75	0.10	-1.24	1.75	-0.63	-1.19	-0.54	0.85	-6.04	-0.34	-2.54
Business and repair services	0.16	-1.35	0.34	6.71	-0.62	1.07	-0.85	-0.68	2.32	0.19	-0.98	0.21
Personal services	0.21	-0.46	0.05	-0.14	-0.80	-0.11	-0.34	-0.23	-0.80	-0.20	-0.31	0.65
Entertainment and recreation services	0.14	-1.92	0.18	-0.46	-0.61	-0.64	-1.95	0.62	1.08	-0.67	-0.72	0.00
Professional and related services	0.01	0.16	-0.98	-0.24	-0.27	-0.29	-1.32	-1.86	-1.54	-1.93	-1.84	-1.59
Public administration	0.23	2.78	0.22	-0.52	0.96	-0.22	-0.22	0.70	-0.03	-1.43	-0.77	-0.94

Column: From:
A Father to first matrix
B Father to current matrix
C First to current matrix

Column: From:
D Father to first matrix
E Father to current matrix
F First to current matrix

[a] Column

TABLE 9.7

Canonical Weights on First and Second Variates of 14 Industry Categories, Based on Intergenerational and Intragenerational Mobility Matrices, Total Population

Industry	First Variate						Second Variate					
	Father's Industry		First Industry		Current Industry		Father's Industry		First Industry		Current Industry	
	A[a]	B	C	D	E	F	A	B	C	D	E	F
Agriculture, forestry and fisheries	0.25	0.07	0.08	-0.58	-0.34	-0.67	1.61	1.55	0.70	1.09	0.41	1.59
Mining	-4.36	-4.03	-6.06	-0.29	-7.00	-0.40	0.08	1.60	0.26	3.83	2.99	4.82
Construction	0.19	0.33	0.09	0.00	0.23	-0.27	0.24	0.10	0.24	0.84	0.29	0.77
Manufacturing, durable goods	0.18	-0.52	0.08	-0.32	-0.57	-0.43	-2.07	-1.90	-1.81	0.65	-1.65	0.69
Manufacturing, non-durable goods	0.33	0.05	0.22	-0.29	0.09	-0.34	-0.21	-0.38	-0.22	-0.43	-0.28	-0.46
Transportation, communication, other public utilities	0.22	0.23	0.10	-0.28	0.04	-0.39	0.32	0.37	0.48	0.05	0.52	0.09
Wholesale trade	0.27	0.50	0.30	-0.16	0.36	-0.23	1.13	0.33	1.14	-0.87	0.74	-0.78
Retail trade	0.25	0.53	0.15	-0.26	0.25	-0.41	0.91	0.97	0.66	-0.77	0.76	-0.76
Finance, insurance, and real estate	0.32	0.92	0.43	-0.32	1.03	0.16	1.08	1.54	1.03	-2.39	1.44	-2.24
Business and repair services	0.15	-0.35	0.07	-0.30	-0.09	-0.26	0.84	-0.14	1.05	-0.04	-0.82	-0.09
Personal services	0.14	0.42	0.22	-0.29	0.47	-0.44	0.33	0.00	0.18	-0.85	0.38	-0.76
Entertainment and recreation services	0.10	0.90	0.35	-0.28	0.88	0.19	0.35	0.40	1.17	-0.44	0.17	-1.31
Professional and related services	0.27	0.74	0.27	4.07	0.65	3.14	0.59	0.18	0.81	0.35	0.32	0.30
Public administration	0.23	0.60	0.28	0.59	0.41	0.12	0.40	0.37	0.60	-0.96	0.44	-0.57

[a]Column: From:
A   Father to first matrix
B   Father to current matrix
C   Father to first matrix

Column: From:
D   First to current matrix
E   Father to current matrix
F   First to current matrix

TABLE 9.8

Canonical Correlations[a] Among Industry Variates for Three Mobility Matrices, by Population Group

	Groups			
Type of Mobility	Nonblack, Native Parentage	Nonblack, Non-Native Parentage	Black	Total
(A) First Canonical Correlation				
Father's industry to first industry	.4679	.5660	.6346	.5012
Father's industry to current industry	.2618	.3042	.3872	.2596
First industry to current industry	.4991	.4651	.5097	.4788
(B) Second Canonical Correlation				
Father's industry to first industry	.2809	.3222	.4175	.2697
Father's industry to current industry	.2028	.2670	.3490	.2028
First industry to current industry	.3413	.3699	.4214	.3339

SOURCE: Tables 9.4 - 9.7.

[a]The canonical correlations shown here are maximum likelihood estimates (Kendall and Stuart, 1967:568-75).

236

sition reveals a clear pattern. The blacks consistently have the highest correlations. The whites of native parentage have the least predictable relationship, while those of foreign parentage are at intermediate levels (with a single exception for the career transition). Similar comments apply to the correlations between the second canonical variates. These linear relationships are similar to those observed for the index of dissimilarity of the log-linear models in Table 9.2.

Rather than describe the actual weights assigned to each industry variate and attempt to discern any patterns therein, we analyze the product–moment correlations among the canonical weights of each variate as summary measures of the regularities, if any.[8] In Table 9.9, the comparison of the correlations of the variates for the same transition (e.g., correlation among weights in the father's occupation and the son's current occupation variates in the father-to-current transition—r_{BE} in Table 9.9) indicates the degree of stability in the weighting of the industry categories over the period of the transition. For the two white groups and for the total population, the magnitude of these correlations is quite high (.95 to 1.00 for the first variates and .83 to .99 for the second variates), indicating extreme intertemporal stability. The stability for the blacks is somewhat less, ranging from .70 to .99 for the first and from .56 to .84 for the second variates.

The comparison of the correlation of variates between industry categories of different transitions (e.g., correlation among weights in father's occupation in the father-to-first-job and father-to-current transitions—r_{AB} in Table 9.9) indicates the degree of similarity of structure of the different mobility matrices of each population group. For the two white groups, the correlations of the first variates are high for the intergenerational transitions (.74 to .99) but are not so large for the second variates (virtually nil for those of foreign parentage and between .41 and .62 for those with native-born parents). For blacks, no intergenerational regularities occur for either the first or the second variates, the highest correlation attained between the variates of different transitions reaching only .45. The weights of the intragenerational variates do not correlate highly in a regular fashion with those of the intergenerational transitions for any of the population groups for either the first or second variates. Substantively then, these correlations demonstrate that the only sizable regularity between the

---

[8]All of the correlations presented are those obtained by assigning unit population weights to the industries. These correlations were also calculated, weighting the industries by their proportions in the 1962 total population, but these did not differ in any systematic or sizable fashion from the correlations obtained with unit weights.

TABLE 9.9

Pearsonian Correlations of Industrial Variates Between Industry Variables for the Same and for Different Mobility Matrices, by Population Group

Industry Variable		First Variate						Second Variate					
		A	B	C	D	E	F	A	B	C	D	E	F
		Nonblacks of Native Parentage Below Each Diagonal and Nonblacks of Non-native Parentage Above											
Father's Industry	A[a]	--	.75	1.00	.19	.91	.29	--	.11	.83	-.19	-.01	-.13
	B	.94	--	.74	.21	.95	.36	.62	--	.11	.58	.93	.54
First Industry	C	.99	.96	--	.20	.89	.28	.85	.49	--	-.03	.06	.00
	D	.11	.23	.11	--	.18	.95	-.47	-.34	-.49	--	.81	.99
Current Industry	E	.96	.99	.99	.18	--	.32	.49	.93	.41	-.18	--	.79
	F	.10	.24	.11	.98	.19	--	-.47	-.31	-.45	.98	-.13	--
		Blacks Below Each Diagonal and Total Population Above											
Father's Industry	A	--	.94	1.00	.10	.98	.13	--	.78	.90	.25	.45	.19
	B	.30	--	.96	.20	.99	.26	.45	--	.69	.10	.84	.18
First Industry	C	.99	.30	--	.11	.99	.14	.44	.41	--	.29	.44	.28
	D	.60	-.48	.57	--	.16	.97	.56	.24	.20	--	.30	.98
Current Industry	E	.35	.70	.35	-.44	--	.21	.44	.76	.27	.34	--	.39
	F	.97	-.35	.96	.73	-.39	--	.67	.17	.37	.84	.34	--

SOURCE: Tables 9.4 - 9.7.

[a]Column: From:
A   Father to first matrix
B   Father to current matrix
C   Father to first matrix

Column: From:
D   First to current matrix
E   Father to current matrix
F   First to current matrix

structure of the mobility matrices for the white groups is that between the intergenerational matrices (and only for the first variates). For the blacks, no regularity in the structure of the different transition matrices occurs.

Table 9.10 presents the product–moment correlations of the industry variates among the population groups. These correlations will be high whenever the underlying structure of their respective mobility matrices is similar for the different subgroups. The correlations demonstrate that the first variate is essentially the same for the two white groups for each variable in each transition (ranging from .80 to 1.00). The father-to-first and career matrices for these two groups on the second variate are moderately high (.50 to .74), while those for the father-to-current matrix are quite low. In contrast, the only similarity in structure between the blacks and either of the other groups is the first variate of the father-to-first matrix. Essentially then, the two white subgroups do not differ from each other in the major structures underlying their respective industrial mobility matrices. The important differences are between racial groups.

To this point, we have established the credibility of substantial and significant associations between the industry of father and industry of son and between a man's first and later industry. These associations were due largely to inheritance, though significant off-diagonal association remains. The structure underlying the association in the industrial matrices is the same for the two intergenerational transitions (for whites) which in turn differ from the structure of the career matrix. Nativity among the whites is virtually meaningless; the racial distinction appears essential, though the small black sample renders this conclusion tentative. The major remaining question is whether this situs (industry) dimension exists independently of the status (occupation) dimension or whether the associations observed here are dependent upon it. It is toward this issue that the final portion of the analysis is directed.

SITUS AND STATUS AS CORRELATED
DIMENSIONS OF MOBILITY

The mobility matrices analyzed above were two-dimensional; it is possible to study intertemporal mobility matrices of four dimensions—origin and destination industry by origin and destination occupation—using the log-linear modeling techniques for multidimensional contingency tables (Goodman, 1970, 1971, 1972a). The

TABLE 9.10

Pearsonian Correlations of Industrial Variates Between U.S. Population Groups

		Population Groups Correlated				
		Nonblacks, Native Parentage With Nonblacks Non-native Parentage	Nonblacks, Native Parentage With Blacks	Nonblacks, Native Parentage With Total Population	Nonblacks, Non-native Parentage With Blacks	Nonblacks, Non-native Parentage With Total Population	Blacks With Total Population
First Variate							
Father's Industry	A[a]	.99	.99	1.00	.99	1.00	1.00
	B	.81	.44	.99	.16	.86	.43
First Industry	C	.99	.98	1.00	.98	1.00	.98
	D	.96	-.15	.98	-.22	.96	-.13
Current Industry	E	.92	.31	.99	.35	.94	.38
	F	.96	-.10	1.00	-.26	.93	-.14
Second Variate							
Father's Industry	A	.67	.05	.78	-.15	.88	.08
	B	.23	.09	.68	.56	.48	.31
First Industry	C	.50	.42	.81	.00	.85	.31
	D	.74	.75	.95	.27	.90	.59
Current Industry	E	.44	.41	.80	.76	.70	.65
	F	.71	.58	.91	.10	.90	.43

SOURCE: Tables 9.4 - 9.7.

[a]Column: From:
A   Father to first matrix
B   Father to current matrix
C   Father to first matrix

Column: From:
D   First to current matrix
E   Father to current matrix
F   First to current matrix

240

goal of the analysis is to find the most elegant model accounting for as much of the total association in the four-way table as can significantly be explained. The unique contribution of each effect parameter included in the final model is the datum of interest. In order to estimate such unique effects without making any a priori assumptions as to which parameters should be included in the model prior to others, the association in each four-way table is partitioned using the forward stepwise procedures cited above (Goodman, 1971). The categorizations of the industry and occupation dimensions used for this analysis are presented in Figures 9.1 and 9.2. Because of the earlier findings indicating the importance of the racial distinction and the unimpor-

Agriculture, forestry, and fisheries
Mining
Construction
Manufacturing, durable goods
Manufacturing, nondurable goods
Transportation, communications, and other public utilities
Wholesale trade
Retail trade
Finance, insurance, and real estate
Business and repair services
Personal services
Entertainment and recreation services
Professional and related services
Public administration

Figure 9.1   Fourteen-category industry distribution.

Professional, technical, and kindred workers
Managers, officials, and proprietors, excluding farm
Sales workers
Clerical and kindred workers
Craftsmen, foremen, and kindred workers
Operatives and kindred workers
Service workers, including private household
Laborers, excluding farm and mine
Farmers, farm managers, laborers and foremen [not included
   in occupation of father dimension]

Figure 9.2   Nine-category occupation distribution.

tance of the nativity distinction, we confine this log-linear analysis to whites. (Sampling error and sample size prohibits analysis of blacks.)

Tables 9.11–9.13 present the partition of association in the four-way table for each transition matrix.[9] Several features of the table merit comment. For each matrix, the same model provides the best fit—that model incorporating the association explained by each possible joint variable pair while excluding each higher-order (three- or four-way) parameter. Furthermore, each variable pair ultimately included in the fitted model enters in the same stepwise order (with a single exception for the father-to-first matrix). The two-way associations always account for about 70% of the association in the table. The associations of industry and occupation at the time of origin and again at time of destination for each matrix account for a considerable proportion of this two-way association. This covariation of industry and occupation, of course, has been widely reported and comes as no surprise (Horan, 1972; Mueller, 1973). What is of greater interest is the fairly substantial association due to origin and destination industry relative to that due to the origin and destination occupation association. This industry association comparison is *net* of the association due to occupation. Finally, a rather minor (though significant) percentage of the association is due to the association of earlier industry with later occupation and earlier occupation with later industry. Apparently, the industry in which one originates has effects not only on the subsequent industrial career, but also on occupation and occupational status as well. Likewise, a man's initial full-time occupation affects both his occupational and industrial career.

SUMMARY AND CONCLUSIONS

This analysis documents the existence of a situs dimension (industry) in the organization of the labor market and in the process of social stratification. Just as intertemporal status (occupation) associations can be observed across generations and within a career, intertemporal situs associations of comparable magnitudes can be identified. This association is largely (though not entirely) due to inheritance, that is, em-

---

[9] In order to expedite the rate of convergence of the iterative fit of the log-linear model, a value of .5 was added to each cell of the matrix. This resulted in a small inflation of the baseline Chi-square value for the intergenerational matrices and a deflation in the value for the career matrix. Since the results of the statistical tests are so clear-cut, it is improbable that this computational procedure is of any substantive importance. The relative percentage of association explained by each parameter is essentially unaffected by the addition of a constant to each cell.

TABLE 9.11

Forward Stepwise Partition of Association of Father to First Industry by Occupation Matrix: Nonblacks

Parameters of Model[a]	χ^2_{LR}	Father to First df	p	χ^2_H/χ^2_T
Total association net of marginal variation	13,411.0	14,070	.000	100.00
Total two-way association	9,300.1	615	.000	69.35
Origin occupation by origin industry	3,200.4	91	.000	23.86
Destination occupation by destination industry	3,590.4	104	.000	26.77
Origin by destination occupation	671.6	56	.000	5.01
Origin by destination industry	1,522.0	169	.000	11.35
Origin occupation by destination industry	144.3	91	.000	1.08
Origin industry by destination occupation	171.4	104	.000	1.28
Total three-way association[b]	2,374.1	3,991	>.5	17.70
Total four-way association	1,736.8	9,464	>.5	12.95

[a]The association due to each parameter is net of all association accounted for by parameters included earlier in the model (all those parameters listed above the one in question).

[b]Each three-way parameter was tested individually for association net of all two-way effects; none was significant.

TABLE 9.12

Forward Stepwise Partition of Association of Father to Current Industry by Occupation Matrix: Nonblacks

Parameters of Model[a]	Father to Current			
	X^2_{LR}	df	P	X^2_H/X^2_T
Total association net of marginal variation	11,663.8	14,070	.000	100.00
Total two-way association	7,910.7	615	.000	67.82
Origin occupation by origin industry	3,325.4	91	.000	28.51
Destination occupation by destination industry	2,751.7	104	.000	23.59
Origin by destination occupation	719.7	56	.000	6.17
Origin by destination industry	834.1	169	.000	7.15
Origin industry by destination occupation	158.6	104	.000	1.36
Origin occupation by destination industry	121.2	91	.013	1.04
Total three-way association[b]	2,102.5	3,991	>.5	18.03
Total four-way association	1,650.6	9,464	>.5	14.15

[a] The association due to each parameter is net of all association accounted for by parameters included earlier in the model (all those parameters listed above the one in question).

[b] Each three-way parameter was tested individually for association net of all two-way effects; none was significant.

244

TABLE 9.13

Forward Stepwise Partition of Association of First to Current Industry by Occupation Matrix: Nonblacks

Parameters of Model[a]	First to Current			
	X^2_{LR}	df	p	X^2_H/X^2_T
Total association net of marginal variation	15,549.3	15,833	.000	100.00
Total two-way association				
Origin occupation by origin industry	10,942.2	649	.000	70.37
Destination occupation by destination industry	4,050.6	104	.000	26.05
Origin by destination occupation	2,947.6	104	.000	18.96
Origin by destination industry	1,568.2	64	.000	10.09
Origin by destination industry	1,922.6	169	.000	12.36
Origin industry by destination occupation	232.0	104	.000	1.49
Origin occupation by destination industry	221.2	104	.000	1.42
Total three-way association[b]	2,756.2	4,368	> .5	17.73
Total four-way association	1,850.9	10,816	> .5	11.90

[a] The association due to each parameter is net of all association accounted for by parameters included earlier in the model (all those parameters listed above the one in question).

[b] Each three-way parameter was tested individually for association net of all two-way effects; none was significant.

245

ployment in roughly the same general industry as father's. The structure of the intergenerational matrices were quite similar (for whites), but that structure differed from the one characterizing the intragenerational matrices. Furthermore, this structure of the industrial situs dimension can be viewed as linear in nature. This is similar to the structure of occupational status, as seen in Chapter 1 of this volume.

The industry associations differ rather little by nativity but substantially by race.[10] The absence of any large nativity differential for the situs structure is similar to the findings of Blau and Duncan (1967: Chapter 6) concerning the occupational structure. Compared to the occupational analysis of Chapter 8 of this volume, the observed differentials by race may be somewhat greater for industry than for occupation. Such an interpretation is supportive of theories reviewed at the beginning of this chapter, which suggested that differential allocation of the races to industrial situses is one mechanism by which inequality of socioeconomic opportunity arises and persists in the social structure.

This situs structure is analytically independent of any status association, so that the situs and status dimensions can be said to be separable, though complementary: The situs and status dimensions characterizing the labor market do intersect. Large associations between concurrent situs and status variables abound; associations between intertemporal situs and status variables are much smaller and less obvious, though still significant. This evidence offers strong confirmation for the soundness of the conceptualization of social space as composed of vertical and horizontal dimensions as proposed by Sorokin and Benoit-Smullyan. Whether these relationships hold within the black male labor force as well as within the white labor force remains problematic.

The explanation of the complex associations of status and situs between generations and within the filial career are important next steps in this line of research. One possible factor which a priori seems likely to account for at least some of the association is community of origin and community of destination (both size and regional location). To the extent that the industrial structure of communities differ and association of origin and destination community occurs, some intertemporal association of industry would be expected. Insofar as a similar process has been observed for occupation (Blau and Duncan, 1967; Chapters 7 and 8 of this volume) and concurrent occupation and industry are

---

[10] This conclusion regarding the racial difference must remain tentative due to the large amounts of possible sampling variability in the small black sample.

associated, at least part of the association of origin industry with later occupation and origin occupation with destination industry would be explicable. Other possible factors accounting for the situs associations could doubtless be suggested but this issue will not be further explored here.

One can also consider the consequence of an individual's situs for other aspects of social behavior. Situs seems likely to be associated with class of worker. Industrial effects (apart from any occupation effects) on unemployment, underemployment, and earnings are probable. Industries may also have consequences for such social psychological variables as job satisfaction, perceived control over job situation and worker alienation. The consequences of industrial position have been the foci of some of the research efforts reviewed in the introduction of this chapter. The fact that current industrial position is not a random event but is to some extent dependent on the industry of one's father and one's own first industry renders this analysis of the consequences of situses even more meaningful sociologically.

10

Socioeconomic Achievements and City Size

Stratification analysts in the Blau and Duncan tradition not only have been interested in identifying additional important determinants of socioeconomic achievements but they also have been concerned with whether the processes of status allocation vary across different subpopulations and different social and ecological contexts. With reference to subpopulation variation, much of the research has focused on racial differences (e.g., Blau and Duncan, 1967: Chapter 6; Duncan, 1968b; Coleman *et al.*, 1972; Blum, 1972; Siegel, 1970). Interest in the effect of different contexts has appeared, for example, in the form of studies on neighborhood (Sewell and Armer, 1966), on school effects (Hauser, 1969, 1971; Alwin, 1974; Duncan, Featherman, and Duncan, 1972), on industrial situs (see Chapter 9 of this volume), and on city effects (Lane, 1968; Mueller, 1974). The research reported in this chapter concerns cities and their effects on the socioeconomic achievements of workers, a research topic which has provided neither conclusive nor consistent results. This inconclusiveness is largely the result of imprecise conceptualization, inadequate data, and inappropriate statistical analysis. This chapter is directed toward remedying some of these inadequacies. Its major objectives are to (*1*) determine if the socioeconomic achievements of occupation and income vary by size of community of residence when other variables known to influence these two outcomes are controlled statistically (additive city effects);

This chapter is based on the 1973 Ph.D. dissertation of Charles W. Mueller, "City effects on socioeconomic achievements," carried out at the Universtiy of Wisconsin, Madison.

(2) determine if the process of socioeconomic achievement, as represented by an extended Blau and Duncan (1967: Chapter 5) model, varies by city size (nonadditive city effects); (3) determine if the effects described above differ for the black and nonblack (white) populations (racial interactions); and (4) determine if there is differential racial discrimination by city size.

THEORY AND PAST RESEARCH

Behind claims of additive and nonadditive city effects is the general premise that a person's socioeconomic achievements are affected not only by individual level variables such as years of schooling or parental income but also by the social and economic context in which the individual lives and works. Past literature has not offered a well-organized explication of how cities of various sizes or functional types affect socioeconomic achievements. Nor has it identified the critical features of cities and residential places for the socioeconomic stratification of persons. Nevertheless, several rationales have been offered which shed some light on underlying factors as well as on expected effects. Our review of these rationales and associated research will consider occupation and income separately, and for each of these, differentiate between additive and nonadditive city effects.

Most of the arguments for additive effects on occupational attainment have centered on the importance of city size. The expectation has been that the mean level of occupational status will increase monotonically with city size. The claim is not that city size per se is responsible for these differences among cities, but that certain city characteristics which vary concomitantly with city size are the causal factors. The characteristics receiving the most attention, either explicitly or implicitly, are economic structure and functional specialization. Duncan and Reiss (1956) argue that because there is greater functional specialization and complexity in the division of labor of larger cities, there will be an associated increase in the white-collar occupations which are responsible for record keeping and coordination. Overall, this and related changes in the industrial and occupational structures result in a greater proportion of higher ranked occupations, and thus, a higher mean level of occupational status in the larger cities. Research does support a near perfect monotonic relationship between city size and occupational status (Schnore and Varley, 1955; Duncan and Reiss, 1956; Schnore, 1963; Blau and Duncan, 1967: Chapter 7). However, these positive correlations are not sufficient proof for the proposition that city contexts have an independent influence on a person's occupational attainment. Instead, we prefer (in accordance with Blau and Duncan, 1967: 249) to interpret differences in mean socioeconomic status as indicators of the differences in occupational opportunities which exist across cities of different size.

In order to determine if size and other city characteristics in themselves have causal consequences for occupational and other socioeconomic achievements, compositional differences among cities must be taken into account. This is necessary, since the stratification literature identifies a variety of individual level variables (which are the compositional variables for the city population aggregate) which are major determinants of occupation and income. Thus, these compositional, or individual-level, differences must be controlled before statistically separable city effects can be estimated, since equilibrating mechanisms tend to match populations and labor force opportunities. For example, selective migration tends to adjust labor supply to labor demand; and the location of business and industry frequently takes advantage of certain labor supply conditions. In short, we expect compositional differences to account for some of the socioeconomic differences which are so consistently observed across the city-size categories. Unfortunately, few data are published which allow for assessing *net* city-size differences, namely, those which remain after compositional factors are controlled. Blau and Duncan (1967: Chapter 7), however, do present data which suggest that the size variation is not entirely accounted for by composition.

The theory which attempts to explain nonadditive city effects on occupation is post hoc. As with additive effects, city size has been the explanatory variable receiving the greatest attention. Two studies have shown that the influence of several of the important determinants of occupational level decreases with an increase in city size. Hochbaum *et al.* (1955) compared zero-order correlations among income, education, and occupational status for a metropolitan community (Minneapolis) and a small nonurban community (Warner's Jonesville). When they found lower correlations among these variables for Minneapolis, they concluded that city size must affect the tightness of the relationships among socioeconomic variables. Lane (1968) in examining the "Six Cities" data (Palmer, 1954), found an inverse relationship of city size with the influence of education on occupation and father's occupation on occupation. She claimed that the larger cities have more complex industrial structures, which would result in the blending of a number of job hierarchies. This "results in more shallow slopes for the effects of education and father's occupation on son's occupational status than in smaller cities" (1968: 748). However, Lane (1972) reassesses this interpretation and argues essentially the opposite. She states (1972: 131):

> The argument concerning the significance of the city size goes as follows. Increase in size leads to more complex division of labor which, in turn, implies not only increased size in the occupational structure but especially greater variation. In turn, a diversified occupational structure signifies a greater probability that some specialized position will exist such that a given individual, with his particular set of qualifications, can fill it to his advantage.

Lane correctly argues, we believe, that both her data and the Hochbaum et al. data are inadequate for drawing inferences about nonadditivity and city size. The size range is too restricted in the "Six Cities" data, and two cities do not constitute a sufficiently representative sample.

A recent study by Artz et al. (1971) lends support to Lane's second argument for a positive relationship. Based on data from different-sized communities (Indianapolis and Phoenix of metropolitan size; Columbus, Indiana, and Yuma, Arizona, of about 25,000; Linton, Indiana, and Safford, Arizona, of about 6000), Artz et al.report that the correlations between the individual's education and occupational status, on the one hand, and father's occupational status and son's occupational status, on the other, decrease in magnitude as city size decreases, although the pattern is not entirely consistent. In addition, Duncan (1968d) has reported an almost perfect positive monotonic relationship between city size and the influence of father's occupational attainment on son's occupational attainment; however, Duncan does not choose to interpret this as a city effect.

There are reasons not to make too much of these inconsistencies in ideas and findings. First, the specific relationships being considered are not the same in all of these studies. Lane's first argument (1968), in which she theorizes an inverse relationship, is for the influence of both father's occupation and respondent's education. However, her subsequent argument for a positive relationship is stated only for the influence of education. Hochbaum et al. consider only the zero-order relationship between education and occupational attainment, whereas Artz et al. analyze the influence of both education and father's occupation simultaneously, Finally, Duncan reports only the zero-order influence of father's occupational attainment. In brief, the data and findings are not directly comparable. Second, the accompanying theoretical rationales (when present) have at least implicitly posited that the influence of both son's education and father's occupation will vary *similarly* across cities of different size. We believe this assumption is problematic, but we would suggest that the interaction of paternal occupation and city size is not identical to the interaction of size and filial education.

Our thinking on these matters is influenced by Treiman's theory of the relationships among industrial organization, urbanization, and stratification. When discussing differences in the process of stratification which vary with industrialization, Treiman (1970) hypothesizes that the influence of social origin (e.g., father's occupation) will vary inversely and the influence of own education will vary directly with industrialization. Father's occupation will have less influence on son's because increased rationalization or bureaucratization of work, the greater number of jobs, and a more complex occupational structure will make it less likely, by chance alone, that the occupations will be similar in the two generations. Education will become more important because it is a mechanism for learning the occupationally relevant skills and is a major resource in job competition. Even though we are unwilling to argue that cities of different size mirror the changes a given society undergoes as it industrializes, we think Treiman's hypotheses and reasoning are suggestive for understanding city size differences.

Aside from size, other city characteristics have been brought to bear upon the interpretation of both additive and nonadditive city effects. These include the form and degree of functional specialization, the rate of economic growth or decline, the spatial and economic relations with other cities, the industrial composition, and occupational diversity. However, the past research has indicated that these additive effects, whatever may be their cause, are small in magnitude, especially when size is controlled. Lane (1968) reports significant but small occupational attainment differences among the "Six Cities," after controlling on the educations and fathers' occupations of 45- to 64-year-old (but not younger) men. In subsequent analysis (Lane 1972), she found support for her reasoning that this between-city variation reflects differences in industrial composition. However, Mueller (1974), in a similar analysis of 15 U.S. SMSAs, found no additive city effects for any age cohort in the OCG sample when important compositional variables were controlled statistically.

Nonadditive city effects also have been examined in places of constant size. Mueller (1974) finds no significant interactions in the 15 largest SMSAs in 1962. Lane's (1968) "Six Cities" reanalysis attempts to explain significant interactions for the two older age cohorts (ages 45–54 and 55–64) by controlling on occupational diversity (measured as the variance of the occupational prestige measure). Education has a stronger influence in cities with more diversified structures, but the relationship between occupational diversity and the influence of father's occupation is indeterminate.

The impact of size of place on earnings and income differentials is studied extensively by economists, although research on city effects per se is not vast. Some economists of "human capital" formation (e.g., Mincer, 1958; Becker, 1964; Ashenfelter and Mooney, 1968; Blaug, 1967; Bowman, 1969; Daniere and Mechling, 1970; Denison, 1964; Weisbrod and Karpoff, 1968; Weiss, 1970; Griliches and Mason, 1972; Hansen, Weisbrod, and Scanlon, 1970) have constructed causal models of labor income quite similar to the Duncan, Featherman, and Duncan (1972) research in sociology. "Contextual analysis" enters these researches as an anlaysis of labor market homogeneity, which is the economists' analog to our phrasing of additive city effects. With considerable simplification, the issue is whether or not the interplay between labor demand and labor supply is sufficiently homogeneous across regions, cities or other market contexts to produce similar earnings levels. Research has been consistent in demonstrating the heterogeneity of labor markets (e.g., Hanoch, 1967; Hansen, Weisbrod, and Scanlon, 1970; Griliches and Mason, 1972; Hanushek, 1973). In addition, and more relevant to the research undertaken here, city size has been found to be monotonically related to mean income level (Schnore and Varley, 1955; Duncan and Reiss, 1956; Schnore, 1963). As is well recognized, however, inferences concerning these differences are usually clouded by the influences of cost-of-living differences across place.

In view of the inconsistencies in these literatures regarding the additive and nonadditive effects of city size on occupational and economic statuses and on the process of socioeconomic stratification, we are loathe to advance hypotheses about cities as contexts for mobility and achievement. Instead, this chapter describes our exploration of the evidence of city effects on occupation and income within the 1962 Occupational Changes in a Generation (OCG) data.

ESTIMATING CITY EFFECTS IN LIFE CYCLE
MODELS OF ACHIEVEMENT

Our structural equation model reflects a life cycle approach to socioeconomic achievements (e.g., Blau and Duncan, 1967; Duncan, Featherman, and Duncan, 1972); it allows us to view city of residence as another variable in the model.[1] We may then speak of additive city effects when there remain statistically significant and substantively meaningful differences in mean level of achievement after other variables thought to influence these achievements are controlled. In addition, if there are nonadditive city effects, the structural coefficients of the attainment model will vary across city-size categories. We estimate our life cycle model with analysis of covariance (ANCOVA). In that framework, cities are the treatments and the other exogenous variables (e.g., paternal occupation, son's education) are the covariates.

For our analysis, we draw a subset from the March 1962 OCG population; namely, men in the experienced civilian labor force, aged 25–64 and residing in urban places of 2500 or more persons. The size categories are: "very large," 1 million +; "large," 250,000–1 million; "middle-sized," 50,000–250,000; and "small," 2500–50,000. A set of dummy variables is used to represent these city-size categories.

Occupational status (OC) is the individual's current occupation measured by Duncan's (1961) socioeconomic index (SEI) of occupational status. Income (INC) is total income for the previous year. Although INC does not measure market earnings exclusively, we shall assume that it is a reliable proxy for earnings. In addition, some error is introduced by considering 1961 income to be causally subsequent to 1962 occupational attainment. We must necessarily assume that such specification error is minimal.

The covariates include: father's (family head's) occupation, in units of Duncan's SEI (OCF); paternal (head's) education, in years completed (EDF); nativity (NAT) and nativity of father (NATF) dichotomies distinguishing whites who are native from those born outside the U.S.; farm origin (FARM), a dichotomy distinguishing men whose family heads were employed as farmers, farm managers, farm laborers, or farm foremen; family type (FAM), a dichotomy designating men who were reared in an intact family; and number of siblings (SIBS). Covariates which do not index a man's social origin include his education (ED), in years; his first full-time civilian occupation after schooling (OC1), in units of SEI; labor force experience (EXPER), the difference between age at first job and age in March 1962; marital

---

[1] We will not attempt to develop and estimate a causal model which delineates the causal ordering of all of the variables to be considered. Such a model would require that present city of residence be unambiguously positioned with regard to other determinants. The causal model assumed is one in which place of residence and all other determinants are viewed as exogenous variables determining occupational attainment and income.

status (*MAR*), a dichotomy distinguishing the married spouse-present and widowed from the divorced, separated, and married spouse-absent; residential migration (*RESMIG*), a dichotomy distinguishing natives in their cities of residence from in-migrants; regional migration (*REGMIG*), distinguishing natives in census regions from in-migrants to current region; and current region (*REG*), a dichotomy distinguishing south from non-south.

Nonadditive effects are examined first. Although the regression coefficients will be examined visually, a statistical significance test is possible by comparing the explained sum of squares for two regression models.[2] In one model, occupation (or income) is regressed on a set of dummy variables for the city-size categories and the covariates. In the other model, occupation (or income) is regressed on the city-size dummy variables, the covariates, and a set of variables representing the city size interactions with the covariates. An F-ratio is used to test the increment in R^2 for statistical significance (Cohen, 1968: 435). Not only does this particular test provide evidence for answering the substantive question of interest, but it also tells us whether or not there exist common within-group slopes, a statistical necessity for adjusting category means and for testing for additive effects. Finding statistically significant interactions is not a sufficient condition for inferring nonadditive effects, however (Hauser, 1971: 26). There must exist a pattern of the coefficients to which a meaningful substantive interpretation can be attached.

Next, if the interactions are not statistically significant, or if they are small in magnitude and not substantively meaningful, additive effects

---

[2] All regression analysis utilizes pair-wise present data, that is, only data from those respondents who provided information on both variables in the pair. In addition, the procedures for conducting significance tests had to be modified somewhat. This was necessary, since a sampling design less efficient than simple random sampling was utilized. To take this into account, the sample size, n, used to estimate standard errors and for computing F-ratios was obtained by multiplying the actual pair-wise present n (in which the dependent variable of interest is included) by the sample design correction factor of .62 (see Appendix F). This correction factor is an estimate of the relative efficiency, as compared with simple random sampling, of the sampling design used in the OCG survey. The n obtained is referred to as degrees of freedom (df) in the tables. Finally, data on income were obtained for persons in households of the March CPS sample which also were in the CPS sample in February, the month in which income data were elicited. Since there is approximately a three-fourths overlap in persons sampled from one CPS to the next, this resulted in loss of 25% of the cases for income analysis. In practical terms, this means that less reliable estimates will be obtained for the income variable. The representativeness of the sample remains unaffected, however.

are examined. An estimate of the magnitude of these additive effects, whatever their source, may be obtained by regressing occupational attainment (or income) on the set of dummy variables for the city-size categories. The R^2 value gives the upper limit for the sum of squares explained by the between-category differences (Hauser, 1971: 430) as in one-way ANOVA and may be used here to test for significant between-category differences (Cohen, 1968: 430).

Finally, the between-category differences, net of the influence of the covariates, are estimated. This also involves comparing two regression models, one in which occupation (or income) is regressed only on the compositional variables, and another in which occupation (or income) is regressed on the compositional variables and the categorical (city) variables. The F-ratio for the R^2 increment indicates whether the city size categories make a significant independent contribution to the explanation of the dependent variable. An additional procedure consists of making the covariance adjustment in order to obtain category means adjusted for compositional differences. This last step is especially important when, as with the study here, there is an hypothesized ordering of the means.

CITY SIZE AND OCCUPATIONAL ACHIEVEMENT

Table 10.1 presents gross (zero-order) and net regression coefficients for the four city-size categories for relationships receiving attention in the literature reviewed above. The net coefficients among nonblacks (whites) for the influence of father's occupation on son's occupation do not form a monotonic pattern in either direction with city size; the relationship is curvilinear with the strongest influence appearing in the large-sized cities. Differences over size categories are not large, however. The pattern for the black population does not match the pattern for whites, and the relationship is neither monotonically positive nor negative. The net coefficients for the influence of education on occupation do suggest that the effect is greatest in the very large and largest cities, although the variation over size categories is not perfectly monotonic and the differences are not large. This is not true for the black population, where the influence is noticeably weaker in the small cities.

A summary of the tests for nonadditive and additive effects for both the black and the white population is presented in Table 10.2. The tests for nonadditivity are represented by a comparison of Models 3 and 4 and a comparison of Models 7 and 8. The first comparison allows

TABLE 10.1

Selected Metric Regression Coefficients for Different City Size Categories by Race: Men in the Experienced Civilian Labor Force, Aged 25-64 in March 1962

Race and City Size	Effect of OCF on OC[a]		Effect of ED on OC		Effect of OC on INC		Effect of ED on INC	
	Gross	Net	Gross	Net	Gross	Net	Gross	Net
Nonblack[b]								
Very Large	.397	.072	4.41	3.29	81	55	466	177
Large	.420	.125	4.37	3.46	70	48	361	130
Middle-Sized	.411	.113	4.06	2.93	68	48	441	156
Small	.400	.108	4.12	3.01	68	48	379	135
Total	.407	.099	4.30	3.21	74	51	425	151
Black[c]								
Very Large	.138	.048	1.60	1.66	27	22	77	35
Large	.249	.051	2.15	1.72	40	18	205	111
Middle-Sized	-.133	-.230	1.85	1.95	44	29	197	182
Small	-.127	.020	.98	.94	26	8	115	59
Total	.141	.025	1.60	1.51	37	22	150	62

[a] See text for definition of variables.

[b] All variables which had coefficients twice the size of their standard errors were controlled. For occupation: OC1, OCF, ED, SIBS, RESMIG, FAM, MAR, NAT, EXPER, and REG. For income: OC, OC1, OCF, ED, REGMIG, REG, MAR, NAT, and EXPER.

[c] All variables which had coefficients at least twice the size of their standard errors were controlled. For occupation: OC1, ED, and EXPER. For income: OC, MAR, EXPER, and REGMIG.

TABLE 10.2

Summary of Tests for Additive and Nonadditive Effects of Community of Residence on Occupational Attainment by race: Men in the Experienced Civilian Labor Force, Aged 25-64 in March 1962

Model[a]	Nonblack	Black
	Coefficients of Determination (R^2)	
1	.0046	.0192
2	.4213	.1957
3	.4227	.2030
4	.4236	.2294
5	.4383	.2074
6	.4396	.2136
7	.4261	.2136
8	.4283	.2259
Tests	F-Ratio	
1	9.514^b	3.563^c
4 vs. 3	.801	1.513
7 vs. 8	1.121	.631
3 vs. 2	4.988^b	1.655
6 vs. 5	4.765^b	1.403
df	6180	550

[a]Model 1 includes three dummy variables for size of community of residence (3). Model 2 includes OCF, EDF, OC1, and ED (4). Model 3 is the same as model 2, plus the three dummies for size of community (7). Model 4 is the same as model 3, plus city interactions with the four independent variables (19). Model 5 includes OCF, EDF, OC1, ED, SIBS, EXPER, REG, RESMIG, FAM, MAR, FARM, and REGMIG (and NAT and NATF for nonblacks) (12 for blacks, 14 for nonblacks). Model 6 is the same as model 5, plus three dummies for city size. Model 7 includes OCF, EDF, OC1, ED, SIBS, FAM, FARM, RESMIG, REGMIG, REG, NATF (for nonblacks only), and the three city size dummies (14 for nonblacks and 13 for blacks). Model 8 is the same as model 7, plus city inateractions with each of the independent variables (47 for nonblacks and 43 for blacks).

[b]Significant at the .01 level.

[c]Significant at the .025 level.

for interactions only with the variables in the basic Blau–Duncan model (*OCF, EDF, ED,* and *OC1*), whereas the second comparison is for an extended model and allows for the additional interactions with number of siblings, family type, farm origin, residential migration, regional migration, region, and nativity of the father. The finding for blacks and whites is the same: no statistically significant interactions.[3]

[3] Since this overall test for interactions might mask interactions with particular variables, we conducted tests for interactions with each variable. Not one was significant for blacks; regional migration just reached the .05 level for the whites.

TABLE 10.3

Size of Community of Residence Effects on Occupational Status for Nonblacks and Blacks: Men in the Experienced Civilian Labor Force, Aged 25-64 in March 1962

City Size	Gross Effects		Net Effects[a]	
	Mean	Deviation[b]	Mean	Deviation[b]
Nonblacks				
1 mil.+	43.68	0.72	43.32	0.36
250,000–1 mil.	45.08	2.11	44.21	1.25
50,000–250,000	41.08	-1.88	41.54	-1.42
2,500–50,000	40.44	-2.52	42.22	-0.74
Blacks				
1 mil.+	19.38	1.01	18.12	-0.25
250,000–1 mil.	18.47	0.10	19.54	1.17
50,000–250,000	20.63	2.25	21.42	3.05
2,500–50,000	13.92	-4.45	16.47	-1.90

[a]This covariance adjustment was obtained by controlling on only those variables having net regression coefficients twice the size of their standard errors: OC1, ED, EXPER for blacks; OCF, OC1, SIBS, ED, RESMIG, FAM, MAR, NAT, EXPER, and REG for nonblacks.

[b]These are deviations from the respective grand means: 18.37 for blacks; 42.96 for nonblacks.

Consequently we find no evidence to contradict the assertion that the basic process of occupational stratification is the same in all cities.

The tests for additive effects are represented by a comparison of Models 3 and 2 and Models 6 and 5 in Table 10.2; both the basic model and an extended model are examined. The results indicate quite clearly the consequences of different-sized samples. For the white data, an increment in R^2 of .0013 is statistically significant, whereas an increment of .0073 for blacks is not significant.

The net effects in Table 10.3 show the direction of the relationship between city size and occupational attainment after compositional factors are controlled (i.e., the covariance adjustments are made). For whites, a perfect monotonic relationship is not found; only by collapsing and comparing large and very large with middle-sized and small cities is the customary positive relationship between size and status

observed. However, the differences are small. For blacks, we are reluc-
tant to discuss the relationship between city size and occupational
level, since the criterion of statistical significance is not met. Overall,
we observe no substantial variation in mean occupational attainment
across different sized cities.

VARIATIONS IN INCOME ATTAINMENTS
BY CITY SIZE[4]

The influence of occupational attainment on income among whites is
essentially the same for all city sizes except for the very large, where
the influence is somewhat stronger (see Table 10.1, Column 3). For
blacks, no monotonic relationship by size is apparent. The influence of
education on income, for both blacks and whites, is not monotonically
related to city size (Table 10.1, Column 4). By comparing Models 3
and 4 and Models 7 and 8 in Table 10.4, we test for interactions; both a
basic and an extended model are considered. There are statistically
significant interactions for the white population, although the additional variance attributable to interaction (.0052 for Models 3 and 4,
and .0155 for Models 7 and 8) is small. Nevertheless, additional procedures were carried out to determine precisely which variables are
interacting with city categories. In Table 10.5, we report statistically
significant interactions between city size and each of nativity of father,
region, and number of siblings. An examination of the differences in
influence of nativity of father indicates that this variable exerts a
unique influence in the middle-sized cities; those with foreign fathers
are greatly advantaged in such places. We have no ready explanation
for this result. Residents in all southern cities, irrespective of size,
receive lower incomes than those in other regions (compare net coefficients), but this disadvantage is greatest in the middle-sized and small
cities. This would suggest that the regional disadvantages generally
found in the South might be counteracted or diminished by properties
and processes associated with increased city size (urbanization). The
gross coefficients for the influence of number of siblings indicate a
negative influence in all city-size categories, but the pattern does not
take a form that is readily interpreted. In short, it is only the interaction
of region and city size which is explicable in our analysis of process in
income determination.

---

[4] Equivalent analyses of income equations were performed with income transformed
into logarithms to the base 10. The results were only trivially different from these
reported, and in no way could different substantive conclusions be drawn.

TABLE 10.4

Summary of the Tests for Additive and Nonadditive Effects of Community of Residence on Income by Race: Men in the Experienced Civilian Labor Force, Aged 25-64 in March 1962

	Nonblack	Black
Model[a]	Coefficients of Determination (R^2)	
1	.0106	.1062
2	.2151	.1182
3	.2216	.1945
4	.2268	.2170
5	.2498	.2474
6	.2528	.2840
7	.2326	.2130
8	.2481	.2443

Tests	F-Ratio	
1	18.377[b]	20.041[b]
4 vs. 3	2.300[b]	.931
7 vs. 8	4.008[b]	1.098
3 vs. 2	14.310[b]	15.819[b]
6 vs. 5	6.867[b]	8.400[b]
df	5150	510

[a]Model 1 includes three dummy variables for size of community of residence (3). Model 2 includes OCF, EDF, OC1, ED, and OC (5). Model 3 is the same as model 2 plus the 3 city size dummies (8). Model 4 is the same as model 3, plus city interactions with the 5 independent variables (23). Model 5 includes OCF, EDF, OC1, ED, SIBS, EXPER, REG, RESMIG, FAM, MAR, FARM, REGMIC, and OC (and NAT and NATF for nonblacks) (13 for blacks; 15 for nonblacks). Model 6 is the same as model 5, plus 3 dummies for city size. Model 7 includes OCF, EDF, OC1, ED, SIBS, FAM, FARM, RESMIG, REGMIG, REG, OC, NATF (for nonblack only), and the 3 city size dummies (15 for nonblacks and 14 for blacks). Model 8 is the same as model 7 plus city size interactions with each of the independent variables (51 for nonblacks and 47 for blacks).

[b]Significant at the .01 level.

Statistically significant additive effects exist for both the black and the white population (see Table 10.4), even after we control for the variables in the extended model. Despite the absence of a perfectly monotonic relationship between mean income and city size, white residents of very large cities appear to be advantaged (see Table 10.6, Column 2). Black residents of very large and large cities are advantaged when compared with residents of middle-sized and small communities. For both racial groups, these data are consistent with the published findings that indicate higher economic rewards, and in this case net rewards, in larger communities.

TABLE 10.5

Examination of Variables which Interact with City Size in Influencing Income for Nonblacks: Men in the Experienced Civilian Labor Force, Aged 25-64 in March 1962[a]

	City Size			
Variable	Very Large	Large	Middle-Sized	Small
NATF	69 (-604)[b]	12 (-292)	1086 (1680)	-180 (-490)
REG	-370 (319)	-506 (-634)	-1603 (-2123)	-919 (-918)
SIBS	-16 (-199)	88 (-75)	-85 (-293)	-20 (-167)

[a] Separate within-city size regression models were estimated. The values for NATF and REG are deviations from the omitted category: for NATF they indicate the deviation from residents whose fathers were native; for REG they indicate the deviation from residents not living in the South. The coefficients for SIBS indicate the change in income for a unit change in the SIBS variable.

[b] The values in parentheses are zero-order coefficients, whereas the others are net coefficients obtained with controls on ED, OC1, EXPER, REGMIG, MAR, NAT, and OC, all of which have a significant influence on income.

TABLE 10.6

Size of Community of Residence Effects on Income for Nonblacks and Blacks: Men in the Experienced Civilian Labor Force, Aged 25-64 in March 1962

City Size	Gross Effects		Net Effects[a]	
	Mean	Deviation[b]	Mean	Deviation[b]
Nonblacks				
1 mil.+	7349	446	7171	268
250,000–1 mil.	6725	-178	6691	-212
50,000–250,000	6733	-170	6852	-51
2,500–50,000	6269	-634	6600	-303
Blacks				
1 mil.+	3779	445	3631	296
250,000–1 mil.	3556	221	3629	294
50,000–250,000	2834	-501	2720	-614
2,500–50,000	2054	-1281	2503	-831

[a]These covariance adjustments were obtained by controlling on only those variables having net regression coefficients twice the size of their standard errors: OC, OC1, OCF, ED, REGMIG, REG, MAR, NAT, and EXPER for nonblacks; OC, OC1, ED, RESMIG, MAR, and REG for blacks.

[b]All deviations are from the respective grand means: 6903 for nonblacks; 3334 for blacks.

RACIAL DISCRIMINATION AND CITY SIZE

Research has been cited (Blau and Duncan, 1967: Chapter 6; Duncan, 1968b; Coleman *et al.*, 1972; Blum, 1972; Siegel, 1970) which indicates that the black–white gaps in occupational attainments and earnings remain, even after one controls for other relevant differences between the races. Here, we shall determine if racial discrimination differs by city size. Theoretical and empirical literature which speaks directly to this question could not be found.[5] Nevertheless, it is not

[5] Taeuber and Taeuber (1965) did examine the relationship between city size and racial segregation but found no relationship between the two variables. However, "discrimination," as used here, is conceptually and empirically distinct from "segregation." Also, see Stolzenberg and D'Amico (1976) and research cited therein.

difficult to derive, from the material already discussed, an expected pattern. It could be argued that the criteria utilized in occupation screening, selecting, promoting, and rewarding differ by city size. In particular, the use of more universalistic and less particularistic criteria can be expected in the larger cities, as the consequence of a more complex division of labor, the associated diversity of the occupational structure, and the specialization within segments of the structure. These conditions would necessitate that employers judge potential employees and present employees on achievement-based characteristics rather than on ascribed traits. If this is true, then both occupational and economic discrimination based on race can be expected to diminish as city size increases.

The procedure used for determining the extent of racial discrimination is similar to that used by Duncan (1968b) for the same purpose. The technique standardizes on the white regression model and hypothetically gives the white population the black population means for those variables known to influence the dependent variables of interest. Since the white regression coefficients are used, the procedure removes any disadvantages associated with the differences in how these variables influence either occupation or income. In short, handicaps in terms of mean differences in determinants and in terms of differences in the influence of these variables are controlled. Because the objective is to obtain an estimate of discrimination for each city-size category, the procedure is applied separately to each category.

The results of this analysis for occupational achievement are presented in Table 10.7. In making these estimates, the black means for each city-size category were substituted into the single nonblack equation for all city-size categories, since it has already been shown that a single white equation fits all city sizes.[6] The initial gaps indicate that the differences are the greatest in the large and small cities, next largest in the very large cities, and smallest in the middle-sized cities. After making the adjustments described above, the gaps which remain were greatest in the very large and small-sized cities, with the large and middle-sized cities having somewhat smaller gaps. As with the initial gaps, a monotonic relationship of the magnitude of the gap with city size is not revealed; only if small cities are excluded from the examination is a monotonic relationship apparent, and it is in the direction opposite from that hypothesized.

[6] The analysis was also conducted with separate nonblack equations for each city-size category; the pattern of data presented in Table 10.7 was not significantly changed.

TABLE 10.7

Black and Nonblack Mean Occupational Status and Income Gaps by Size of City of Residence Obtained by Indirect Standardization: Men Aged 25-64 in the Experienced Civilian Labor Force, March 1962

City Size	Occupation		Income	
	Initial Gap	Remaining Gap[a]	Initial Gap	Remaining Gap[b]
1 mil. +	24.30	10.48 (43.1)[c]	3581	1696 (47.4)[c]
250,000 – 1 mil.	26.60	7.20 (27.1)	3153	785 (24.9)
50,000 – 250,000	20.96	6.41 (30.6)	3880	1696 (43.7)
2,500 – 50,000	26.53	9.33 (35.2)	4239	1120 (26.4)

[a] Since nonadditive effects were not found for the nonblack population, the regression model for the total nonblack sample was used for standardizing. In addition, only those variables having significant net regression coefficients in total sample models for either the black or nonblack samples were used for standardizing: OCF, SIBS, FAM, OCl, ED, RESMIG, MAR, and EXPER.

[b] Since nonadditive city effects were found for the nonblack population, a separate regression model was used for each city size category. In addition, only those variables having significant net regression coefficients for either the black or nonblack total samples were used for standardizing: OCF, ED, OCl, RESMIG, EXPER, MAR, and REGMIG.

[c] Percent of the initial gap which remains is in parentheses.

Examination of the *proportion* of the initial gap left unexplained shows a pattern consistent with the findings for actual differences; more of the initial gap is accounted for in the large and middle-sized communities. Thus, no new insights are provided.

The same procedure was adopted for examining racial differences in income. The major change is that separate white regression equations were used for each city-size category. This was necessary since significant nonadditive city-size effects were found. As with the examination of occupational attainment, only those variables having significant net influences on income for either black or nonblack total samples were controlled. The initial gaps are large, with no obvious pattern, and the gaps remaining after controls are not much more informative. The gap is smallest for the large-sized cities; the greatest gap remains for the very large and middle-sized cities. If attention is given to the proportion of the initial gap accounted for by the control variables, the conclusions are not substantially altered. More of the initial gap is accounted for in the large and small cities than in the very large and middle-sized cities. In short, a monotonic relationship of discrimination with city size is not indicated by the data.

CONCLUSIONS AND DISCUSSION

Our analysis of occupational stratification in urban places of the U.S. in 1962 uncovers no variation in the process of status allocation across cities of different size. We conclude that contextual differences which vary concomitantly with city size do not alter the process of stratification in significant ways. In that sense, we detect a remarkable homogeneity in the process of occupational achievement in the United States (cf. Mueller, 1974, for fuller treatment).

In most respects, the process of income attainment is homogeneous across urban places as well. No interactions were found for the black population, and only small (but significant) nonadditive effects were observed for whites; interpretable differences by city size were found only for region of current residence. The impact of region was largest for residents of middle-sized and small communities, suggesting that the characteristics associated with more urbanized communities counteract the strong regional effects noted for the smaller communities.

In that both mean occupational status and income are positively related to size, past research findings are supported. However, the observed patterns are not very convincing. Occupational opportunity (unadjusted means) is positively related to city size, but even this is not a perfect monotonic relationship. After controlling for composition, significant differences with the same pattern remain, but whether one examines the absolute differences or the explained sum of squares, one must conclude that the differences are small. These differences can be interpreted in several ways. First, they may reflect imperfections in the equilibrating mechanisms whereby opportunity structures are matched with population compositions. That is, the selectivity of migration may be imperfect, as may be the training of nonmigrants and the industrial adjustment to labor supply conditions. Second, it is possible that such equilibrating mechanisms are operating effectively, but we may not have controlled on the important compositional variables. Finally, it is possible that mechanisms are working adequately, that we have adjusted properly for composition, and that individuals attain higher-status positions because they reside and work in larger communities. The data do not allow us to determine which of these or which combination of these is the most likely. However, we would argue for two conclusions with regard to occupational attainment. First, there do exist predictable differences in occupational attainment for whites by size of city of residence. Second, these differences are so small that we must conclude that city contextual differences, whatever they may be, contribute only slightly to an individual's occupational achievements.

The data for income did suggest some advantages to residents of the very large cities. However, we would argue that such an advantage is small and could easily be accounted for by differences in cost of living. In particular, data presented by the U.S. Census Bureau (1968; Table 507) indicate that, in 1966, the average total budget costs for residents of metropolitan areas was $9376, whereas the budget costs in nonmetropolitan areas (places with 2500 to 50,000 population in 1960) was $8366. Such a difference in cost of living would explain most, if not all, of the differences which remain.

The findings for differential racial discrimination by city size do not readily lend themselves to a meaningful interpretation. We had hypothesized that discrimination would be inversely related to city size, but found no supporting monotonic pattern for either occupation or income. In fact, the data suggested that discrimination is greatest in the very large cities. Although the absence of a monotonic relationship in either direction weakens generalization, we suggest that racial discrimination does not decrease as city size increases.

These conclusions cannot be left without some qualifications. First, if the objective is to assess the maximum possible influence exerted by city contextual differences on socioeconomic achievements, then the actual cities themselves should be included as a set of dummy variables in the covariance analysis. We have been forced, as have most researchers, to aggregate by city-size categories. Categorization by city size, however, does not necessarily capture other city characteristics which might influence the achievements of their residents. Characteristics such as the community's spatial, economic, and social relationships with large metropolitan cities, the magnitude of population growth and decline, and the type and degree of functional specialization all could influence the compositional characteristics of a community and may affect levels of achievement in some form. It must be admitted that these factors produce within-city size variation which could either conceal or accentuate differences observed by city size. For this reason, the findings should not be expressed in terms of city effects in general; they must be qualified as referring to differences by city size.

Second, the city-size categories are arbitrary and broad. Consequently, they may not capture the differences by city size that do exist. Thus, small reversals in near-perfect monotonic patterns should not be viewed as carrying much substantive meaning.

Third, the black sample is small, and sampling variability is greater than we would desire. As a consequence, fairly large differences by size (relative to the white findings) were rejected as not being statistically significant. Therefore, generalizations about the black population cannot be made with the certainty attached to those for whites.

Finally, since mean income increases with city size and since cost of living has been reported to follow the same pattern, one must seriously question whether the adjusted income differences are real income differences. Since these differences were not large, cost-of-living variations could account for them.

With these qualifications in mind, we conclude that U.S. society is rather homogeneous in the manner by which the determinants of socioeconomic achievements exert their influence. That is, processes of allocation to positions in the socioeconomic hierarchy operate in a consistent fashion regardless of the size of the community in which a person resides. At the same time, an individual is slightly advantaged, both in terms of occupational status and income, by being employed in the larger cities.

11

Intergenerational Transmission of Income: An Exercise in Theory Construction

This chapter reports an attempt to introduce paternal income into the Blau–Duncan model of the process of status attainment among men in the United States (Blau and Duncan, 1967; Duncan, Featherman, and Duncan, 1972). Our analysis is motivated by suggestions that the specification of socioeconomic background in terms of paternal education and occupational status does not adequately reflect the strictly economic dimension of family background (Bowles, 1972; Huber and Form, 1973: 179–193). Our results should be assessed in conjunction with the parallel efforts of other researchers to elaborate the representation of family background in models of the stratification process (Duncan, 1968a; Duncan, Featherman, and Duncan, 1972; Jencks *et al.*, 1972; Hauser and Dickinson, 1974; Jencks, 1974; Bowles, 1972; Bowles and Gintis, 1972; Bowles and Nelson, 1974).

No direct measures of parental income were included in the 1962 Occupational Changes in a Generation (OCG) survey, nor are validated measurements of this variable included in any national survey of U.S. men (but see Featherman and Hauser, 1975; Sewell and Hauser, 1975). For this reason, we use indirect means to assess the possible impact of parental income on the socioeconomic life-chances of U.S. men, and our numerical estimates should be interpreted with caution. Indeed, all of our calculations might better be regarded as quantitative speculations than as "estimates" in the usual sense.

This chapter was prepared by Donald J. Treiman and Robert M. Hauser.

Several variations of the Blau–Duncan model have been published, but we will begin with the path model in Figure 11.1, which is a modified version of Figure 3.1 of Duncan, Featherman, and Duncan (1972: 39); "number of siblings" has been dropped from the model for computational convenience. The model summarizes the main features of the process of stratification in the U.S. as it is currently understood. Numerical values are shown for the 45- to 54-year-old cohort of nonblack (white) men of nonfarm origin in the experienced civilian labor force (ECLF) in 1962, but the pattern of coefficients is similar for other cohorts of adult white men of nonfarm origin in the ECLF. Educational attainment depends directly on father's educational and occupational attainment to a moderate degree. Occupational status is strongly affected by educational attainment and slightly by father's occupational status but is only indirectly dependent upon father's education. Last, income (in 1961) is moderately dependent upon occupational status, but the direct effect of schooling on income is small, and income depends only indirectly on father's education and occupational status.

However, as the reader will immediately note, the model has an obvious omission. While the model incorporates educational attainment, occupational status, and income in the son's generation, among fathers, only the first two aspects of social standing are represented; father's income is not included. The reasons for this come readily to mind. It would be difficult, if not impossible, for both conceptual and practical reasons, to obtain valid retrospective reports of father's income.

The same conceptual problem which occurs in the measurement of father's occupation appears in the case of income, but with even

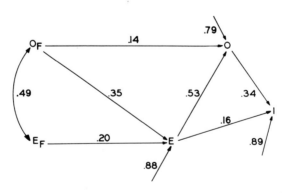

Figure 11.1 A basic model of social stratification: Nonblack men of nonfarm background in the experienced civilian labor force, aged 45 to 54 in 1962.

greater force: At what point in a man's life should his father's income be measured? One reasonable choice would be the period when the son was attending high school, on the assumption that parental income would have its greatest impact on status attainment by influencing the decision to drop out of high school, graduate from high school, or go on to college. However, it might be argued that, at least in the upper portions of the status hierarchy, the greatest impact would occur later in the son's life, involving the decision to attend graduate school or to launch a business or professional practice. Alternatively, rather than considering parental income purely as a facilitating resource, it is possible to view income as helping to set a style of life into which a child is socialized. Parental education and occupation may set a given life style while income provides the wherewithal to carry it out; hence, the size of income, relative to education and occupation, may determine the "comfort" in which a family lives and may thereby generate the basic attitudes an individual has regarding income acquisition. To the extent that this is the case, the important impact of parental income should occur during early childhood. At the present state of our understanding, we cannot choose between these alternatives, and indeed both may be correct.

Even if we were to choose one appropriate time to measure parental income, say, when the son was about 16 years old, there would be other problems in obtaining a valid measure. First, income fluctuates widely from year to year, at least relative to the degree of fluctuation in occupational status; thus, an accurate report of annual income would be an unreliable measure of "true" income during the high school years. One might surmount this problem by averaging incomes over a period of years, but this presents obvious practical difficulties in a retrospective survey. However, William H. Sewell and his associates have obtained 4-year averages of parental income from tax records in a statewide Wisconsin sample of high school graduates (Sewell and Hauser, 1975). Second, except in the case of a narrowly defined cohort (like that in the Wisconsin sample), it may be necessary to adjust incomes for temporal or geographic variations in price levels. Moreover, it is not clear whether current dollar incomes, real dollar incomes, or some relative measure of standing in the income distribution will best represent the economic aspect of social background.

These conceptual problems could probably be overcome with sufficient ingenuity, but the task of measuring parental income in a retrospective survey might still founder on the rock of practical impossibility. It is unreasonable to expect people to recall their fathers' incomes in a specific year with any degree of accuracy. Indeed, it is probable that a teenager does not know his family income in any given year, much less the specific contribution of each member of the household. Even in the case where individuals can provide contemporaneous information, the interannual instability in income may preclude reliable reporting for any point in the past. Most survey researchers believe that individuals cannot recall their own incomes with any degree of accuracy more than a very short time in the past.

In the 1973 OCG survey, Featherman and Hauser (1975) included the question, "When you were about 16 years old, what was your family's annual income?" Pretest results showed that respondents would answer the query, and their responses were about as reliable as reports of parental education or occupational status. However, it is not clear what the item measures, that is, whether it should be regarded as a report of annual income, as a global perception of relative economic standing, or as a distorted and perhaps ideologically colored reconstruction of the past with no validity as a measure of one's actual conditions of upbringing. Fortunately, Featherman and Hauser are attempting to validate similar reports against U.S. Census records for a sample of Wisconsin men, and Sewell and Hauser have used the 1973 OCG item in an 18-year follow-up survey of their Wisconsin panel. Thus, we may soon know a great deal more about the feasibility of using retrospective reports of family income. At present, the only viable strategies for direct measurement of parental income are the use of public records and, perhaps, the cumulation of contemporaneous reports from panel studies (as in the National Longitudinal Surveys of H. L. Parnes and his associates at Ohio State University).

Ultimately, it may be possible to measure directly the effects of paternal income on socioeconomic achievements in a national sample of U.S. men of diverse ages. However, for the time being, we can only introduce paternal income into a model of achievement as an unmeasured or hypothetical variable.

DATA AND METHODS

Starting with the correlations given in Table 11.1, which are taken from Duncan, Featherman, and Duncan (1972: 38, Table 3.1), we introduce a variety of assumptions about the relations between "father's income," our unmeasured variable, and the other variables in the model. These assumptions provide enough information to estimate the parameters in a model which specifies the effects of "father's income." We estimate two alternative models in order to establish a set of plausible limits within which the parameters involving father's income can

TABLE 11.1

Correlations between Status Variables by Age: Non-Negro Men with Nonfarm Background in the Experienced Civilian Labor Force, March 1962

Variable	O_F	E	O	I	Mean	Standard deviation
Age 25 to 34						
E_F	.4885	.4017	.3420	.1534	9.17	3.53
O_F		.4133	.3534	.2019	34.59	22.35
E			.6510	.2726	12.38	3.04
O				.3369	43.34	25.01
I					6.14	4.29
Age 35 to 44						
E_F	.5300	.4048	.3194	.2332	8.55	3.72
O_F		.4341	.3899	.2587	34.41	23.14
E			.6426	.3759	11.95	3.20
O				.4418	44.78	24.71
I					7.50	5.36
Age 45 to 54						
E_F	.4863	.3685	.2517	.1902	8.15	3.69
O_F		.4454	.3777	.3032	32.99	22.35
E			.5949	.3635	11.25	3.28
O				.4376	42.41	23.76
I					7.74	6.81
Age 55 to 64						
E_F	.5313	.3534	.3022	.1595	8.38	3.66
O_F		.3879	.3543	.1871	34.06	23.16
E			.5576	.3071	10.47	3.61
O				.3799	42.73	24.62
I					6.99	6.37

NOTE: Source is Duncan, Featherman and Duncan, 1972:38, Table 3.1. Variables are E_F = father's educational attainment, O_F = father's occupational status (Duncan SEI), E = son's educational attainment, 0 = son's 1962 occupational status (Duncan SEI), I = income in 1961 ($1,000).

reasonably be supposed to lie, and then we correct the known correlations for attenuation (a step suggested by earlier results) and estimate adjusted parameters of both the earlier models. Finally, we work "backward" by positing a very high intergenerational income correlation and showing that it leads to implausible results.[1]

[1] Larry Bumpass suggested this strategy to us.

The variables entering the model are defined as follows: Respondent's and father's education are scaled in years of school completed. Father's occupation and son's current occupation were first coded into the 1960 U.S. Census detailed classification and then assigned scores on Duncan's socioeconomic index (Duncan, 1961). Income is total dollar income in 1961, including both earnings and other income (U.S. Bureau of the Census, 1964b: x–xi). Father's occupation refers to the occupation of the father when the son was about 16 years old. Of course, father's income is unmeasured, but implicitly it is taken to refer to the father's income when the son was 16 years old. The analytic sample for this chapter is representative of the white male experienced civilian labor force of nonfarm origin, aged 25 to 64 in March 1962; it includes about 15,000 men.

It should be emphasized that our results are generalizable to the white, nonfarm-origin male experienced civilian labor force of the U.S. While inclusion of the farm-origin population would probably have made little difference in the results (Duncan, Featherman, and Duncan, 1972: 38), we avoid the question of the comparability of farm and nonfarm occupations with respect to status by excluding the farm-origin population, which has the effect of excluding the current agricultural labor force as well, since virtually all farmers are sons of farmers. Exclusion of blacks is another matter. Although the results might have changed little if blacks were included, simply because

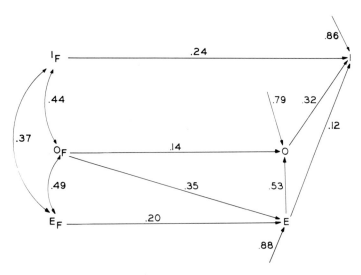

Figure 11.2 Model I: Lower-bound estimates of intergenerational income persistence without correction for measurement error.

they comprise only about 10% of the population, it is well known that the process of status attainment differs markedly between whites and non-whites (Duncan, 1968b; Winsborough, 1967). In addition, the patterns of response errors (about which we shall make assumptions in correcting for attenuated variances) are substantially dissimilar for blacks and whites (Bielby, Hauser, and Featherman, 1977).

MODEL I: DIRECT INTERGENERATIONAL INCOME EFFECTS

To begin, consider the model in Figure 11.2, ignoring for the moment the numerical coefficients appearing in the diagram. The model assumes that the three components of father's status—education, occupation, and income—are correlated, but it makes no assumption about their causal ordering. Education of the son depends on father's education and father's occupation, but not father's income. Similarly, son's occupation depends on his education and father's occupation, but not father's income; we know from the work of Blau and Duncan (1967: 173) that father's education has no direct influence upon occupational attainment. By specifying the model in this way, we estimate a lower bound of the effect of father's income on son's educational and occupational attainment. It is inconceivable that the effects of father's income on each of these variables could be negative, but it is not clear whether one or both should be positive or just how large they should be. Analyses of educational attainment among men in Sewell's Wisconsin panel show a direct positive effect of parental income on post-secondary schooling which is about as large as that of father's occupational status or the schooling of either parent (Hauser, 1972; Sewell and Hauser, 1972). In the same sample, there is no direct effect of father's income on son's occupational status 7 years after high school graduation, once the length of post-secondary schooling has been taken into account (Sewell and Hauser, 1975: 73). These findings suggest that Model I may be wrong in leaving out a direct path from father's income to son's schooling. Later, we introduce an alternative model which yields plausible upper bounds of the effects of father's income on son's education and occupational status. In this way, we can generate a range within which the true values of the various coefficients can reasonably be expected to lie.

Finally, in the present model, we assume that son's 1961 income is directly dependent upon son's occupational status and education and father's income, but only indirectly upon father's occupational status and education. It should be stressed that when we refer to the "inheritance" or "transmission" of income, we mean nothing more than the propensity for high-income men to be the sons of high-income fathers and low-income men to be the sons of low-income fathers. We take no explicit position regarding the mechanism of *direct* income transmission. There are several plausible mechanisms and, in a later model, we also allow the *indirect* transmission of income through the effect of father's income on son's educational and occupational attainment and the effect of these on son's income. Of course, income may be directly inherited; or, more properly, income-producing capital may be directly inherited. But this possibility cannot account for a large proportion of the variance in total income, since income from sources other than employment constitutes only a very small fraction of total income for the overwhelming bulk of the population. In 1960, over 90% of average family income consisted of earnings, and, even among families then enjoying an income of at least $15,000 per year (the top 5% of all families), 87% of income consisted of earnings (computed from U.S. Bureau of the Census, 1964b: Table 7).

A second way in which parental income may affect son's income is by affecting the level of parental support for individuals just getting started on careers. Fathers may directly aid sons in setting up a business, may tide them over lean periods, or may simply provide the security necessary to launch a risky venture. Conversely, the absence of adequate parental income may require that individuals take on responsibility for support of parents or siblings and in this way may tie them to secure but low-paying jobs. For example, consider the difference between a high school graduate who must immediately find a job to help support his family and who must—entirely apart from the question of what sort of occupation he enters—be sure that the conditions of employment are secure, and another high school graduate who is secure in the assurance that his parents will continue to support him, or at least that they do not need his support. The second may end up doing the same sort of work as the first, but he is much more likely to be able to afford to wait until the right opportunity develops, with the right sort of pay and possibility of advancement, or to quit an unsuitable job and wait until a better one comes along. In short, he can afford the risk required to secure a well-paying job.

Finally, a third way in which parental income may influence the income propensities of offspring is by helping to determine attitudes regarding money and its importance. It may well be the case that in relatively high-income families, children are socialized to regard money as important and to act so as to maximize their own income. Individuals who have been socialized in this way may be more inclined than others to switch jobs simply to secure higher pay and to accord less importance to other aspects of work.

It is difficult to imagine how father's occupational status could affect son's chances for income except insofar as it helps determine father's income or son's education or occupational status, which in turn influence son's income. Indeed, it turns out that positing a direct path from father's occupational status to son's income hardly alters the three paths initially posited, at least in the 45- to 54-year-old cohort. As predicted on theoretical grounds, the path from father's occupation to son's income is hardly different from zero; $p_{IO_F} = .04$ for this cohort[2] when all four direct paths are posited. Sewell and Hauser's (1975: 73) results also support our specification. Once paternal income is controlled, neither a father's educational attainment nor his occupational status affect the earnings of his son 8 to 10 years after high school graduation.

Suppose we accept this model of the causal relations among the included variables. How can we estimate its parameters? The paths to son's education and occupational status entail no special difficulty but are estimated by the usual procedures of path analysis. For example, applying the basic theorem of path analysis (Duncan, 1966c), we may write the correlation between father's and respondent's education as

$$r_{EE_r} = p_{EE_F} + p_{EO_F} r_{O_F E_F} \tag{1}$$

and, similarly, the correlation between education and father's occupation as

$$r_{EO_F} = p_{EE_F} r_{E_F O_F} + p_{EO_F}. \tag{2}$$

Since all the correlations are known, we have two simultaneous linear equations in two unknowns, which we solve to estimate the path coefficients relating father's education and occupational status to respondent's education. A similar application of the basic theorem yields two equations from which we estimate the path coefficients relating son's occupational status to son's education and father's occupational status. In both these cases, the path coefficients are just regression coefficients for variables in standard form (expressed as ratios of deviations from their mean to their standard deviation). In regressing son's occupational status on its measured causes, we ignore father's educational attainment and its correlation with son's occupational status. It is statistically inefficient to use that correlation in estimating p_{OO_F} and p_{OE} (Goldberger, 1970), and had we estimated p_{OE_F}, it would have been

---

[2] This and all other numerical estimates reported in text and tables have been rounded, but were originally calculated to a larger number of decimal places.

very close to zero in each cohort. In this part of Model I, the estimates are identical to those in Figure 11.1, since the two models are identical with respect to the determination of education and occupational status. The estimated coefficients for 45- to 54-year-old men are presented in Figure 11.2, while those for all cohorts are shown in Table 11.2.

We now have three remaining path coefficients to estimate, those pertaining to son's 1961 income. Using the basic theorem, we can write expressions for each of the four correlations relating income to the other measured variables. Of course, we could express the correlation r_{II_F} in the same way, but since this is an unobserved correlation we are trying to estimate, rather than one which is known, such an exercise would be premature. We have

$$r_{IE} = p_{IE} + p_{IO}r_{OE} + p_{II_F}r_{I_FE},$$
$$r_{IO} = p_{IE}r_{EO} + p_{IO} + p_{II_F}r_{I_FO},$$
$$r_{IO_F} = p_{IE}r_{EO_F} + p_{IO}r_{OO_F} + p_{II_F}r_{I_FO_F}, \qquad (3)$$

and

$$r_{IE_F} = p_{IE}r_{EE_F} + p_{IO}r_{OE_F} + p_{II_F}r_{I_FE_F}.$$

If we assign values to all the correlations in this set of equations (a problem to which we shall return shortly), this is a system of four linear equations in three unknowns. The system is thus "overidentified" and admits of no unique solution for the values of the path coefficients in a sample, even if the specification of the model is correct. In order to obtain a solution, we simply add together the last two equations of (3), which is the equivalent of taking their arithmetic average. Were all of the correlations in Expression (3) directly observable and our sample not so large, we should prefer a statistically efficient set of weights to our arbitrary averaging procedure (Hauser and Goldberger, 1971). However, given the necessity of guessing values of $r_{I_FE_F}$ and $r_{I_FO_F}$ (see below), we do not know the sampling properties of our estimates. With so large a sample, we suspect sampling error is the least of our troubles. Thus, in place of the last two equations of (3), we use

$$r_{IO_F} + r_{IE_F} = p_{IE}(r_{EO_F} + r_{EE_F}) + p_{IO}(r_{OO_F} + r_{OE_F}) + p_{II_F}(r_{I_FO_F} + r_{I_FE_F}). \quad (4)$$

Putting together the top two equations of (3) along with (4), we appear to have a system of three equations in three unknowns, which can be solved directly for p_{IO}, p_{IE}, and p_{II_F}. However, these equations include the four correlations $r_{I_FE_F}$, $r_{I_FO_F}$, r_{EI_F} and r_{OI_F}, which are unknown because I_F is unmeasured. Thus, before we can estimate the path

TABLE 11.2

Path Coefficients of Model I by Age: Lower-Bound Estimates of Inter-generational Income Persistence without Correction for Measurement Error

Dependent variable	Predetermined variable					Coefficient of determination (R^2)
	O	E	I_E	O_E	E_F	
Age 25 to 34						
E				.29	.26	.22
O		.61		.10		.43
I	.27	.07	.14			.14
Age 35 to 44						
E				.31	.24	.23
O		.58		.14		.43
I	.33	.12	.19			.25
Age 45 to 54						
E				.35	.20	.23
O		.53		.14		.37
I	.32	.12	.24			.26
Age 55 to 64						
E				.28	.21	.18
O		.49		.16		.33
I	.30	.13	.07			.16

NOTE: Variables are I_F = father's income (hypothesized construct), O_F = father's occupational status (Duncan SEI), E_F = father's educational attainment, E = son's educational attainment, 0 = son's 1962 occupational status (Duncan SEI), I = son's income in 1961.

coefficients, we must choose suitable values for these correlations. The problem is less than it may first appear, since values of r_{EI_F} and r_{OI_F} are implied by other parameters of the model. That is, expanding each of these correlations by the basic theorem, we get

$$r_{EI_F} = p_{EO_F} r_{O_F I_F} + p_{EE_F} r_{E_F I_F} \tag{5}$$

and

$$r_{OI_F} = p_{OE} r_{EI_F} + p_{OO_F} r_{O_F I_F}$$
$$= p_{OE}(p_{EO_F} r_{O_F I_F} + p_{EE_F} r_{E_F I_F}) + p_{OO_F} r_{O_F I_F}. \tag{6}$$

It is evident that all the coefficients on the right side of Equations (5) and (6) can be estimated directly from observed correlations except $r_{I_F E_F}$ and $r_{I_F O_F}$, the remaining two of the unknown correlations involving I_F. Thus, in order to estimate the remaining path coefficients in Model I, we must first ascertain the values of the two correlations relating father's income to his occupation and education.

What are reasonable values for these correlations? The most obvious device is to assume that the associations between income and occupation and education, respectively, are the same in the fathers' generation as in the sons' generation. If this be so, we are justified in simply taking as values for $r_{E_F I_F}$ and $r_{O_F I_F}$ those which we observe for r_{EI} and r_{OI}. However, it is incorrect to view the joint distribution of fathers' statuses as merely an earlier instance of a joint distribution of sons' statuses (Duncan, 1966a). Fathers' statuses are really measurements of status origins in a population of sons. They do not pertain to a population of men at an earlier time. Their distributions aggregate differentially weighted slices of joint status distributions of men over a period of years in which the weights not only represent the timing of births among fathers with each combination of status characteristics, but also reflect differential fertility. Thus, in our view, two criteria must be satisfied to justify the assumption of intergenerational similarity in the associations between income and the other two status attributes: (a) temporal stability in the cross-sectional relationships among components of status, and (b) lack of a differential fertility effect. That is, we must be able to ignore historical trends in the association between each pair of status variables and also to ignore interactions between the joint status distributions and the quantity and tempo of male fertility. Let us consider these criteria one at a time.

Substantial evidence of the historic stability of relations among the status characteristics of U.S. men is presented by Blau and Duncan (1967: 177–180; also, see Duncan, 1968d). For men of nonfarm origin, Blau and Duncan show the essential stability over cohorts in the intercorrelations of father's education, father's occupational status, son's education, and status of son's first job. These four status characteristics pertain to fixed points in the lives of fathers and sons and are not potentially confounded by age effects. While we have not looked into the temporal stability of income's correlations with schooling and occupational status, we feel reasonably confident that historical trends in correlations among status variables are not large enough to warrant our assuming that the correlations between income and the other two status variables in our model are either higher or lower for fathers than they are for sons.

Regarding differential fertility, it is known that very low-status men tend to remain unmarried (Bogue, 1959: 255) and hence, as a group, tend to have disproportionately few sons; also, there is a negative correlation between fertility and the social standing of married men. For example, Duncan, Featherman, and Duncan (1972: 38) show negative correlations on the order of .2 to .3 between number of siblings and father's education and occupation for all cohorts. Consequently, within any given cohort of men, the variance in status attributes of fathers is likely to be reduced relative to the variance of the corresponding characteristics of men of the same age as fathers in the male labor force at the time the cohort reached age 16.

We also considered the possibility that the secular trend toward increased educational and occupational attainment would *increase* the variance in these characteristics for the fathers of each cohort relative to the variance among men in the labor force at the time the cohort reached age 16, because the fathers of men in a given cohort vary substantially in age. However, in Table 11.1, there is no trend in mean levels of father's occupation and father's education (unless one is willing to count the slight increase in the level of education of the fathers of the youngest cohort). Hence, it comes as no surprise that the standard deviation of these variables in each cohort is about the same as in the total sample (compare our Table 11.1 with Duncan, Featherman, and Duncan, 1972: Table A.2).

Ceteris paribus, a reduction in the variance of a variable will lower the correlation between it and other variables, so a strong enough differential fertility effect should reduce correlations between status characteristics of fathers relative to those in a sample of men of roughly the same age as the fathers. In the absence of historical trends in these correlations, differential fertility should effect lower correlations between fathers' characteristics than between corresponding characteristics of sons. This is what we observe in the case of the one status correlation measured in both generations, that between education and occupation. In the two middle cohorts, where age of son and of father are similar, the correlation in the father's generation is about 11 points lower than in the son's generation. However, it is also possible to attribute this difference to unreliability in reports of fathers' statuses, a point we will consider in some detail below. For this reason, it is important to assess the effect of differential fertility on the correlation between schooling and occupational status.

A few rough calculations suggest that differential fertility does not explain a large share of the difference between education–occupation correlations of fathers and sons. Among 25- to 64-year-old white men of nonfarm origin in the experienced civilian labor force in 1962, the observed correlation between father's educational attainment and father's occupational status was .50. We recomputed this same correlation, weighting each observation by the reciprocal of the number of male siblings in each family of orientation, obtaining a correlation of .51 between the same two variables. Thus, we infer that differential fertility does not account for the intergenerational difference in the size of the association between education and occupational status. Again, we have little reason to believe that the correlations between father's income and father's other status characteristics should be very different from those in the current generation.

Having considered and rejected the possibility that intercorrelations among fathers' status characteristics systematically deviate from those for sons, we have added confidence in applying correlations observed in the present generation to the father's generation. However, one troubling observation remains—the fact that the correlation between education and occupation is higher in the current generation than in the father's generation for all four cohorts. Since we have ruled out both historical trends and differential fertility as influences on the relative size of these correlations, we must entertain a different possibility—that father's characteristics are reported less reliably than corresponding characteristics of sons. Random measurement error could easily produce differences in correlations of the magnitude which concern us here. The idea that the correlations in the father's generation are attenuated by unreliability is especially plausible when one considers the nontrivial errors which are known to occur in reports of respondents' own characteristics. Hence, in a later section, we will return to the issue of reliability and will attempt to correct our estimates for attenuation.

For the present, we complete the estimation of Model I without adjustment for measurement error. We have argued that the correlations among education, occupation, and income are of about the same size in the father's generation as in the son's, so we can borrow correlations from the son's generation to estimate unknown correlations in the father's generation. However, it is not plausible to borrow these correlations on a cohort-by-cohort basis since relationships among status variables vary over the life cycle. Letting "father's income" refer to the son at age 16, as in the case of father's occupation, we estimate the correlations between father's income and father's education and occupational status as the average of the corresponding correlations in the two middle cohorts of sons: that is, $r_{E_f I_f} = .37$ and $r_{O_f I_f} = .44$ for all cohorts. It is comforting that these values are not too dissimilar from correlations between a 4-year average of family income and paternal educational attainment ($r = .320$) and occupational status ($r = .457$) among nonfarm Wisconsin high school graduates (Sewell and Hauser, 1975: 72).

Substituting these two correlations in Equation (5), we estimate $r_{I_F E}$ as .22, .22, .23, and .20, going from the youngest to the oldest cohort. Similarly, from Equation (6), we estimate $r_{I_F O}$ as .18, .19, .18, and .17, respectively, in the four cohorts. That these figures may be unrealistically low is suggested by observed correlations between parental income and son's educational attainment and occupational status of .279 and .237, respectively, in the Wisconsin cohort (Sewell and Hauser, 1975: 72). Moreover, the differences between the Sewell–Hauser findings and our estimates in Model I may be understated, for their Wisconsin sample was truncated at both the upper and lower ends of the schooling distribution (Sewell and Hauser, 1975: 45–49). Among all male Wisconsin high school graduates, Hauser (1972: 165) reported a correlation of $r = .319$ between average parental income in 1957 to 1960 and completed years of post-secondary schooling. However, it should be recalled that Model I was deliberately specified to produce lower-bound estimates of the influence of paternal income, and this is reflected in Equations (5) and (6), from which $r_{I_F E}$ and $r_{I_F O}$ have been estimated.

We now have all the information needed to estimate Model I from Equations (3) and (4). Estimated coefficients of the paths leading to income are shown in Figure 11.2 for the 45- to 54-year-old cohort and are presented in Table 11.2 for all cohorts. The fit of model and data is reasonably good. The values of r_{IO_F} and r_{IE_F} implied by our estimated path coefficients deviate from the observed values by no more than .02 (among 45- to 54-year-olds) and by as little as .001 (among 55- to 64-year-olds). By our standards, we have come acceptably close to satisfying the overidentifying restriction in Equation (3).

In all but the oldest cohort, the direct effect of father's income upon son's income falls midway between the effect of the son's occupational status, which is strongest, and his educational attainment, which has the weakest direct effect of the three. Among the oldest men, father's income is very weak in its effect. Since Model I gives lower-bound estimates of the influence of father's income, we can conclude only that father's income plays a significant role in income attainment, but we cannot yet say just how strong its effect might be. However, at a minimum, father's income apparently has a stronger direct effect on son's income than does son's own education. This undoubtedly reflects the fact that one-half to two-thirds of the effect of education on income is mediated by occupational status. Apparently, education contributes to income by enabling one to get a high-paying job but makes relatively little difference apart from that. By contrast, father's income has at least a modest effect on son's income, even when his education and occupation are taken into account.

In addition to estimating the direct effect of father's income on son's income, we can estimate the total correlation between father's and son's income. This allows us to compare the extent of income "inheritance" with our direct measures of the amount of occupational status and educational "inheritance." Using the basic theorem of path analysis to expand the intergenerational income correlation, we write

$$r_{II_F} = p_{II_F} + p_{IO}r_{OI_F} + p_{IE}r_{EI_F}. \tag{7}$$

Since the solution of Equations (3) through (6) has given us values for all the coefficients on the right side of the equation, we estimate r_{II_F} in each cohort by substitution. These estimates are in the third column of the top panel of Table 11.3. For comparative purposes, the intergenerational education and occupational status correlations are shown in the first two columns of the table. We withhold comment on the intergenerational income correlations from Model I for now, except to note that they are lower than the corresponding correlations of occupational status and educational attainment. This should not be surprising since they are lower-bound estimates.

MODEL II: DIRECT AND INDIRECT INCOME EFFECTS

Having obtained lower-bound estimates of the correlations and path coefficients involving father's income, we turn to estimation of upper-bound values. We respecify the model to allow father's income to affect educational and occupational attainment directly, as well as son's income. Thus, in Model II, father's income may have both direct and indirect effects on son's income, as shown in Figure 11.3. At least in the early career, there is evidence that the correct specification of the income equation lies between the extremes of Model I and Model II. Among nonfarm Wisconsin high school graduates, Sewell and Hauser (1975: 73) find a direct effect of paternal income on son's postsecondary schooling, but none on his occupational status 7 years after high school graduation.

On its face, Model II is more substantively appealing than is Model I. It is likely that continuation in school, especially at the higher

TABLE 11.3

Intergenerational Correlations of Status Variables in Several Models of the Stratification Process

Age cohort	Educational attainment	Occupational status	Income		
			Model I (min.)	Model II (max.)	Average of I, II
		Uncorrected correlations			
25 to 34	.40	.35	.20	.31	.26
35 to 44	.40	.39	.28	.42	.35
45 to 54	.37	.38	.33	.46	.39
55 to 64	.35	.35	.15	.26	.20
		Correlations corrected for attenuation			
25 to 34	.48	.46	.24	.36	.30
35 to 44	.47	.49	.32	.47	.39
45 to 54	.45	.49	.39	.54	.47
55 to 64	.41	.44	.15	.28	.22

NOTE: See text for explanation.

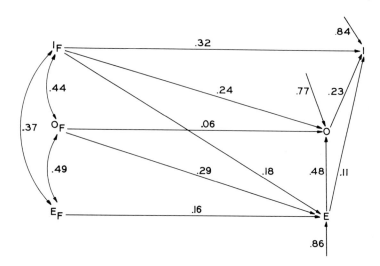

Figure 11.3 Model II: Upper-bound estimates of intergenerational income persistence without correction for measurement error.

levels, depends upon whether one has enough money to pay for school or to support oneself while going to school. Even with respect to high school, it may be the case that, in very poor families, there are strong pressures to drop out of school and go to work in order to help contribute to the support of one's parents and siblings (see B. Duncan, 1965: Chapter 3). While the potential contribution of father's income to son's occupational status is not so obvious, it is possible that entry into some enterprises or occupations entails a degree of risk which an individual might be more willing to undertake were he insured of the support of his father to tide him through difficult times. Moreover, entry into some occupations requires the investment of a substantial amount of capital and family resources may be used to provide such funds directly or to improve access to lending institutions.

What effect does the introduction of these additional paths have upon the parameters of the model? Instead of assuming that p_{OI_F} and p_{EI_F} are zero and estimating the corresponding correlations (r_{OI_F} and r_{EI_F}) from Equations (5) and (6), we assign values to the correlations and estimate the path coefficients as in ordinary regression analysis. Of course, this also revises our estimates of coefficients on the other paths leading to education and occupation.

What are reasonable upper-bound values for $r_{I_F O}$ and $r_{I_F E}$? Given the functional interrelations among schooling, occupational incumbency, and remuneration, it is virtually inconceivable that the intergenerational correlations could be larger than the corresponding intragenerational correlations. That is, it is unlikely that father's income is more highly associated with son's education or occupational status than is son's education or occupational status with his own income. Hence, if we use the intragenerational correlations for sons as estimates of the two intergenerational correlations in question, we obtain maximum estimates of the influence of father's income upon son's statuses. As above, we use the average intragenerational correlations for the 35- to 44- and 45- to 54-year-old cohorts as estimates of $r_{I_F O}$ and $r_{I_F E}$ in each of the four cohorts.

With numeric values assigned to $r_{I_F O}$ and $r_{I_F E}$, as well as $r_{I_F E_F}$ and $r_{I_F O_F}$ (as in Model I), we estimate coefficients for paths leading to E and O as if by ordinary regression. Then we estimate coefficients in the income equations in each cohort as in Model I, except $r_{I_F O}$ and $r_{I_F E}$ are larger in Model II. It is consistent with our effort to set upper bounds on the effects of paternal income in Model II that the assigned numeric values ($r_{I_F O} = .44$ and $r_{I_F E} = .37$) are substantially larger than the observed values of these correlations in the Wisconsin study (Sewell and Hauser, 1975: 72). The estimated path coefficients in Model II are shown in Table 11.4 for each cohort, and the results for 45- to 54-year-old men are also given in Figure 11.3.

As in the case of Model I, the estimates of Model II come close to satisfying the overidentifying restrictions of the model, that is, they can be used to reproduce r_{OE_F}, r_{IO_F}, and r_{IE_F} with reasonable accuracy and with no consistent tendency toward over- or underestimation across the four cohorts. It is a corollary observation that the "tests" of the model using these overidentifying restrictions do not help us to choose between the specifications of Model II and Model I. Both appear to be consistent with the data. At the same time, there are indications that the numeric value of $r_{I_F O}$ may be too large. For example, in the Wisconsin data, $r_{I_F E}$ is larger than $r_{I_F O}$, but we have assumed the opposite in estimating Model II. Further, in the Wisconsin data, father's income has no effect on son's occupational standing, while father's occupational status does affect that of the son. However, in our estimates of Model II, we obtain nearly the opposite result; father's income has a larger effect on son's occupational status than does father's occupational status. Again, these anomalies are consistent with our attempt in Model II to place an upper bound on the influence of father's income.

In Table 11.4, several interesting results can be noted. First, all three parental status characteristics appear to have moderately strong effects on educational attainment. This is about as one might expect, at

TABLE 11.4

Path Coefficients of Model II by Age: Upper-Bound Estimates of Inter-generational Income Persistence without Correction for Measurement Error

Dependent variable	Predetermined variable					Coefficient of determination (R^2)
	O	E	I_F	O_F	E_F	
Age 25 to 34						
E			.19	.22	.22	.25
O		.56	.22	.02		.47
I	.21	.06	.19			.15
Age 35 to 44						
E			.19	.24	.21	.26
O		.54	.21	.06		.46
I	.25	.12	.27			.27
Age 45 to 54						
E			.18	.29	.16	.25
O		.48	.24	.06		.41
I	.23	.11	.32			.29
Age 55 to 64						
E			.22	.20	.16	.22
O		.44	.24	.08		.38
I	.27	.12	.10			.17

NOTE: Variables are I_F = father's income (hypothesized construct), O_F = father's occupational status (Duncan SEI), E_F = father's educational attainment, E = son's educational attainment, O = son's 1962 occupational status (Duncan SEI), I = son's income in 1961.

least if credence is given to the notion of a multidimensional status system in which the effect of various status variables is cumulative. Second, education is by far the most important determinant of occupational status, even though we probably have overestimated the influence of family income. Father's occupation plays almost no role, and, of course, father's education has no effect at all, while the influence of father's income is moderate. Third, except in the oldest cohort, father's income has about as large a direct influence on son's income as does son's occupation and a considerably stronger direct influence than son's education. It is substantively reassuring that the effects of paternal on filial income are small in the oldest cohort in both Model I and Model II, for our rationale for the existence of this path applies mainly to the early career and not at all to the influence of long-deceased fathers on aging sons.

Compared to Model I, the direct effects of schooling on income are not reduced much in Model II; the major effect of the respecification of the income equation is to increase the direct effect of paternal income and decrease that of son's occupational status. However, the respecification also does lower both components of the indirect influence of schooling on income as well as the direct effect, and in combination, these changes are noteworthy. For example, in Model I at ages 25 to 34, the total effect of schooling on income is $.07 + .61(.27) = .23$, but, in Model II at the same ages, the total effect of schooling on income is $.06 + .56(.21) = .18$, or only 80% as large. At ages 25 to 34, the simple correlation of educational attainment and income is .27, so our estimate of specification bias in the simple regression of income on schooling ranges from 16% under Model I to 33% under Model II. We have carried out these same calculations for each of the cohorts with the results shown in Table 11.5. The main finding is that our estimates of bias in the schooling–earnings regression range from 10% to 20% under Model I and from 25% to 40% under Model II. Even under extreme assumptions, most of the association between schooling and earnings represents an effect of the former on the latter.

Finally, to complete our discussion of this model, we estimate the intergenerational income correlations by substituting the appropriate values into Equation (7) for each cohort. The results are presented in Column 4 of the top panel of Table 11.3. These may be regarded as *maximum* estimates of the size of the intergenerational correlations (conditional on the effects of measurement error). Hence, it is of interest to note they are about as large as the correlations of educational

TABLE 11.5

Effects of Schooling (E) on Income (I) (Standardized Reduced Form Coefficients) under Alternative Specifications of the Stratification Process

Age	Uncorrected coefficients			Corrected coefficients		
	r_{EI}	Model I	Model II	r_{EI}	Model I	Model II
25 to 34	.27	.23	.18	.31	.24	.19
35 to 44	.38	.31	.25	.42	.33	.28
45 to 54	.36	.29	.22	.41	.29	.21
55 to 64	.31	.27	.24	.34	.30	.26

attainment and occupational status across generations; the correlations of incomes in the two middle cohorts are slightly larger than the education and occupation correlations, while those in the oldest and youngest cohorts are smaller than the comparable education and occupation figures. Taking these correlations together with those estimated from Model I (the averages of the two estimates are presented in Column 5), we are led to conclude that the degree of income "inheritance" in the U.S. is about as great as the degree of occupational or educational inheritance. Conversely, there is about as much income mobility as there is occupational or educational mobility, which is to say, quite a lot.

CORRECTING FOR RANDOM MEASUREMENT ERROR

Thus far, we have used correlations reported in Duncan, Featherman, and Duncan (1972), assuming all variables were measured without error. This is an untenable assumption on its face. Moreover, in dismissing effects of historical trends and fertility differentials on correlations between father's education and father's occupation, we suggested that the differential reliability of father's and son's characteristics explains the observed differences in the size of the education–occupation correlations in the two generations. In the two middle cohorts—the cohorts for which an intergenerational comparison is least affected by age differences between fathers and sons—the difference in the size of the correlations is about 11 points. For this reason, our findings may have been distorted by our use of correlations observed in the son's generation to estimate the unknown correlations involving father's income at the same time we used the observed correlation between father's education and father's occupation.

Thus, it seems worthwhile to assess the effects of measurement error on our findings and interpretations. We proceed by taking explicit account of the differential reliability of reports about sons and their fathers, first correcting the observed correlations for unreliability and then reestimating each of the path models. Last, we compare the corrected and uncorrected path coefficients to see whether any of our earlier conclusions are affected.[3]

Using reliability coefficients for educational attainment, occupa-

---

[3] A more elaborate specification of error structure and estimation of "corrected" structural coefficients is made possible by the Featherman and Hauser (1975) replication of the OCG study; see Bielby, Hauser, and Featherman (1976, 1977).

tional status, and income obtained from data of the 1960 census (Siegel and Hodge, 1968: 37), it is possible to develop reliability estimates for all of the variables in our models. Consider Figure 11.4, which is like Model I, except the values of each of the observed variables are completely determined by a true score plus a random error term. The latter is uncorrelated both with the true score and with the errors in other variables in the system. True scores are designated by an asterisk, for example, E is observed educational attainment while E^* is the true length of schooling. The assumption of uncorrelated errors is not entirely realistic, since men who overestimate the value of one variable may be likely to overestimate the value of another, and vice versa, as where a son attributes an incorrectly high education and occupation to his father. However, the assumption of random error or some statistically equivalent assumption must be made before we can estimate the parameters of the model. We think it unlikely that correlations among errors are very large or that they would substantially affect our results (see Bielby, Hauser, and Featherman, 1976).

We start by correcting the three correlations between variables which pertain only to sons. Consider first the correlation between O and E, the observed levels of occupational status and educational attainment. From Figure 11.4, it is evident that this correlation may be written as

$$r_{OE} = p_{OO^*} r_{O^* E^*} p_{EE^*} . \qquad (10)$$

Then, rearranging terms, we have

$$r_{O^*E^*} = \frac{r_{OE}}{p_{OO^*} p_{EE^*}} . \qquad (11)$$

Using Equation (11), we can estimate $r_{O^*E^*}$; r_{OE} is observed directly, and we use the square roots of census reliability estimates for p_{OO^*} and p_{EE^*}. From Siegel and Hodge (1968: 37), we obtain $p_{EE^*} = \sqrt{.9332} = .9660$, $p_{OO^*} = \sqrt{.8610} = .9279$, and, in the case of income, $p_{II^*} = \sqrt{.8522} = .9231$. (There is some slippage in population coverage here, since the reliability of education pertains to the total adult population and those of income and occupational status to adult white males.) We use similar equations to estimate $r_{O^*I^*}$ and $r_{E^*I^*}$; these correlations are shown for each cohort in Table 11.6.

To correct correlations within the father's generation, we follow the same logic as in the previous section. We assume that the true correlations in the father's generation are equal to the means of the corrected correlations in the son's generation at ages 35 to 44 and 45 to 54. Thus,

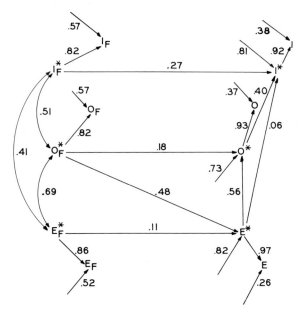

Figure 11.4 Model I: Lower-bound estimates of intergenerational income peristence with adjustment for random errors of measurement.

as before, the values of these correlations in the father's generation are the same in all four cohorts.

Having the corrected correlations in hand, with one further assumption, we can estimate validity coefficients for father's education and father's occupation, that is, $p_{E_F E_F^*}$ and $p_{O_F O_F^*}$. While these validities do not directly enter the final estimation of the model, we need them to correct the intergenerational correlations among observed variables. The additional assumption is that the reliabilities of father's educational attainment and occupational status are proportionate to those of the son's education and occupation. Even though all variables in the father's generation may be measured less reliably than the corresponding variables pertaining to the son's generation, this assumption appears to be plausible. The reader will recall that respondent's education is more reliable than is respondent's occupation. Similarly, we think that a son will recall how much schooling his father completed with greater accuracy than the kind of work the father did during a particular year in the son's life. Under this assumption, we have, for example

$$p_{O_F O_F^*} = a p_{E_F E_F^*}, \tag{12}$$

where

$$a = \frac{p_{OO^*}}{p_{EE^*}}.$$

Consider the observed correlation between father's education and his occupation. From Figure 11.4, we can write the correlation as

$$r_{O_F E_F} = p_{O_F O_F^*}\, r_{O_F^* E_F^*}\, p_{E_F E_F^*},$$

so

$$p_{O_F O_F^*}\, p_{E_F E_F^*} = \frac{r_{O_F E_F}}{r_{O_F^* E_F^*}}.$$

Then, substituting Equation (12) for $p_{O_F O_F^*}$, we have

$$a\left(p_{E_F E_F^*}\right)^2 = \frac{r_{O_F E_F}}{r_{O_F^* E_F^*}}$$

or

$$p_{E_F E_F'} = \sqrt{\frac{r_{O_F E_F}}{a\, r_{O_F^* E_F^*}}} \tag{13}$$

Thus, we can express the validity of father's education in terms of known coefficients. With this result in hand, the validity coefficient for father's occupation can be obtained immediately from Equation (12). (Starting with the youngest cohort, our estimates of $p_{E_F E_F^*}$ are .86, .89, .86, and .90; the estimates of $p_{O_F O_F^*}$ are .82, .86, .82, and .86.) From this point, it is a simple matter to correct the remaining six intercorrelations among observed variables using formulas like Equation (11). These estimates, like those developed above, are presented in Table 11.6 for each cohort. Estimates of the three intergenerational correlations involving father's income are, as before, derived directly from the models, but are presented in Table 11.6 for convenience.

We now reestimate both Model I and Model II, using the corrected correlations but otherwise following the same scheme as before. The estimated coefficients for each cohort under Model I and Model II are shown in Tables 11.7 and 11.8, respectively. With a few exceptions, the corrected estimates satisfy the overidentifying restrictions of Models I and II as well as did the uncorrected estimates.

Inspecting the two tables, it is evident that our corrections for measurement error have had little effect on the results. In both cases, the relative sizes of various coefficients remain essentially unchanged. Indeed, the correlation between the size of the 28 path coefficients reported in Table 11.7 and the corresponding coefficients reported in

TABLE 11.6

Correlations between Status Variables by Age, Adjusted for Random Errors of Measurement

Variable	O_F	I_F	E	O	I
Age 25 to 34					
E_F	.69	.41	.48	.43	.19
O_F		.51	.52	.46	.27
I_F (Model I)			.28	.25	.24
I_F (Model II)			.41	.51	.36
E				.73	.31
O					.39
Age 35 to 44					
E_F	.69	.41	.47	.39	.28
O_F		.51	.52	.49	.33
I_F (Model I)			.28	.26	.32
I_F (Model II)			.41	.51	.47
E				.72	.42
O					.52
Age 45 to 54					
E_F	.69	.41	.45	.32	.24
O_F		.51	.56	.49	.40
I_F (Model I)			.29	.26	.39
I_F (Model II)			.41	.51	.54
E				.66	.41
O					.51
Age 55 to 64					
E_F	.69	.41	.41	.36	.19
O_F		.51	.47	.44	.24
I_F (Model I)			.25	.23	.15
I_F (Model II)			.41	.51	.28
E				.62	.34
O					.44

NOTE: Variables are E_F = father's educational attainment, I_F = father's income (hypothesized construct), O_F = father's occupational status (Duncan SEI), E = son's educational attainment, 0 = son's 1962 occupational status (Duncan SEI), I = son's income in 1961.

Table 11.2 is .97; similarly, the correlation between the 28 coefficients in Table 11.8 and the corresponding coefficients in Table 11.4 is .97. Thus, the relative magnitudes of relationships estimated in each of the

TABLE 11.7

Path Coefficients of Model I by Age: Lower-Bound Estimates of Inter-
generational Income Persistence with Adjustment for Random Errors of
Measurement

Dependent variable	Predetermined variable					Coefficient of determination (R^2)
	O	E	I_F	O_F	E_F	
Age 25 to 34						
E				.35	.24	.30
O		.67		.12		.54
I	.35	.01	.15			.18
Age 35 to 44						
E				.38	.21	.30
O		.63		.16		.53
I	.42	.07	.19			.30
Age 45 to 54						
E				.48	.11	.32
O		.56		.18		.46
I	.40	.06	.27			.34
Age 55 to 64						
E				.35	.16	.23
O		.53		.20		.42
I	.27	.10	.04			.21

NOTE: Variables are I_F = father's income (hypothesized construct), O_F = father's occupational status (Duncan SEI), E_F = father's educational attainment, E = son's educational attainment, O = son's 1962 occupational status (Duncan SEI), I = son's income in 1961.

models is not strongly affected by our corrections. To some degree, this validates the usual procedure of estimating path coefficients directly from observed data of the kind used here. However, we would urge caution in the application of these findings to other situations.

On the other hand, despite the several arbitrary assumptions required to effect the correction for attenuation, we believe the estimates in Tables 11.7 and 11.8 are superior to those in Tables 11.2 and 11.4. In Model I, the corrections for attenuation have increased the size of most effects (and the proportions of variance explained), but there are im-

TABLE 11.8

Path Coefficients of Model II by Age: Upper-Bound Estimates of Inter-generational Income Persistence with Adjustment for Random Errors of Measurement

Dependent variable	Predetermined variable					Coefficient of determination (R^2)
	O	E	I_F	O_F	E_F	
Age 25 to 34						
E			.18	.27	.22	.32
O		.61	.25	.01		.58
I	.27	.02	.21			.19
Age 35 to 44						
E			.18	.30	.18	.32
O		.59	.24	.06		.57
I	.32	.09	.27			.33
Age 45 to 54						
E			.16	.41	.09	.34
O		.51	.26	.07		.51
I	.27	.07	.37			.37
Age 55 to 64						
E			.23	.26	.14	.27
O		.47	.28	.08		.47
I	.35	.10	.06			.21

NOTE: Variables are I_F = father's income (hypothesized construct), O_F = father's occupational status (Duncan SEI), E_F = father's educational attainment, E = son's educational attainment, O = son's 1962 occupational status (Duncan SEI), I = son's income in 1961.

portant exceptions. The direct effects of father's education on son's education decline in each cohort, as do the direct effects of son's schooling on his income. However, there is very little change in the effect of father's income on son's income, which increases in two cohorts and declines in one cohort when the corrections are made. As shown in Table 11.5, the total effects of schooling on income are slightly larger after the corrections than before in three of the four cohorts. At the same time, the bias in the simple regression of income on schooling is consistently greater in the corrected estimates for

Model I; it ranges from 13% in the oldest cohort to 29% among 45- to 54-year-old men. Finally, in Model I, the corrected intergenerational income correlations are slightly larger than the earlier estimates (see the lower panel of Table 11.3), but in no case are they large as any of the corrected intergenerational correlations of educational attainment or occupational status. The effects of our corrections on the estimates under Model II are much the same as in the case of Model I. Overall, we are impressed that failure to correct for measurement error does not lead to very large or consistent understatement of the tightness or rigidity of the stratification system. This is perhaps most evident in our finding that "corrected" estimates give larger estimates of returns to schooling in occupational status and income at the same time they tell us that we had previously underestimated the bias in those same coefficients.

A MODEL ASSUMING HIGH-INCOME INHERITANCE

Finally, we briefly consider what the process of stratification would look like if son's income were as heavily influenced by parent's income as some writers on poverty appear to believe (Council of Economic Advisors, 1966: 102). We arbitrarily choose a large value for r_{II_F} and, otherwise retaining our earlier assumptions, we use this assumed correlation between father's and son's incomes to estimate the path coefficients of a model like those treated above. For want of a better value, we arbitrarily set $r_{II_F} = .7$, which implies that about half of the variance in son's income can be accounted for (directly or indirectly) by father's income. While some might defend the choice of an even larger value, we think even this figure is unrealistically large. For example, recall from Table 11.3 that in only one instance did an estimate of r_{II_F} under Model II exceed .5, and Model II was constructed to yield maximal estimates of the persistence of incomes across generations. Moreover, .7 is about as large as the largest of the corrected correlations among variables in the model, that between education and occupation. In short, we investigate a model in which the inheritance of income or the propensity to acquire income is assumed to be stronger than any other linkage in the process of status attainment, except that between educational attainment and occupational achievement in the generation of sons. In illustrating the implications of this assumption, we use the correlations corrected for attenuation for the 45- to 54-year-old cohort.

Our estimation procedure is identical to that in Models I and II, except we use a different set of equations to estimate the coefficients of paths leading to income. Given our assumption about the size of the intergenerational income coefficient, this choice of estimating equations gives us a means of assessing the adequacy of the model. Since we not start with a value of $r_{I_F I_F}$, we can solve a system of equations

$$
\begin{aligned}
r_{I I_F} &= p_{I I_F} + p_{I O} r_{O I_F} + p_{I E} r_{E I_F} \\
r_{I O} &= p_{I I_F} r_{I_F O} + p_{I O} + p_{I E} r_{E O} \\
r_{I E} &= p_{I I_F} r_{I_F E} + p_{I O} r_{O E} + p_{I E}
\end{aligned} \tag{14}
$$

to estimate the coefficients of the income equation. All the correlations in this set of equations are known, including $r_{E I_F}$ and $r_{O I_F}$ to which we earlier assigned values under the specifications of Model I or Model II. Table 11.9 gives the estimated coefficients of the income equations in Models I and II. Inspection of the coefficients suggests their rejection out of hand. It is most implausible that income *directly* depends upon father's income to a much higher degree than upon occupational status, especially considering that most income of American men derives from occupational performance. Presumably, even those who believe that income "inheritance" is a major feature of the stratification system would expect that the principal mechanism of income persistence is the creation by wealthy fathers of educational and occupational opportunities for their sons. But we have, in a sense, considered this possibility in Model II, which assumes that the association of son's education and occupation with father's income is as strong as that with his own income. While it would be possible to imagine a society in which the *inter*generational effects of status were actually greater than the corresponding *intra*generational effects, it is not possible to imagine this of mid-twentieth-century America.

TABLE 11.9

Estimated Effects on Income where Intergenerational Income Correlation is r = .7

Predetermined variable	Model I	Model II
I_F	.61	.59
E	-.01	.04
O	.36	.18

NOTE: Variables are I_F = father's income (hypothesized construct), E = son's educational attainment, O = son's 1962 occupational status (Duncan SEI).

Even though the results in Table 11.9 (and thus the assumption of an intergenerational income correlation as large as .7) can be rejected on purely theoretical grounds, we can also show other ways in which the model is untenable if such a large correlation is assumed. The system of Equation (14) is highly overidentified, since we could have written an equation for each of the five correlations of income with other variables in the model. By writing only the three equations in (14), we assumed that the paths leading from father's education and father's occupation to income are zero, that the model is identical in that respect to one of those estimated earlier. If there are zero coefficients on paths leading from father's education and occupation to son's income, it will be possible using the basic theorem of path analysis to reproduce r_{IE_F} and r_{IO_F} within the limits of sampling error. However, this is far from the case. From the model we may write the implied correlations,

$$\hat{r}_{IO_F} = p_{II_F}r_{I_FO_F} + p_{IO}r_{OO_F} + p_{IE}r_{EO_F} \tag{15}$$

and

$$\hat{r}_{IE_F} = p_{II_F}r_{I_FE_F} + p_{IO}r_{OE_F} + p_{IE}r_{EE_F}. \tag{16}$$

The observed (corrected values of r_{IO_F} and r_{IE_F} are, respectively, .32 and .28, while the corresponding correlations calculated from Model I are .49 and .36, and from Model II they are .42 and .32. It is evident that both models, but especially Model I, reproduce the observed correlations rather poorly. In both cases, the calculated correlations are substantially larger than the observed values. To state the matter in a different, but equivalent way, had we estimated all five possible path coefficients in the income equation, we would have found substantial negative paths from father's occupational status and educational attainment to son's income. However stated, these results lead us to reject the idea that the correlation of paternal and filial incomes could be as large as .7.

CONCLUSIONS

Starting with a set of intercorrelations among five variables that enter into the process of status attainment and a set of plausible assumptions about the structure of the relationships between these variables and father's income, we have derived various estimates of income's persistence across generations of men in the U.S. Our major conclusion is quite simple: The extent of income mobility is no less than that of occupational or educational mobility, father's income accounts for no more than 15% to 25% of the variance in son's income, which is comparable to the proportion of variance in son's occupational status explained by father's occupational status and the proportion of variance in son's educational attainment explained by father's education. Whatever the exigencies of life which make successes or failures of men, it is clear that their social origins are of modest importance, at least in comparison with the host of factors which do not vary systematically with social origins.

While it is tempting to conclude here, one final *caveat* is in order: It must be strongly emphasized that the results reported above do not have the status of direct empirical findings but, rather, are inferences based on the many assumptions underlying our estimation procedures. While most of the assumptions we have made are plausible enough— and we made some effort to assess their plausibility—our results must still stand as a poor substitute for direct empirical evidence regarding the role of parental income in the stratification process. What is needed is careful empirical study of the ways in which parental income influences the life chances of children.

Appendix A

1970 Detailed Industry and Occupation Codes, U.S. Bureau of the Census

INDUSTRIAL CLASSIFICATION SYSTEM

Equivalent alphabetic codes follow some codes. Either code may be utilized, depending upon the processing method. Numbers in parentheses following the industry categories are the SIC definitions. "N.e.c." means "not elsewhere classified."

Industry Code

AGRICULTURE, FORESTRY, AND FISHERIES

017 (A) Agricultural production (01)
018 Agricultural services, except horticultural (07 except 0713 and 073)
019 Horticultural services (073)
027 Forestry (08)
028 Fisheries (09)

MINING

047 Metal mining (10)
048 Coal mining (11, 12)
049 Crude petroleum and natural gas extractions (13)
057 Nonmetallic mining and quarrying, except fuel (14)

CONSTRUCTION

067 General building contractors (15)
068 General contractors, except building (16)
069 (B) Special trade contractors (17)
077 Not specified construction

MANUFACTURING

Durable goods

Lumber and wood products, except furniture
107 Logging (241)
108 Sawmills, planing mills, and mill work (242, 243)
109 Miscellaneous wood products (244, 249)
118 Furniture and fixtures (25)

Stone, clay, and glass products
119 Glass and glass products (321–323)
127 Cement, concrete, gypsum, and plaster products (324, 327)
128 Structural clay products (325)
137 Pottery and related products (326)
138 Miscellaneous nonmetallic mineral and stone products (328, 329)

Metal industries
139 Blast furnaces, steel works, rolling and finishing mills (3312, 3313)
147 Other primary iron and steel industries (3315–3317, 332, 3391, part 3399)
148 Primary aluminum industries (3334, part 334, 3352, 3361, part 3392, part 3399)
149 Other primary nonferrous industries (3331–3333, 3339, part 334, 3351, 3356, 3357, 3362, 3369, part 3392, part 3399)
157 Cutlery, hand tools, and other hardware (342)
158 Fabricated structural metal products (344)
159 Screw machine products (345)
167 Metal stamping (346)
168 Miscellaneous fabricated metal products (341, 343, 347, 348, 349)

MANUFACTURING—Continued

169 Not specified metal industries

Machinery, except electrical
177 Engines and turbines (351)
178 Farm machinery and equipment (352)
179 Construction and material handling machines (353)
187 Metalworking machinery (354)
188 Office and accounting machines (357 except 3573)
189 Electronic computing equipment (3573)
197 Machinery, except electrical, n.e.c. (355, 356, 358, 359)
198 Not specified machinery

Electrical machinery, equipment, and supplies
199 Household appliances (363)
207 Radio, T.V., and communication equipment (365, 366)
208 Electrical machinery, equipment, and supplies, n.e.c. (361, 362, 364, 367, 369)
209 Not specified electrical machinery, equipment, and supplies

Transportation equipment
219 Motor vehicles and motor vehicle equipment (371)
227 Aircraft and parts (372)
228 Ship and boat building and repairing (373)
229 Railroad locomotives and equipment (374)
237 Mobile dwellings and campers (3791)
238 Cycles and miscellaneous transportation equipment (375, 3799)

Professional and photographic equipment, and watches
239 Scientific and controlling instruments (381, 382)

247 Optical and health services supplies (383, 384, 385)
248 Photographic equipment and supplies (386)
249 Watches, clocks, and clockwork-operated devices (387)
257 Not specified professional equipment
258 Ordnance (19)
259 Miscellaneous manufacturing industries (39)

Nondurable goods
Food and kindred products
268 Meat products (201)
269 Dairy products (202)
278 Canning and preserving fruits, vegetables, and sea foods (203)
279 Grain mill products (204, 0713)
287 Bakery products (205)
288 Confectionery and related products (207)
289 Beverage industries (208)
297 Miscellaneous food preparation and kindred products (206, 209)
298 Not specified food industries
299 Tobacco manufactures (21)

Textile mill products
307 Knitting mills (225)
308 Dyeing and finishing textiles, except wool and knit goods (226)
309 Floor coverings, except hard surface (227)
317 Yarn, thread, and fabric mills (221–224, 228)
318 Miscellaneous textile mill products (229)

Apparel and other fabricated textile products
319 (C) Apparel and accessories (231–238)

Industry Code	
	MANUFACTURING—Continued

Paper and allied products

327   Miscellaneous fabricated textile products (239)

328   Pulp, paper, and paperboard mills (261–263, 266)
329   Miscellaneous paper and pulp products (264)
337   Paperboard containers and boxes (265)

Printing, publishing, and allied industries

338   Newspaper publishing and printing (271)
339   Printing, publishing, and allied industries, except newspapers (272–279)

Chemicals and allied products

347   Industrial chemicals (281)
348   Plastics, synthetics and resins, except fibers (282, except 2823 and 2824)
349   Synthetic fibers (2823, 2824)
357   Drugs and medicines (283)
358   Soaps and cosmetics (284)
359   Paints, varnishes, and related products (285)
367   Agricultural chemicals (287)
368   Miscellaneous chemicals (286, 289)
369   Not specified chemicals and allied products

Petroleum and coal products

377   Petroleum refining (291)
378   Miscellaneous petroleum and coal products (295, 299)

Rubber and miscellaneous plastic products

379   Rubber products (301–303, 306)
387   Miscellaneous plastic products (307)

Leather and leather products

388   Tanned, curried, and finished leather (311)
389   Footwear, except rubber (313, 314)

397   Leather products, except footwear (312, 315–317, 319)
398   Not specified manufacturing industries

TRANSPORTATION, COMMUNICATIONS, AND OTHER PUBLIC UTILITIES

Transportation

407 (D)   Railroads and railway express service (40)
408   Street railways and bus lines (411, 413–415, 417)
409   Taxicab service (412)
417   Trucking service (421, 423)
418   Warehousing and storage (422)
419   Water transportation (44)
427   Air transportation (45)
428   Pipe lines, except natural gas (46)
429   Services incidental to transportation (47)

Communications

447   Radio broadcasting and television (483)
448   Telephone (wire and radio) (481)
449   Telegraph and miscellaneous communication services (482, 489)

Utilities and sanitary services

467   Electric light and power (491)
468   Electric gas utilities (493)
469   Gas and steam supply systems (492, 496)
477   Water supply (494)
478   Sanitary services (495)
479   Other and not specified utilities (497)

WHOLESALE AND RETAIL TRADE

Wholesale trade

507   Motor vehicles and equipment (501)

WHOLESALE AND RETAIL TRADE—Continued

508 Drugs, chemicals, and allied products (502)
509 Dry goods and apparel (503)
527 Food and related products (504)
528 Farm products—raw materials (505)
529 Electrical goods (506)
537 Hardware, plumbing, and heating supplies (507)
538 Not specified electrical and hardware products
539 Machinery equipment and supplies (508)
557 Metals and minerals, n.e.c. (5091)
558 Petroleum products (5092)
559 Scrap and waste materials (5093)
567 Alcoholic beverages (5095)
568 Paper and its products (5096)
569 Lumber and construction materials (5098)
587 Wholesalers, n.e.c. (5094, 5097, 5099)
588 Not specified wholesale trade

Retail trade

607 Lumber and building material retailing (521–524)
608 Hardware and farm equipment stores (525)
609 (E) Department and mail order establishments (531, 532)
617 Limited price variety stores (533)
618 Vending machine operators (534)
619 Direct selling establishments (535)
627 Miscellaneous general merchandise stores (539)
628 (F) Grocery stores (541)
629 Dairy products stores (545)
637 Retail bakeries (546)
638 Food stores, n.e.c. (542–544, 549)
639 Motor vehicle dealers (551, 552)

647 Tire, battery, and accessory dealers (553)
648 Gasoline service stations (554)
649 Miscellaneous vehicle dealers (559)
657 Apparel and accessories stores, except shoe stores (56 except 566)
658 Shoe stores (566)
667 Furniture and home furnishings stores (571)
668 Household appliances, TV, and radio stores (572, 573)
669 (G) Eating and drinking places (58)
677 Drug stores (591)
678 Liquor stores (592)
679 Farm and garden supply stores (596)
687 Jewelry stores (597)
688 Fuel and ice dealers (598)
689 Retail florists (5992)
697 Miscellaneous retail stores (593–595, 599 exc. 5992)
698 Not specified retail trade

FINANCE, INSURANCE, AND REAL ESTATE

707 Banking (60)
708 Credit agencies (61)
709 Security, commodity brokerage, and investment companies (62, 67)
717 Insurance (63, 64)
718 Real estate, incl. real estate-insurance-law offices (65, 66)

BUSINESS AND REPAIR SERVICES

727 Advertising (731)
728 Services to dwellings and other buildings (734)
729 Commercial research, development, and testing labs (7391, 7397)

BUSINESS AND REPAIR SERVICE—Continued

737 Employment and temporary help agencies (736, 7398)
738 Business management and consulting services (part 7392)
739 Computer programming services (part 7392)
747 Detective and protective services (7393)
748 Business services, n.e.c. (732, 733, 735, 7394, 7395, 7396, 7399)
749 Automobile services, except repair (751, 752, 754)
757 Automobile repair and related services (753)
758 Electrical repair shops (762, 7694)
759 Miscellaneous repair services (763, 764, 769, except 7694)

PERSONAL SERVICES

769 (H) Private households (88)
777 Hotels and motels (701)
778 Lodging places, except hotels and motels (702, 703, 704)
779 Laundering, cleaning, and other garment services (721, 727)
787 Beauty shops (723)
788 Barber shops (724)
789 Shoe repair shops (725)
797 Dressmaking shops (part 729)
798 Miscellaneous personal services (722, 726, part 729)

ENTERTAINMENT AND RECREATION SERVICES

807 Theaters and motion pictures (78, 792)
808 Bowling alleys, billiard and pool parlors (793)

809 Miscellaneous entertainment and recreation services (791, 794)

PROFESSIONAL AND RELATED SERVICES

828 Offices of physicians (801, 803)
829 Offices of dentists (802)
837 Offices of chiropractors (804)
838 (J) Hospitals (806)
839 Convalescent institutions (8092)
847 Offices of health practitioners, n.e.c. (part 8099)
848 Health services, n.e.c. (807, part 8099)
849 Legal services (81)
857 (K) Elementary and secondary schools (821)
858 Colleges and universities (822)
859 Libraries (823)
867 Educational services, n.e.c. (824, 829)
868 Not specified educational services
869 Museums, art galleries, and zoos (84)
877 Religious organizations (866)
878 Welfare services (part 867)
879 Residential welfare facilities (part 867)
887 Nonprofit membership organizations (861–865, 869)
888 Engineering and architectural services (891)
889 Accounting, auditing, and bookkeeping services (893)
897 Miscellaneous professional and related services (892, 899)

PUBLIC ADMINISTRATION

907 Postal service (part 9190)
917 (L) Federal public administration (part 9190, 9490)
927 State public administration (9290)
937 (M) Local public administration (9390)

999   INDUSTRY NOT REPORTED[1]

ALLOCATION CATEGORIES[2]

029 Agriculture, forestry, and fisheries—allocated
058 Mining—allocated
078 Construction—allocated
267 Manufacturing, durable goods—allocated
399 Manufacturing, nondurable goods—allocated
499 Transportation, communications, and other public utilities—allocated

599 Wholesale trade—allocated
699 Retail trade—allocated
719 Finance, insurance, and real estate—allocated
767 Business and repair services—allocated
799 Personal services—allocated
817 Entertainment and recreation services—allocated
899 Professional and related services—allocated
947 Public administration—allocated

OCCUPATIONAL CLASSIFICATION SYSTEM

Equivalent alphabetic codes follow some codes. Either code may be utilized, depending on the processing method. "N.e.c." means "not elsewhere classified."

*Occu-
pation
Code*   PROFESSIONAL, TECHNICAL, AND
        KINDRED WORKERS

001 Accountants
002 Architects
    Computer specialists
003 Computer programmers
004 Computer systems analysts
005 Computer specialists, n.e.c.
    Engineers
006 Aeronautical and astronautical engineers

010 Chemical engineers
011 Civil engineers
012 Electrical and electronic engineers
013 Industrial engineers
014 Mechanical engineers
015 Metallurgical and materials engineers
020 Mining engineers
021 Petroleum engineers
022 Sales engineers
023 Engineers, n.e.c.
024 Farm management advisors
025 Foresters and conservationists

[1] This code is used to identify not reported industries in surveys where the not reported cases are not allocated.

[2] Those returns from the Population Census which do not have an industry entry are allocated among the major industry groups during computer processing. These cases are labeled with the code for the "allocation" category to which they are assigned.

Occupation Code

PROFESSIONAL, TECHNICAL, AND KINDRED WORKERS—Continued

026 Home management advisors

Lawyers and judges
030 Judges
031 Lawyers

Librarians, archivists, and curators
032 Librarians
033 Archivists and curators

Mathematical specialists
034 Actuaries
035 Mathematicians
036 Statisticians

Life and physical scientists
042 Agricultural scientists
043 Atmospheric and space scientists
044 Biological scientists
045 Chemists
051 Geologists
052 Marine scientists
053 Physicists and astronomers
054 Life and physical scientists, n.e.c.
055 Operations and systems researchers and analysts
056 Personnel and labor relations workers

Physicians, dentists, and related practitioners
061 Chiropractors
062 Dentists
063 Optometrists
064 Pharmacists
065 Physicians, medical and osteopathic
071 Podiatrists
072 Veterinarians

073 Health practitioners, n.e.c.

Nurses, dietitians, and therapists
074 Dietitians
075 Registered nurses
076 Therapists

Health technologists and technicians
080 Clinical laboratory technologists and technicians
081 Dental hygienists
082 Health record technologists and technicians
083 Radiologic technologists and technicians
084 Therapy assistants
085 Health technologists and technicians, n.e.c.

Religious workers
086 Clergymen
090 Religious workers, n.e.c.

Social scientists
091 Economists
092 Political scientists
093 Psychologists
094 Sociologists
095 Urban and regional planners
096 Social scientists, n.e.c.

Social and recreation workers
100 Social workers
101 Recreation workers

Teachers, college and university
102 Agriculture teachers
103 Atmospheric, earth, marine, and space teachers
104 Biology teachers
105 Chemistry teachers
110 Physics teachers
111 Engineering teachers
112 Mathematics teachers

PROFESSIONAL, TECHNICAL, AND KINDRED WORKERS—Continued

113 Health specialties teachers
114 Psychology teachers
115 Business and commerce teachers
116 Economics teachers
120 History teachers
121 Sociology teachers
122 Social science teachers, n.e.c.
123 Art, drama, and music teachers
124 Coaches and physical education teachers
125 Education teachers
126 English teachers
130 Foreign language teachers
131 Home economics teachers
132 Law teachers
133 Theology teachers
134 Trade, industrial, and technical teachers
135 Miscellaneous teachers, college and university
140 Teachers, college and university, subject not specified
    Teachers, except college and university
141 Adult education teachers
142 (N) Elementary school teachers
143 Prekindergarten and kindergarten teachers
144 Secondary school teachers
145 Teachers, except college and university, n.e.c.
    Engineering and science technicians
150 Agriculture and biological technicians, except health

151 Chemical technicians
152 Draftsmen
153 Electrical and electronic engineering technicians
154 Industrial engineering technicians
155 Mechanical engineering technicians
156 Mathematical technicians
161 Surveyors
162 Engineering and science technicians, n.e.c.
    Technicians, except health, and engineering and science
163 Airplane pilots
164 Air traffic controllers
165 Embalmers
170 Flight engineers
171 Radio operators
172 Tool programmers, numerical control
173 Technicians, n.e.c.
174 Vocational and educational counselors
    Writers, artists, and entertainers
175 Actors
180 Athletes and kindred workers
181 Authors
182 Dancers
183 Designers
184 Editors and reporters
185 Musicians and composers
190 Painters and sculptors
191 Photographers
192 Public relations men and publicity writers
193 Radio and television announcers
194 Writers, artists, and entertainers, n.e.c.
195 Research workers, not specified

MANAGERS AND ADMINISTRATORS, EXCEPT FARM

201 Assessors, controllers, and treasurers; local public administration
202 Bank officers and financial managers
203 Buyers and shippers, farm products
205 Buyers, wholesale and retail trade
210 Credit men
211 Funeral directors
212 Health administrators
213 Construction inspectors, public administration
215 Inspectors, except construction, public administration
216 Managers and superintendents, building
220 Office managers, n.e.c.
221 Officers, pilots, and pursers; ship
222 Officials and administrators; public administration, n.e.c.
223 Officials of lodges, societies, and unions
224 Postmasters and mail superintendents
225 Purchasing agents and buyers, n.e.c.
226 Railroad conductors
230 Restaurant, cafeteria, and bar managers
231 Sales managers and department heads, retail trade
233 Sales managers, except retail trade
235 School administrators, college
240 School administrators, elementary and secondary
245 Managers and administrators, n.e.c.

SALES WORKERS

260 Advertising agents and salesmen
261 Auctioneers
262 Demonstrators
264 Hucksters and peddlers
265 Insurance agents, brokers, and underwriters
266 Newsboys
270 Real estate agents and brokers
271 Stock and bond salesmen
280 Salesmen and sales clerks, n.e.c.[1]

CLERICAL AND KINDRED WORKERS

301 Bank tellers
303 Billing clerks
305 (P) Bookkeepers
310 Cashiers
311 Clerical assistants, social welfare
312 Clerical supervisors, n.e.c.
313 Collectors, bill and account
314 Counter clerks, except food
315 Dispatchers and starters, vehicle
320 Enumerators and interviewers
321 Estimators and investigators, n.e.c.
323 Expediters and production controllers
325 File clerks
326 Insurance adjusters, examiners, and investigators
330 Library attendants and assistants
331 Mail carriers, post office

[1] Category "280 Salesmen and sales clerks, n.e.c." was subdivided in the Census into 5 occupation groups dependent on industry. The industry codes are shown in parentheses.

281 Sales representatives, manufacturing industries (Ind. 107–399)
282 Sales representatives, wholesale trade (Ind. 017–058, 507–599)
283 Sales clerks, retail trade (Ind. 608–699 except 618, 639, 649, 667, 668, 688)
284 Salesmen, retail trade (Ind. 607, 618, 639, 649, 667, 668, 688)
285 Salesmen of services and construction (Ind. 067–078, 407–499, 707–947)

CLERICAL AND KINDRED WORKERS—Continued

332 Mail handlers, except post office
333 Messengers and office boys
334 Meter readers, utilities
Office machine operators
341 Bookkeeping and billing machine operators
342 Calculating machine operators
343 Computer and peripheral equipment operators
344 Duplicating machine operators
345 Key punch operators
350 Tabulating machine operators
355 Office machine operators, n.e.c.
360 Payroll and timekeeping clerks
361 Postal clerks
362 Proofreaders
363 Real estate appraisers
364 Receptionists
Secretaries
370 Secretaries, legal
371 Secretaries, medical
372 (Q) Secretaries, n.e.c.
374 Shipping and receiving clerks
375 Statistical clerks
376 Stenographers
381 Stock clerks and storekeepers
382 Teacher aides, exc. school monitors
383 Telegraph messengers
384 Telegraph operators
385 Telephone operators
390 Ticket, station, and express agents

391 Typists
392 Weighers
394 Miscellaneous clerical workers
395 Not specified clerical workers

CRAFTSMEN AND KINDRED WORKERS

401 Automobile accessories installers
402 Bakers
403 Blacksmiths
404 Boilermakers
405 Bookbinders
410 Brickmasons and stonemasons
411 Brickmasons and stonemasons, apprentices
412 Bulldozer operators
413 Cabinetmakers
415 (R) Carpenters
416 Carpenter apprentices
420 Carpet installers
421 Cement and concrete finishers
422 Compositors and typesetters
423 Printing trades apprentices, exc. pressmen
424 Cranemen, derrickmen, and hoistmen
425 Decorators and window dressers
426 Dental laboratory technicians
430 Electricians
431 Electrician apprentices
433 Electric power linemen and cablemen
434 Electrotypers and stereotypers
435 Engravers, exc. photoengravers
436 Excavating, grading, and road machine operators; exc. bulldozer
440 Floor layers, exc. tile setters

Occu-
pation
Code

CRAFTSMEN AND KINDRED WORKERS—Continued

Code	Occupation
441	Foremen, n.e.c.
442	Forgemen and hammermen
443	Furniture and wood finishers
444	Furriers
445	Glaziers
446	Heat treaters, annealers, and temperers
450	Inspectors, scalers, and graders; log and lumber
452	Inspectors, n.e.c.
453	Jewelers and watchmakers
454	Job and die setters, metal
455	Locomotive engineers
456	Locomotive firemen
461	Machinists
462	Machinist apprentices
	Mechanics and repairmen
470	Air conditioning, heating, and refrigeration
471	Aircraft
472	Automobile body repairmen
473 (S)	Automobile mechanics
474	Automobile mechanic apprentices
475	Data processing machine repairmen
480	Farm implement
481	Heavy equipment mechanics, incl. diesel
482	Household appliance and accessory installers and mechanics
483	Loom fixers
484	Office machine
485	Radio and television
486	Railroad and car shop
491	Mechanic, exc. auto, apprentices
492	Miscellaneous mechanics and repairmen
495	Not specified mechanics and repairmen
501	Millers; grain, flour, and feed
502	Millwrights
503	Molders, metal
504	Molder apprentices
505	Motion picture projectionists
506	Opticians, and lens grinders and polishers
510	Painters, construction and maintenance
511	Painter apprentices
512	Paperhangers
514	Pattern and model makers, exc. paper
515	Photoengravers and lithographers
516	Piano and organ tuners and repairmen
520	Plasterers
521	Plasterer apprentices
522	Plumbers and pipe fitters
523	Plumber and pipe fitter apprentices
525	Power station operators
530	Pressmen and plate printers, printing
531	Pressman apprentices
533	Rollers and finishers, metal
534	Roofers and slaters
535	Sheetmetal workers and tinsmiths
536	Sheetmetal apprentices
540	Shipfitters
542	Shoe repairmen
543	Sign painters and letterers
545	Stationary engineers
546	Stone cutters and stone carvers
550	Structural metal craftsmen
551	Tailors

CRAFTSMEN AND KINDRED WORKERS—Continued

552 Telephone installers and repairmen
554 Telephone linemen and splicers
560 Tile setters
561 Tool and die makers
562 Tool and die maker apprentices
563 Upholsterers
571 Specified craft apprentices, n.e.c.
572 Not specified apprentices
575 Craftsmen and kindred workers, n.e.c.
580 Former members of the Armed Forces

OPERATIVES, EXCEPT TRANSPORT

601 Asbestos and insulation workers
602 (T) Assemblers
603 Blasters and powdermen
604 Bottling and canning operatives
605 Chainmen, rodmen, and axmen; surveying
610 Checkers, examiners, and inspectors; manufacturing
611 Clothing ironers and pressers
612 Cutting operatives, n.e.c.
613 Dressmakers and seamstresses, except factory
614 Drillers, earth
615 Dry wall installers and lathers
620 Dyers
621 Filers, polishers, sanders, and buffers
622 Furnacemen, smeltermen, and pourers
623 Garage workers and gas station attendants
624 Graders and sorters, manufacturing
625 Produce graders and packers, except factory and farm

626 Heaters, metal
630 Laundry and dry cleaning operatives, n.e.c.
631 Meat cutters and butchers, exc. manufacturing
633 Meat cutters and butchers, manufacturing
634 Meat wrappers, retail trade
635 Metal platers
636 Milliners
640 Mine operatives, n.e.c.
641 Mixing operatives
642 Oilers and greasers, exc. auto
643 Packers and wrappers, except meat and produce
644 Painters, manufactured articles
645 Photographic process workers
    Precision machine operatives
650 Drill press operatives
651 Grinding machine operatives
652 Lathe and milling machine operatives
653 Precision machine operatives, n.e.c.
656 Punch and stamping press operatives
660 Riveters and fasteners
661 Sailors and deckhands
662 Sawyers
663 Sewers and stitchers
664 Shoemaking machine operatives
665 Solderers
666 Stationary firemen
    Textile operatives
670 Carding, lapping, and combing operatives
671 Knitters, loopers, and toppers
672 Spinners, twisters, and winders
673 Weavers
674 Textile operatives, n.e.c.
680 Welders and flame cutters

Occu- pation Code	
	OPERATIVES, EXCEPT TRANSPORT—Continued
681	Winding operatives, n.e.c.
690	Machine operatives, miscellaneous specified
692	Machine operatives, not specified
694	Miscellaneous operatives
695	Not specified operatives
701	Boatmen and canalmen
703	Bus drivers
704	Conductors and motormen, urban rail transit
705	Deliverymen and routemen
706	Fork lift and tow motor operatives
710	Motormen; mine, factory, logging camp, etc.
711	Parking attendants
712	Railroad brakemen
713	Railroad switchmen
714	Taxicab drivers and chauffeurs
715 (U)	Truck drivers
	LABORERS, EXCEPT FARM
740	Animal caretakers, exc. farm
750	Carpenters' helpers
751 (V)	Construction laborers, exc. carpenters' helpers
752	Fishermen and oystermen
753	Freight and material handlers
754	Garbage collectors
755	Gardeners and groundskeepers, exc. farm
760	Longshoremen and stevedores
761	Lumbermen, raftsmen, and woodchoppers
762	Stock handlers
763	Teamsters
764	Vehicle washers and equipment cleaners
770	Warehousemen, n.e.c.
780	Miscellaneous laborers
785	Not specified laborers
	FARMERS AND FARM MANAGERS
801 (W)	Farmers (owners and tenants)
802	Farm managers
	FARM LABORERS AND FARM FOREMEN
821	Farm foremen
822	Farm laborers, wage workers
823	Farm laborers, unpaid family workers
824	Farm service laborers, self-employed
	SERVICE WORKERS, EXC. PRIVATE HOUSEHOLD
	Cleaning service workers
901	Chambermaids and maids, except private household
902	Cleaners and charwomen
903 (X)	Janitors and sextons
	Food service workers
910	Bartenders
911	Busboys
912	Cooks, except private household
913	Dishwashers
914	Food counter and fountain workers
915 (Y)	Waiters
916	Food service workers, n.e.c., except private household
	Health service workers
921	Dental assistants

SERVICE WORKERS, EXC. PRIVATE
HOUSEHOLD—Continued

922 Health aides, exc. nursing
923 Health trainees
924 Lay midwives
925 Nursing aides, orderlies, and attendants
926 Practical nurses
Personal service workers
931 Airline stewardesses
932 Attendants, recreation and amusement
933 Attendants, personal service, n.e.c.
934 Baggage porters and bellhops
935 Barbers
940 Boarding and lodging house keepers
941 Bootblacks
942 Child care workers, exc. private household
943 Elevator operators
944 Hairdressers and cosmetologists
945 Personal service apprentices
950 Housekeepers, exc. private household
952 School monitors
953 Ushers, recreation and amusement
954 Welfare service aides
Protective service workers
960 Crossing guards and bridge tenders

961 Firemen, fire protection
962 Guards and watchmen
963 Marshals and constables
964 Policemen and detectives
965 Sheriffs and bailiffs
980 Child care workers, private household
981 Cooks, private household
982 Housekeepers, private household
983 Laundresses, private household
984 (Z) Maids and servants, private household
995 OCCUPATION NOT REPORTED[2]

ALLOCATION CATEGORIES[3]

196 Professional, technical, and kindred workers—allocated
246 Managers and administrators, except farm—allocated
296 Sales workers—allocated
396 Clerical and kindred workers—allocated
586 Craftsmen and kindred workers—allocated
696 Operatives, except transport—allocated
726 Transport equipment operatives—allocated
796 Laborers, except farm—allocated
806 Farmers and farm managers—allocated
846 Farm laborers and farm foremen—allocated
976 Service workers, exc. private household—allocated
986 Private household workers—allocated

---

[2] This code is used to identify not reported occupations in surveys where the not reported cases are not allocated.

[3] Those returns from the Population Census which do not have an occupation entry are allocated among the major occupation groups during computer processing. These cases are labeled with the code for the "allocation" category to which they are assigned.

Appendix B

Duncan Socioeconomic Index
and Siegel Prestige Scores for
1970 Census Detailed
Occupation Codes

1970 Census occupation code	Duncan SEI[a]		Siegel (1965 NORC) Prestige[a]	
	Male scores	Total scores	Male scores	Total scores
001	76.8	76.9	55.9	56.0
002	85.2	85.3	66.7	
003	65.0		50.6	
004	65.0		50.6	
005	65.0		50.6	
006	87.0		71.1	
010	89.9		67.2	
011	84.0		67.8	
012	84.0		69.4	
013	85.5		55.6	
014	80.2		62.1	
015	83.1		58.4	
020	85.0		61.6	
021	81.0		57.1	
022	87.0		50.6	
023	86.9		67.0	
024	83.0		53.9	
025	48.0		53.9	
026	83.0		53.9	
030	93.0		75.7	
031	92.3		75.1	
032	60.0		54.6	
033	74.6		59.6	
034	81.0		55.4	
035	80.0		65.0	
036	81.0		55.4	
042	80.0		55.8	
043	62.0		47.0	
044	80.0		67.7	
045	79.4		67.1	67.3
051	80.0		67.2	
053	80.0		73.8	
054	77.2	77.4	64.8	65.1
055	65.7		50.8	
056	83.6	82.4	55.8	55.2
061	75.0		60.0	
062	96.0		73.6	
063	79.0		62.0	
064	81.3	81.4	60.3	
065	92.1		81.2	
071	58.0		36.7	
072	78.0		59.7	
074	39.0		52.1	
075	44.3		60.1	
076	59.9	58.9	40.5	38.5
080	48.0		61.0	
081	48.0		61.0	
082	60.0		54.6	

(Continued)

1970 Census occupation code	Duncan SEI[a]		Siegel (1965 NORC) Prestige[a]	
	Male scores	Total scores	Male scores	Total scores
083	48.0		61.0	
084	48.0		61.0	
085	52.2	55.2	49.8	51.1
086	52.0		69.0	
090	56.7	57.1	55.0	54.6
091	74.4	74.3	53.6	53.5
093	81.0		71.4	
095	65.0		50.6	
096	81.0		65.6	
100	64.0		52.4	
101	67.0		48.6	
102	84.0		78.3	
103	84.0		78.3	
104	84.0		78.3	
105	84.0		78.3	
110	84.0		78.3	
111	84.0		78.3	
112	84.0		78.3	
113	84.0		78.3	
114	84.0		78.3	
115	84.0		78.3	
116	84.0		78.3	
120	84.0		78.3	
121	84.0		78.3	
122	84.0		78.3	
123	53.2	55.6	46.8	48.6
124	64.0		53.2	
125	84.0		78.3	
126	84.0		78.3	78.3
130	84.0		78.3	
132	84.0		78.3	
133	84.0		78.3	
134	84.0		78.3	
135	84.0		78.3	
140	84.0		78.3	
141	61.3	64.3	44.3	43.9
142	71.2	71.4	58.9	59.2
143	72.0		56.1	
144	70.2	70.5	59.8	60.1
145	62.3	57.7	44.2	44.9
150	62.0		47.2	
151	62.0		47.0	
152	67.0		56.1	
153	62.0		51.6	51.5
154	64.1	64.0	49.5	49.4
155	62.0		47.0	
161	48.4		53.1	
162	62.0		47.0	

(Continued)

321

1970 Census occupation code	Duncan SEI[a]		Siegel (1965 NORC) Prestige[a]	
	Male scores	Total scores	Male scores	Total scores
163	79.0		70.1	
164	69.0		42.8	
165	60.8	60.3	51.7	51.9
170	48.0		48.2	
171	69.0		42.8	
172	62.0		47.0	
173	62.0		47.2	
174	65.0		50.6	
175	60.0		55.0	
180	59.4	60.2	51.8	52.1
181	76.0		59.8	
182	45.0		37.6	
183	70.5	70.4	56.5	
184	82.0		51.2	
185	52.0		46.0	
190	67.0		56.2	
191	50.0		40.5	
192	82.0		56.7	
193	65.0		50.6	
194	40.2	45.4	38.6	41.2
195	65.0		50.6	
201	61.2	58.8	50.9	53.8
202	79.5	80.0	66.1	66.6
203	50.5	50.3	43.0	42.9
205	72.1		50.0	
210	74.0		48.8	
211	59.0		52.2	
212	74.1	56.9	63.8	59.4
213	57.6	57.5	39.6	
215	66.7	66.6	42.3	
216	32.0		38.3	
220	75.1	73.1	57.6	56.0
221	49.9		56.7	
222	67.3	66.5	60.7	60.3
223	59.8	60.0	48.4	48.4
224	61.3	60.8	58.4	58.3
225	74.7	74.8	46.4	
226	58.2		40.9	
230	37.6	38.1	38.7	38.9
231	70.6	69.8	48.5	47.8
233	74.7	74.6	54.2	
235	77.9	77.1	70.6	69.6
240	71.7		61.7	61.6
245	62.0	61.7	50.8	50.7
260	66.1		42.3	
261	40.0		31.9	
262	35.0	38.1	28.3	30.6
264	08.8	12.9	18.6	20.2

(Continued)

1970 Census occupation code	Duncan SEI[a]		Siegel (1965 NORC) Prestige[a]	
	Male scores	Total scores	Male scores	Total scores
265	66.0		46.8	
266	27.0		15.4	
270	62.0		44.0	
271	72.3	72.4	51.2	51.3
281	65.0		49.1	
282	60.9		39.9	
283	39.0		28.7	28.6
284	39.0		28.6	
285	52.7	52.2	35.8	35.4
301	52.0	51.8	49.5	49.0
303	44.0		36.2	
305	50.8	50.9	47.3	47.4
310	44.0	43.9	31.4	31.0
312	43.6	43.8	35.8	36.0
313	43.3	42.5	28.4	27.9
314	44.0		36.2	
315	39.9	40.1	33.3	33.4
320	44.0		36.2	
321	59.2	56.2	42.9	41.2
323	43.7	43.6	36.0	
325	44.0		31.4	30.8
326	62.1		47.6	
330	44.0	43.1	40.4	39.7
331	53.0		42.3	
332	43.0	43.3	35.1	35.5
333	28.2		19.4	19.3
334	44.0		36.2	
341	44.9		43.7	44.3
342	45.0		44.9	
343	45.0		44.9	
344	45.0		44.9	
345	45.0		44.9	
350	45.0		44.9	
355	45.0		44.9	
360	44.0		41.2	41.3
361	44.7	44.6	42.3	42.4
362	44.0		36.2	
363	67.8		43.0	
364	44.0		37.1	38.9
370	61.0		45.8	
371	61.0		45.8	
372	61.9	61.0	46.5	45.8
374	24.2	24.1	29.9	
375	43.7	43.9	35.8	36.0
376	61.0		43.3	
381	44.0	43.9	25.0	25.2
382	63.2	62.4	49.3	48.8
383	22.0		29.8	

(Continued)

1970 Census occupation code	Duncan SEI[a]		Siegel (1965 NORC) Prestige[a]	
	Male scores	Total scores	Male scores	Total scores
384	47.0		43.5	
385	45.0		40.4	
390	59.8		35.4	
391	61.0		41.3	
392	41.9	41.8	35.5	35.4
394	43.7		36.2	36.5
395	44.0		36.2	
401	21.6		32.5	
402	21.9	21.7	34.0	33.8
403	16.0		35.5	
404	32.6		30.6	
405	39.0	38.0	31.3	31.4
410	27.0		35.7	
411	32.0		40.8	
412	19.7		32.3	
413	22.3		38.1	
415	18.9		39.7	39.6
416	31.0		40.8	
420	12.0		32.8	
421	19.0		31.6	
422	52.0		38.0	
423	40.0		40.8	
424	21.0		38.7	
425	40.0		37.4	
426	48.0		61.0	
430	44.0		49.2	
431	37.0		40.8	
433	49.0		39.2	
434	55.0		38.0	
435	47.0		41.2	
436	22.8		31.5	
440	17.3	17.4	31.4	31.8
441	49.7	49.5	45.3	45.3
442	23.0	22.8	35.5	
443	17.8		29.1	
444	39.5	33.4	35.2	32.3
445	25.2	25.3	26.7	
446	21.7		35.3	
450	22.4	22.5	31.0	
452	41.2	41.0	31.3	
453	36.4		37.5	37.5
454	33.5		46.4	
455	57.8		50.8	
456	45.0		36.2	
461	32.9		47.7	
462	41.0		40.8	
470	27.0		36.7	
471	48.0		48.2	

(Continued)

1970 Census occupation code	Duncan SEI[a]		Siegel (1965 NORC) Prestige[a]	
	Male scores	Total scores	Male scores	Total scores
472	19.0		36.7	
473	19.0		36.7	
474	25.0		40.8	
480	27.0		32.6	
481	26.6		32.8	
482	27.0		32.6	
483	10.0		30.4	
484	35.9		33.8	
485	36.0		35.0	
486	20.5		35.6	
491	34.0		40.8	
492	26.5		32.8	
495	27.0		32.6	
501	19.0		25.2	
502	31.0		40.3	
503	12.0		39.1	
504	33.0		40.8	
505	43.0		33.9	
506	39.0		51.4	
510	16.4		29.9	29.8
511	29.0		40.8	
512	13.7	13.5	27.7	27.5
514	43.0		38.7	38.7
515	63.0	61.1	40.1	39.7
516	38.0		32.0	
520	25.0		33.2	
521	29.0		40.8	
522	34.0		40.6	
523	33.0		40.8	
525	50.0		38.8	
530	46.3	45.6	39.3	39.1
531	40.0		40.8	
533	22.0		36.0	
534	15.1		31.5	
535	33.0		36.8	
536	33.0		40.8	
540	34.0		35.5	
542	12.0	11.9	32.6	
543	16.9	16.8	30.7	
545	45.2		34.9	32.9
546	24.0		31.7	
550	33.7	33.4	35.6	
551	22.0	21.4	34.0	
552	48.8		39.1	
554	49.0		39.2	
560	28.2		38.4	
561	49.2		42.3	
562	41.0		40.8	

(Continued)

1970 Census occupation code	Duncan SEI[a]		Siegel (1965 NORC) Prestige[a]	
	Male scores	Total scores	Male scores	Total scores
563	21.1	21.2	29.9	
571	34.5	34.6	40.8	
572	39.0		40.8	
575	25.7	25.3	42.1	41.7
601	32.0		28.4	
602	17.2		27.5	
603	11.0		32.1	
604	18.4	16.1	23.3	23.5
605	25.0		39.4	
610	19.2	18.4	36.1	
611	17.8	16.8	21.9	20.7
612	18.8	18.9	28.8	28.5
613	23.0	22.4	31.7	31.0
614	21.6		26.2	
615	24.5	24.4	36.4	36.3
620	12.0		25.0	
621	18.7	18.7	23.1	23.5
622	18.1		32.9	
623	17.9		21.2	
624	17.0	16.6	32.9	32.6
625	12.2	13.7	23.6	24.5
626	29.0		32.9	
630	15.0		18.2	
631	28.8		32.0	
633	16.4	16.2	23.6	23.5
634	18.0		19.4	
635	19.8	19.7	30.3	30.2
636	46.0		33.4	
640	16.5	16.5	26.4	
641	17.6	17.3	27.5	27.3
642	15.0		24.2	
643	18.0	18.1	19.5	
644	18.1		29.0	28.8
645	42.1	41.2	35.9	35.5
650	21.8	22.0	31.7	31.8
651	21.9		19.0	
652	21.5	21.6	31.9	31.9
653	21.0	20.9	31.1	
656	19.4	19.5	30.4	30.3
660	20.1	20.6	31.6	31.5
661	16.0		33.7	
662	04.9		27.6	
663	18.2		25.2	25.1
664	09.2		31.6	
665	23.8	24.4	35.4	36.1
666	16.6		31.7	
670	03.1	03.3	28.9	
671	21.0		29.4	

(Continued)

1970 Census occupation code	Duncan SEI[a]		Siegel (1965 NORC) Prestige[a]	
	Male scores	Total scores	Male scores	Total scores
672	03.8	04.1	28.2	
673	05.9		25.0	25.1
674	06.1	08.6	28.8	
680	24.0		40.1	
681	19.6	21.7	32.0	33.6
690	19.0		28.4	28.5
692	19.3	19.3	29.3	
694	19.2	18.8	29.1	28.9
695	19.2	19.5	29.1	
701	24.0		36.8	
703	24.0	24.0	32.4	
704	32.5		28.0	
705	31.0		28.2	28.3
706	16.8	16.8	28.4	28.4
710	03.0		27.2	
711	18.8		22.0	
712	42.0		34.7	
713	44.0		32.8	
714	10.0		21.5	
715	15.1		32.1	
740	16.9	17.5	28.7	30.3
750	07.2	23.0		
751	07.1	07.1	74.4	
752	10.6	30.3		
753	08.7	08.9	18.8	19.0
754	06.0	06.0	17.3	
755	10.9		22.1	
760	11.0		24.4	
761	04.1		25.9	
762	16.7	17.3	20.6	20.7
763	08.0		12.2	
764	08.6	08.6	18.5	18.5
770	08.3		20.3	
780	08.2	08.2	19.1	
785	08.3	08.3	17.5	
801	14.0		40.7	
802	36.0		43.7	
821	20.0		35.0	
822	06.3		18.9	18.8
823	17.0		18.4	18.5
824	22.0		26.8	
901	13.4	11.6	16.6	14.1
902	07.8	09.8	18.4	17.4
903	12.7	12.5	19.5	19.3
910	19.0		19.9	
911	11.0		14.4	
912	15.0		26.4	
913	11.0		21.8	

(Continued)

1970 Census occupation code	Duncan SEI[a]		Siegel (1965 NORC) Prestige[a]	
	Male scores	Total scores	Male scores	Total scores
914	17.0		15.4	
915	16.0		20.3	
916	11.0		20.9	20.8
921	38.0		47.8	
922	25.0	29.4	26.3	40.5
923	51.0		45.1	
924	37.0		23.3	
925	13.7	13.5	36.8	36.4
926	22.0		41.9	
931	31.0		36.4	
932	19.1	19.5	15.6	16.4
933	26.3	28.8	21.7	22.5
934	07.8	07.9	17.5	
935	17.0		37.9	
940	30.0		22.1	
941	08.0		09.3	
942	28.2		24.0	24.1
943	10.0		20.9	
944	17.0		33.2	
945	31.0		40.8	
950	31.0		36.4	
952	26.0		14.1	
953	25.0		14.9	
954	11.0		14.4	
960	17.9	17.5	25.3	24.5
961	37.0		43.8	
962	18.2		22.2	22.3
963	21.0		45.8	
964	40.5	40.4	47.7	
965	34.0		55.0	
980	07.0		22.6	22.9
981	07.0		18.0	
982	10.7	18.6	20.1	24.7
983	12.0		17.6	
984	07.0		18.0	
052	80.0		67.2	
073	58.0		36.7	
092	81.0		71.4	
094	81.0		71.4	
131	72.0		53.2	
156	53.0		46.8	
280	49.4		35.4	
311	44.0		31.4	
475	27.0		40.8	
775	07.9		17.5	
782	07.6		19.1	
795	07.9		17.5	

(Continued)

1970 Census occupation code	Duncan SEI[a]		Siegel (1965 NORC) Prestige[a]	
	Male scores	Total scores	Male scores	Total scores
796	07.9		17.5	
805	17.0		18.4	
882	06.3		18.9	

[a] These scores reflect the male composition of the civilian labor force ("male scores"); scores reflecting the composition of total persons in the civilian labor force are marked "total scores" only in those cases where the latter differ from "male scores." No scores appear for codes 580 (Armed Forces) or 995 (Not ascertained).

Appendix **C**

Regression Models of
Socioeconomic Achievement
for Men by Age and by Race,
March 1962

TABLE C.1

Standardized Regression Coefficients in a Model of Socioeconomic Achievement: U.S. Men in the Experienced Civilian Labor Force by Age and by Race, March 1962

Dependent Variable	Predetermined Variable						R^2
	X	V	F	S	U	Y	
Nonblack men, 35–44 years old							
U	.234 (.024)	.253 (.022)	-.069 (.021)	-.186 (.020)			.294
Y	.137 (.022)	.015 (.020)	-.056 (.019)	-.022 (.018)	.545 (.020)		.428
H	.087 (.026)	.055 (.024)	-.060 (.022)	-.027 (.022)	.150 (.027)	.245 (.026)	.221
lnH	-.009 (.027)	.013 (.025)	-.111 (.024)	-.030 (.023)	.117 (.029)	.211 (.028)	.130
Nonblack men, 45–54 years old							
U	.269 (.025)	.215 (.023)	-.071 (.023)	-.170 (.021)			.273
Y	.161 (.024)	-.012 (.022)	-.043 (.021)	-.026 (.021)	.504 (.022)		.376
H	.153 (.027)	-.012 (.024)	-.002 (.024)	-.009 (.022)	.126 (.028)	.331 (.026)	.254
lnH	.024 (.028)	.008 (.025)	-.072 (.025)	-.027 (.023)	.151 (.029)	.274 (.027)	.189

TABLE C.1 (continued)

Dependent Variable	Predetermined variable						R^2
	X	V	F	S	U	Y	
Black men, 45-54 years old							
U	-.043 (.086)	.308 (.086)	-.187 (.088)	-.145 (.083)			.195
Y	.046 (.090)	-.021 (.094)	.021 (.093)	-.021 (.087)	.361 (.092)		.130
H	.032 (.088)	.126 (.091)	-.106 (.091)	-.065 (.085)	.160 (.096)	.186 (.087)	.174
lnH	.018 (.090)	.164 (.093)	-.131 (.093)	-.049 (.087)	.113 (.098)	.124 (.089)	.139
Black men, 55-64 years old							
U	.353 (.105)	.161 (.098)	-.084 (.099)	.030 (.096)			.208
Y	-.005 (.113)	.042 (.102)	.035 (.101)	.019 (.098)	.423 (.107)		.184
H	-.009 (.108)	-.110 (.097)	-.063 (.096)	-.133 (.093)	.425 (.110)	.146 (.100)	.273
lnH	-.044 (.111)	-.164 (.099)	-.080 (.099)	-.087 (.096)	.432 (.113)	.092 (.103)	.232

NOTE: Source is March 1962 Current Population Survey and the supplement, "Occupational Changes in a Generation." Variables are X = father's occupational status, V = father's educational attainment, F = farm background, S = number of siblings, U = educational attainment, Y = occupational status in March 1962, H = 1961 income. Coefficients in parenthesis are approximate standard errors.

333

TABLE C.1 (continued)

Dependent Variable	Predetermined Variable						R^2
	X	V	F	S	U	Y	
Nonblack men, 55-64 years old							
U	.214 (.033)	.255 (.030)	-.049 (.030)	-.133 (.027)			.232
Y	.136 (.031)	.011 (.029)	-.095 (.028)	-.043 (.026)	.463 (.028)		.346
H	.046 (.035)	-.012 (.032)	-.066 (.031)	-.010 (.028)	.153 (.034)	.312 (.033)	.214
lnH	-.013 (.036)	-.003 (.033)	-.125 (.032)	.024 (.029)	.151 (.035)	.243 (.034)	.152
Black men, 35-44 years old							
U	.163 (.073)	.186 (.073)	-.292 (.070)	-.090 (.069)			.218
Y	.043 (.076)	.069 (.076)	-.075 (.076)	-.077 (.072)	.331 (.079)		.182
H	-.049 (.076)	-.005 (.076)	-.033 (.076)	-.008 (.071)	.327 (.083)	.188 (.077)	.194
lnH	-.010 (.080)	.072 (.080)	.005 (.080)	-.023 (.076)	.220 (.088)	.093 (.082)	.090

TABLE C.2

Regression Coefficients in a Model of Socioeconomic Achievement: U.S. Men in the Experienced Civilian Labor Force by Age and by Race, March 1962

Dependent Variable	Predetermined Variable						Constant
	X	V	F	S	U	Y	
Nonblack men, 35-44 years old							
U	.03637	.2185	-.5322	-.2068			9.564
Y	.1563	.094	-3.126	-.1808	3.979		-8.215
H	20.61	71.77	-704.91	-45.37	227.78	51.01	1416.80
lnH	-.0004	.0034	-.2531	-.0100	.0346	.0085	7.916
Nonblack men, 45-54 years old							
U	.04526	.1887	-.5356	-.1869			8.936
Y	.1853	-.072	-2.215	-.1992	3.455		-1.150
H	42.11	-17.66	-30.50	-15.51	206.52	79.00	677.23
lnH	.0011	.0019	-.1467	-.0081	.0409	.0108	7.715
Nonblack men, 55-64 years old							
U	.03844	.2390	-.3770	-.1527			7.773
Y	.1608	.068	-4.820	-.3260	3.058		6.107
H	11.53	-15.41	-706.31	-15.53	213.54	65.92	1580.31
lnH	-.0008	-.0010	-.3132	.0092	.0493	.0120	7.478

TABLE C.2 (continued)

Dependent Variable	Predetermined Variable						
	X	V	F	S	U	Y	Constant
Black men, 35–44 years old							
U	.05866	.2111	-2.431	-.0998			7.654
Y	.0620	.312	-2.492	-.3402	1.325		8.136
H	-11.52	-3.60	-179.99	-6.07	215.42	30.91	1011.24
lnH	-.0013	.0312	.0162	-.0097	.0840	.0088	6.539
Black men, 45–54 years old							
U	-.01417	.3072	-1.443	-.1509			7.460
Y	.0558	-.077	.592	-.0798	1.325		7.101
H	5.20	62.19	-407.18	-33.28	79.24	25.05	1940.81
lnH	.0014	.0390	-.2410	-.0123	.0269	.0080	7.307
Black men, 55–64 years old							
U	.10458	.1601	-.6223	.0286			3.456
Y	-.0054	.147	.895	.0637	1.479		5.012
H	-1.29	-56.23	-239.85	-64.02	217.35	21.39	1910.61
lnH	-.0036	-.0449	-.1626	-.0225	.1190	.0072	7.192

NOTE: Source is March 1962 Current Population Survey and the supplement, "Occupational Changes in a Generation." Variables are X = father's occupational status, V = father's educational attainment, F = farm background, S = number of siblings, U = educational attainment, Y = occupational status in March 1962, H = 1961 income.

Appendix **D**

Supplementary Occupational Mobility Tables for Married Males and Females, March 1962

TABLE D.1

Mobility from Father's (or Other Family Head's) Occupation to Current Occupation and Labor Force Status: Married U.S. Men Aged 20 to 64 in March 1962

Father's Occupation	March 1962 Occupation																		Total
	(1)	(2)	(3)	(4)	(5)	(6)	(7)	(8)	(9)	(10)	(11)	(12)	(13)	(14)	(15)	(16)	(17)	(18)	
(1) Prof., tech., & kindred, self-employed	30	64	20	9	24	0	5	4	3	10	3	6	4	0	7	2	1	7	198
(2) Prof., tech., & kindred, salaried	17	148	69	27	24	0	41	9	11	35	42	26	17	0	8	5	1	7	486
(3) Mgrs., officials, prop., salaried	23	121	115	43	37	1	40	8	23	76	20	17	8	0	9	3	1	16	561
(4) Mgrs., officials, prop., self-employed	44	159	227	187	59	1	69	30	23	120	56	52	29	1	20	12	2	32	1123
(5) Sales, other	12	60	68	33	39	2	16	6	4	33	15	7	6	0	2	5	1	9	319
(6) Clerical & kindred, stenog & secretaries	1	10	8	1	1	0	0	1	0	0	2	1	0	0	0	0	0	0	24
(7) Clerical & kindred, other	13	98	52	26	27	2	39	6	14	71	26	16	20	0	8	7	0	8	434
(8) Sales, retail	2	34	42	29	27	0	14	7	11	37	21	24	12	0	7	9	0	7	284
(9) Craftsmen, foremen	1	44	34	22	6	0	20	7	16	68	25	25	10	0	9	15	0	13	300
(10) Craftsmen, other	25	263	213	172	78	10	174	36	85	625	209	220	98	1	105	18	9	69	2411
(11) Operatives, other	5	107	58	67	33	2	68	14	41	196	152	105	58	0	67	9	5	32	1019
(12) Operatives, mfg.	9	100	75	75	36	2	71	16	58	240	110	222	55	0	76	8	5	51	1208
(13) Service, other	5	57	54	44	30	0	59	11	28	96	70	58	66	0	34	3	2	12	629
(14) Service, private household	0	1	1	0	0	0	2	3	4	10	12	8	5	0	4	4	0	1	54
(15) Laborers, except farm	2	54	39	37	20	0	59	13	20	179	118	125	67	2	110	11	8	33	895
(16) Farmers, farm mgrs.	28	183	188	290	53	5	163	40	98	703	403	398	186	2	275	662	119	178	3974
(17) Farm laborers	1	9	12	20	1	0	14	5	7	70	46	42	17	0	35	27	33	14	352
(18) Not in labor force, not ascertained	14	78	98	92	23	1	71	19	46	218	134	139	103	2	126	31	16	46	1254
Total	232	1589	1374	1172	518	26	926	235	491	2787	1462	1492	761	6	901	818	201	536	15526

TABLE D.2

Mobility from Father's (or Other Family Head's) Occupation to Current Occupation and Labor Force Status: Married U.S. Women Aged 20 to 64 in March 1962

Father's Occupation	March 1962 Occupation																		
	(1)	(2)	(3)	(4)	(5)	(6)	(7)	(8)	(9)	(10)	(11)	(12)	(13)	(14)	(15)	(16)	(17)	(18)	Total
(1) Prof., tech., & kindred, self-employed	3	29	1	2	0	20	13	1	0	0	5	6	2	3	0	0	0	160	245
(2) Prof., tech., & kindred, salaried	4	57	6	2	6	33	53	13	0	2	6	12	11	4	0	0	1	366	576
(3) Mgrs., officials, prop., salaried	3	41	7	2	1	30	47	5	0	0	4	9	17	4	0	0	2	347	517
(4) Mgrs., officials, prop., self-employed	14	79	17	16	2	40	79	35	2	0	4	24	33	5	1	1	8	627	986
(5) Sales, other	5	20	12	6	0	8	28	9	0	0	2	3	8	1	0	0	1	212	315
(6) Clerical & kindred, stenog & secretaries	0	1	0	0	0	1	1	0	0	0	0	1	0	0	0	0	0	15	19
(7) Clerical & kindred, other	4	33	7	1	2	25	46	8	0	2	1	2	12	1	1	0	3	279	427
(8) Sales, retail	1	12	2	4	1	16	15	8	0	1	2	21	9	2	0	1	0	172	268
(9) Craftsmen, foremen	2	33	3	1	1	23	38	11	0	0	2	10	11	3	1	0	0	207	345
(10) Craftsmen, other	5	87	23	21	8	111	232	63	4	5	25	125	91	26	7	2	10	1563	2408
(11) Operatives, other	2	47	8	3	1	35	89	46	1	1	15	51	64	20	2	0	4	814	1203
(12) Operatives, mfg.	2	44	14	12	8	51	110	42	3	4	8	99	58	15	4	1	5	833	1314
(13) Service, other	2	22	3	1	0	28	56	14	1	5	5	27	31	3	0	1	1	366	566
(14) Service, private household	0	2	0	0	0	0	0	1	0	0	0	1	0	4	0	0	0	18	24
(15) Laborers, except farm	1	20	4	6	2	28	57	19	1	1	11	75	65	26	8	2	3	649	977
(16) Farmers, farm mgrs.	15	153	40	22	5	61	227	117	12	12	46	212	260	97	4	8	88	2149	3526
(17) Farm laborers	0	5	3	1	5	1	21	6	1	1	8	33	22	15	0	1	4	233	359
(18) Not in labor force, not ascertained	6	45	8	12	1	49	91	30	18	3	16	89	99	53	2	1	5	920	1450
Total	68	731	157	112	43	557	1202	427	44	35	161	798	794	281	30	17	135	9932	15525

Appendix **E**

Supplementary Industrial
Mobility Tables for Men,
March 1962

TABLE E.1

Mobility from Father's Industry to First Industry, Total Population: Outflow Percentages

Father's Industry (% of Fathers in Father's industry)	Respondent's First Industry														Total
	1	2	3	4	5	6	7	8	9	10	11	12	13	14	
1. Agriculture, forestry and fisheries (0.81)	39.04	0.00	3.93	7.98	7.35	5.07	3.80	21.65	0.00	6.48	0.83	0.91	1.91	1.05	100.00
2. Mining (4.98)	3.87	37.55	5.29	15.67	9.97	6.04	1.43	12.30	0.30	2.39	1.21	0.49	2.56	0.93	100.00
3. Construction (12.31)	6.46	0.91	21.80	15.76	14.77	7.04	2.66	15.02	2.33	2.32	2.64	1.61	4.08	2.60	100.00
4. Manufacturing, durable goods (16.66)	3.44	0.80	5.15	44.26	12.87	5.42	2.21	13.19	2.02	1.77	2.38	0.90	4.07	1.54	100.00
5. Manufacturing, non-durable goods (13.27)	3.46	0.24	4.34	15.37	39.42	4.21	2.68	15.81	2.86	2.07	1.96	1.78	4.01	1.79	100.00
6. Transportation, communication, other public utilities (12.56)	5.93	0.68	5.81	17.33	14.48	19.05	5.50	15.73	1.91	2.70	2.84	1.08	4.33	2.62	100.00
7. Wholesale trade (3.05)	3.59	1.11	3.33	13.70	13.48	5.75	18.24	15.39	5.89	2.87	2.39	1.04	11.62	1.59	100.00
8. Retail trade (13.29)	4.54	0.76	4.40	13.28	12.97	6.10	5.02	33.78	3.42	3.00	2.03	2.81	5.87	2.01	100.00
9. Finance, insurance and real estate (3.13)	1.46	0.94	4.25	14.75	10.90	6.07	4.93	13.14	14.79	5.01	3.84	6.82	9.39	3.72	100.00
10. Business and repair service (2.78)	8.62	1.11	6.55	14.82	12.33	7.43	1.12	17.31	2.33	17.03	2.89	2.18	4.63	1.64	100.00
11. Personal services (6.06)	6.32	1.70	5.99	19.23	9.62	6.94	3.65	18.55	8.95	2.72	8.79	1.55	3.74	2.25	100.00
12. Entertainment and recreation services (0.68)	2.25	2.09	16.06	19.29	7.78	11.28	2.46	9.58	3.79	0.00	2.08	10.28	7.04	6.01	100.00
13. Professional and related services (5.02)	3.35	0.78	5.46	18.45	8.30	9.16	1.83	15.49	4.23	2.76	2.27	2.83	21.97	3.13	100.00
14. Public administration (5.39)	4.60	0.92	7.31	17.85	13.11	9.23	4.42	18.62	4.72	3.03	1.05	0.61	7.48	7.04	100.00
Total	4.90	2.63	7.29	20.62	16.15	7.90	3.82	17.73	3.46	2.95	2.67	1.77	5.74	2.39	100.00

TABLE E.2

Mobility from Father's Industry to 1962 Industry, Total Population: Outflow Percentages

Father's Industry (% of Fathers in Father's Industry)	Respondent's Industry in March, 1962														
	1	2	3	4	5	6	7	8	9	10	11	12	13	14	Total
1. Agriculture, forestry and fisheries (0.81)	8.46	2.00	13.02	7.14	14.56	10.96	8.25	18.71	1.93	0.00	2.74	0.00	8.50	3.73	100.00
2. Mining (4.92)	3.02	15.33	8.26	22.36	8.62	9.56	4.08	10.82	2.21	2.36	1.59	0.38	5.74	5.68	100.00
3. Construction (12.32)	2.38	0.54	20.93	18.14	9.36	8.15	4.53	11.69	4.11	3.20	1.50	0.48	7.21	7.77	100.00
4. Manufacturing, durable goods (16.65)	1.83	1.29	6.26	36.89	10.67	6.91	3.40	9.90	2.41	4.63	1.73	0.60	7.95	5.52	100.00
5. Manufacturing, non-durable goods (13.20)	2.20	1.09	8.40	19.56	22.63	8.30	5.21	10.30	3.36	2.77	1.95	0.79	7.12	6.30	100.00
6. Transportation, communication, other public utilities (12.61)	2.12	0.77	8.52	16.47	11.51	19.99	4.50	11.57	3.89	2.89	4.60	0.45	6.16	6.63	100.00
7. Wholesale trade (3.09)	0.52	0.76	4.31	19.51	8.38	5.41	13.68	13.71	5.83	3.58	1.99	0.29	14.28	7.75	100.00
8. Retail trade (13.35)	2.42	0.93	6.57	13.31	10.97	5.95	6.12	23.37	6.22	3.25	2.63	1.11	10.05	7.10	100.00
9. Finance, insurance, and real estate (3.14)	0.74	0.96	5.26	11.03	11.38	11.87	7.29	7.80	16.59	2.86	0.96	0.27	12.65	10.33	100.00
10. Business and repair services (2.81)	1.78	2.63	7.67	19.23	10.65	8.52	3.26	14.69	3.75	10.30	1.31	1.33	9.12	5.77	100.00
11. Personal services (6.00)	3.03	0.54	8.05	22.41	6.60	7.95	4.95	11.75	5.85	1.46	7.86	3.27	7.81	8.47	100.00
12. Entertainment and recreation services (0.69)	0.00	0.00	23.58	15.07	4.54	10.91	2.48	8.99	3.31	1.09	2.23	9.77	9.35	8.67	100.00
13. Professional and related services (4.98)	2.23	0.64	5.91	17.29	9.94	6.73	3.45	6.86	5.36	2.33	2.51	1.72	26.71	8.32	100.00
14. Public administration (5.43)	1.36	0.41	11.49	15.77	10.17	10.26	3.15	10.91	7.02	4.85	0.93	0.29	12.38	11.01	100.00
Total	2.15	1.63	9.27	20.62	11.77	9.34	4.86	12.49	4.62	3.41	2.55	0.91	9.25	7.11	100.00

TABLE E.3

Mobility from First Industry to 1962 Industry, Total Population: *Outflow Percentages*

Respondent's First Industry (% of Respondents in Respondent's First Industry)	Respondent's Industry in March, 1962														Total
	1	2	3	4	5	6	7	8	9	10	11	12	13	14	
1. Agriculture, forestry and fisheries (5.86)	17.93	2.29	11.33	19.56	8.29	10.01	3.48	12.84	2.10	0.84	2.99	1.05	3.20	4.08	100.00
2. Mining (2.56)	1.07	24.92	10.50	21.51	6.44	8.75	3.75	8.71	1.63	1.93	0.97	0.38	6.08	3.34	100.00
3. Construction (7.37)	1.65	1.43	31.18	18.13	7.10	7.67	3.37	8.38	1.69	2.49	1.51	0.31	8.73	6.36	100.00
4. Manufacturing, durable goods (20.40)	1.80	1.28	7.56	41.24	9.49	6.73	3.63	8.17	1.76	3.48	2.00	0.59	5.41	6.88	100.00
5. Manufacturing, non-durable goods (16.00)	1.18	0.86	7.57	16.28	29.38	8.17	4.67	11.74	3.06	2.49	1.75	0.88	4.82	7.14	100.00
6. Transportation, communication, other public utilities (7.98)	1.77	1.00	8.72	16.34	7.10	30.50	3.53	8.03	4.11	3.65	2.86	0.56	5.28	6.54	100.00
7. Wholesale trade (3.77)	0.80	0.74	3.80	16.84	10.46	8.96	18.45	11.15	6.12	2.67	8.20	0.00	6.32	5.50	100.00
8. Retail trade (17.65)	1.19	0.64	7.89	14.88	9.56	8.24	6.60	25.48	5.68	4.44	2.61	1.14	5.09	6.57	100.00
9. Finance, insurance, and real estate (3.29)	0.22	0.63	2.76	12.13	7.69	5.12	6.86	5.86	31.36	0.40	1.82	4.35	9.20	11.61	100.00
10. Business and repair services (2.89)	2.61	1.92	6.52	18.82	8.48	6.51	3.38	17.33	4.09	18.24	0.76	0.00	4.80	6.53	100.00
11. Personal services (2.71)	0.00	0.52	7.42	15.38	14.19	5.69	3.91	17.78	3.51	1.32	17.10	0.62	5.32	7.23	100.00
12. Entertainment and recreation services (1.67)	3.49	0.43	13.27	8.62	7.35	12.97	2.98	23.70	1.32	3.67	5.85	4.30	5.16	6.89	100.00
13. Professional and related services (5.49)	0.61	0.65	3.42	5.38	5.00	2.87	2.19	2.51	3.08	1.93	0.52	1.05	64.42	6.37	100.00
14. Public administration (2.35)	1.99	0.00	7.11	9.79	4.74	5.84	5.71	9.45	8.23	1.40	1.14	0.61	12.92	31.07	100.00
Total	2.36	1.63	9.27	20.65	11.85	9.31	4.91	12.63	4.33	3.34	2.69	0.91	8.93	7.19	100.00

Appendix **F**

A Sampling Design Factor for the 1962 Occupational Changes in a Generation Survey

We have very little information about sampling error in the 1962 OCG. There is a table of standard errors of percentages for a range of population bases which pertain to occupation and education reports (U.S. Bureau of the Census, 1964c: Table G, reproduced in Appendix G of Blau and Duncan, 1967: 477). This table is reproduced in Columns (1)–(3) of the attached table. Since the 20,700 OCG respondents represent 44,984,000 men aged 20–64, sample case bases may be estimated by dividing the entries in Column (2) by $\dfrac{44,984,000}{20,700} = 2173.14$ with the results shown in Column (5). For example, 50,000 men are represented by 23 sample cases on the average. Under simple random sampling, the standard error of a proportion is s.e.$(\hat{p}) = \sqrt{\dfrac{pq}{N}}$. Since we know s.e.$(\hat{p})$ and p from Columns (1) and (2), we can compute the size of the random sample needed to obtain a standard error of the given size for each value of p as $N = \dfrac{pq}{\text{s.e.}^2(\hat{p})}$, with results as shown in Column (4). The ratio of entries in Column (4) to those in Column (5) are as the variances of percentages under simple random sampling compared to those in the OCG sample design. Where the population bases are small and true percentages large, so there is little rounding error in the calculations, the several estimates consistently suggest a relative efficiency of the OCG design of .62, so standard errors are about $1/\sqrt{.62} = 1.27$ times as large in the OCG as under simple random sampling. In the absence of any better guideline, this might be used as a rule of thumb in making inferences from the OCG data.

(1) Estimated percentage	(2) Population base	(3) Standard error	(4) Random sample	(5) Estimated sample cases	(6) Ratio (4)/(5)
1 or 99	50,000	.026	14.6453	23.0096	.6365
	100,000	.019	27.4245	46.0193	.5959
	500,000	.008	154.6914	230.0966	.6723
$\sqrt{pq} = .0995$	1,000,000	.006	275.0069	460.1932	.5976
	2,500,000	.004	618.7656	1,150.4830	.5378
	5,000,000	.003	1,100.0277	2,300.9664	.4781
	10,000,000	.002	2,475.0675	4,601.9328	.5378
	25,000,000	.001	9,900.2500	11,504.8320	.8605
	50,000,000	.001	9,900.2500	23,009.6640	.4303
2 or 98	50,000	.037	14.3170	23.0096	.6222
	100,000	.026	28.9941	46.0193	.6300

(Continued)

(1) Estimated percentage	(2) Population base	(3) Standard error	(4) Random sample	(5) Estimated sample cases	(6) Ratio (4)/(5)
$\sqrt{pq} = .140$	500,000	.012	136.1111	230.0966	.5915
	1,000,000	.008	306.2500	460.1932	.6655
	2,500,000	.005	784.0000	1,150.4830	.6815
	5,000,000	.004	1,225.0000	2,300.9664	.5324
	10,000,000	.003	2,177.7777	4,601.9328	.4732
	25,000,000	.002	4,900.0000	11,504.8320	.4259
	50,000,000	.001	19,600.0000	23,009.6640	.8518
5 or 95	50,000	.058	14.1143	23.0096	.6134
	100,000	.041	28.2453	46.0193	.6138
$\sqrt{pq} = .2179$	500,000	.018	146.5445	230.0966	.6369
	1,000,000	.013	280.9492	460.1932	.6105
	2,500,000	.008	741.8814	1,150.4830	.6448
	5,000,000	.006	1,318.9003	2,300.9664	.5732
	10,000,000	.004	2,967.5256	4,601.9328	.6448
	25,000,000	.003	5,275.6011	11,504.8320	.4586
	50,000,000	.002	11,870.1025	23,009.6640	.5159
10 or 90	50,000	.079	14.4208	23.0096	.6267
	100,000	.056	28.6990	46.0193	.6236
$\sqrt{pq} = .30$	500,000	.025	144.0000	230.0966	.6258
	1,000,000	.018	277.7777	460.1932	.6036
	2,500,000	.011	743.8017	1,150.4830	.6465
	5,000,000	.008	1,406.2500	2,300.9664	.6112
	10,000,000	.006	2,500.0000	4,601.9328	.5433
	25,000,000	.004	5,625.0000	11,504.8320	.4889
	50,000,000	.003	10,000.0000	23,009.6640	.4346
15 or 85	50,000	.095	14.1297	23.0096	.6141
	100,000	.067	28.4073	46.0193	.6173
$\sqrt{pq} = .3571$	500,000	.030	141.6893	230.0966	.6158
	1,000,000	.021	289.1619	460.1932	.6283
	2,500,000	.013	754.5586	1,150.4830	.6559
	5,000,000	.009	1,574.3260	2,300.9664	.6842
	10,000,000	.007	2,602.4573	4,601.9328	.5655
	25,000,000	.004	7,970.0256	11,504.8320	.6928
	50,000,000	.003	14,168.9344	23,009.6640	.6158
20 or 80	50,000	.106	14.2399	23.0096	.6189
	100,000	.075	28.4444	46.0193	.6181
$\sqrt{pq} = .40$	500,000	.033	146.9238	230.0966	.6385
	1,000,000	.024	277.7777	460.1932	.6036
	2,500,000	.015	711.1111	1,150.4830	.6181
	5,000,000	.011	1,322.3140	2,300.9664	.5747
	10,000,000	.007	3,265.3061	4,601.9328	.7096
	25,000,000	.005	6,400.0000	11,504.8320	.5563
	50,000,000	.003	17,777.7777	23,009.6640	.7726
25 or 75	50,000	.115	14.1769	23.0096	.6161
	100,000	.081	28.5763	46.0193	.6210

(Continued)

(1) Estimated percentage	(2) Population base	(3) Standard error	(4) Random sample	(5) Estimated sample cases	(6) Ratio (4)/(5)
$\sqrt{pq}$ = .433	500,000	.036	144.6674	230.0966	.6287
	1,000,000	.026	277.3506	460.1932	.6027
	2,500,000	.016	732.3789	1,150.4830	.6366
	5,000,000	.011	1,549.4959	2,300.9664	.6734
	10,000,000	.008	2,929.5156	4,601.9328	.6366
	25,000,000	.005	7,499.5600	11,504.8320	.6519
	50,000,000	.004	11,718.0625	23,009.6640	.5093
35 or 65	50,000	.126	14.3316	23.0096	.6229
	100,000	.089	28.7248	46.0193	.6242
$\sqrt{pq}$ = .477	500,000	.040	142.2056	230.0966	.6180
	1,000,000	.028	290.2156	460.1932	.6306
	2,500,000	.018	702.2500	1,150.4830	.6104
	5,000,000	.013	1,346.3254	2,300.9664	.5851
	10,000,000	.009	2,809.0000	4,601.9328	.6104
	25,000,000	.006	6,320.2500	11,504.8320	.5494
	50,000,000	.004	14,220.5625	23,009.6640	.6180
50	50,000	.132	14.3474	23.0096	.6235
	100,000	.094	28.2918	46.0193	.6147
$\sqrt{pq}$ = .5	500,000	.042	141.7219	230.0966	.6159
	1,000,000	.030	277.7777	460.1932	.6036
	2,500,000	.019	692.5208	1,150.4830	.6019
	5,000,000	.013	1,479.2899	2,300.9664	.6429
	10,000,000	.009	3,086.4198	4,601.9238	.6707
	25,000,000	.006	6,944.4444	11,504.8320	.6036
	50,000,000	.004	15,625.0000	23,009.6640	.6791

References

Acker, Joan
    1973   "Women and social stratification: a case of intellectual sexism." *American Journal of Sociology* 78 (January): 936–945.

Alexander, Arthur J.
    1970   *Structure, Income and Race: A Study of Internal Labor Markets*. Final Report for Office of Economic Opportunity, R-577-OEO. Santa Monica, Cal.: Rand.

Alwin, Duane F.
    1974   "College effects on educational and occupational attainment." *American Sociological Review* 39 (October): 201–223.

Artz, Reta, Dianne Fairbank, Richard Curtis, and Elton Jackson
    1971   "Community rank stratification: a factor analysis." *American Sociological Review* 36 (December): 985–1002.

Ashenfelter, Orley, and Joseph Mooney
    1968   "Graduate education, ability and earnings." *Review of Economics and Statistics* 50 (February): 78–86.

Becker, Gary
    1964   *Human Capital*. New York: Columbia University Press.

Benoit-Smullyan, Emile
    1944   "Status, status types, and status interactions." *American Sociological Review* 9 (April): 151–161.

Bielby, William T., Robert M. Hauser, and David L. Featherman
    1976   "Response errors of nonblack males in models of the stratification process." In Dennis J. Aigner and Arthur S. Goldberger (eds.), *Latent Variables in Socioeconomic Models*. Amsterdam: North Holland.

Bielby, William T., Robert M. Hauser, and David L. Featherman
    1977   "Response errors of black and nonblack males in models of the Intergenerational transmission of socioeconomic status." *American Journal of Sociology* (forthcoming).

Blau, Peter M., and Otis Dudley Duncan
    1967   *The American Occupational Structure*. New York: Wiley.

Blaug, Mark
    1967   "The private and the social returns on investment in education: some results for Great Britain." *Journal of Human Resources* 2 (Summer): 330–346.

Blishen, B. R.
    1967   "A socio-economic index for occupations in Canada." *Canadian Review of Sociology and Anthropology* 4 (February): 41–53.

Blum, Zahava
   1972   "White and black careers during the first decade of labor force experience. Part
          II: Income differences." *Social Science Research* 1 (September): 271–292.
Bogue, Donald J.
   1959   *The Population of the United States.* New York: Free Press.
Boudon, Raymond
   1972   "A note on social immobility and inequality measurement." *Quality and
          Quantity* 6 (June): 17–35.
   1973   *Mathematical Structures of Social Mobility.* San Francisco: Jossey-Bass.
   1974   *Education, Opportunity, and Social Inequality.* New York: Wiley.
Bowles, Samuel
   1972   "Schooling and inequality from generation to generation." *Journal of Political
          Economy* 80 (May/June): S219–S251.
Bowles, Samuel, and Herbert Gintis
   1972   "IQ in the U.S. class structure." *Social Policy* 3 (November): 65–96.
Bowles, Samuel, and Valerie I. Nelson
   1974   "The 'Inheritance of IQ' and the intergenerational reproduction of economic
          inequality." *Review of Economics and Statistics* 56 (February): 39–51.
Bowman, Mary Jean
   1969   "Economics of education." *Review of Educational Research* 39 (December):
          641–670.
Broom, Leonard, and F. Lancaster Jones
   1969a "Career mobility in three societies." *American Sociological Review* 34 (Octo-
          ber): 650–658.
   1969b "Father-to-son mobility: Australia in comparative perspective." *American
          Journal of Sociology* 74 (January): 333–342.
Broom, Leonard, F. Lancaster Jones, and J. Zubrzycki
   1965   "An occupational classification of the Australian workforce." *Australian and
          New Zealand Journal of Sociology* 1 (October): 1–16.
Campbell, Richard T., and Mark Evers
   1974   "An empirical comparison of canonical and log linear approaches to the
          analysis of polytomous dependent variables." Paper presented at the annual
          meeting of the American Sociological Association, Montreal, Canada.
Carter, Nancy Dunton
   1972   The effects of sex and marital status on a social–psychological model of occupa-
          tional status attainment. Unpublished master's thesis, University of
          Wisconsin–Madison.
Chase, Ivan D.
   1975   "A comparison of men's and women's intergenerational mobility in the United
          States." *American Sociological Review* 40 (August): 483–505.
Chinoy, Ely
   1955   "Social mobility trends in the United States." *American Sociological Review*
          20 (April): 180–186.
Cohen, Jacob
   1968   "Multiple regression as a general data-analytic system." *Psychological Bulletin*
          70 (December): 426–443.
Coleman, James S., Zahava D. Blum, Aage B. Sørensen, and Peter H. Rossi
   1972   "White and black careers during the first decade of labor force experience.
          Part I: Occupational status." *Social Science Research* 1 (September):
          243–270.

Council of Economic Advisors
  1966 "What is poverty? Who are the poor?" Pp. 92–106 in Herman P. Miller (ed.), *Poverty: American Style.* Belmont, Cal.: Wadsworth.
Counts, G. S.
  1925 "The social status of occupations: A problem in vocational guidance." *Social Review* 33 (January): 16–27.
Daniere, Andre, and Jerry Mechling
  1970 "Direct marginal productivity of college education in relation to college aptitude of students and production costs of institutions." *Journal of Human Resources* 5 (Winter): 51–70.
Davis, James A.
  1974 "Hierarchical models for significance tests in multivariate contingency tables: an exegesis of Goodman's recent papers." Pp. 189–231 in Herbert L. Costner (ed.), *Sociological Methodology, 1973–74.* San Francisco: Jossey-Bass.
DeJong, Peter Y., Milton J. Brawer, and Stanley S. Robin
  1971 "Patterns of female intergenerational occupational mobility: a comparison with male patterns of intergenerational occupational mobility." *American Sociological Review* 36 (December): 1033–1041.
Deming, W. Edwards
  1943 *Statistical Adjustment of Data.* New York: Wiley.
Denison, E. F.
  1964 "Measuring the contribution of education." In *The Residual Factor and Economic Growth.* Paris: Organization for Economic Cooperation and Development.
Dietrick, Barbara A.
  1974 "Social mobility: 1969–1973." *Annals* 414 (July): 138–147.
Duncan, Beverly
  1965 *Family Factors and School Dropout: 1920–1960.* Final Report, Cooperative Research Project No. 2258, U.S. Office of Education. Ann Arbor: University of Michigan.
Duncan, Otis Dudley
  1961 "A socioeconomic index for all occupations." Pp. 109–138 in A. J. Reiss, Jr., *Occupations and Social Status.* New York: Free Press.
  1965 "The trend of occupational mobility in the United States." *American Sociological Review* 30 (August): 491–98.
  1966a "Methodological issues in the analysis of social mobility." Pp. 51–97 in Neil J. Smelser and Seymour Martin Lipset (eds.), *Social Structure and Mobility in Economic Development.* Chicago: Aldine.
  1966b "Occupation trends and patterns of net mobility in the United States." *Demography* 3 (1): 1–18.
  1966c "Path analysis: sociological examples." *American Journal of Sociology* 72 (July): 1–16.
  1967 "Discrimination against Negroes." *Annals of the American Academy of Political and Social Science* 371 (May): 85–103.
  1968a "Ability and achievement." *Eugenics Quarterly* 15 (March): 1–11.
  1968b "Inheritance of poverty or inheritance of race?" Pp. 85–110 in Daniel P. Moynihan (ed.), *On Understanding Poverty: Perspectives from the Social Sciences.* New York: Basic Books.
  1968c "Patterns of occupational mobility among Negro men." *Demography* 5 (1): 11–22.

1968d "Social stratification and mobility: problems in the measurement of trend." Pp. 675–719 in Eleanor B. Sheldon and Wilbert E. Moore (eds.), *Indicators of Social Change*. New York: Russell Sage Foundation.

Duncan, Otis Dudley, and David L. Featherman
1972 "Psychological and cultural factors in the process of occupational achievement." *Social Science Research* 1 (June): 121–145.

Duncan, Otis Dudley, David L. Featherman, and Beverly Duncan
1972 *Socioeconomic Background and Achievement*. New York: Seminar Press.

Duncan, Otis Dudley, and R. W. Hodge
1963 "Education and occupational mobility." *American Journal of Sociology* 68 (May): 629–644.

Duncan, Otis Dudley, and Albert J. Reiss
1956 *Social Characteristics of Urban and Rural Communities, 1950*. New York: Wiley.

Duncan-Jones, Paul
1972 "Social mobility, canonical scoring, and occupational classification." Pp. 191–210 in John Goldthorpe and Keith Hope (eds.), *The Analysis of Social Mobility: Methods and Approaches*. Oxford: Clarendon Press.

Durbin, J.
1955 "Appendix note on a statistical question raised in the preceding paper." *Population Studies* 9 (July): 101.

Fararo, T.
1973 *Mathematical Sociology*. New York: Wiley-Interscience.

Farley, Reynolds
1968 "The quality of demographic data for nonwhites." *Demography* 5 (1): 1–10.

Featherman, David L.
1971 "The socioeconomic achievement of white religio-ethnic subgroups: social and psychological explanations." *American Sociological Review* 36 (April): 207–222.
1974 "Strategies for the assessment of socioeconomic structures." Paper presented at the Workshop on Socioeconomic Measurement, East–West Population Institute, Honolulu, Hawaii.

Featherman, David L., and Robert M. Hauser
1973 "On the measurement of occupation in social surveys." *Sociological Methods and Research* 2 (November): 239–251.
1975 "Design for a replicate study of social mobility in the United States." Pp. 219–251 in Kenneth C. Land and Seymour Spilerman (eds.), *Social Indicator Models*. New York: Russell Sage Foundation.
1976a "Changes in the socioeconomic stratification of the races, 1962–1973." *American Journal of Sociology* 82 (November): 621–651.
1976b "Prestige or socioeconomic scales in the study of occupational achievement?" *Sociological Methods and Research* 4 (May): 403–422.
1976c "Sexual inequalities and socioeconomic achievement in the U.S., 1962–1973." *American Sociological Review* 41 (June): 462–483.

Featherman, David L., Robert M. Hauser, and William H. Sewell
1974 "Toward comparable data on inequality and stratification." *American Sociologist* 9 (February): 18–25.

Featherman, David L., F. Lancaster Jones, and Robert M. Hauser
1975 "Assumptions of social mobility research in the United States: the case of occupational status." *Social Science Research* 4 (December): 329–360.

Glass, D. V.
  1954 *Social Mobility in Britain*. London: Routledge and Kegan Paul.
Glenn, Norval D., Adreain A. Ross, and Judy Corder Tully
  1974 "Patterns of intergenerational mobility of females through marriage." *American Sociological Review* 39 (October): 683–699.
Goldberger, Arthur S.
  1970 "On Boudon's method of linear causal analysis." *American Sociological Review* 35 (February): 97–101.
Goldthorpe, John, and Keith Hope
  1972 "Occupational grading and occupational prestige." Pp. 19–80 in John Goldthorpe and Keith Hope (eds.), *The Analysis of Social Mobility: Methods and Approaches*. Oxford: Clarendon Press.
  1974 *The Social Grading of Occupations: A New Approach and Scale*. Oxford: Clarendon Press.
Goodman, Leo A.
  1965 "On the statistical analysis of mobility tables." *American Journal of Sociology* 70 (March): 564–585.
  1968 "The analysis of cross-classified data: independence, quasi-independence, and interactions in contingency tables with or without missing entries." *Journal of the American Statistical Association* 63 (December): 1091–1131.
  1969a "How to ransack social mobility tables and other kinds of cross-classification tables." *American Journal of Sociology* 75 (July): 1–40.
  1969b "On the measurement of social mobility: an index of status persistence." *American Sociological Review* 34 (December): 831–850.
  1970 "The multivariate analysis of qualitative data: interactions among multiple classifications." *Journal of the American Statistical Association* 65 (March): 226–256.
  1971 "The analysis of multidimensional contingency tables: stepwise procedures and direct estimation methods for building models for multiple classifications." *Technometrics* 13 (February): 33–61.
  1972a "A general model for the analysis of surveys." *American Journal of Sociology* 77 (May): 1035–1086.
  1972b "Some multiplicative models for the analysis of cross-classified data." Pp. 649–696 in *Proceedings of the Sixth Berkeley Symposium on Mathematical Statistics and Probability*. Berkeley: University of California Press.
Griliches, Zvi, and William Mason
  1972 "Education, income and ability." *Journal of Political Economy* 80 (May/June): S74–S103.
Haberman, Shelby J.
  1974a *The Analysis of Frequency Data*. Chicago: University of Chicago Press.
  1974b "Log-linear models for frequency tables with ordered classifications." *Biometrics* 30 (December): 589–600.
Haller, Archibald O., and Alejandro Portes
  1973 "Status attainment processes." *Sociology of Education* 46 (Winter): 51–91.
Hanoch, Giora
  1967 "An economic analysis of earnings and schooling." *Journal of Human Resources* 2 (Summer): 310–329.
Hansen, W. Lee, Burton Weisbrod, and William Scanlon
  1970 "Schooling and earnings of low achievers." *American Economic Review* 60 (June): 409–418.

Hanushek, Eric
  1973   "Regional differences in the structure of earnings." *Review of Economics and Statistics* 55 (May): 204–213.
Hatt, Paul K.
  1950   "Occupation and social stratification." *American Journal of Sociology* 55 (May): 533–543.
Haug, Marie R.
  1973   "Social class measurement and women's occupational roles." *Social Forces* 52 (September): 86–98.
Hauser, Philip M.
  1969   "The chaotic society: product of the social morphological revolution." *American Sociological Review* 34 (February): 1–19.
Hauser, Robert M.
  1969   "Schools and the stratification process." *American Journal of Sociology* 74 (May): 587–611.
  1971   *Socioeconomic Background and Educational Performance.* Rose Monograph Series. Washington, D.C.: American Sociological Association.
  1972   "Disaggregating a social–psychological model of educational attainment." *Social Science Research* 1 (June): 159–188.
  1973   "Socioeconomic background and returns to education." Pp. 129–145 in Lewis C. Solmon and Paul J. Taubman (eds.), *Does College Matter? Evidence of the Impacts of Higher Education.* New York: Academic Press.
Hauser, Robert M., and Peter J. Dickinson
  1974   "*Inequality* on occupational status and income." *American Educational Research Journal* 11 (Spring): 161–168.
Hauser, Robert M., Peter J. Dickinson, Harry P. Travis, and John N. Koffel
  1975   "Structural changes in occupational mobility among men in the United States." *American Sociological Review* 40 (October): 585–598.
Hauser, Robert M., and David L. Featherman
  1973   "Trends in the occupational mobility of U.S. men, 1962–1970." *American Sociological Review* 38 (June): 302–310.
  1974a "Socioeconomic achievements of U.S. men, 1962–1972." *Science* 185 (July): 325–331.
  1974b "White–nonwhite differentials in occupational mobility among men in the United States, 1962–1972." *Demography* 11 (May): 247–265.
  1976   "Equality of schooling: Trends and prospects." *Sociology of Education* 49 (April): 99–120.
Hauser, Robert M., and Arthur S. Goldberger
  1971   "The treatment of unobservable variables in path analysis." Pp. 81–117 in Herbert Costner (ed.), *Sociological Methodology, 1971.* San Francisco: Jossey-Bass.
Hauser, Robert M., John N. Koffel, Harry P. Travis, and Peter J. Dickinson
  1975   "Temporal change in occupational mobility: evidence for men in the United States." *American Sociological Review* 40 (June): 279–297.
Havens, Elizabeth M., and Judy Corder Tully
  1972   "Female intergenerational occupational mobility: comparisons of patterns?" *American Sociological Review* 37 (December): 774–779.
Havighurst, Robert J.
  1947   "The influence of recent social changes on the desire for social mobility in the United States." In L. Bryson, L. Finkelstein, and R. M. Maciver (eds.), *Conflicts of Power in Modern Culture.* New York: Harper and Bros.

Hertzler, J. O.
  1952 "Some tendencies toward a closed class system in the United States." *Social Forces* 30 (March): 313–323.
Hochbaum, Godfrey, John Darley, E. Monachesi, and Charles Bird
  1955 "Socioeconomic variables in a large city." *American Journal of Sociology* 61 (July): 31–38.
Hodge, Robert W.
  1966 "Occupational mobility as a probability process." *Demography* 3 (1): 19–34.
Hodge, Robert W., Paul M. Siegel, and Peter H. Rossi
  1964 "Occupational prestige in the United States, 1925–63." *American Journal of Sociology* 70 (November): 286–302.
Hodge, Robert W., Donald J. Treiman, and Peter H. Rossi
  1966 "A comparative study of occupational prestige." Pp. 309–321 in Reinhold Bendix and Seymour Martin Lipset (eds.), *Class, Status and Power*. New York: Free Press.
Hogan, Dennis P.
  1973 Industrial mobility and the situs effects of industry. Unpublished master's thesis, University of Wisconsin–Madison.
Hollingshead, August B.
  1952 "Trends in social stratification: a case study." *American Sociological Review* 17 (December): 679–686.
Hope, Keith
  1972 "Quantifying constraints on social mobility: the latent hierarchies of a contingency table." Pp. 121–190 in Keith Hope (ed.), *The Analysis of Social Mobility: Methods and Approaches*. Oxford: Clarendon Press.
  1974 "Trends in the openness of British society in the present century." Paper presented at the Mathematical Social Sciences Board Conference on Measurement and Models in Comparative Social Stratification, Toronto, Canada, August.
Horan, Partick M.
  1972 The structure of occupational mobility: A comparative approach. Unpublished doctoral dissertation, University of Wisconsin–Madison.
Huber, Joan, and William H. Form
  1973 *Income and Ideology*. New York: Free Press.
Jackson, Elton F., and Harry J. Crockett, Jr.
  1964 "Occupational mobility in the United States: a point estimate and trend comparison." *American Sociological Review* 29 (February): 5–15.
Jencks, Christopher S.
  1974 Comments on "*Inequality* on occupational status and income," by Robert M. Hauser and Peter J. Dickinson. *American Educational Research Journal* 11 (Spring): 169–175.
Jencks, Christopher S., Marshall Smith, Henry Acland, Mary Jo Bane, David Cohen, Herbert Gintis, Barbara Heyns, and Stephan Michelson
  1972 *Inequality: A Reassessment of the Effect of Family and Schooling in America*. New York: Basic Books.
Jones, Frank E., and F. Lancaster Jones
  1972 "Occupational prestige in Australia and Canada: a comparison and validation of some occupational scales." *Australian and New Zealand Journal of Sociology* 8 (June): 75–82.
Jones, F. Lancaster
  1969 "Social mobility and industrial society: a thesis reexamined." *Sociological Quarterly* 10 (Summer): 292–305.

1971   "Occupational achievement in Australia and the United States." *American Journal of Sociology* 77 (November): 527–539.

1975   "Measures of father-to-son mobility: a liberal or radical criterion of evaluation?" *Quality and Quantity* 9 (December): 361–369.

Jöreskog, Karl, G. Gruvaeus, and M. van Thillo

1970   *ACOVS: A General Computer Program for the Analysis of Covariance Strutures.* Research Bulletin RB-70-15. Princeton, N.J.: Educational Testing Service.

Kendall, M. G., and A. Stuart

1967   *The Advanced Theory of Statistics.* Vol. 2. New York: Hafner.

Kerckhoff, Alan C., William M. Mason, and Sharon S. Poss

1973   "On the accuracy of children's reports of family social status measures." *Sociology of Education* 46 (Spring): 219–247.

Kish, Leslie, and Martin R. Frankel

1974   "Inferences from complex samples." *Journal of the Royal Statistical Society* (Series B): 1–22.

Klatzky, Sheila R., and Robert W. Hodge

1971   "A canonical correlation analysis of occupational mobility." *Journal of the American Statistical Association* 66 (March): 16–22.

Koffel, John N.

1974   Subjectivity in mobility trend literature: sociology of knowledge and statistical approaches. Unpublished master's thesis, University of Wisconsin–Madison.

Ku, Harry H., and Solomon Kullback

1974   "Loglinear models in contingency table analysis." *American Statistician* 28 (November): 115–122.

Lane, Angela

1968   "Occupational mobility in six cities." *American Sociological Review* 33 (October): 740–749.

1972   Contexts of socioeconomic attainment: the role of community, industry of employment and spatial mobility. Unpublished doctoral dissertation, University of Chicago.

Lasswell, Thomas E., and Sandra L. Benbrook

1974   "Social stratification: 1969–1973." *Annals* 414 (July): 105–137.

Lebergott, Stanley

1968   "Labor force and employment trends." Pp. 97–144 in Eleanor B. Sheldon and Wilbert E. Moore (eds.), *Indicators of Social Change.* New York: Russell Sage Foundation.

Lenski, Gerhard E.

1958   "Trends in inter-generational occupational mobility in the United States." *American Sociological Review* 23 (October): 514–523.

Levine, Joel Harvey

1967   Measurement in the study of intergenerational status mobility. Unpublished doctoral dissertation, Department of Social Relations, Harvard University, Cambridge, Mass.

Lipset, Seymour Martin

1972   "Social mobility and equal opportunity." *Public Interest* 29 (Fall): 90–108.

Lipset, Seymour Martin, and Reinhard Bendix

1960   *Social Mobility in Industrial Society.* Berkeley: University of California Press.

Martin, J. David

1970   "A comment on whether American women do marry up." *American Sociological Review* 35 (April): 327–328.

Mason, William M., Robert M. Hauser, Alan C. Kerckhoff, Sharon Sandomirsky Poss, and Kenneth Manton
  1976 "Models of response error in student reports of parental socioeconomic characteristics." Pp. 443–494 in William H. Sewell, Robert M. Hauser, and David L. Featherman (eds.), *Schooling and Achievement in American Society*. New York: Academic Press.

McClendon, McKee J.
  1976 "The occupational status attainment processes of males and females." *American Sociological Review* 41 (February): 52–64.

McFarland, David D.
  1969 "Measuring the permeability of occupational structures: an information-theoretic approach." *American Journal of Sociology* 75 (July): 41–61.
  1970 "Intra-generational social mobility as a Markov process." *American Sociological Review* 35 (June): 463–476.

Miller, S. M.
  1960 "Comparative social mobility." *Current Sociology* 9: 1–89.
  1975 "Social mobility and equality." Pp. 394–433 in *Education, Inequality and Life Chances*. Vol. 1. Paris: Organization for Economic Cooperation and Development.

Milner, M., Jr.
  1973 "Race, education and jobs: trends, 1960–1970." *Sociology of Education* 46 (Summer): 280–298.

Mincer, Jacob
  1958 'Investment in human capital and personal income distribution." *Journal of Political Economy* 66 (August): 281–302.

Moore, Wilbert E.
  1966 "Changes in occupational structures." Pp. 194–212 in Neil J. Smelser and Seymour Martin Lipset (eds.), *Social Structure and Mobility in Economic Development*. Chicago: Aldine.

Morris, Richard T., and R. J. Murphy
  1959 "The situs dimension in occupational structure." *American Sociological Review* 24 (April): 231–239.

Mosteller, Frederick
  1968 "Association and estimation in contingency tables." *Journal of the American Statistical Association* 63 (March): 1–28.

Mueller, Charles W.
  1973 City effects on socioeconomic achievement. Unpublished doctoral dissertation, University of Wisconsin–Madison.
  1974 "City effects on socioeconomic achievements: the case of large cities." *American Sociological Review* 39 (October): 652–667.

National Opinion Research Center
  1972 Codebook for the Spring 1972 General Social Survey, National Data Program for the Social Sciences, University of Chicago (July).

Palmer, Gladys
  1954 *Labor Mobility in Six Cities*. New York: Social Science Research Council.

Parkin, F.
  1971 *Class Inequality and Political Order*. New York: Praeger.

Parnes, Herbert S., Robert C. Miljus, and Ruth S. Spitz
  1970 *Career Thresholds: A Longitudinal Study of the Educational and Labor Market Experience of Male Youth*. Vol. 1 (1966 survey). Manpower Research Monograph No. 16. Washington, D.C.: U.S. Department of Labor.

Parnes, Herbert S., Belton M. Fleisher, Robert C. Miljus, and Ruth S. Spitz
  1970   *The Pre-Retirement Years: A Longitudinal Study of the Labor Market Experience of Men.* Vol. 1 (1966 survey). Manpower Research Monograph No. 15. Washington, D.C.: U.S. Department of Labor.
Pease, J., W. Form, and J. Rytina
  1970   "Ideological currents in American stratification literature." *American Sociologist* 5 (May): 127–137.
Priebe, John A.
  1968   *Changes between the 1950 and 1960 occupation and industry classifications.* U.S. Bureau of the Census Technical Paper No. 18. Washington, D.C.: U.S. Government Printing Office.
Priebe, John A., Joan Heinkel, and Stanley Greene
  1972   *1970 occupation and industry classification systems in terms of their 1960 occupation and industry elements.* U.S. Bureau of the Census Technical Paper No. 26. Washington, D.C.: U.S. Government Printing Office.
Ramsøy, Natalie Rogoff
  1973   "Patterns of female intergenerational occupational mobility: a comment." *American Sociological Review* 38 (December): 806–807.
Reiss, Albert J.
  1961   *Occupations and Social Status.* New York: Free Press.
Robinson, J. P., R. Athanasiou, and K. B. Head
  1969   *Measures of Occupational Attitudes and Occupational Characteristics.* Ann Arbor, Mich.: Institute for Social Research.
Rogoff, Natalie
  1953a *Recent Trends in Occupational Mobility.* New York: Free Press.
  1953b "Recent trends in urban occupational mobility." Pp. 442–454 in Reinhard Bendix and Seymour Martin Lipset (eds.), *Class, Status, and Power: A Reader in Social Stratification.* New York: Free Press.
Routh, G.
  1965   *Occupations and Pay in Great Britain, 1906–1960.* Cambridge: Cambridge University Press.
Rubin, Zick
  1968   "Do American women marry up?" *American Sociological Review* 33 (October): 750–760.
  1969   "Reply to Scott." *American Sociological Review* 34 (October): 727–728.
Schnore, Leo
  1963   "The socioeconomic status of cities and suburbs." *American Sociological Review* 28 (February): 76–85.
Schnore, Leo, and David Varley
  1955   "Some concomitants of metropolitan size." *American Sociological Review* 20 (August): 388–414.
Scott, John Finley
  1969   "A comment on 'Do American Women Marry Up?' " *American Sociological Review* 34 (October): 725–727.
Sewell, William H.
  1971   "Inequality of opportunity for higher education." *American Sociological Review* 36 (October): 793–809.
Sewell, William H., and Michael Armer
  1966   "Neighborhood context and college plans." *American Sociological Review* 31 (April): 159–168.

Sewell, William H., Archibald O. Haller, and G. Ohlendorf
1970 "The educational and early occupational status attainment process." *American Sociological Review* 35 (December): 1014–1027.

Sewell, William H., and Robert M. Hauser
1972 "Causes and consequences of higher education: models of the status attainment process." *American Journal of Agricultural Economics* 54 (December): 851–861.
1975 *Education, Occupation and Earnings: Achievement in the Early Career.* New York: Academic Press.

Sibley, Elbridge
1942 "Some demographic clues to stratification." *American Sociological Review* 7 (June): 322–330.

Siegel, Paul M.
1970 "On the cost of being a negro." Pp. 727–743 in Edward O. Lauman *et al.* (eds.), *The Logic of Social Hierarchies.* Chicago: Markham.
1971 Prestige in the American occupational structure. Unpublished doctoral dissertation, University of Chicago.

Siegel, Paul M., and Robert W. Hodge
1968 "A causal approach to the study of measurement error." Pp. 28–59 in Hubert M. Blalock, Jr., and Ann B. Blalock (eds.), *Methodology in Social Research.* New York: McGraw-Hill.

Sjoberg, Gideon
1951 "Are social classes in America becoming more rigid?" *American Sociological Review* 16 (December): 775–783.

Sörensen, Aage
1974 "A model for occupational careers." *American Journal of Sociology* 80 (July): 44–57.

Sorokin, Pitirim A.
1959 *Social and Cultural Mobility.* New York: Free Press.

Spilerman, Seymour
1968 The distribution of Negro males among industries in 1960. Unpublished doctoral dissertation, Johns Hopkins University, Baltimore, Maryland.
1969 "Industry differences in stability of the rate of Negro employment." Discussion Paper No. 59–69. Madison: University of Wisconsin, Institute for Research on Poverty.

Steinmetz, Suzanne K.
1974 "The sexual context of social research." *American Sociologist* 9 (August): 111–116.

Stolzenberg, Ross M., and Ronald J. D'Amico
1976 "City differences and nondifferences in the effect of race and sex on occupational distribution." Center for Metropolitan Planning & Research, and Department of Social Relations. Baltimore: Johns Hopkins University.

Suter, Larry, and H. Miller
1973 "Income differences between men and women." *American Journal of Sociology* 78 (January): 962–974.

Svalastoga, K.
1972 "The determination of occupational prestige." Unpublished paper, Copenhagen, Denmark.

Sweet, James
1973 *Women in the Labor Force.* New York: Seminar Press.

Taeuber, Karl E., and Alma F. Taeuber
  1965 *Negroes in Cities: Residential Segregation and Neighborhood Change.*
        Chicago: Aldine.
Theil, Henri
  1972 *Statistical Decomposition Analysis.* Amsterdam: North Holland.
Titmuss, R.
  1962 *Income Distribution and Social Change.* London: Allen & Unwin.
Treiman, Donald J.
  1970 "Industrialization and social stratification." Pp. 207–234 in Edward O.
        Laumann (ed.), *Social Stratification: Research and Theory for the 1970's.* In-
        dianapolis: Bobbs-Merrill.
  1975 Problems of concept and measurement in the comparative study of occupa-
        tional mobility. *Social Science Research.* 4 (September): 183–230.
Treiman, Donald J., and Kermit Terrell
  1975a "Sex and the process of status attainment: a comparison of working women and
        men." *American Sociological Review* 40 (April): 174–200.
  1975b "The process of status attainment in the United States and Great Britain."
        American Journal of Sociology 81 (November): 563–583.
  1975c "Women, work, and wages—trends in the female occupation structure." Pp.
        157–199 in Kenneth C. Land and Seymour Spilerman (eds.), *Social Indicator
        Models.* New York: Russell Sage Foundation.
Tully, Judy Corder, Elton F. Jackson, and Richard F. Curtis
  1970 "Trends in occupational mobility in Indianapolis." *Social Forces* 49 (Decem-
        ber): 186–200.
Tyree, Andrea
  1973 "Mobility ratios and association in mobility tables." *Population Studies* 27
        (November): 577–588.
Tyree, Andrea, and Judith Treas
  1974 "The occupational and marital mobility of women." *American Sociological
        Review* 39 (June): 293–302.
U.S. Bureau of the Census
  1953 *Annual Report on the Labor Force: 1952.* Current Population Reports, Series
        P-50, No. 45 (July): Tables D and 3. Washington, D.C.: U.S. Government
        Printing Office.
  1956 *Occupational Characteristics.* 1950 Census of Population, Special Report P-E,
        No. 1B. Washington, D.C.: U.S. Government Printing Office. Tables 4 and 5.
  1960 *Alphabetical Index of Occupations and Industries.* Washington, D.C.:
        Superintendent of Documents.
  1964a *Lifetime Occupational Mobility of Adult Males: March 1962.* Current Popula-
        tion Reports, Series P-23, No. 11 (May 12). Washington, D.C.: U.S. Govern-
        ment Printing Office.
  1964b *U.S. Census of Population: 1960.* Subject Reports. Sources and Structure of
        Family Income. Final Report PC (2)-4C. Washington, D.C.: U.S. Government
        Printing Office.
  1964c *Educational Changes in a Generation: March, 1962.* Current Population Re-
        ports, Series 132 (September 22, 1964). Washington, D.C.: U.S. Government
        Printing Office.
  1968 *Statistical Abstract of the United States: 1968.* 89th ed. Washington, D.C.:
        U.S. Government Printing Office.

1971a *Alphabetical Index of Industries and Occupations, 1970 Census of Population.* Washington, D.C.: U.S. Government Printing Office.

1971b *Classified Index of Industries and Occupations, 1970 Census of Population.* Washington, D.C.: U.S. Government Printing Office.

U.S. Department of Labor

1965 *Dictionary of Occupational Titles.* Vol. 1. *Definition of Titles.* Washington, D.C.: U.S. Government Printing Office.

1970 *Dual Careers: A Longitudinal Study of Labor Market Experience of Women.* Vol. 1. Manpower Research Monograph No. 21. Washington, D.C.: U.S. Government Printing Office.

Walsh, T.C., and P.J. Buckholdt

1970 *Accuracy of Retrospectively Reporting Work Status and Occupation Five Years Ago.* U.S. Bureau of the Census Working Paper PA-(75).

Wang, Linda

1972 The female status attainment process and occupational mobility. Unpublished master's thesis, University of Wisconsin–Madison.

Watson, Walter B., and Ernest A. T. Barth

1964 "Questionable assumptions in the theory of social stratification." *Pacific Sociological Review* 7 (Spring): 10–16.

Weber, Max

1958 "Class, status, and party." In Hans Gerth and C. Wright Mills (eds.), *From Max Weber.* New York: Oxford Press.

Weisbrod, Burton, and P. Karpoff

1968 "Monetary returns to college education, student ability and college quality." *Review of Economics and Statistics* 50 (November): 491–497.

Weiss, Randall

1970 "The effect of education on the earnings of blacks and whites." *Review of Economics and Statistics* 52 (May): 150–159.

White, Harrison C.

1963 "Cause and effect in social mobility tables." *Behavioral Science* 7 (January): 14–27.

1970 *Chains of Opportunity.* Cambridge, Mass.: Harvard University Press.

Winsborough, Halliman H.

1967 "Components of Negro–white income differences." Paper presented at the Population Association of America Meeting, April.

Yasuda, Saburo

1964 "A methodological inquiry into social mobility." *American Sociological Review* 29 (February): 16–23.

Subject Index

DATE DUE

BRODART, INC.

Cat. No. 23-221